The Western Paradox

A Conservation Reader

Bernard DeVoto

EDITED BY

Douglas Brinkley and

Patricia Nelson Limerick

with a foreword by

Arthur M. Schlesinger, Jr.

NB Yale Nota Bene

YALE UNIVERSITY PRESS

New Haven & London

First published as a Yale Nota Bene book in 2001.
Copyright © 2000 by Mark DeVoto.

Mark DeVoto thanks the Green Library of Stanford University and archivists Maggie Kimball and Linda Long.

For information about this and other Yale University Press publications, please contact:

| U.S. office | sales.press@yale.edu |
| Europe office | sales@yaleup.co.uk |

Printed in the United States of America

Library of Congress Cataloging-in-Publication Data

DeVoto, Bernard Augustine, 1897–1955.
  The Western paradox : a conservation reader / Bernard DeVoto ; edited by Douglas Brinkley and Patricia Nelson Limerick ; with a foreword by Arthur Schlesinger, Jr.
      p. cm. — (Yale Western Americana)
Includes bibliographical references and index.
  ISBN 0-300-08422-6 (cl.) — ISBN 0-300-08423-4 (pbk.)

  1. Conservation of natural resources—West (U.S.) 2. Public lands—West (U.S.) 3. West (U.S.) I. Brinkley, Douglas.
II. Limerick, Patricia Nelson, 1951– III. Title. IV. Yale Western Americana series (Unnumbered)
S932.W37 D4 2001
333.7`2`0978—dc21   00-012507

A catalog record for this book is available from the British Library.

10 9 8 7 6 5 4 3 2 1

in memory of T. H. Watkins, mentor,
historian, and ardent conservationist

Contents

Foreword

I owe many things to Bernard DeVoto, but three in particular stand out in memory.

He taught me how to write. In my second year at Harvard, I took his course in English composition. He read one's sophomoric efforts with meticulous care, exposed pretentiousness and phoniness with pitiless eye, scrawled scathing but unanswerable comments on the margin, and goaded students to think through what they were trying to say and to say it plainly, concisely, and concretely. After three months I wrote in my undergraduate diary that he had "improved (or at least changed) my style by about 100 percent."

And he taught me how to appreciate the dry martini. His glorious little tract *The Hour* is a hymn to six o'-clock—"the violet hour, the hour of hush and wonder, when the affections glow and valor is reborn." At six the martini is carefully mixed, "the healer, the weaver of forgiveness and reconciliation, the justifier of us to ourselves and one another." I suppose such sentiments are incomprehensible to a generation that turns to white wine after a hard day's work; but how much the boomers miss of the savor of life.

Most important, DeVoto introduced me to the West. Though he loved his life in Cambridge, Massachusetts, he taught me that the nation stretched far beyond New England into the magnificent, wild, disorderly, troubled land across the wide Missouri, filled with beauty and surprise and possibility but betrayed by its own inhabitants, a "plundered province," a region at war with itself.

In 1940, preparing to write *The Year of Decision: 1846,* he felt an urgent need to refresh his physical sense of the West, to follow the Santa Fe and Oregon Trails once again, to inspect the weather-beaten forts and smell the alkali plains and watch the distant snow melting on the mountains. And he wonderfully invited me to accompany him on the long journey west.

Driving Benny's Buick with that best-informed and most zestful of guides resurrected the dusty past. But the insistent present could not be escaped. This was May 1940, and we lived divided lives on the journey, half absorbed by thoughts of the mountain men who had blazed the trails across hostile country a century before, half absorbed by reports over the car radio of Nazi *Panzer* divisions striking at the heart of France.

The West, Benny taught me, lived a divided life, too. The mountain men were brave but they were careless, and those who followed the mountain men—the stockmen and timbermen and ranchers and mine owners and railroad men and bankers—were pillagers, trading in nature's great patrimony for fast bucks. The consequence—overgrazing and deforestation—would weaken the defenses of the land afforded by grass and trees and speed the process of erosion. This book is the fascinating record of DeVoto's crusade to save the West from itself.

DeVoto was born in Ogden, Utah, in 1897. He had by birthright an abiding identification with the frontier and an abiding concern with the process by which the United States became a continental nation. He defined himself as a Populist—a term out of fashion in the 1930s and 1940s, but he was a man who greatly enjoyed being out of fashion. I think, however, he would be outraged by the way the word *populist* is flung around today.

He was the son of a Mormon-Catholic marriage. Suspended in his own family between two revelations authoritatively certified as divine but totally incompatible, he developed a profound mistrust of revelation in general. "I early acquired," he later wrote, "a notion that all gospels were false, and all my experience since then has confirmed it. . . . I came to conclude that absolutes were a mirage. And in my desert country, mirages are also commonplace." The collision in his parentage made him a relativist and a skeptic.

He was by temperament a contrarian, instinctively hostile to what his great friend John Kenneth Galbraith was soon to call the "conventional wisdom." So, confronting New Deal ideologues in the 1930s, DeVoto had seemed for a season a conservative. But the nation's drift to the right after the war redirected his contracyclical impulse, and he soon emerged as a liberal.

He took up the problems of segregation and racial justice—not the "private business" of the South, he wrote: "They are our business too. They are national problems." He denounced J. Edgar Hoover and Joe McCarthy. "I like a country where it's nobody's damned business what magazine anyone reads, what he thinks, whom he has cocktails with. . . . We had that kind of country only a little while ago, and I'm for getting it back."

But the West remained his passion. *The Year of Decision,* in 1943, was followed by *Across the Wide Missouri* in 1947, *The Course of Empire* in 1952, and his edition of *The Journals of Lewis and Clark* in 1953. Even his single novel of the period was entitled *Mountain Time.* An extended trip across the West in 1946 rekindled his concern over the fate of "the plundered province." He now saw more clearly than ever the extent to which westerners themselves were complicit in the policy of plunder. The West's "willingness to hold itself cheap and its eagerness to sell out" constituted a historical betrayal. The West had certainly been raped by the East, DeVoto said, but its posture had always invited rape.

The election of General Eisenhower in 1952 brought into power a party that had long since rejected the conservationist gospel of Theodore Roosevelt and an administration eagerly responsive to interests calling for the transfer of public lands to the states. State ownership would be a preliminary to turning the grazing land and forest land over to private ownership at forced sale and at bargain prices (as little as ten cents an acre). The result might be the biggest landgrab in American history.

"In a year and a half," DeVoto wrote in 1954, "the businessmen in office have reversed the conservation policy by which the United States has been working for more than seventy years to substitute wise use of its natural resources in place of reckless destruction for the profit of special corporate interests. . . . Every move in regard to conservation that the Administration has made has been against the public interest—which is to say against the future."

The withdrawal of great tracts from federal control would encourage overgrazing and other abuses of the land, damage the watersheds, lower the water table, and accelerate the whole terrible process of erosion. The assault on the public resources of the West, he wrote, "is an assault which in a single generation could destroy the West and return it to the processes of geology."

His eloquent articles helped stop the landgrab. He was the first conservationist—we would call him today an environmentalist—in nearly half a century, except for Franklin D. Roosevelt, to command a national audience. No one did more in the postwar years to rouse public opinion against the spoilers than DeVoto. He was, in the phrase of the journalist and senator Richard Neuberger of Oregon, "the most illustrious conservationist who has lived in modern times."

The fight DeVoto waged against the spoilers is far from over. His arguments, insights, and passion are as relevant and urgent today as they were when he first put them on paper. It would hardly have surprised him that the fight continues. "Democracy," Benny once said, "is not a pathway to the stars but only the articles of war under which the race fights an endless battle with itself."

Arthur M. Schlesinger, Jr.

Introduction

> The achieved West had given the United States something
> that no people had ever had before, an internal, domestic
> empire.
> Bernard DeVoto, *The Year of Decision,* 1943

As the twenty-first century dawns, Bernard DeVoto, the iconoclastic Pulitzer Prize–winning historian, would be outraged to learn that his battle to preserve the American West has met numerous defeats in places like the Mojave Desert and Humboldt County, the Cascades and Alaska. In fact, his strident conservationist cause remains as timely as it was fifty years ago when he first wrote his fervid pleas. For DeVoto was no detached, dispassionate historian: he was a hard-nosed, full-bore conservationist who vigorously denounced the exploitation of the West, no matter whether the pillagers were private corporations, the federal government, or environmentally heedless ranchers. "He was a fighter for public causes," novelist Wallace Stegner recalled of his dear friend, "for conservation of our natural resources, for freedom of the press and freedom of thought." Alas, many of the earth-scorching dragons DeVoto set out to slay never disappeared from their lairs belching an all too familiar fire.

DeVoto is best remembered for his historic trilogy—
The Year of Decision: 1846 (1943), *Across the Wide
Missouri* (1947), and *The Course of Empire* (1952)—
followed in 1953 by his abridged and one-volume edition
of *The Journals of Lewis and Clark.* All four books have
remained in print since their original publication, ce-
menting DeVoto's place in the top tier of American historians. But DeVoto was haunted far more by the future
of the American West than by its past. In his time, the
region seemed to be reckoning with the twin dangers
of overpopulation and overdevelopment. The scarcity of
water in particular, DeVoto argued, would force those
who went West to make sensible judgments to both
limit their numbers and adapt their ways of life. Those
adaptations, he believed, would save the region from
the consequences of too much development too soon—or
at all.

No such luck. No one who reads *Western Paradox*—a
conservationist manifesto broken off at DeVoto's death
at age fifty-eight and published here for the first time—
can possibly dismiss it as a hoary relic of a bygone era.
That goes for the ten (also fifty years old) *Harper's* articles and columns included in this volume as well. Presented chronologically and culminating with DeVoto's
unfinished manuscript, this book paints the portrait of
a firebrand of a conservationist and a tireless scribe
whose work and life remained unfinished.

As depressing as their author would find it, the
pieces in *The Western Paradox: A Bernard DeVoto Conservation Reader* are as relevant today as they were
when DeVoto wrote them. Had he lived to see the so-
called Reagan Revolution—with antienvironment zealot
James Watt as secretary of the interior deeming the
wilderness as any asphalt parking lot without lines and
the president declaring that caribou pollute more than
cars—DeVoto would have jumped into the ring with fists
and wit flying. After all, in such pieces as "Sacred Cows

and the Public Lands," "Statesmen on the Lam," "Billion Dollar Jack Pot," and "The Sturdy Corporate Homesteader," he lit into conservation's foes with not just zeal but irresistible humor to boot. Today a procession of earnest environmentalists may parade through the hallowed offices of senators, congressmen, and other "Wise Use" advocates to protest the latest demands for the privatization of public lands, but none comes close to doing so with anything like DeVoto's intellect, fulmination, or sense of fun.

In 1948, as he launched himself fully into the campaign for conservation, DeVoto offered an exuberantly mixed metaphor to describe his passion: "If you listen late at night . . . you will hear an odd, steady sound. That is me boiling. I don't know when I came to a boil or just why I suddenly realized that it had happened. I've just been knocking up practice flies in this game so far. Now I'm coming up to bat. Give me some offstage noises for I'm in the saddle again, off the reservation and out for blood. Somehow I seem to have got mad."

So what use can we make today of such a legacy of righteous fury? Can DeVoto still inspire, energize, and move us to action?

It seems to depend on which stage of DeVoto's thinking one is looking at and which hat he was wearing at the time. In a November 1954 letter to his literary agent's secretary, he described himself as "a journalist, a novelist, a critic, a historian, and an editor"—an assessment supported by the bibliography at the end of this volume. "I am," as DeVoto once told his wife, "a literary department store."

His political identity was equally complex. In an early 1950s column for *Harper's*, DeVoto proclaimed, with dubious mathematics, that "I am a half Mugwump, 60 percent New Dealer, 90 percent Populist dirt-roads historian." In fact, however, the multifaceted writer had one true calling that infused his entire body of work: a passionate dedication to the American West and the need to save it both from outsiders and from westerners themselves. "Debunking or correcting Western myths, scorning the things the West had become, he would continue to love, to the point of passion, Western openness, freedom, air, scenery, violence; and would accept some of the myths as eagerly as the most illiterate cowhand reading *Western Stories* in the shade of the cookhouse," Stegner wrote of his colleague.

Bernard DeVoto was born on January 11, 1897, in Ogden, Utah, not far from the town of Promontory, where the transcontinental railroad was completed in 1869. The young man's formative experience amid the snow-peaked mountains, dense forests, butted arroyos, arid deserts, and big skies thrilled him, giving DeVoto the native's knowledge and appreciation for the lands of the West that would remain with him all his life. As the son of a Roman Catholic father and a Mormon mother, the young DeVoto was at odds with his peers from the very start in his predominantly Mormon hometown, a circumstance that hardened his enthusiasm for taking on any opponent, real or imagined. As Stegner's 1974 book *The Uneasy Chair: A Biography of Bernard DeVoto* emphasizes, it was as a boy in Ogden that DeVoto first demonstrated what would become his trademark pugnacity and relish for rebuttal. An unhealthy child too bookwormish to access a Western culture that prized brawny machismo above school smarts, the young DeVoto quickly developed a strong sympathy for the underdog. "Birth made him a Westerner," his friend the historian Arthur Schlesinger, Jr., wrote in 1962. "It gave him an identification with the experience of the frontier and a permanent concern with the process by which America became a continental nation. It also made him a Populist. . . . It meant a broad sympathy for the pioneer over the capitalist, for the men who opened up and settled a region as against those who came along later and drained it of its wealth."

In 1915, after a year at the University of Utah, De-Voto enrolled as a sophomore at Harvard and began a lifelong love affair with New England: its rolling hills, autumn stillness, winter snows, and most of all the sparkling intellectual opportunities of Cambridge. But the Utah teenager who crossed the continent to be educated at the most elite of Eastern establishment institutions was, as Schlesinger put it, "still at heart a Western radical." *Harper's* editor Lewis Lapham wrote in 1997, "DeVoto's presence in the East strengthened his fierce affection for the West, and his writing is everywhere marked by poignant remembrances of Western landscapes, Western grasses, Western animals and birds."

DeVoto spent much of the next forty years in Cambridge and New York, producing a prodigious amount of both fiction and nonfiction prose. Much of it is witty as well as cogent; all of it reveals a mind at once inordinately honest, sensitive, devoted to fact, and enamored of the written word. Through much of his life DeVoto struggled to write the "Great American Novel," at which he failed alongside virtually everyone else self-assured and overoptimistic enough to try. Nevertheless, his fiction remains of interest. His first novel, for example— *The Crooked Mile,* published in 1924—showcases what would become the linchpin through all of DeVoto's writings: the impact of the West on American society. Coming as it did during the 1920s heyday of the pulp Western, the likes of Zane Grey's purple-sage potboilers perpetually on the best-seller lists, *The Crooked Mile* reads as an admirable precursor to the serious Western fiction of Wallace Stegner, Larry McMurtry, and A. B. Guthrie.

In *The Crooked Mile* and his half-dozen other novels, some written under the nom de plume John August, De-Voto spun tales about building families and communities in the American West, without so much as a nod to the OK-Corral-remember-the-Alamo-shoot-'em-up tradition of the frontier fiction genre. DeVoto's novels instead detailed how the West was never just an outpost for solitary, hard-living range riders rebelling against authority but was an evolving society of sturdy, everyday folk who understood that they lived in an interdependent culture and wanted to raise their families to fit into it. As Lapham noted, DeVoto's greatest gift— his sense of universal human nature—allowed him to appreciate that all generations belong "to the same repertory company, succeeding one another on the same stage."

DeVoto may have only partially succeeded as a novelist, but he earned critical accolades as a literary provocateur in 1932 with his book *Mark Twain's America,* a clever refutation of critic Van Wyck Brooks's 1920 standard, *The Ordeal of Mark Twain.* A few years later DeVoto was named editor of *Harper's* popular Easy Chair column, which provided a perfect platform for his inimitable biting commentary for the remaining twenty years of his life. It was through the bully pulpit of this column that DeVoto began to give full voice to his love for the West and for the land, rivers, and mountains of all of America. But unlike the myriad writers who romanticized the West in tall tales of cowboys drenched in sunset, DeVoto instead set to waging a political war in defense of the region's resources.

In *The West Against Itself,* the preeminent conservationist writer between Theodore Roosevelt and Rachel Carson dissects the West's curious attitude toward the federal government. "It shakes down to a platform," DeVoto wrote: "Get out and give us more money."

His take on the West and on the origins of its environmental dilemmas developed in two distinct stages. The first began in August 1934 with the publication in *Harper's* of DeVoto's article "The West: A Plundered

Province," a classic harangue against the region's victimization. His litany of plaints was hardly new and boiled down to the old lament that the hardy frontier was being overtaken by the established might of Eastern capital and industry. Mining, for instance, may have made the region a treasure trove, but it had not "made the West wealthy," as DeVoto pointed out; in fact, "to be brief, it made the East wealthy." Congress did its part to aid the Eastern pirates, he added, by "passing a series of imbecile laws" that led to "inconceivably stupid government" that practiced "prodigal stupidity."

As ever, he was nothing if not frank. Thus DeVoto drew his battle lines, purposely precipitating a public-lands controversy through his magazine essays. He went with a vengeance after the cattle and sheep ranchers of the Stockmen's Association, who had long enjoyed the considerable privilege of grazing their livestock on certain public lands in exchange for minimal fees and for promises to observe a few rules. He came to full boil pledging to derail any bills before Congress that would give power over public lands to the Western states or to the ranchers whose livestock were permitted to graze on those lands. "Nothing in history suggests," he growled, "that the states are adequate to protect their own resources, or even want to, or suggest that cattlemen and sheepmen are capable of regulating themselves even for their own benefit, much less the public's." To DeVoto, it was despicable to compel the U.S. Forest Service to rehabilitate lands ravaged into uselessness by business interests, only to transfer the property back to private ownership as soon as it could produce timber again. The unprotected public lands of the American West contained an estimated 4 billion barrels of crude oil and 324 billion tons of coal; DeVoto had reason to worry about private interests hell-bent on exploiting the West's resources as cheaply as possible, damn the environment.

He would not let up. Encouraged and supported by the "imbecile laws," DeVoto said, all the corrupt parasites were lined up to feed off the West: water companies, railroad companies, land companies, grain-storage companies, mortgage companies, and banks, "all of them looting the country in utter security." The West could not win, he raged, because it could "fight the battle only on the terms [others] have laid down." As DeVoto summed up at the time: "Looted, betrayed, sold out, the Westerner is a man whose history has been just a series of large-scale jokes."

This was not exactly a complex or subtle portrait of the West or of its history of resource use. It was, rather, the roiling indignation of a prickly personality eager to vent his own vituperative disapproval of greedy developers. A porcupine of a writer had made himself spokesman for a porcupine of a region.

Over the next twelve years, however, the porcupines' relationship deepened, evolved, and in the end turned inside out, leaving the writer shooting his quills straight into the region's fondest delusions and pretensions. The West was no longer simple to DeVoto, and no longer simply victimized. The turning point for the writer as a conservationist came in 1946 when he took a long, leisurely car trip through the Rocky Mountain states. DeVoto—who had been closely reading the works of naturalist John Muir—slowly began to see "the plundered province" from a broader perspective than he had in 1934, and when he returned East he put forth a new thesis in *Harper's:* that a schizophrenic West was destroying itself.

According to Schlesinger, who had accompanied "Benny" on another such trek in 1940, DeVoto now saw the American West as a confused yet apparently willing victim, repeatedly violated by the East but willingly cemented in the sort of gun-toting libertarianism that made it vulnerable to gross exploitation. The problem, he had come to believe, was that the West's "historic willingness to hold itself cheap and its eagerness to sell out" were the products of the region's own weaknesses: in essence, if the East didn't destroy the West's resources, the West itself surely would do so in time.

"There is intended," DeVoto wrote in *Harper's*, "an assault on the public resources of the West which is altogether Western and so open that it cannot possibly be called a conspiracy. It is an assault in which a single generation could destroy the West and return it to the processes of geology."

This stage two of DeVoto's Western analysis appeared in *Harper's* in December 1946 and January 1947 in two remarkable articles, "The Anxious West" and "The West Against Itself." Westerners, DeVoto wrote in the former, had become the "fall guys of the United States, victimized by everybody," and it was "most disastrously by themselves." Oh, they might talk of declaring independence and seceding from a nation that neither respected nor rewarded them, but such dreams of a separate, regional utopia ran aground on the fact that Westerners "have never been able to work together or trust one another." What's more, DeVoto wrote, they persisted in looking toward the future "with hope and confidence, and they ignore the elements in themselves which bring both [hope and confidence] into question. They are children of paradox and begetters of paradox."

Then he really got down to the bare bones: "Westerners, too many of them, have an urge to dramatize themselves to strangers as the Old Ranger or the Old Trail Boss." The West, he continued, "has always been facile at self-deception; that it has chosen this illusion to erect into myth may be comic to outsiders but could end by being tragic to the West." In a wonderful passage that still packs a punch, DeVoto derided the sort of ersatz cowboy festivals he mocked as "Frontier Week": "There is no harm," he said, "in people's dressing up in the costumes of their ancestors, though silk coats, flow-ered vests, black mitts, and hoop skirts are tolerably grotesque. There is no harm in growing beards, though the urgency with which the modern West grows them suggests a fear that it has not inherited all the frontier masculinity that beards are supposed to signify."

But to the extent that such nostalgia "conditions po-litical behavior," DeVoto went on, there was a real dan-ger of self-delusion in acting out and promoting the old Wild West myths. Doing so perpetuated "a faint fantasy and a nostalgia for something idiotically misconceived. If the druggist and the bank clerk were to wear peaked denim caps to Rotary luncheons and once a year were to put on striped bibbed overalls and go to the carnival car-rying engine waste and an oil can with a long spout, by-standers would be moved to laughter rather than disbe-lief." The celebration of "Frontier Week," DeVoto sniffed in summation, "is rather conducted without reference to history, it is empty of idea and emotion, its data are anachronistic and preposterous." But it *was* revealing of the way the modern West still denies its reality in favor of an imaginary past—and through that fantasy pushes itself closer to political, economic, and environmental disaster. A region clinging to a false, mythological past was, in DeVoto's estimation, destined to be ill prepared for coping with the difficult future.

Thus in stage two of DeVoto's thinking the West was no longer an innocent victim but was an active partici-pant in its own decline. "The basic problems," he wrote, "are internal. The West has always suppressed domestic criticism while cringing before criticism from outside. Forever in rebellion against exterior exploitation, it has nevertheless always cooperated with the exploiters when the chips were down." Then came the key point: "No destruction by absentee-owned corporations of the West's natural resources could be forestalled, because anything that could forestall it would also forestall the

West's own destruction of those same resources." In other words, the issues might look economic, but in the end they were also psychological. The developments that triggered DeVoto's recognition of this split personality remain familiar as we enter the twenty-first century: a movement begins in the West, prompting Congress to debate whether to return the resources of the public lands to the states or to privatize them through direct sale to corporations or well-heeled individuals. The rhetoric would accept the rights of the little guy; the actual practice would increase the profits of companies and corporations.

DeVoto—who seldom concerned himself with matters of logical consistency—believed the West was divided into two main camps: one made up of permanent residents determined to put down lasting roots and to build a workable future in the region with a view toward posterity, the other of transients interested only in "liquidating the West's resources." With the region's congressmen leading the campaign for the latter, the West again betrayed its bipolar disorder. "The West," DeVoto sighed, "does not want to be liberated from the system of exploitation that it has always violently resented. It only wants to buy into it."

Irascible pragmatist that he was, DeVoto was often wrong about his predictions—such as when he opined of the thirty-eighth state, Nevada, "Not much more can happen; there are plenty of square miles but there are no more water sources. Outside the present centers the population density cannot increase more than microscopically. Nevada will remain the least populous state and the one with the widest open spaces. It will be the first Western state to attain a stable equilibrium with the desert." Since then Nevada has been called many things, but "a stable equilibrium" has never been among them; for a decade now Las Vegas has been the fastest growing city in the nation. Of course, DeVoto ig-

nored the effects of Nevada's decision in 1931 to legalize what remain its two most lucrative and ever-thriving
industries: gambling and quickie divorces. Clearly, De-
Voto was far off the mark on the power of natural limits
in determining the evolution of Nevada. DeVoto—like
most environmentalists today—believed that the distribution of water would govern human settlement patterns and set a limit on the Western population in states
like Nevada with a clearly defined carrying capacity. To
some extent he considered Nevada a mistake—or, groan
aside, a mis-state—in that there was no logical reason
for people to live there; Nevada attained statehood in
1864, he proclaimed, only because Abraham Lincoln
needed it to secure ratification of the Thirteenth Amendment to the Constitution abolishing slavery. "It was a
notable service to the United States," DeVoto explained,
"and would justify maintaining the area as a National
Historic Park on the same basis as Jamestown or Washington's headquarters at Morristown. What other benefits has the United States had from Nevada in ninety
years?"

But right or wrong DeVoto was always ripe for the
good fight. In 1948, for example, he used his Easy Chair
column to finger Senator Wesley D'Ewart of Montana
and Representative Frank Barrett of Wyoming as "landgrabbers." Both lost their seats in the election that year,
thanks in part to DeVoto's influence. The crusading
writer had become, in the words of his political ally Senator Richard Neuberger of Oregon, "the most illustrious
conservationist who has lived in modern times." In
recognition, in January 1948, Secretary of the Interior
Julius Krug appointed DeVoto to the Advisory Board for
National Parks, Historical Sites, Buildings, and Monuments, a congressionally commissioned citizens group
responsible for advising the secretary on conservation
matters.

Today it seems inconceivable that such an honor could be bestowed upon such a pugnacious firebrand. In the 1990s, we ritually sigh over how public discourse has declined as civility has been besieged and reduced. DeVoto's works make for a lively corrective to our scripted lamentation: his unabashedly surly screeds are peppered with reckless references to "stupidity" and "imbecility" and "catastrophe" and "greed" and "disaster." Would it have been more politically effective to be more civil, more tactful, more respectful of opponents' positions? Even to suggest such a dilution to DeVoto would surely have secured a prominent slot on his generously proportioned list of imbecilities—in this case that of ignoring the claims of posterity to fuss over manners. And perhaps he would have been right. After all, it's the very bluntness of DeVoto's language that raises the question of whether civility is all it's cracked up to be.

DeVoto obviously didn't think so. In a letter written in 1943, he outlined the ambitions he had set for his middle age: "To do good work; to do work in which I may take some satisfaction and my friends some pleasure; at the utmost, as Frost once said of Robinson, to put something on the record that will not easily be dislodged." To put something on the record that will not easily be dislodged, to put it where posterity might actually be able to use it, is surely the finest and should be the foremost goal of any activist writer. Bernard DeVoto attained that goal—time and time again. What would he have considered to be the best way to honor his achievements? To continue his crusade, one suspects he would say, as loudly as he had conducted it in his lifetime.

As economist Robert Heilbroner pointed out in his essay "What Has Posterity Ever Done For Me?" the willingness to make sacrifices in the interests of future generations is an illogical inclination. After all, as Heilbroner put it, why "should I lift a finger to affect the events that will have no meaning for me seventy-five years after my death? There is no rational answer to that terrible question. No argument based on reason will lead me to care for posterity or to lift a finger on its behalf. Indeed, by every rational consideration, precisely the opposite answer is thrust upon us with irresistible force."

But what has posterity ever done for anybody, or needed to? Absolutely nothing on either score; by definition posterity *can't* do anything for the living. So, Heilbroner exhorted, we have to search for "the personal responsibility that defies all the homicidal promptings of reasonable calculation." In other words, as DeVoto himself had clearly concluded, go with your gut and do what you know is right: do whatever you can to make the world a better place for those who come after you.

Only passion can sustain this "unreasonable" determination to govern the present in the interests of the future, and it was passion that drove Bernard DeVoto. He threw himself into the task of persuading the public to embrace the value of posterity, to make others see with him that humankind's future progeny are our kinfolk. DeVoto knew by instinct that posterity not only deserved but demanded our consideration and respect. He had anticipated and answered Heilbroner's question, "What has posterity ever done for me?" As DeVoto noted—"What we want posterity to do for us is to value us as ancestors and predecessors; what we want posterity to do for us is to appreciate and enjoy the undiminished natural heritage we passed on to them."

DeVoto practiced what he preached. In spite of the unending deadlines that harry every professional writer, on one occasion, for example, he took the time to pen seven dense pages to an unmotivated teenager he'd never met who had written him for advice regarding college. In response to the young man's admission that he was not a very good student and often found teachers rather dull, DeVoto wrote: "My dear boy, the world is under no obligation to entrance you. There was no thought of pleasing you when it was created." He reminded the lad that "the world presents itself to you and whether you find it a magical drama or whether you find it an intolerably dull tale is equally indifferent to the world, which goes about its cycle without reference to your pleasure or ennui. There is nothing interesting or dull in any subject you have studied or will ever study. The interest and the dullness inhere in you, and in studies as in most other things, you will get out of them what you bring, and no more." He went on more gently, ending with an invitation to continue the correspondence and the assurance: "And don't consider my time. I always have plenty of time for such discussions as these." To Bernard DeVoto, posterity mattered—no matter how or by whom he was reminded of its due. In the end, for all his rage DeVoto was a hopeless optimist. "Sure the people are stupid; the human race is stupid," he sighed from his Easy Chair in *Harper's* in 1950. "Sure Congress is an inefficient instrument of government. But the people are not stupid enough to abandon representative government for any other kind."

This book brings us into DeVoto's spirited company and reminds us that many of his causes and campaigns remain concerns of ours. In his long endnote to *The Easy Chair*—a twentieth-anniversary collection of his essays from *Harper's,* published in 1955—DeVoto wrote: "I am treating the whole subject in a book which I am writing as this one goes to press." This book in progress was to be a summary peroration on two decades' thinking on conservation and public lands policy, understood in the context of the history of the American West. He did not finish it. On November 13, 1955, barely two weeks after *The Easy Chair* hit bookstore shelves, Bernard DeVoto died in New York of a massive heart attack. *Western*

Paradox remained in typescript at the DeVoto Archive in the Stanford University Library until this publication. With this release, though, we are once again graced with an all too familiar warning crossing nearly half a century to echo in our ears as the booming and profound voice of Bernard DeVoto.

Douglas Brinkley
Patricia Nelson Limerick

Select *Harper's*
Conservation Essays

The West

A Plundered Province

First published in the August 1934 edition of *Harper's,* this essay plunges into DeVoto's rails against the Eastern financial establishment. He draws the line in the sand in the fight over Western resource rights and the autonomy of the region. Written nearly a year after DeVoto's participation in the annual Bread Loaf Writer's Conference, this essay appeared a month before DeVoto's novel *We Accept with Pleasure* was released on September 21.

The Westerner remains a bewildering creature to the rest of the nation. Socially he has never fused with the energetic barbarian that for many decades symbolized the Middle Westerner to the appalled East. Politically, also, he has remained distinct from the Middle Westerner, to whom our cartoonists allot a more genial grin, a better-filled-out frame, and a neater suit of overalls. To cartoonists, the Middle Westerner is the Dirt Farmer and he lives in the Corn Belt and, except occasionally, he is admitted to be a person of some consequence. On the contrary, it is established that the Westerner is gaunt, ragged, and wild-eyed; also he is a mendicant and rapacious. Under one arm he clasps a concrete dam or a bundle labeled Government-Built Hard Roads. Other labels dangling from his pocket announce that he has grabbed a lot of pork. They allude to Reclamation Projects, Forest Reserves, Experiment Stations, Grazing Acts, the Desert Land Act, Crop Surveys,

3

Home Loan Banks, and similar privileges. Sometimes, with a quaint candor, they mention Land Grant Railroads, and nearly always a caption informs the reader how much Massachusetts paid in Federal taxes and how many miles of concrete in Idaho were laid by the sum. The mendicant's mouth is open: you are to understand that he is bawling for more Privilege and Paternalism. This is his routine appearance when the cartoonists are merely amused, are even willing to tip him a dam or two for the sake of quiet as you would give a child a nickel to go play somewhere else. When, however, the spectacle of human greed dismays the artist the Westerner ceases to be a mere beggar. Gaunt and wild-eyed still, he now rides a whirlwind or rushes over a cliff, invariably dragging the Republic with him, and the lightning round his head is labeled Socialism, Bolshevist Daydreams, or National Bankruptcy. Instead of being merely a national pensioner, he is now a national danger.

This is the symbolism of the Westerner in our metropolitan press—the national wild man, the thunder-bringer, disciple of madness, begetter of economic heresy, immortal nincompoop deluded by maniac visions, forever clamoring, forever threatening the nation's treasury, forever scuttling the ship of state. And yet, a queer thing: a mere change of clothes gives him a different meaning on quite as large a scale. Put a big hat on his head, cover the ragged overalls with hair pants and let high heels show beneath them, knot a bandanna round his neck—and you have immediately one of the few romantic symbols in American life. He has ceased to be a radical nincompoop and is now a free man living greatly, a rider into the sunset, enrapturer of women in dim theaters, solace of routine-weary men who seek relief in wood pulp, a figure of glamour in the reverie of adolescents, the only American who has an art and a literature devoted wholly to his celebration. One perceives a certain incompatibility between these avatars.

The land he inhabits has a further symbolism. The West is the loveliest and most enduring of our myths, the only one that has been universally accepted. In that mythology it has worn many faces. It has meant escape, relief, freedom, sanctuary. It has meant opportunity, the new start, the saving chance. It has meant oblivion. It has meant manifest destiny, the heroic wayfaring, the birth and fulfillment of a race. It has, if you like, meant what the fourth house of the sky has meant in poetry and all religions—it has meant Death. But whatever else it has meant, it has always meant strangeness. That meaning may serve to reconcile the incompatibles.

Much energy has been spent in an effort to determine where the West begins. The definitions of poetry and the luncheon clubs are unsatisfactory: vagueness should not be invoked when a precise answer is possible. The West begins where the average annual rainfall drops below twenty inches. When you reach the line which marks that drop—for convenience, the one-hundredth meridian— you have reached the West. And it is a strange country.

The first part of its strangeness is that it was the last frontier to fall. The American migration leaped across it and in part returned to it from beyond, Californians and Oregonians invading it eastward from their region of plentiful rain. It lingered on invincible after all other frontiers had disappeared, into a time when pioneering was only a memory shimmering with the rainbow of the never-never. The pioneers' grandchildren were now citizens of orderly manufacturing towns, and when they read of to-day's happenings over the hill they necessarily thought of them as belonging to grandfather's romance. It must clearly be a strange country where the legendary saga of redskins and first-fruits was still going on.

It was strange too in that the westward-making Americans, when they came to their last frontier, found that what they had learned on the way there would do

them little good. They were the world's great frontiersmen. The whole continent had been frontier, and in subduing it they had learned an exquisite craftsmanship,
an exquisite technique, round which much of the national culture had formed. Yet four-fifths of their travel
had lain among trees, and the forests had conditioned
their craftsmanship. Was not the first chapter in the
heroic legend called "The Cabin in the Clearing"? The
roadways through the wilderness were forest-fed streams
down which produce could be floated to market and up
which the pioneers could make their way by canoe. It
was a hard labor, but the very core of American significance was that its results were certain. A man made a
clearing with his axe, raised his cabin, fenced his fields,
and grew old in security. During the last fifth of the westward journey craftsmanship had had to be somewhat
modified, for the Americans had reached the prairies.
Yet the problems here differed in degree rather than in
kind, for the rivers were still navigable, there was wood
for fuel and for the cabin and the fences, and the pioneers
could count on even greater security, since this was the
richest land in the world. But when they reached the
West a craftsmanship refined through more than two
centuries, and now felt to be a hereditary way of life,
was simply useless.

There could be no cabin in the clearing, for there
were no trees to clear and no logs to shape into walls:
the pioneer's axe, his greatest tool, was as ineffective as
its prototype of the smooth-flint age. The rivers ran
contrariwise, most of them ran too shallowly to float a
barge or even a canoe, ran brackish water, and in summer sometimes did not run at all. The redskins of the
forest had been cruel, pestiferous, and obstinate, but
they had never been a match for the Americans.
Whereas the mounted Indians of the plains for many
years exercised a boisterous superiority over their invaders, easily dominating them because of superior

equipment and superior adaptation to the land's necessities. Even the fauna gave the pioneer problems his legendary technique was not adequate to solve. Bear and venison were not to be butchered in the door-yard but had to be followed over the horizon and perhaps could not be met with at all; and the buffalo, the West's beef, had had no precedent in the forests. Not only the fauna was unfamiliar—the tight-fisted land would not grow most of the crops which the pioneers had grown to the eastward, would grow little dependably, and nothing at all except under methods radically different from anything the East had known.

It was a strange land, and all its strangeness came from the simple arithmetic of its rainfall. A grudging land—it gave reluctant crops only. A treacherous land—its thin rain might fail without reason or warning, and then there were no crops at all and the pioneer, who had been ignorant of droughts, promptly starved. An inventive land—besides drought it had other unprepared-for plagues: armies of locusts and beetles, rusts and fungi never encountered in the forests, parasites that destroyed grains and cattle which had been habituated to an Eastern climate. A poisoned land—it was variously salted with strange earths which must be leached away before seeds could germinate. And in the end as in the beginning, a dry land—so that all problems returned to the master problem of how to get enough water on land for which there could never be water enough. In sum, conditions that made unavailing everything that the pioneers had learned, conditions that had to be mastered from scratch if the last frontier was to be subdued.

And, therefore, the final strangeness of the West: it was the place where the frontier culture broke down. The pioneer's tradition of brawn and courage, initiative, individualism, and self-help was unavailing here. He could not conquer this land until history caught up with him. He had, that is, to ally himself with the force which our sentimental critics are sure he wanted to escape from: the Industrial Revolution.

Professor Webb's fine book, *The Great Plains,* catches the era in the actual process which can only be alluded to here. The country had no rivers for the transportation of goods—so settlement had to await the railroads. It had, except for the alpine regions, no forests. The pioneer might cut sod or mold adobe bricks for a shanty, but he could not fence his claim until industrialism brought him barbed wire. The Plains Indians were better equipped than he for the cavalry campaigns that had to be the West's warfare—so the Industrial Revolution had to give him repeating rifles and repeating pistols, especially the latter. So far as the Winning of the West was a war of conquest, victory waited upon the Spencer, the Winchester, and especially the Colt. And always the first condition: to grow crops where there was not enough water. The Revolution's railroads had to bring westward the Revolution's contrivances for deep cultivation, bigger and tougher plows, new kinds of harrows and surfacers and drills, and its contrivances for large-scale operations, new harvesters and threshers, steam and then gasoline group-machines which quadrupled cultivating power and then quadrupled it again. Finally, the problem of the water itself. The axe-swinging individualist had farmed his small claim with methods not much different from those of Cain's time. The Western pioneer could not farm at all until the Revolution gave him practicable windmills, artesian wells, and the machinery that made his dams possible. When he crossed the hundredth meridian, in order to be Cain at all he had first to become Tubal-Cain.

II

The West, then, was born of industrialism. When the age of machinery crossed the hundredth meridian the frontier, which had so long resisted conquest, promptly came under the plow. But industrialism has other products than machines. Drawn to his heritage partly by advertising, which is one of them, the pioneer found prepared and waiting there for him the worst of all: financial organization.

In one sense the California gold rush won the Civil War, and that has its importance for history; but a greater importance is that it developed a mechanism for the exploitation of the West. The inventive men who devised ways of preventing gold-washers from retaining any outrageous profit from their labors skipped eastward into the true West with a perfected system. From 1860 on, the Western mountains have poured into the national wealth an unending stream of gold and silver and copper, a stream which was one of the basic forces in the national expansion. It has not made the West wealthy. It has, to be brief, made the East wealthy. Very early the West memorized a moral: the wealth of a country belongs to its owners, and the owners are not the residents or even the stockholders but the manipulators. Gold, silver, copper, all the minerals, oil—you need not look for their increase in the West, nor even among the generations of widows and orphans thoughtfully advised to invest in them by trust companies. The place to look for that increase is the trust companies, and the holding companies.

All this was demonstrated by the mines even before the Westerners arrived in force. The demonstration was repeated on a magnificent scale by the railroads, which added refinements in their ability to loot the Westerner directly as real-estate agencies and common carriers. Meanwhile the Government, the press, the whole nation were expediting the rush of settlement. It was *Zeitgeist,* by God! The continent had to be occupied—a bare spot on the map was an affront to the eagle's children. The folk migration, now in its last phase, was speeded up. Manifest destiny received the valuable assistance of high-pressure publicity. Congress, even less aware than the rail splitters that this was a strange country, helped out by passing, during fifty years, a series of imbecile laws which, even if no other forces had been working to that end, would have insured the West's bankruptcy. To inconceivably stupid government was added the activity of the promoter, who in the West had his last and greatest flowering as a statesman. Able to invade the last wilderness after fifty years of frustration, the migrating folk settled on the West like locusts. And they found finance—the finance of the East—waiting for them.

The catch phrase is "a debtor section." This was not, let me repeat, a problem of shouldering an axe and walking into the forest. The country had to be developed with the tools of the Industrial Revolution, and these cost money. The fencing, the wells, the canals and dams, the windmills, the gang plows, the cultivators, the tractors had to be paid for. The pioneers have been a debtor class all through history, and the Westerners as debtors differed only in having to pay more. What distinguished them from the rail-splitters was the fact that history had got ahead of them. They had to pay for the development of the country because the financiers were there first, whereas on the earlier frontiers that development had paid for itself.

Costs are not always apparent on the surface. The financing of an expertly wrecked and re-wrecked railroad may be like the salesman's overcoat—you don't see it on the expense account but it's there just the same. The railroads have been made symbolic; but in comparison with some of the other devices of exploitation their watered capitalizations, rigged bankruptcies, short and long-haul differentials, and simple policy of getting what they could seem social-minded and almost sweet. There were the water companies, the road companies, the land companies, the grain-storage companies. There were the mortgage companies. There were the banks. All of them learned from the mines and railroads, improving on instruction, and all of them looted the country in utter security, with the Government itself guaranteeing them against retributive action by the despoiled. There was also the Deacon Perkins formula which, because it contains the basic principle, will suffice to describe the whole process.

When money was easy, Deacon Perkins got three percent for it in his little back-room bank at East Corner, Massachusetts. When money was tight, he raised the rate to three and a half or four percent. So from a thousand East Corners, a thousand Deacon Perkinses each sent a nephew West, trusting him just so far as it was impossible to find further legal safeguards. Then borrowing from his own bank at three or four percent, the Deacon had Nephew Jim lend it in the West at twelve percent. I say twelve percent but it was more likely to be sixteen or eighteen percent, and in the newest districts it went to two percent a month. If Nephew Jim wanted to kite the rate a little by charging his client a commission for getting the loan, that was his own affair and had nothing to do with the system, which was concerned solely with the spread in interest rates, East and West. A good many Deacon Perkinses got rich on the system. A good many of them also got into the real estate business; but, with both Government and tradition sending the come-ons West in a steady stream, it was an easy business to get out of with another profit. The point, however, is that this system, a little complicated by the law of corporations, was precisely that of the manipulators. They were Eastern corporations and they financed themselves at two percent in order to charge twenty percent interest against the West, over and beyond the profits of trade, finance, monopoly, combination, and the normal increase of development. They had learned how to make the country pay. Their system was automatic and self-adjusting, an excellent system—for the East.

Besides taking over the country, then, the East added direct usury. The customary justification has mentioned empire-building—this tax was merely the fee which the strong men, the leaders, assessed for opening up the country. The explanation sounds sufficiently like that of other empire-builders, who got theirs without risk of loss, to sound convincing; and it probably satisfies the principles of imperial expansion in the textbooks. It has not, however, had a wide popularity in the West. The Westerner has seen palaces rise on Fifth Avenue and the endowments of universities and foundations increase with a rapidity that establishes the social conscience of his despoilers. The water company that took a mortgage on his farm grew into a bank, joined a network of interlocked pilfering agencies, changed into a holding company, and ended as an underwriter of railroad bonds and a depressant of farm prices in the interest of someone's foreign trade. In this whole country no one has ever been able to borrow money or make a shipment or set a price except at the discretion of a board of directors in the East, whose only interest was to sequester Western property as an accessory of another section's finance. He has contributed to those palaces and endowments just precisely what his predecessors in the pioneering system were enabled to keep for themselves. Meanwhile, the few alpine forests of the West were leveled, its minerals were mined and smelted, all its resources were drained off through perfectly engineered gutters of a system designed to flow eastward. It may be empire-building. The Westerner may be excused if it has looked to him like simple plunder.

Meanwhile the *Chicago Tribune,* the *New York Times,* and similar organs of his despoilers have maintained their amusing howl about those Federal taxes. Look how New York and Illinois, Massachusetts and Pennsylvania, contribute fifty- or a hundredfold to the national treasury, and look how their money is commandeered to build roads and maintain bureaus in the begging West. So long as this appears to be mere cynicism, the West enjoys the show, having had an experience that begets an enjoyment of cynicism. But sometimes the spokesmen seem really to believe what they are saying, seem really to be protesting against a form of confiscation, and then one hears above the sage the sound of prolonged and acid laughter.

III

So far as there is any theory in the politics of sectional warfare beyond the simple one of "them who can, gets," it is this: that the plundering of one section for the benefit of another is justifiable if the prosperity of the second spills over enough to compensate the first for what it has been robbed of. The theory sanctioned the tariffs, trusts, and service charges that the dominant East used as implements of exploitation. Since, however, the West flouted theory by going and staying bankrupt, it has for fifty years been customary to supplement the theory, which may be described as the horse-feathers school of thought, with occasional bakshish. The West has sometimes been tipped a fractional percent of its annual tribute in the form of Government works or social supervision. This bakshish is what the Eastern press so regularly laments, and yet is the time-honored way of dealing with agrarian unrest. Throughout history, governments have found it expedient to buy off the farmers when they grow troublesome, in order to sell them out at a profit later on. East of the hundredth meridian the agrarians have satisfactorily responded to that method. It has failed in the rainless country because the manipulators took too large an equity to begin with—they set the empire-builder's fee too high. The West has never had enough to come back on. It is the one section of the country in which bankruptcy, both actuarial and absolute, has been the determining condition from the start.

Newspapers are practicing relativists. A proposal to widen the scope of the horse-feathers policy has always been statesmanship. If you are a creditor seeking by tariffs or mergers to expedite the plundering of the West you become *ipso facto* a person of patriotic vision. If, however, you try to slow up the rate of exploitation, you are just an anarchist pushing the Republic over the cliff in the name of Utopia. Fair enough, but at least it may be explained that the cartoonists are wrong about Utopia. The West exists only by rigorous adaptation to a realistic climate. It has no vision of perfection and has been unable to sprout belief in planned economies. Millennial visions in America are native to areas of forty inches annual rainfall or above. Nevertheless, the accepted symbol is accurate: throughout its existence the West has produced much of the agitation known in the East as "radical" and has wholeheartedly supported all it did not produce. Most notably, schemes to debase the currency. Greenbackery, bimetallism, proposals for the cancellation of mortgages, for the reduction of usury, for even more direct methods with debt—all of them have either been born in the West or have had their apogee there. Nothing can exceed the horror of a banker who owns the mortgages or receives the usury or has participated in the mergers at which the reduction would be aimed. He knows that the Republic would be brought down by the collapse of its cornerstone, the sanctity of property; and in his way he is quite right. Only, the Westerner in his madness has experienced the fall of the Republic. It was property private to him that proved to lie outside the churchyard. The Republic crumbled fifty years ago, about the time a bank took over his first cooperative water-company, and his radicalism consists of inability to see wherein lies the heinousness of trying to get back some part of what was stolen from him at the muzzle of a gun.

The late flurry of doom, which agitated literary folk and frightened customers' men and young communists, anticipated a revolution so vague that one could make out little except that it would be bloody and soon. The prospect was stimulating but uncorrected by the historical approach. Agrarian revolutions in America, as I have pointed out, have always yielded to simple bribery, and our political revolutions have been hamstrung by the more economical method of enlisting their leaders on the side of the virtuous. If American history shows anything, it makes clear that revolution by means of the class struggle is inconceivable. The one revolution by means of class struggle that did come to actual warfare in America was a sectional revolution, and it is likely that any new one would take the same form. If the nation weakened sufficiently, conceivably it might split along the cleavage-lines of the sections. (Perhaps intra-sectional revolution could then follow the classics. While the united soviets of the steel country marched out to liquidate the kulaks of Western Pennsylvania, we might find General Dawes's minutemen arming themselves with castor oil to extirpate the La Follettes, take over the cooperative creameries of the Green Bay region, and exile the last Socialist councilman of Milwaukee.) The prospect of such fission would not appall the West. When empires crumble it is the provinces that go first, and the plundered province would slide into the sea with a perceptible exhilaration. Imagine repossessing the mines, the oil, the power lines, the cattle ranges and the wheat fields—imagine going into the first conference of independent sections prepared to bargain as proprietors, not as tenants or peons! The West could correct the interest-spread and realign the tariffs on a basis of realism. It could demand something more than the *pourboire* of a dam or some hard roads. Conceivably,

Massachusetts and Pennsylvania would learn something from federated bargaining that they have omitted to infer from Federal taxes.

This, however, is a virtual movement, an economic pipe dream kin to the editorials in liberal journals but unrelated to the actual pressures exerted by people who are carrying on economic struggles. The West has no hope of such dissolution, being able to estimate the strength of chains from their weight. It anticipates neither a breakup of the American economy nor any substantial readjustment of its part in that drainage system. It can fight the battle only on the terms laid down. If you can't win the campaign you try to win the individual engagement; if you can't reduce the salient you make a sortie against a limited portion of the front line. Reversal of the intersectional system is beyond hope, no return to the West of its equity in the nation is conceivable. In effect, no matter how the exterior alters, the East will go on producing protected goods for the West to buy in produce which the East's protection has depreciated. The West cannot modify the conditions but will continue to make sorties against the front line. The equity is not recoverable, but here and there the forced debt may be in part reduced. Cartoonists may as well dig in for a long winter; the West will remain radical. Necessarily, it will always be shoving the Republic over the same old cliff, bellowing one or another insanity. The actual form of insanity will change with chance and opportunism, but the force behind it will remain constant, a desire to rob the robbers of some fraction of their loot. That is part of the West's strangeness: it has always had an inexplicable hankering to get back its own.

Those of its spokesmen who resisted purchase have always been regarded as near relatives of the wild jackass. This too has an irony of its own, considering the politicians who have been the West's governors when they have not been simply the agents of its despoilers.

With the greatest kindness, Congress has frequently taken time off to help the West develop institutions fitted to its conditions. Amiable thinkers, who had the traditions of the well-watered country to guide them, produced a series of inconceivable stupidities for the formation of the West—and had the power to convert stupidity into law. Hence another part of the West's strangeness, its lawlessness. Quoting Professor Webb: "No law has ever been made by the Federal Government that is satisfactorily adapted to the arid region."

The West soon realistically phrased the Homestead Act under which the Government invited occupation: Uncle Sam bets you a hundred and sixty acres that you'll starve in less than five years. It was a safe bet and all alterations made in the odds were just as safe. Two only of such alterations need be mentioned. Congress, perceiving a generation too late that the country could not be farmed but might be grazed, authorized patents fully one-tenth the size of the minimum that would permit grazing. But that was enlightened vision compared to another bounty—one of Pennsylvania's little gratuities to Wyoming—under whose terms the Westerner might occupy his land provided he would grow trees on it. God's forestry had not been that ambitious, but it was just lawlessness that withheld the West from complying. The Homestead Act itself provided for units of settlement that had made forests and prairies productive but just one-eighth the size required in the region of thin rain.

The Westerner had his choice. He could become a social producer by occupying and developing the country illegally, in flat defiance of the law, or he could become a social charge by obeying the law and pauperizing himself. He did both. Survival in the West has been won at the price of actual or constructive illegality; beyond the hundredth meridian, the basic social institutions have always been beyond the law of the land, which catches up with them slowly and only in part. And of course, Governmental stupidity cooperating with promotional skin-games, hundreds of thousands of Westerners have failed in their pioneering efforts. These bankrupts form the unlovely finale of the westward wayfaring, the squalor in which the folk movement ended. Brought West by *Zeitgeist* and advertising, they were asked to make the country produce what it could not produce and to do the job under regulations that doubled the grim humor of the farce. They are the West's paupers, victims of the East's advertising campaign for unearned increment; and both Government and the East have forgotten them except as exasperating dependents who must be fed at someone's expense. Probably at the expense of the land-grant railroads or those Federal taxpayers in Pennsylvania.

Government's prodigal stupidity abetted them throughout. They were brought to a country unfitted to produce the crops they were asked to grow—a country which, under the conditions Congress laid on them, could support them at best only two years in five, and one year in five would wipe them out altogether. It was among these foreordained victims of a country which Congress could not understand that Pennsylvania's *pourboires* were expended. Here the dams and canals were built and the whole stupendous asininity of Reclamation enacted. God couldn't grow trees in this country but Congress would.

So now, after sprinkling those taxes on the alkali, Congress, we hear, proposes to buy back the land and let the alkali have its turn at reclamation. The dams and canals built, the generations bankrupted, the land is discovered to be what the maps label it, desert. It was, we are told, sub-marginal land all along. This discovery, in view of its history, is hardly of this world—belonging rather to the cosmic reaches. But let it go: the West is a strange country.

IV

Remember that this sub-marginal land, the sage and greasewood of the West's ultimate barrens, witnessed the end of a historic process. The rainless country was the last frontier, and in its poisoned areas, without dignity, the wayfaring Americans came to the end of their story. Reclamation is a shining image of something or other—aspiration, it may be, or futility. Confronted by the last acres of the tradition and finding them incapable of producing, the Americans wasted millions trying to enforce their will on the desert. The impulse and the glory of the migration died hard but, when the desert was conceded to be desert in spite of will power, they died at last, in something between pathos and farce. So here ends ingloriously what began gloriously on the Atlantic littoral, below the falls line; and the last phase of the westward wayfaring has the appearance of a joke.

Yet, this having always been a country of paradox, there is something more than a joke. Before that ending the Westerner learned something. Implicit in the westward surge, both a product and a condition of it, was the sentiment that has been called, none too accurately, "the American dream." It has a complex sentiment not too easily to be phrased. The plain evidence of the frontier movement, from the falls line on, indicated that there could be no limit but the sky to what the Americans might do. The sublimate of our entire experience was just this: here was a swamp and look! here is Chicago. Every decade of expansion, every new district that was opened, backed up the evidence till such an expectation was absolutely integral with the national progress. There was no limit but the sky: American ingenuity, American will power, American energy could be stopped by nothing whatever but would go on forever building Chicagos. It was a dream that, in the nature of things, had to be wrecked on reality sometime, but in actual fact the West was the first point of impact. Just as the pioneer had to give up his axe and learn mechanics when he crossed the hundredth meridian, just as he had to abandon his traditional individualism, so he had to reconcile himself to the iron determinism he faced. In the arid country just so much is possible, and when that limit has been reached nothing more can be done. The West was industry's stepchild, but it set a boundary beyond which industrialism could not go. American ingenuity, will power, and energy were spectacular qualities but, against the fact of rainfall, they simply didn't count. The mountains and the high plains, which had seen the end of the frontier movement and had caused the collapse of the pioneer culture, thus also set the first full stop to the American dream. Of the Americans, it was the Westerners who first understood that there are other limits than the sky. To that extent they led the nation. It may be that to the same extent they will have a better adjustment to the days ahead.

There at least, and not in the symbolism that has attached to them, is to be looked for the national significance of the West. They learned adaptation: they built their institutions, illegally for the most part and against the will of their plunderers, in accordance with the necessities of a climate that rigorously defined the possible. It was the necessities of the mining codes that first gave the clue of collectivism, and these codes were the nucleus round which the commonwealths coalesced. The law of real estate in part and the law of water rights in entirety followed this lead; the axe-swinger's individualism, in the desert, yielded to an effort much more cooperative. There was no other way in which the land could be occupied; this was determinism, and the Westerners accepted it, and not even their manipulators could do much against the plain drift of necessity. To the dismay of bondholders and cartoonists, the West is integrated collectively. It will stay that way while climate is climate. That also may be a portent for the nation whose dream is receded.

Looted, betrayed, sold out, the Westerner is a man whose history has been just a series of large-scale jokes. That comicality has helped to form the image which the dominant East has chosen to recognize. But it is not altogether a comic image. The wild-eyed figure of the cartoons attests to a certain Eastern uneasiness, and there is always the strangeness of the chaps and sombrero. It is wise to end on that strangeness. For the romantic clothes are only occupational garments, a work suit, the sign of the Westerner's adaptation to the conditions of his trades. Their true symbolism is not romance but intelligent acceptance of the conditions. The American dream was ended, but cattle could be grazed in this country, and these were the best outfit for the job, so he put them on. Thus dressing himself, he has become a romantic symbol to people who live in areas of greater rain; but do not be fooled. He is a tough, tenacious, overworked, and cynical person, with no more romance to him than the greasewood and alkali in which he labors. He is the first American who has worked out a communal adaptation to his country, abandoning the hope that any crossroads might become Chicago. The long pull may show—history has precedents—that the dispossessed have the laugh on their conquerors.

The Anxious West

On August 3, 1946, DeVoto wrote Arthur Schlesinger, Jr., that he intended to use the Easy Chair to strike a blow for conservation against the "western hogs." He wrote Schlesinger that he would time his blow so as to cripple the legislative programs that he and the Forest Service antici- pated the Stockmen to introduce in Congress. In December 1946 this article appeared not as an Easy Chair column in *Harper's*, but as a full-length article. In it DeVoto danced around the Stockmen issue, but did not fully bare his fangs in this attack. He would save his full-scale attack for January 1947, when he would strike a deep blow against the Stock- men and Land-grabbers in his article "The West Against It- self."

The West is plains, mountains, and desert. Its land- scape is dramatic, its climate violent. Its history is dramatic and paradoxical, and parts of it im- portant to both East and West never happened. Its nat- ural wealth is enormous and belongs mostly to the East and the national government. Its inhabitants, products of landscape, climate, and history, are a volatile, expan- sive people, energetic extroverts at the base of whose consciousness are tensions and conflicts. They are the fall guys of the United States and have been victimized by everybody, most disastrously by themselves. They have repeatedly scared the nation at large and now dream of seceding from it but have never been able to work together or trust one another. They have worked out an adaptation to their incredible environment which is one of the pleasantest ways of life ever known and this culture holds a shining promise for the United States, a promise which is countersigned by the world movements. They are the only Americans today who look toward the future with hope and confidence and they ignore the elements in themselves which bring both in question. They are children of paradox and begetters of paradox.

The first clue to them is their language. They speak standard American and speak it with fewer local tunes and shadings than any other section. The Western voice has none of the nasality and flatness of the Midwest. There is a Western drawl and it is on the increase but it is a phony. It is part Southern and part Hoosier. The Southern ingredients arrived with deserters from the armies during the Civil War—their trail can be traced on the map in various Virginia Cities, Richmonds, Davisvilles and the like, and innumerable Secesh Creeks, Confederate Bars, and Rebel Gulches. It was supplemented after the war by a migration that amounted to a stampede and is still known in the West as the left wing of Price's army. There was a third increment when the cattle began to move to the northern range. All three, however, were soon diluted to the vanishing point and there was no revival of the drawl till the West began to succumb to the most damaging of its illusions, the notion that it is universally a race of cowpokes.

That revival was self-conscious and originally it was for comic purposes only—which brought in the Hoosier tune by affinity, the Hoosiers having dedicated themselves to bucolic humor unto all eternity. But the illusion has proved so comforting and has received such support from the movies and radio that the future looks ominous. Whereas twenty-five years ago switching on the drawl notified the listener that a joke was in process, now it is histrionic. Westerners, too many of them, have an urge to dramatize themselves to strangers as the Old

Ranger or the Old Trail Boss. So far it is only drama but the role is taking hold. Increasingly the West sees itself as a congeries of big cow outfits before the freeze of 1886. It has always been facile at self-deception; that it has chosen this illusion to erect into a myth may be cosmic to outsiders but could end by being tragic to the West.

A good ear can make out some Westernisms. The habitual use of "home" for "house" is not confined to the West and neither is a characteristic handling of *eg* sounds, but the universal substitution of "lady" for "woman" comes close to being diagnostic and the Westerner gives himself away by the mayhem he commits on the sounds represented by *au* and *ol*. You can compose a shibboleth that will unmask him at the passages of Jordan—any such sequence as "Aunt Augusta's naughty daughter and her autumnal doll." He may have been educated at Oxford and lived for fifty years in Brooklyn but when he speaks such words he reverts to his childhood on Nine Mile.

Western speech is poetic, shot with fantasy, running over with metaphor. The figures of all the tongues in the melting pot and all the romantic occupations that are commonplace in the West have left a deposit on the common speech, superimposed on a similar deposit from violent frontier. The common humor is also specific. Southern humor is oratorical and anecdotal; as the world knows, Yankee humor runs to dryness and underemphasis; Midwestern humor is nervous and hyperbolic—but Western humor is self-deprecating, disparagement suspended in a medium of irony. It is partly explained by the fundamental fact that the West is at the mercy of the physical environment but the rest of the explanation is more revealing still: much Western humor expresses an inner chagrin.

Westerners are big men, according to the Army the biggest in the country. Also they are heavy men; an extraordinary percentage of them are fat. Elsewhere metropolitan America has adopted a diet proper to the sedentary life, but the Western city dweller eats a cowhand's meals. His breakfast egg is plural and is usually accompanied by meat, frequently a steak, and always by fried potatoes. Fried potatoes are the West's seasoning, in fact; they are served with practically everything except ice cream. The breakfast steak is likely to be served with pancakes as well and they are likely to be a side dish at lunch. The excellence of Western pastry increases the consumption of starch. You may know that you have reached the true West when you are served salads embedded in gelatin or cottage cheese and when you begin to encounter good pies in restaurants. Public or private, Western pies and cakes are the best in the country; so are Western breads and, in spite of the literary cliché about the South, Western rolls and biscuits too. They help to produce the Western waistline.

Western cooking has vastly improved in the past quarter of a century. But the West only reluctantly gives up the idea that the thing to do with a steak is to fry it—fry it hard—with the result that the hostesses and waitresses habitually set out several kinds of bottled sauces to make it edible and there is a big business in bicarbonate of soda. A sense of the salad has grown too. You seldom encounter the mixtures of cold veal, grapes, and boiled dressing that meant salad when I was a boy in the West, but you seldom encounter a plain green salad either. Only an occasional restaurant carries it on the menu and at some of those that do you may still have to explain that you don't want boiled carrots and lima beans in it. Western vegetables and fruits, which the unexhausted mineral soil makes the best in the country, have come into their own during the past generation; Westerners now eat them passionately. But they have added them to, rather than substituted them for, the proteins, fats, and starches which they have always eaten passionately. The word is revealing: Westerners are passionate about eaters, and this passion may be a displacement of others.

The diet is proper for ranch hands, farmers, and outdoor workers in general, who really have the lean, muscular look that is Western to illustrators and the movies. But it tends to bring the townsman's chest down to his waist at thirty and to pad his neck with fat at forty. I should like to speak more agreeably of Western women, young women, and girls—to call them buxom, deep-breasted, strong-thewed, fit to be the mates and mothers of big men. Mathematics forbids; too high a percentage of them are just fat. Overeating gives them thick ankles, cylindrical calves, big behinds, wide waists, heavy breasts. They must be the bulwark of the corset industry but all in vain. Elizabeth Arden could make a killing by establishing a chain of her Maine Chance reducing farms from the Missouri to the Pacific.

The cosmetic end of Miss Arden's business is a more fundamental necessity in the West than elsewhere, for the environment levies a heavy tax on women. There is no escape from an alleviation of Western sun, wind and dryness. Women's hair fades and grows brittle. Their skin dries, coarsens, and wrinkles. They tend to look older than they are and this effect is progressive. A girl of eighteen may look matronly only because she eats too much, but by the time she is forty she may look fifty because the climate has had its way with her.

II

Sun, wind, aridity—they condition life in the West, where men and society are more dominated by the natural environment than anywhere else in the United States. That Western society has survived at all is proof of a successful adaptation to them, and it is an engaging adaptation. The Western way of life is a good one. Westerners, I think, have a better time than any other Americans: they enjoy themselves more. The paradox is that mastering their environment has not given them self-confidence. They brag, they are obsessive and coercive and gang-minded; an awareness that something is wrong gnaws at them.

Basic in the Western way of life is the naturalness of living much in the open. You do not need the weather forecast in order to set the date for a picnic, a camping trip, a hunting or fishing or skiing expedition; for a calendar will do. The climate is violent but it is also stable, and in the seasons when rain is not to be expected there will be no rain. Winters are short except in the high country, which lengthens the season for summer sports, and the high country is so accessible that the season for winter sports lasts through June and in some places all year. The great fact is the mountains. Mountains are within the driving range of all Westerners, even those on the eastern edge of the high plains who can reach the Black Hills. They are a refuge from heat and dust, from the aridity that dehydrates you and the intensity of sun that shrinks the ego. The forests are in the mountains, with the fish and game, the trails, the creeks, the ski runs, and the cliffs that need rope work. More important still, they put solitude and silence at the disposal of everyone. Western life has come to incorporate mountain living. A national forest near large towns—the Wasatch Forest for instance, which straddles the range it is named for just above Salt Lake City—will have a million or more visitors in the course of a year, practically all of them from the immediate vicinity.

As a result most Westerners are hunters and fishermen and campers. Most of them are in some degree mountain climbers, naturalists, geologists. They know nature at first hand and intimately, are adept at outdoor skills, can maintain themselves comfortably in the wilderness. Furthermore, since they have grown up to these things naturally they have not romanticized or stylized them—except, that is, for the myth of the cattle business. There are no rituals. A Westerner cooking a meal in the forest is simply cooking a meal in the best way with the means at hand—there is none of the High-Church nonsense that accompanies outdoor cooking in Westchester or Long Island. Westerners are habituated to firearms and the right to bear them has not been abridged, but not even the movies have succeeded in tricking out Western firearms with the twaddle that has developed about them in the South.

Such folkways have produced the West's happiest contribution to architecture. I do not mean the bungalow, which is an eyesore, but the mountain cabin. It is made of logs, usually lodgepole pine, which are peeled and varnished with clear shellac; sometimes for the exterior surfaces a little burnt sienna is added to the shellac. The logs are chinked with concrete; chimneys and fireplaces are made of stones ("rocks" in the West) from the nearest creek. The result is a charming, comfortable, functional dwelling which blends with the landscape, warm in winter, cool in summer, almost vermin-proof. It is excellent everywhere except when the resort business parodies it by covering steel and concrete hotels with a veneer of logs.

An astonishingly large number of Westerners own such cabins or still more inexpensive camps in the mountains. They visit them at all seasons, not only for the annual vacation and at weekends but on momentary impulse. Similar cabins and camps can be rented everywhere. And almost no one is too poor to own an automobile and a camping outfit; those who use them, in fact, get farther into the wilderness and come to know it better than those with fixed camps. So the frontier's mastery of the outdoors has remained a part of Western life. It has contributed alike to the realism and the mysticism that makes so striking a mixture in the Western consciousness. Familiarity with the skills of Western occupations is also widespread; most Westerners know something about mining, prospecting, engineering, lumbering, sheep growing, and cattle raising. The Westerner is the best American outdoorsman and he is almost the only remaining American who rides a horse naturally, not as one practicing a cult.

All these sports and occupations have pleasantly vivified Western dress, especially the cattle business. The working cowpoke, of course, wears levis, a Big Yank shirt, and a pair of nine-dollar Acme boots. But the dress-up tradition of his trade, supported by the same tradition in lumbering and mining, has given Western clothes a moderate, satisfying flamboyance: half-gallon hats, saddle-shop belts with silver buckles, bright but not insistent colors in shirts and scarves, a species of riding trousers better than breeches or jodhpurs and for women much more attractive. (Turquoises, ninety-dollar boots, boots anywhere away from the presence of horses, hats beyond a gallon, and purple, orange, magenta, and vermilion shirts mean dudes or professional entertainers.)

The cattle business has also supplied the West's autochthonous festival, the rodeo. (Accent the first syllable.) It has been so commercialized and stylized that the pure form is to be seen only in small towns where cowhands from neighboring ranches do the riding. Nevertheless, the circuit shows, whose performers are as much professionals as baseball players, are an important contribution to entertainment. Their spectacles and skills are derived from a still living reality and their roots go down to an authentic past.

Not so much can be said for another Western festival whose generic name might be Frontier Week. It is the property of the Chamber of Commerce, a bad custodian for the expansive spirit. It is aimed at the tourist trade and retail sales. It is a fake and it is objectionable. (Montana, the most urbane and most skeptical of Western states, is least given to it.) There is no harm in people's dressing up in the costumes of their ancestors, though silk coats, flowered vests, black mitts, and hoop-skirts are tolerably grotesque. There is no harm in growing beards, though the vehemence with which the modern West grows them suggests a fear that it has not inherited all the frontier masculinity they are supposed to signify. There is no harm in celebrating the past if the celebration involves some knowledge of what it was or some respect for it, but Frontier Week seldom involves either. It is conducted without reference to history, it is empty of idea and emotion, its data are anachronistic and preposterous. Unlike a rodeo or a county fair, it has no cultural validity. Even its much-advertised release from restraints is pumped-up and cold.

It is, however, extremely revealing. Western towns by the hundred submit to Frontier Week and make a big noise about it at the direction of the Chamber of Commerce, for business reasons. They grow beards as an assist to sales—at the same command. They submit to being fined, ducked, or otherwise penalized if the beards won't grow. The kind of Westerner whom Frontier Week is supposed to commemorate would have slugged or if need be taken a shot at anyone who ventured to tell him how to wear his hair. He was an individualist with all that individualism implied in the West for both good and ill, but the contemporary beard-grower is just a coerced advertiser. He accommodates his behavior to sales talk and gang dictation and what is worse, he is advertising a myth. He symbolizes several of the unhealthiest forces in Western life.

In twenty-five years the celebration of the Western past has grown enormously. It has grown, however, chiefly in business sagacity and in noise; little increase in knowledge or understanding is visible. The West has found its history a valuable asset but remains widely uninterested in doing anything about it beyond hoking it up for tourists. Western antiquarians, local historians, collectors, and annalists are as enthusiastic and expert as those anywhere else, but they are few and forlorn; the historical societies (several of them very distinguished), societies for the preservation of antiquities, and similar groups, are small, handicapped by poverty, and under some public derision. Apart from advertising or at most ancestor worship, public feeling for the past is lethargic. In three months of Western travel I saw only one private enterprise devoted to celebrating local history which was both sincerely intended as a public service and likely to succeed. That was the work of Charles A. Bovey, who began by making the amazing collection at Great Falls, Montana, that is called Old Town and has gone on to restore Virginia City. I cannot praise it too highly, but what struck me was not only Mr. Bovey's success but the fact that he had been privileged to use his own money exclusively. Practically all the other non-utilitarian efforts to recover the Western past or to preserve its vestiges are the work of the federal government, and they are usually conceived and carried out by Easterners.

The effort to expand the tourist business is not, however, the only explanation for the uninformed noise which the West is making about its past. Much of it shows the influence of the horse operas, which are the West's favorite movies, and of the radio programs which alternate supposedly Western songs and allegedly frontier dramas all day long, with a large part of the West listening. But the ultimate responsibility cannot be charged to Hollywood and Tin Pan Alley, for the urge they satisfy originates in the West itself and reveals a tension in the Western consciousness. The past quarter century has transferred the myth of the Old West from fiction and the screen square into that consciousness, where it is beginning to show resemblances to the myth of the Old South.

The most significant aspect of this revelation is that the West has chosen to base its myth on the business that was of all Western businesses most unregardful of the public rights and decencies, most exploitative, and most destructive. The Cattle Kingdom did more damage to the West than anything else in all its economy of liquidation. As a mythology it will do even worse damage hereafter.

III

Much other evidence suggests psychic conflict. For instance, Jesus is advertised in the Northwest as insistently as in southern California and if possible more vulgarly. Innumerable small crank religions saturate Oregon and Washington and fan out across the neighboring states. They range from simple but extreme evangelism far into mental disease. Their emotional content is squalid and their compulsiveness attests a widespread inner frustration. Or take public attitudes toward liquor, which in the Northwest, Idaho, and Utah are downright schizophrenic.

These states desire drinking to be surreptitious, excessive, and uncivilized and have preserved all the evils of prohibition. In Utah this is understandable, since teetotalism is a tenet of the Mormon Church and all drinking has to be officially attributed to the Gentiles, though inquiry develops that the state liquor stores do their highest per capita business in purely Mormon communities. (The hamlet of Wendover is trying to secede from Utah and attach itself to the franker if frowsier culture of Nevada.) Idaho somewhat reduces the worst absurdities of the common system—the prohibition of liquor with meals and the refusal to sell it in less than bottle lots—by licensing cocktail bars at hotels so long as they pretend to be under a different management. It nevertheless refuses to let you drink less than a bottle in a hotel room; and it requires a temperate person to seek out the institution called a private club.

That institution is the worst result of the liquor laws in Washington and Oregon, where the system is most vicious—and most characteristic, since both states have always done some of the most brutal drinking in the United States and both had prohibition societies before they had local governments. The club is the customary answer to prohibitory laws: it is a speakeasy. It is unregulated, protected, frequently gang-owned, a place for getting drunk, and it serves prohibition liquor. Romantic Easterners nostalgic for the indecencies of the Incredible Era are advised to try Portland or Seattle.

The attitude thus revealed is pointed up by another one. Nothing is more shocking to a resident of the East than to come out of the speakeasy where he has had to go for his six o'clock cocktail and enter a restaurant, hotel, grocery, drugstore, railroad station, barber shop, beauty parlor, or department store where the natives are lined up by the dozen playing slot machines. They are universal from the Dakotas on, though of course in Utah they are more or less under cover, and they are in all public places except churches. And in a town which shall be nameless I saw the Episcopal rector dropping a stack of half-dollars into one, no doubt in the hope of increasing his poor fund—a vain hope since the slot machine is the most openly crooked and cynical of all gambling devices, in fact is not a gambling device at all. The machines are owned by syndicates, which implies widespread corruption of police officials and occasional gang wars, and they are played constantly and obsessively by everyone more than four feet tall, male or female. The obsessiveness is what strikes a visitor. The universal patronage of admittedly crooked machines cannot be explained by the Westerner's traditional eagerness to take a chance or by his liking for being treated as a sucker. It stems from unconscious anxiety and dissatisfaction.

Genuine gambling is wide open in the West (again Utah requires a veneer of hypocrisy) but appears to be conducted with decency everywhere except in Nevada. I am not referring to such places as Reno and Las Vegas which are organized to trim Easterners who can afford to be trimmed and which, I suppose, maintain the institutional honesties of gambling as rigorously as Monte Carlo. As a Westerner I cannot weep at the sight of Eastern dudes leaving their money in the West, nor refrain from reflecting that the take is only a small percentage of the sum lifted from well-heeled Westerners by New York alone. I am referring to the repulsive little dives in unknown Nevada hamlets which are patronized wholly by local residents.

No town is too small to have a combination lunchroom, bar, and gambling joint where a fish-eyed house man sits at his frowsy table dealing for a handful of customers—a couple of high school girls, a couple of phony cowpokes and a couple of real ones, some machinists from the railroad, a grade school teacher, and a bum who had cadged a dollar from a tourist. They absorb a percentage of the town's earnings every day. And they have a discernible relation to the signs set up along the roads leading to Fernley, the only signs I have ever seen advertising the desirability of getting drunk. In those signs there may be expansive Western humor and in the squalid dives there may be some of the Western freedom which the State of Nevada itself advertises at all its borders, adding that it has no sales tax, no income tax, no inheritance tax, and no corporation tax. But also they testify to the West's inner awareness that something is lacking in the way it lives.

IV

To Eastern eyes Western cities, most of which are just
big towns, seem clean, neat, glistening, even new. Part
of this shininess is due to the fact that few have slums
and very few have industrial slums, and part to the thin
air. Most of it, however, comes from the drama of the
Western landscape. You cross a long stretch of treeless
country and suddenly you reach such a town as Pierre
or Miles City which has been growing shade trees ever
since the first settlers came. The overwhelming Western sun is diffused, the wind is splintered, there are
coolness and dampness. The shade has a spiritual, even
a mystical quality, and as it assuages you it gives you a
vivid sense of the desperate and dogged aspiration that
produced it. Or the drama may be the mountains where
they seem to rise straight out of the town square—at
Missoula, Ogden, Colorado Springs, dozens of other
places. But the greatest drama comes from the miracle
on which the entire life of the West rests, irrigation.

Climb, for instance, out of the valley of the Snake at
Glenn's Ferry and head into the desert. For those who
love the desert there is great beauty here but it is a
beauty of sterility, in the imminence of death, sagebrush flats leading the eye across nothingness till barren mountains put a bound to space. Eventually you will
come to a river and will instantly understand why it was
named the Boise—and how infinitely more worthy its
valley is of the name now because its waters have been
diverted across the land. You cross the great canals with
a kindling awareness of the achievement they represent
and the tremendous imagination they realize. So you
come into the town of Boise. After such a prologue,
against such a backdrop, a drab and obsolescent town
would seem resplendent, but Boise is neither. Its trees
and lawns, the contemporaneousness of its hotels, its
shop windows, its inbound and outbound freight traffic,

the multifarious matériel of ranching, farming, mining, lumbering, and engineering which it is busily distributing—well, a complex culture is at work in circumstances that never permit you to forget that that culture has been created in a land originally lifeless. This touch of miracle might suggest to a newcomer that Boise is an extraordinary town, but it is a typical Western town, like Carson City, Billings, Walla Walla, Pendleton, like any town where irrigation has made a dead land live.

Such settings and such achievements, with the violent drama of the climate, have shaped the Western consciousness. Moreover, the towns are set not only in drama but in vastness. Enormous distances have been a master-condition of Western life from the beginning and they have altered conceptions of space and therefore of time, too. The reduction of space began with the railroads but its conquest awaited the automobile, which has reoriented Western society, business, and thinking.

The Western orientation always startles even the most mobile Easterner. Your hostess is going to make a three-hundred-mile round trip tomorrow to buy a blouse she has seen advertised in a big-town paper. Your host will be going to his ranch, fifty miles away, after breakfast but will be back for lunch and glad to take your son to a rodeo, fifty miles in the opposite direction, and have him back well before dinner. Your friend won't be in San Francisco over the weekend, having decided to go fishing on the Madison River at the edge of Yellowstone Park, or the Salmon River in Idaho, or the Deschutes in central Oregon. To take you picnicking at the cabin the family will drive a distance equal to that between New York and Buffalo and while there will drive you the width of Massachusetts to take in a movie or a dance. And why not? The family income probably derives from a business whose routine transport is done by truck at distances elsewhere thought proper only for railroad freight, in areas where a railroad could not possibly penetrate, at a steady reduction of the ratio of space to time.

The conquest of space is not enough, however, and the West is now in a fair way to annihilate it by means of aviation. Where sowers, foresters, prospectors, survey-ors, vermin-exterminators, and even cowpunchers adapt the airplane to their daily job it is natural for all kinds of businesses to turn to it. Even before the war munici-palities down to village size were building excellent air-ports, and the war compressed the development of a quarter century into five years. There are airports every-where in the desert now and landing fields in the most inaccessible mountains. The interior West is less than twenty-four hours from the Atlantic coast and much less than twelve hours from the Pacific coast.

This alteration of time-space is one leg of the tripod—electric power and war industries are the other two—on which the West rests the glorious vision that it may at last emancipate itself from absentee control and com-pete with other sections. Moreover, if markets are only fractions of a day away, littoral fashions, clip-joints, lux-ury shops, theaters, and smart gossip are at the same radius. Hayseed America has practically ceased to exist everywhere, of course, and the West was never hayseed in terms of "The Old Homestead." It has always had a cosmopolitan overtone and has always been nearer the Atlantic than the Midwest. But the airplane is an addi-tional reason why Boise and Missoula seem so spruce and why the girl at the slot machine seems to have stepped in off Fifth Avenue.

Airplane and automobile underscore the historic role of technology in the development of the West. Technol-ogy made the West possible, revolutions in firearms and mining machinery, the technology of railroading and conservation, of wells and dams, of windmills and barbed wire. It is another reason why Western towns are so clean. In the past quarter-century a network of natural-gas mains has crisscrossed the West and wiped the grime of bituminous coal from many towns. The girl in the Fifth Avenue dress cooks on an electric range, heats her bath water by electricity, and has filled her air-conditioned bungalow with more labor-saving gadgets than the bourgeois household has anywhere else. During the war she added to them a deep-freeze unit, which her husband keeps filled with meat bought at wholesale and at the bottom of the market, and with the fish, elk, deer, and game birds he gets at the mountain camp. She is living in an approximation of the America of tomorrow as the fantasies of engineers describe it.

These Western towns would be, thousands of tourists must decide, excellent places for the children to grow up in. So much space, so much sparkling air, so much lawn and forest, so much sunlight, so much natural beauty, such easy access to wilderness and silence, such facilities for recreation. Moreover, their social system is uncomplicated. If the Westerners are not quite free they are at least free and easy, spontaneous equalitarians, open-hearted if not precisely open-minded, friendly, buoyant. There is no anti-Semitism. Though Jim-Crow-ism appeared during the war, there is very little of it. (The West has always had its own color lines: Chinese and Japanese on the coast, Indians in the upper interior and the southwest, Mexicans everywhere.) It would be good, so the day-dream runs, for the children to have such things from their earliest years. And it would be good for them to acquire the West's feeling for the mountains, deserts, and forests, and especially its ever present, dualistic awareness of the struggle between man and nature, the tension between survival and disaster, the conduct of life under the threat of flood, drought, forest fires, and insect plagues. Western realism and Western mysticism, in both of which the idea of man's fate is objectified as the Western environment, make an equipoise that promises much for satisfaction in life.

I have heard this reverie many times from Easterners whom the West has taken by storm. They are right. The West always was a good place for children to grow up in and has steadily become a better one. How good a place it is and will henceforth be for them to stay in when they are grown, however, is a different, not necessarily related question.

V

How important the West is to the postwar United States is insufficiently realized in the West and hardly realized at all anywhere else except at the centers of industrial and financial power.

New Deal measures, war installations, and war industries have given the West a far greater and more widely distributed prosperity than it has ever had before. Moreover, during the war a fundamental revolution took place: power and industrial developments in the West have made a structural change in the national economy. That change is certain to increase and have increasingly important results, for if the developments that have occurred are revolutionary those already planned and sure to be carried out are even more revolutionary, and some of those which so far are only dreams but may be achieved stagger the mind. Finally, the world movements which are working out a long-term reorientation of human societies whose focus is the Pacific Ocean will be increasingly favorable to the West.

The West sees all this in terms of its historical handicaps: colonial economic status and absentee control. The ancient Western dream of an advanced industrial economy, controlled at home and able to compete nationally, is brighter now than it has ever been before. For the first time there are actual rather than phantasmal reasons for believing that the dream can be realized. I will discuss them in a later article. But the West cannot escape history and especially its own history. Nor can it escape psychology, its own historic psychology. If their dream is to be realized at all it must be realized within the Western culture and the limits of Western consciousness. Psychology will have quite as much to do with it as economics. I have described here certain ambiguities in the culture and psychology of the West which at least tinge the dream with doubt.

For some kinds of people the West is something of a paradise and those who have worked out an effective adaptation to it seem to be happier than the average run of Americans. Even they, however, show symptoms of psychic insecurity. That insecurity shows most plainly in the two kinds of Westerners who are most obviously unhappy and most obviously out of harmony with Western culture, the intellectuals and the rich. It must be significant that both are obsessed by a feeling of inferiority and that the Western colonialism by which they explain it is not economic but cultural.

The rich are easily explained. In the overwhelming majority they are either local representatives and managers of, or else are necessarily allied with, the system of absentee exploitation that has drained the West's resources eastward and channeled its wealth in the same direction. As parties to or dependents on that system they are really adversaries of the West. Their intellectual and spiritual loyalties are to its enemies. They have no function in the indigenous culture but they must live in the most of it as remittance men, émigrés, and expatriates. Forty years ago Harry Leon Wilson described them as Spenders, and a generation has only made their phantasy-life sillier and more vulgar. In that phantasy-life they see themselves as exiles from reality, but their reality is only the advertising pages of *Vogue*. They are the silliest (and one observer of them is here substituting that adjective for "most hoggish") members of that class for whom the clip-joints of the Atlantic and Pacific Coasts are run: the gaudy restaurants, the vulgar shops, the meretricious resorts, the whole falsely veneered world which has been expertly designed to take them in and whose phoniness they understand to be Elegance and Fashion. Their ambition may be summed up as to be mistaken for the kind of millionaire who was born within this world either in Hollywood or better still New York, night-club New York. It is hard to manage in the desert and impossible in New York. They are America's stupidest fall guys and the West's only hicks.

The rich derive no sustenance from Western culture and contribute nothing to it. There would be no particular significance in that, since it is by their own choice, if it were not the fact that the West's intellectuals come out much the same, if for reasons as different as possible, reasons which are seldom their fault.

Effective radicalism in the West has originated in the economic struggle, as a direct product of the exploitation. The West's intellectual radicals, however, have been and remain something else. They are charming as the millionaires assuredly are not, but theirs is a charm of irresponsibility. They are at once fiery and sweet—red in tooth and claw and buoyed up by the knowledge that they will never have to do anything at all about it. The barricades they fight on are imaginary and the deaths they undergo are mere formulas. Their radicalism is a species of aesthetics. But the point is that if it were anything else they could not survive in the West.

Intellectuals have always been a Western export. In the United States at large the professions—the learned professions—journalism, literature, and the arts contain a disproportionate number of men and women who grew up on Nine Mile over against Dead Man but whose address is now Westport or Winnetka or Palo Alto. They found the going too hard and so they got out. They refused to waste their strength fighting an unfavorable environment.

In the past generation that environment has become somewhat more favorable but not much. Let writers stand for them all. Only a small handful of first-rate writers have stuck it out in the West—men who write as Americans without Western provinciality or who write about Western experience without neuroticism. I do not know what inner resources have been required of such men as, say, Edwin Corle, Thomas Hornsby Ferril, Vardis Fisher, and Joseph Kinsey Howard, but that such achievement as theirs requires unusual strength is obvious from what has happened to the generality of Western writing. It has got mired in the spongy, self-conscious regionalism that has devitalized American writing wherever it has broken out, though for the South's forty acres and a poet the spacious West has substituted six hundred and forty acres and a mystic. Or else it has fled into coterie literature, with the result that the little magazine is making its last stand in the sagebrush and the writer who stayed there is trying to be Eugene Jolas. He has his own *Vogue* and *Spur* and is trying to erect a Left Bank on Nine Mile. This escapism is pathetic rather than vulgar because it is forced on him, but if escapism is a means of survival it nevertheless ranges him with the millionaire. He has found no roots in the common culture and so regards it as colonial.

What has denied him roots, however, is not a colonial state of mind but the state of mind of the vigilantes, the vigilantes who were always as useful for suppressing nonconformity as for getting rid of stage-robbers. I have suggested that the coercive beard-growing of Frontier Week, the developing myth of the Old West, and the compulsive mass-hypnotism of the slot machines are not casual surface-phenomena of Western life but symptoms of conflicts that come close to being organic. They go back in history as far as the West goes but they are more important now than ever before, because the fulfillment of the great dream will depend on whether the West resolves them as it undertakes to seize its hour.

Western freedom has always been extended to certain kinds of behavior only; freedom has always been denied to other kinds of behavior and has hardly existed at all in thought and opinion. Western individualism has different appearances in different lights but it has always been less a matter of letting my neighbor go his way as he chooses than of waiting for him to make some mistake that will allow me to jump his claim. That Chambers of Commerce have taken over the gang function of the Vigilance Committee has only made Western business more timorous, an easier setup for absentee exploitation. It has only increased the West's historic willingness to hold itself cheap and its eagerness to sell out. The West has certainly been raped by the East but its ads and its posture have always invited rape.

Thus the basic problems are internal. The West has always suppressed domestic criticism, while cringing before criticism from outside, and has treated nonconformity of idea and innovation of any kind especially in business, as dire social evils. Forever in rebellion against exterior exploitation, it has nevertheless always co-operated with the exploiters against itself when the chips were down. Worst of all, its own interior exploitation has always worked to the same end. No destruction by absentee-owned corporations of the West's natural resources—all it has—has ever been forestalled, because anything that could forestall it would also forestall the West's own destruction of those same resources. At this moment there is intended an assault on the public resources of the West which is altogether Western and so open that it cannot possibly be called a conspiracy. It is an assault which in a single generation could destroy the West and return it to the processes of geology. That such an intent publicly flourishes and may succeed—at the very moment when the West is undertaking, with some possibility of success, to emancipate itself and establish an advanced industrial economy—is plain proof of schizophrenia.

Will the effort to achieve the status of an equal in the national economy turn out in the end to have been just one more Western boom? Is the West's contemplated secession from the Union premised on getting the federal government to subsidize the secession and Wall Street to pay the carrying charges? Will the revolution now gathering momentum end with the same old masters of the throttle still?

The issue will be settled in terms of steel, aluminum, water, electric power, freight rates, and credit. But the determinant will be the Western consciousness. Westerners have always thought of the East as their worst enemy, but they have always acted as if their worst enemies were the Westerners who wanted their children to live in the West, who wanted to make something of the country and keep it. They have been chary of trusting one another and with good cause: what has always wrecked co-operation has been their willingness to sell one another out. Unless that changes in the course of the revolution, Wall Street can view the future of its Western satrapy with detached claim.

The West Against Itself

This January 1947 essay in *Harper's*—later reprinted in *The Easy Chair*—marked a critical turning point in DeVoto's conservation writing. His close friends in the National Forest Service kept him abreast of the hostility of Eastern stock interests to the range of regulations DeVoto and other environmentalists hoped for. Not only did DeVoto use his influence as a senior writer and columnist for *Harper's* to procure twice the normal amount of space for an article, but he also timed this piece to appear a few weeks before Congress resumed regular session.[1] Though "The West Against Itself" may seem from the beginning to be a continuing conservationist rally cry, DeVoto does turn his gaze to the Westerners themselves. His critical eye and sharp pen turn inward as he takes to task a West seemingly stuck between independence and development. "The West Against Itself," as well as DeVoto's career as an unapologetic conservationist writer and activist, led to his appointment exactly a year later—January 1948—to the Advisory Board for National Parks, Historic Sites, Buildings, and Monuments. The Board members served as advisors to Secretary of the Interior Julius Krug, providing DeVoto yet another platform from which to save the West from the East and its own schizophrenic tendencies.

I n *Harper's* for August 1934, I called the West "the plundered province." This phrase has proved so useful to Western writers and orators that it has superseded various phrases which through two generations of Western resentment designated the same thing. We must realize that it does designate a thing; that whatever the phrases, there is a reality behind them. Economically the West has always been a province of the East and it has always been plundered.

The first wealth produced in the West was furs, mainly beaver furs. It made a good many Easterners rich. Partnerships and corporations sent technical specialists—trappers and Indian traders—into the West to bring out the furs. No producer ever got rich; few were ever even solvent. The wealth they produced—from the West's natural resources—went east into other hands and stayed there. The absentee owners acted on a simple principle: get the money out. And theirs was an economy of liquidation. They cleaned up and by 1840 they had cleaned the West out. A century later, beaver has not yet come back.

In the early eighteen-forties emigrants began to go west. They leapfrogged over the plains and mountains, which were settled much later, in order to get to Oregon west of the Cascade Mountains and California west of the Sierra. Their settlements were the first permanent local interests in the West and (with Mormon Utah) for decades the only ones. The emigrants expected to stay in the West and expected their descendants to go on living off the country. They made farms and set up local systems of production, trade, export of surpluses, and even manufacture. The interests of these people, the permanent inhabitants, have always been in conflict with the interests of transients, of those who were liquidating the West's resources. Their interests have not been in conflict with those of the East, in fact they have been worth more to the East than all other Western sources of wealth put together—so long as the East has been able to control and exploit them, that is from the beginning up to now. The East has always held a mortgage on the permanent West, channeling its wealth eastward, maintaining it in a debtor status, and confining its economic function to that of a mercantilist province.

The development of the mineral West began in 1849. Mining is the type-example of Western exploitation. Almost invariably the first phase was a "rush"; those who participated were practically all Easterners whose sole desire was to wash out of Western soil as much wealth as they could and take it home. Few made a stake. Of those who did practically everyone carried out his original intention and transferred Western wealth to the East. The next and permanent phase was hard-rock mining or mining by placer or dredge on so large a scale that the same necessity held: large outlays of capital were required and the only capital that existed was Eastern. So the mines came into Eastern ownership and control. They have always channeled Western wealth out of the West; the West's minerals have made the East richer. (The occasional Westerner who fought his way into the system—called a "nabob" in his era—became a part of that system, which is to say an enemy of the West.)

Mining is liquidation. You clean out the deposit, exhaust the lode, and move on. Hundreds of ghost towns in the West, and hundreds of more pathetic towns where a little human life lingers on after economic death, signalize this inexorable fact. You clean up and get out—and you don't give a damn, especially if you are an Eastern stockholder. All mining exhausts the deposit. But if it is placer mining, hydraulic mining, or dredging, it also kills the land. Nothing will come of that land again till after this geological epoch has run out.

In witness of what I said last month about the West's split personality, consider this: that in the West no rights, privileges, or usurpations are so vociferously defended by the West—against itself—as the miner's. The miner's right to exploit transcends all other rights whatsoever. Even the national government is unable to effect enough control over mineral property rights to harmonize them with conflicting or even merely different rights.

Oil and natural gas follow the pattern of mines. Because their development is comparatively recent the national government is able to exercise some control over them in the common interest, by using the lease system instead of the patents which it must issue to miners. But just because that development is recent, Eastern capital has been able to monopolize oil and gas even more completely than it ever monopolized mining. The wells, pipelines, and refineries belong to Eastern corporations. They pump Western wealth into Eastern treasuries. It is possible for a Western independent to make a mineral discovery, finance it, and maintain his local control in defiance of the absentee system; it has happened occasionally in the past and it happens occasionally now. But the wildcatter in oil, the independent, has no chance at all except to submit to the system. He may find oil without its assistance; in fact the system hopes he will. But he cannot refine or transport or sell oil except to the system, on the system's terms.

Western psychology prevents him from desiring to do anything else. Last summer I talked with the manager of a small, locally owned refinery which, with much good luck but mostly because the necessities of war had set up exactly the right conditions, had cleared its debts, secured contracts which seemed to guarantee it permanent independence, and built up an impressive surplus and reserve. It was a minute item of fulfillment of the West's great dream, the dream of economic liberation, of local ownership and control. And what had been done with that surplus and that reserve? They had been invested in Standard Oil of New Jersey. The West does not want to be liberated from the system of exploitation that it has always violently resented. It only wants to buy into it.

So we come to the business which created the West's most powerful illusion about itself and, though this is not immediately apparent, has done more damage to the West than any other: the stock business. Now there was stock raising along the Pacific Coast before there was American agriculture there, long before there were American settlements. But the cattle business of the West as such has been conducted east of the Cascades and Sierra and in great degree east of the Rockies, and it began when cattle were brought to the open range— first to Wyoming, Montana, and the Dakotas, then else-where. Its great era lasted from about 1870 to the terminal winter of 1886–87, which changed its condi-tions forever. Changed them, I repeat, forever. But the practices, values, and delusions developed in that era, like the Cattle Kingdom of romance, dominate the cat-tle business today.

The cattlemen came from Elsewhere into the empty West. They were always arrogant and always deluded. They thought themselves free men, the freest men who ever lived, but even more than other Westerners they were peons of their Eastern bankers and of the railroads which the bankers owned and the exchanges and stock-yards and packing plants which the bankers established to control their business. With the self-deception that runs like a leitmotif through Western business, they wholeheartedly supported their masters against the West and today support the East against the West. They thought of themselves as Westerners and they did live in the West, but they were the enemies of everyone else who lived there. They kept sheepmen, their natural and eventual allies, out of the West wherever and as long as they could, slaughtering herds and frequently herds-men. They did their utmost to keep the nester—the farmer, the actual settler, the man who could create local and permanent wealth—out of the West and to ter-rorize or bankrupt him where he could not be kept out.

And the big cattlemen squeezed out the little ones wherever possible, grabbing the water rights, foreclosing small holdings, frequently hiring gunmen to murder them. And, being Western individualists and therefore gifted with illusion, the little cattlemen have always fought the big ones' battles, have adopted and supported their policies to their own disadvantage and to the great hurt of the West.

Two facts about the cattle business have priority over all the rest. First, the Cattle Kingdom never did own more than a minute fraction of one percent of the range it grazed: it was national domain, it belonged to the people of the United States. Cattlemen do not own the public range now: it belongs to you and me, and since the fees they pay for using public land are much smaller than those they pay for using private land, those fees are in effect one of a number of subsidies we pay them. But they always acted as if they owned the public range and act so now; they convinced themselves that it belonged to them and now believe it does; and they are trying to take title to it. Second, the cattle business does not have to be conducted as liquidation but throughout history its management has always tended to conduct it on that basis.

You have seen the Missouri River at Kansas City, an opaque stream half saturated with silt. A great part of that silt gets into it from the Yellowstone River, above whose mouth the Missouri is, comparatively, clear. The Yellowstone is fed by many streams, of which those from the south carry the most silt, the Tongue, the Rosebud, especially the Powder River, and most especially the Big Horn. Above the mouth of the Big Horn the Yellowstone is comparatively clear. These plains rivers are depressing and rather sinister to look at, and they always have been helping to carry the mountains to the sea. But one reads with amazement descriptions of them written before the Civil War. They were comparatively clear streams, streams whose gradual, geological erosion of the land had not been accelerated—as it was when the cattle business came to Wyoming and Montana. The Cattle Kingdom overgrazed the range so drastically—fed so many more cattle than the range could support without damage—that the processes of nature were disrupted. Since those high and far-off days the range has never been capable of supporting anything like the number of cattle it could have supported if the cattle barons had not maimed it. It never will be capable of supporting a proper number again during the geological epoch in which civilization exists.

That should be, though it mostly isn't, important to the citizens of Wyoming, whose heritage the West's romantic business in part destroyed. It is directly important to everyone who lives in the lower Missouri Valley or the lower Mississippi Valley, and only a little less directly important to everyone who pays taxes for flood control, relief, or the rehabilitation of depressed areas. For when you watch the Missouri sliding greasily past Kansas City you are watching those gallant horsemen out of Owen Wister shovel Wyoming into the Gulf of Mexico. It is even more important that their heirs hope to shovel most of the remaining West into its rivers.

There remains lumbering. It perpetuated greater frauds against the people of the United States than any other Western business—and that is a superlative of cosmic size. It was a business of total liquidation: when a tree is cut, a century or two centuries may be required to grow another one and perhaps another one cannot be grown at all. Also it killed the land. A logged-out forest does not take so much geological time to come back as a place where a gold dredge has worked but during the generations of men it is even more evil. The effects of denuding a forest extend as far as fire may go and be-

yond that as far as any of the streams on the watershed
it belongs to may be used for human purposes or are capable of affecting life, property, or society.

Lumbering, however, shows several deviations from
the Western pattern. First, though the greater part of
the timber came into Eastern ownership, with the consequent disregard of Western interests and the usual
transfer of wealth out of the West, nevertheless an important bulk of it came into the hands of Westerners.
Second, the national government got on the job in time
to protect vast areas of forest from liquidation—and to
protect the heart of the West from geological extinction.
Third, a good many of the big operators got the idea in
time and it is mainly they who are now trying to maintain
privately owned Western forests as a permanent source
of wealth, whereas the drive to liquidate all forests
comes most vociferously from small operators, who have
neither the capital nor the timber reserves for long-term
operation. But with lumbering as with the cattle business we see revealed the psychic split that impels the
West to join its enemies against itself.

These then, with power and irrigation which we may
skip for the moment, are the businesses founded on the
West's basic natural resources. While these businesses
were developing, the rest of the West's economic structure, the parts which are like similar businesses everywhere, was also developing. There came to be in the
West agriculture, transportation, wholesale and retail
distribution, all the multifarious activities necessary to
society. As I have already said, they are in sum much
more important to the East than the basic businesses it
owns—so long as it can control them in its own interest.

II

We lack space to describe the system by which the East
maintains the West as an economic fief. It has been de-

scribed many times and several recent books discuss it in relation to the current Western hope of breaking it up. Mr. A. G. Mezerik's *The Revolt of the South and West* is sound but in some contexts emotional rather than factual and commits the fallacy of assuming that the modern Far West can have the same relation to the South that the Middle West had before the Civil War. Mr. Wendell Berge's *Economic Freedom for the West* is more analytical and much more realistic. Mr. Ladd Haystead's *If the Prospect Pleases* is less comprehensive than either but Mr. Haystead deals with the Western psychology that imperils the Western hope, as Mr. Mezerik and Mr. Berge do not.

The bases of the system are simple. In a striking analogy to eighteenth-century mercantilism, the East imposed economic colonialism on the West. The West is, for the East, a source of raw materials for manufacture and a market for manufactured goods. Like the colonies before the Revolution the West is denied industry. Natural evolution concentrated industry and financial power in the East but the same evolution gave all other sections but the West a sizable amount of both. By the time the development of the West began it was possible to control the evolutionary process—to finance the West in such a way that the growth of locally owned industry became all but prohibited.

The control of capital is, of course, the basic process. There is an amazing spread of interest rates between the East and the West. For such purely individual financing as real estate loans the West pays from two to three times as high a rate as the East. For the ordinary conduct of business it pays exactly what the East cares to charge and always enough to constitute a handicap in competition. But also as Western business becomes large enough to compete the Eastern financial network can either dictate to it absolutely or destroy it. This is at the simplest level. Above it is the interconnected structure of finance: the monopolies, cartels, inter-industry agreements, control of transportation, and the many other instruments of power.

Take freight rates. They are devised so that the East pays lightly for the transport of Western raw materials but the West pays heavily for the transport of Eastern manufactured goods—and is prevented from manufacturing its own goods. The cowpoke at a ranch fifty miles from Sheridan, Wyoming, does not wear boots made in Sheridan. He wears boots made of leather from hides shipped from Sheridan to Massachusetts, processed and manufactured there, and then shipped back to Sheridan. The businessman of an Oregon town does not buy a desk made where the lumber is made, but in Grand Rapids whither the lumber is shipped and whence the desk is returned to his home town, paying two freight charges where he should pay none at all. The wheat rancher in Washington or Montana has to buy agricultural machinery made not in rational proximity either to his ranch or to Western deposits of iron and coal but in Illinois, Ohio, or Pennsylvania—and is mentioned here because he pays not only that tax to Eastern control of business but another one, the tariff that protects the manufacturer but builds no wall round the wheatgrower. Finally, the businessman who erects an office building in Denver or the county commissioners who build a bridge in northern Utah may indeed use steel produced within a hundred miles of the operation—but they pay on it, for the maintenance of the system, a tax assessed by the "basing point" principle that makes a satisfactory substitute for the outlawed "Pittsburgh plus."

The West is permitted to engage in preliminary operations that reduce the bulk of raw material so that the East can save freight costs in transporting them to the mills where the finishing operations are performed. It is not permitted to perform those finishing operations, to manufacture finished materials into consumers' goods, or to engage in the basic heavy industries which would give it the power to blow the whole system wide open. So far as the West is industrialized, it has a low-level industry. But there are necessarily loopholes in the system: kinds of industry which cannot be prevented from developing in the West. Such loopholes do not disturb the Eastern masters. Control of credit enables them to buy them out or dictate the terms on which they may be operated. Or they manipulate patent rights or trade agreements to the same end. Or they establish a branch plant of their own which cuts the throat of the Western-owned plant. Or they merely mention these possibilities and the Western industrialist, a fiery secessionist in his oratory, joins the system.

The result is an economy bound to the industrial system of the East even where it is not in fact owned and managed by that system. That is to say, the West is systematically looted and has always been bankrupt.

There has never been a time when the West did not furiously resent all this nor a time when some elements in the West were not trying to do something about it. All the furious agitations that have boiled out of the West and terrified Eastern *rentiers* (but have seldom caused the actual engineers of plunder to turn a hair) have had the sole purpose of securing for the West some fractional control over its economic future. None of them have ever succeeded except when they could perform an ancillary service to the absentee system—like the permanently inflated price of silver, as outrageous a robbery of the American people as any ever devised by the steering committee of a patent pool. At most they have got the West an occasional tip amounting to a nickel or a dime, tossed back out of the millions drained eastward. There was never a chance that they could accomplish more. That is, there was never a chance till recent years. But now there is.

The New Deal began it. New Deal measures slowed the liquidation of resources and substituted measures of permanent yield. They operated to rehabilitate depleted sources, halt and repair erosion, rebuild soil, and restore areas of social decay. They eased credit, opened small gaps in the master system, and created much local prosperity. Such things improved the economic system and more important measures widened its base. Public power and rural electrification dented the power monopoly which I have not touched on here but which is a basic tool of the system. A great expansion of reclamation projects increased agricultural wealth and, what is much more important, made a start toward the production of surplus electric power. Finally, with such enterprises as the Central Valley Project and the stupendous, integrated plans for the development of the Columbia River basin, the New Deal laid the groundwork for a fundamental attack on the system.

The West greeted these measures characteristically: demanded more and more of them, demanding further government help in taking advantage of them, furiously denouncing the government for paternalism, and trying to avoid all regulation. But the measures began to make possible what had not been possible before. They would provide electric power so cheaply and in such quantity that great industrial development must follow in the West. The Western economic structure must be revolutionized and reintegrated—which would imply tremendous changes in the national economic structure. And for the first time the West had a chance to seize control over its own economic destiny.

The war came and the process begun by the New Deal was accelerated. Factories of many kinds sprang up everywhere. (Except in Montana, long the private fief of Anaconda Copper and Montana Power, which succeeded in preventing any serious threat to their control of labor and production.) Mr. Berge has shown how, even in the stress of war, the absentee Eastern masters were able to direct much of this development in the old pattern, to restrain it to plants that performed only preliminary or intermediate processes. But not altogether. The West got airplane plants, shipyards, plants that manufactured such complex things as tanks and landing craft, heavy machinery, packing plants, innumerable processing plants. At Fontana in California and Geneva in Utah it got basic steel production. The war also produced something else the West had never had, a large body of skilled industrial labor. Also, by building landing fields and modern airports everywhere it made at least a fissure in the monopoly of transport and took out of transport much of the handicap of time which the West has always had to carry. Finally, it exhausted the new surplus of electric power and so hastened the already contemplated production of more power.

In short, the West now has an industrial plant and the conditions for its use are favorable—and certain to become more favorable. That is the fact on which the reinvigorated dream of economic liberation rests. The plant is too heavily concentrated along the Columbia, Puget Sound, the Willamette Valley, and the Pacific Coast—more so than it would have been if the development had been more gradual—but it does extend through much of the West. And with the production of, for instance, ingots and rolled steel and aluminum, heavy industrial goods, and many kinds of finished consumers' goods, and with the certainty that the production of power will increase, the terms are changed forever. The West can at last realistically envision developing a high-level economy with all that that implies: stability, prosperity, rising standard of living, successful competition with other sections, a full participating share in an expanding economy.

Realization that the dream can be fulfilled has made the West all but drunk. It is looking forward to the future with hope and confidence. I cannot list here the sectional and interstate associations and committees engaged in implementing the dream, the plans they are working out, the measures they are preparing, or any other specific details that have been born of a strange wedlock—the dynamics of boom which any trigger whatever has always been able to release in the West and the unique opportunity which the last few years have brought about. Enough that the West understands the opportunity, understands the possibilities of success and of failure that are inherent in it, and is taking every conceivable measure to avert failure and insure success.

With a conspicuous exception. The West seems unaware of one possibility of failure, the one that is inherent in its historic psychology.

III

Some doubts will occur to anyone. Thus if the upheaval should merely transfer financial power from Wall Street to Wall Street's California branch office, the basic system would be changed no more than it was years ago by the entrance of Chicago finance into the Western exploitation that had previously been monopolized by New York and Boston. A coastal dictatorship would merely be substituted for a trans-Mississippi one. Certain assurances will also occur to anyone and of these the principal one is that the Northwest has a better chance of pulling it off than the West as a whole. Its natural resources are more compactly concentrated and have been less impaired. The Northwest is a more self-contained unit with fewer internal frictions and the Columbia system is more uniform and manageable than the Missouri system or any other possible focus of future development. Most important of all, the Northwest seems to have got the idea that sustained use of natural resources—which is to say simply, the future—is incompatible with the liquidation of those resources in the present.

I have described a basic split in the Western psyche. Whether the great dream will fail or be fulfilled depends on how that split works out. Western individualism has always been in part a belief that I stand to make more money from letting my neighbor down than from co-operating with him. Westerners have always tended to hold themselves cheap and to hold one another cheaper. Western resentment of its Eastern enslavement has always tended to be less a dislike of the enslavement than a belief that it could be made to pay.

The oil refinery that invested its surplus in Standard Oil was hardly warring on absentee control and the same thing is to be seen throughout the West. The Wolfville Chamber of Commerce which is campaigning almost rabidly for local investment, local manufactures locally owned, integration of the local commercial system—all surcharged with violence about Wall Street, "foreign" corporations, the freight rates, and the East as such—that Chamber of Commerce is also campaigning by advertisement and paid agents to bring Eastern corporations to Wolfville. At the moment when its rhapsody of insurrection is loudest its agents are spreading out their charts on the desks of Eastern industrial managers. Look, we've got this cheap federal power at Wolfville and a labor surplus, too. The unions are feeble in Wolfville and in fact throughout the state—it's not Paterson, it's not Akron, it's a setup. We'll give you a site free and build your spur. Now as for tax abatement, just what do you need? Just what additional advantages do you need, that is, over the locally owned businesses of Wolfville we are trying to build up in order to break the stranglehold of the East?

The symptoms of the division in the Western mind show more clearly in the Western press, the newspapers, and the specialty journals of mining, lumbering, cattle and sheep growing, engineering. It is, to begin with, an astonishingly reactionary press. The Western radical who occasionally scares the East usually turns out to be advocating on his native plains something of a couple of decades earlier than Mark Hanna. An average Democratic newspaper in the West would seem by, say, the advanced liberalism of the Pennsylvania state machine, to be expressing a point of view much too backward for Boies Penrose. A typical Republican editorial page in the West is written out of the economic and social assumptions of avalanche capitalism just after the Civil War. The point is that these conceptions, assumptions, and values are improperly labeled when they are called Democratic or Republican. They are Western.

One image of the West that the East accepts is that of the West not as economic peon but as pensioner of the East, as beggar. The West with its hat held out beseeching the expenditure on its behalf of federal money which must be raised from Eastern corporation and income taxes. Considering how much of that income is plundered from the West, the image is both comic and profoundly ironical. But there are ways in which it is also true. You can hardly find an editorial page in the West that is not demanding as Western right, as compensation for the West, and as assistance toward Western liberation, the expenditure of more federal funds. More government money for public health, hospitals, inspection, treatment; for schools; for service by the Bureau of Mines to the mining industry; for the improvement of Western agriculture, the replenishment of soils, the instruction of farmers; for the instruction and protection of cattle and sheep growers, the improvement of stock and range, quarantine, research; for fire protection in the logging business; for drainage; for reseeding and reforestation of private lands; for roads; for weather service; and always for dams, canals, and the whole program of reclamation.

But at the same time: hands off. The West has been corrupted, its press believes all but unanimously, by a system of paternalism which is collectivist at base and hardly bothers to disguise its intention of delivering the United States over to communism. The second column of the editorial page is sure to be a ringing demand for the government to get out of business, to stop impeding initiative, to break the shackles of regulation with which it has fettered enterprise, to abjure its philosophy of suppressing liberty, and to stop giving money to people who will only store coal in the new bathtub. The editorial is certain to have a few lines about bureaucrats in desk chairs, impractical theorists, probably professors and certainly long-haired, who are destroying the West by interfering with the men who know how. Also it is certain to be horrified by the schools, which the bureaucrats are using to debauch our young people with Russian propaganda.

An editorial typical of scores I read this summer begins, "Next to getting over our complex that we have to appease labor and give it more money every Monday A.M., our next task is to go over to the schoolhouse." It denounces a handful of revolutionary notions, including the dreadful one that "the people should own the water power and the forests," and goes on to suggest measures, of which the first is, "we could call in the principal, or the president of the university and quiz him on why do his teachers recommend socialism. And if his answer was dubious we would get a pinch hitter to take his place."

It shakes down to a platform: get out and give us more money. Much of the dream of economic liberation is dependent upon continuous, continually increasing federal subsidies—subsidies which it also insists shall be made without safeguard or regulation. This is interesting as economic fantasy but is more interesting because it reveals that the Western mind is interfusing its dream

of freedom with the economic cannibalism of the post–
Civil War Stone Age. It is still more interesting as it reveals the West's attitude toward the federal intervention which alone was powerful enough to save Western
natural resources from total control and quick liquidation by the absentee Eastern ownership.

For that preservation the West is grateful to the government. But there was and still is a fundamental defect:
federal intervention has also preserved those resources
from locally owned liquidation by the West itself. So, at
the very moment when the West is blueprinting an
economy which must be based on the sustained, permanent use of its natural resources, it is also conducting
an assault on those resources with the simple objective
of liquidating them. The dissociation of intelligence
could go no farther but there it is—and there is the West
yesterday, today, and forever. It is the Western mind
stripped to the basic split. The West as its own worst
enemy. The West committing suicide.

IV

The National Parks are composed of lands that were
once part of the public domain (plus a few minute areas
that had previously passed out of it). Exceedingly small
in total area, they are permanently reserved and dedicated to their present uses: the preservation of wilderness areas, the protection of supreme scenic beauties,
and the pleasure and recreation of the American people.
By the terms of the original dedication and by policy so
far kept inviolate they are to be maintained as they are,
they are not to be commercially exploited at all. But they
contain timber, grazing land, water, and minerals. And
that, in the West's eyes, is what is wrong with them.

The Olympic National Park contains a virgin stand of
Sitka spruce, which yields a wood that was once essential for airplanes. During the war a violent agitation was

conducted by logging interests (unobtrusively backed by other interests with an eye on natural resources) to open these forests to logging. It presented itself as patriotism and skillfully assimilated itself to the emotions of wartime. There was more than enough Sitka spruce in privately owned and national forests to take care of any demand but no matter: victory depended on our opening the Olympic National Park to logging. The persistence and power of that agitation and its accompanying propaganda (some of it conducted in the public schools, which are supposed to be poisoned with collectivism) would be unbelievable to anyone who had not looked into them.

The National Park Service, backed by conservation associations and by other lumbering interests which have seen the light, was able to hold fast—the Olympic Park was not logged. But immediately the war ended the same interests, augmented by a good many others, began an even more violent campaign of agitation, commercial pressure, and political pressure. We must now house the veterans and clearly we could not do so unless we opened all the national parks to logging.

That onslaught has been held in check and it will not win this time. But it will be repeated many times and the West intends it to win.

This campaign had nothing to do with Sitka spruce, winning the war, or housing veterans. Its purpose was to make a breach in the national parks policy with the aid of war emotions, and to create a precedent. Once that precedent should be set, the rest would follow. Lumber companies could log the parks. Cattle and sheep associations could graze them. Mining companies could get at their mineral deposits. Power companies could build dams in them, water companies could use their lakes and rivers. Each of those objectives has been repeatedly attempted in the past and the sun never sets on the West's efforts to achieve them. Success would mean not only the destruction of the national parks but, as we shall see, far worse.

The parks are trivial in extent, though the destruction of their forests, many of which have critical locations, would have a disproportionately destructive effect on the watersheds—the watersheds which must be preserved if the West is to continue to exist as a society. They are trivial—the main objectives of the Western assault on the natural resources are the remnants of the national domain, the Taylor Act grazing lands, and the national forests.

I have heard this assault called a conspiracy but it is in no way secret or even surreptitious; it is open and enthusiastically supported by many Westerners, by many Western newspapers, and by almost all the Western specialty press. Openly engaged in it are parts of the lumber industry (though other important parts of that industry are opposing it), some water users (though water users would be its first victims), the national associations of cattle and sheep growers and a majority of the state and local associations, large parts of the mining industry, the U.S. Chamber of Commerce (some of whose local chambers are in opposition), and those Western members of Congress who represent these interests. Obscure but blandly co-operative in the background are Eastern interests perennially hostile to the West and concerned here because they greatly desire to halt and reduce government regulation and to open additional Western wealth to liquidation—notably the power companies.

Right now the cattlemen and sheepmen are carrying the ball. We must confine ourselves to them and their principal objectives—remembering that the organized assault aims at many other objectives which would benefit other groups. Their limited objectives are:

1.) Conversion of the privilege which cattlemen and sheepmen now have of grazing their stock on Taylor Act

and Forest Service lands—a privilege which is now subject to regulation and adjustment and for which they
pay less than it is worth—into a vested right guaranteed
them and subject to only such regulation as they may
impose upon themselves.

2.) Distribution of all the Taylor Act grazing lands,
which is to say practically all the public domain that still
exists, to the individual states, as a preliminary to dis-
posing of them by private sale. (At an insignificant price.
At an inflammatory meeting of committees of the American National Livestock Association and the National
Woolgrowers Association in Salt Lake City in August
1946, the price most commonly suggested was ten cents
an acre.)

3.) Reclassification of lands in the national forests
and removal from the jurisdiction of the Forest Service
of all lands that can be classified as valuable for grazing,
so that these lands may be transferred to the states and
eventually sold. Immediately in contemplation is the removal of all government regulation of grazing in about
27,000,000 acres of forest lands and their distribution to
the states—and to stockmen and woolgrowers as soon
thereafter as possible.

These tracts compose the Minidoka and Caribou
Forests in Idaho, all the forests in Nevada, most of the
forest land in the southern half of Utah, and some ten or
twelve million acres in Arizona and New Mexico. But
that is just a start: a further objective is to wrest from
Forest Service control all lands in all forests that can be
grazed. And beyond that is the intention ultimately to
confine the Forest Service to the rehabilitation of land
which lumbermen and stockmen have made unproduc-
tive, under compulsion to transfer it to private ownership as soon as it has been made productive again. The
ultimate objective, that is, is to liquidate all public ownership of grazing land and forest land in the United
States. And the wording of the resolution in which the

U.S. Chamber of Commerce came to the support of the program *excepted no government land whatever*. That represents the desire of most of the leaders of the assault.

The immediate objectives make this attempt one of the biggest landgrabs in American history. The ultimate objectives make it incomparably the biggest. The plan is to get rid of public lands altogether, turning them over to the states, which can be coerced as the federal government cannot be, and eventually to private ownership.

This is your land we are talking about.

The attack has already carried important outposts. Regulation of the use of Taylor Act lands, the vast public range outside the national forests, was vested in the Grazing Service. Over the last few years that service was so systematically reduced in staff and appropriations that some cattlemen and sheepmen have been grazing the public range just as they see fit. Violation of the Taylor Act is widespread, flagrant, systematic, and frequently recommended to their members as policy by various local cattle and sheep associations. The Grazing Service was organized to assist grazers and to protect the public interest. When it took the latter purpose seriously it was emasculated and this year has been killed by Western members of Congress, under the leadership of Senator McCarran of Nevada.[2] But Senator McCarran is by no means so extreme as the majority of the big stockmen whose interests he serves so brilliantly in Washington. His more limited purpose is to get the public lands away from those he calls "the swivel-chair oligarchy," that is, federal officials who cannot be coerced, and into the hands of the states, that is, officials who can be coerced. His model is his own state government, a small oligarchy dominated by stockmen. At the Salt Lake City meeting I have mentioned he warned the associations that demands for private ownership were prema-

ture and might embarrass his efforts, and he is understood to have been furious when, after he had left, the
combined committees declared for ultimate private
ownership of all public lands.

Senator McCarran has been the ablest representa-
tive of cattle and sheep interests in Washington, against
the West and the people of the United States. But from
time to time he has had the help of more than half the
Western delegation in Congress—most surprisingly of
Senator Hatch—and especially of Congressman Barrett[3]
and Senator Robertson of Wyoming. (New Mexico and
Wyoming are the only states whose delegates to the Salt
Lake City meeting were unanimous for the program.)
Let us look at some of the measures they have proposed.

Senator McCarran has fathered a number of bills
aimed at small or large objectives of the program. The
one in point, however, is the "McCarran grazing bill" (S
33 in the last Congress) which has now been defeated
four times but will certainly be reintroduced in the next
Congress. This measure would give present owners of
grazing permits in the national forests fee simple property rights in those permits, on the theory that if you
have leased an apartment from me (at half price or less)
you have become its owner. The purpose was to convert
a privilege (and one that is subject to regulation) into a
vested right, to confine the use of grazing rights in the
national forests to the present holders of permits or
those who might buy them from the present holders,
and to deny the Forest Service the greater part of its
present power to regulate the use of grazing lands.

The Barrett Bill of last session (HR 7638) provided
for the sale of disconnected tracts of unorganized Taylor
Act grazing land, up to four sections per tract and to the
total of over 11,000,000 acres. Priority in purchase was
to be granted to present lessees of those tracts. Its purpose was to let present users of public grazing lands,

who pay considerably less than a fair rental, buy that land at less than it is worth—and to get public grazing land out of public regulation and control.

But the most revealing bill was last session's S 1945, introduced by Senator Robertson. The Senator is, it should be noted, the owner of one of the largest and finest sheep and cattle ranches in Wyoming. He holds a grazing permit in his own name in the Shoshone National Forest for 2400 sheep, has a financial interest in an association that grazes 1200 sheep there, and acts in various ways as agent for individuals and associations that graze nearly 8000 more sheep in the same forest. His bill is a sweetheart.

The Robertson Bill would transfer to thirteen Western states all unappropriated and unreserved lands, *including the minerals in them;* all oil and mineral reserves; all minerals, coal, oil, and gas rights related to them in the public lands; and all homestead lands that have been forfeited to the United States. It would empower the states to dispose of these lands as they might see fit—that is, to sell them—except that coal, oil, and gas lands must be leased, not sold, and the federal government would retain power to prorate production.

The guts of the bill, however, are the provisions which set up in each state a commission ordered to reexamine every kind of reservation of public land—national forests, national parks and monuments, Carey Act (irrigation district) withdrawals, wildlife reserves, *reclamation reserves,* power sites, and certain less important ones. The commission's duty would be to determine whether parts of the national forests in its state are more valuable for grazing and agriculture (practically no Forest Service land can be farmed at all) than for timber production, and if it should decide that any were, to certify them for transfer to the state for sale—that is, the commission is intended to get forest grazing land into private ownership. The commission's duty in regard to other reservations is to do the same in regard to grazing and agricultural land—and also to determine whether the original purposes of the reserve can be achieved by state ownership or "individual enterprise," and whether the reserves may not have lost their importance or perhaps do not justify national administration.

The Robertson Bill is both transparent and carnivorous. It would liquidate the public lands and end our sixty years of conservation of the national resources. And this single bill would achieve all the main objectives of the whole program of the Western despoilers at one step, except that purely timber lands in the forests would still be protected and would have to be attacked by other means. In some respects it goes beyond anything that had been publicly advocated by the despoilers. Nowhere else, for instance, has it been proposed to turn public power sites or reclamation reserves over to private hands. But it expresses the program.

The public lands are first to be transferred to the states on the fully justified assumption that if there should be a state government not wholly compliant to the desires of stockgrowers, it could be pressured into compliance. The intention is to free them of all regulation except such as stockgrowers might impose upon themselves. Nothing in history suggests that the states are adequate to protect their own resources, or even want to, or suggests that cattlemen and sheepmen are capable of regulating themselves even for their own benefit, still less the public's. And the regulations immediately to be got rid of are those by which the government has been trying to prevent overgrazing of the public range. Cattlemen and sheepmen, I repeat, want to shovel most of the West into rivers.

From the states the public lands are to be transferred to private ownership. Present holders of permits are to be constituted a prior and privileged caste, to the exclusion of others except on such terms as they may dictate. They are to be permitted to buy the lands—the public lands, the West's lands, your lands—at a fraction of what they are worth. And the larger intention is to liquidate all the publicly held resources of the West.

Everyone knows that the timber of the United States is being cut faster than replacements are being grown, that the best efforts of the government and of those private operators who realize that other generations will follow ours have not so far sufficed to balance the growth of saw timber with logging. Everyone knows that regulation of grazing is the only hope of preserving the range. Open the public reserves of timber, the national forests, to private operation without government restriction and not only the Western but the national resources would rapidly disintegrate. (And presently the government, on behalf of our society as a whole, would have to wipe out private property in forests altogether.) Turn the public range over to private ownership, or even private management, and within a generation the range would be exhausted beyond hope of repair.

But that is, by a good deal, the least of it. Most of the fundamental watersheds of the West lie within the boundaries of the Taylor Act lands, the national forests, and the national parks. And overgrazing the range and liquidating the forests destroys the watersheds. In many places in the West today property in land, irrigating systems, and crops is steadily deteriorating because the best efforts of the government to repair damage to watersheds—damage caused by overgrazing the ranges and overcutting the forests—have not been enough.

Stream beds choke with silt and floods spread over the rich fields on the slopes and in the bottoms, always impairing and sometimes destroying them. Dams and canals and reservoirs silt up, decline in efficiency, have to be repaired at great expense, cannot be fully restored. Fields gully, soil blows away. Flash floods kill pro-

ductive land, kill livestock, kill human beings, sometimes kill communities.

Less than a month before the joint committees met
in Salt Lake City this summer, a hundred and twenty-
five miles away in the little town of Mount Pleasant,
Utah, the annual parade was forming for the celebration
of July 24, the greatest Mormon feast day. That parade
never got started. A heavy summer storm struck in the
hills and gulches above town and what marched down
Mount Pleasant's main street was not a series of deco-
rated floats but a river of thick mud like concrete that,
in a town of twenty-five hundred people, did half a million dollars' worth of damage in ten minutes. The range
above town had been overgrazed and the storm waters
which would have been retained by healthy land could
not be retained by the sick, exhausted land. They rushed
down over Mount Pleasant, bringing gravel, stones, and
boulders with them, depositing several feet of mud,
damaging many buildings and much of the town's real
estate, leaving much of the grazing land above town ruined and much more damaged and dangerous.

This destruction had been predictable—and predicted; in a small way it had happened before. The government had been working for many years to restore
the range but had not been able to begin the infinitely
slow process soon enough. It knew and had repeatedly
said that such a catastrophe might happen just as and
where it did happen.

The same thing has happened repeatedly in Utah, in
some places more destructively, in others less so. It has
happened and goes on happening throughout the West
wherever the grazing land of watersheds has been exhausted or their forests overcut. Mud flows and flash
floods are dramatic but only occasional, whereas the
steady deterioration of the watersheds and the slow destruction of their wealth go on all the time. Overgrazing
and overcutting—and fire, the hazard of which is greatly

increased by heavy cutting—are responsible. The program which is planned to liquidate the range and forests
would destroy the natural resources of the West, and
with them so many rivers, towns, cities, farms, ranches,
mines, and power sites that a great part of the West
would be obliterated. It would return much of the West,
most of the habitable interior West, to the processes of
geology. It would make Western life as we now know it,
and therefore American life as we now know it, impossible.

There you have it. A few groups of Western interests,
so small numerically as to constitute a minute fraction
of the West, are hell-bent on destroying the West. They
are stronger than they would otherwise be because they
are skillfully manipulating in their support sentiments
that have always been powerful in the West—the home
rule which means basically that we want federal help
without federal regulation, the "individualism" that has
always made the small Western operator a handy tool of
the big one, and the wild myth that stockgrowers constitute an aristocracy in which all Westerners somehow
share. They have managed to line up behind them many
Western interests that would perish if they should succeed. And they count on the inevitable postwar reaction
against government regulation to put their program
over.

To a historian it has the beauty of any historical continuity. It is the Western psychology working within the
pattern which its own nature has set. It is the forever recurrent lust to liquidate the West that is so large a part
of Western history. The West has always been a society
living under threat of destruction by natural cataclysm
and here it is, bright against the sky, inviting such cataclysm.

But if it has this mad beauty it also has an almost cosmic irony, in that fulfillment of the great dream of the
West, mature economic development and local owner-

ship and control, has been made possible by the developments of our age at exactly the same time. That dream envisions the establishment of an economy on the natural resources of the West, developed and integrated to produce a steady, sustained, permanent yield. While the West moves to build that kind of economy, a part of the West is simultaneously moving to destroy the natural resources forever. That paradox is absolutely true to the Western mind and spirit. But the future of the West hinges on whether it can defend itself against itself.

Sacred Cows and Public Lands

Never deviating from his course, Bernard DeVoto rode again
in this essay, which first appeared in *Harper's* in July 1948.
"Sacred Cows and Public Lands" could be considered De-
Voto's Federalist number 10; like Madison before him, De-
Voto acknowledges the need for "pressure groups" in American society, but quickly moves towards his task at hand:
exposing the truths and falsehoods of the public lands grazing rights debate. Never one to back down, DeVoto denounces public officials by name for their refusal to protect
the people's land from the sheep and heifers that ranchers
are eager to sic on public grass. Senator Pat McCarran of
Nevada—who ran the state like it was his own—bears a large
amount of DeVoto's fire. Though the "Landgrabbers" paint
the National Forest Service as the prodigal son of Congress,
ready to return home and pay the piper, DeVoto criticizes
this metaphor and argues for more autonomy from Washington. This essay marked the second time in DeVoto's
Harper's writings when he was given double space by editor
Frederick Lewis Allen. Though stockmen and ranchers tried
to dissuade Allen from publishing DeVoto, Allen ignored
their demands. And when they wanted to answer DeVoto's
claims they were refused, because DeVoto had already effectively disproved their arguments. Amidst his personal war
on the "Landgrabbers" and the Eastern financial establishment, DeVoto enjoyed immense critical success. Two months
before this essay appeared in *Harper's* DeVoto was awarded
the Pulitzer Prize for history; in June an honorary degree
from the University of Colorado was conferred upon him,
and with the Bancroft Prize in July for his book *Across the
Wide Missouri*, DeVoto's place in the canon of historiogra-
phy was cemented.

The Constitution of the United States does not provide for Congressional blocs, pressure groups, and corporate lobbies but under our unwritten Constitution they have become organized in our government. They are instruments for applying political power in the solution of specific political problems and by now it would be impossible to govern a hundred and fifty million people without them. But their development has given journalism an additional political function, that of keeping their operations publicized.

This article describes the application of political pressure to a specific problem of administration. It shows a committee of the House of Representatives acting in obedient response to a pressure group. The committee is the Subcommittee on Public Lands of the House Committee on Public Lands. The pressure group consists of certain Western cattlemen and sheepmen operating through various of their state associations, their two national associations, a joint committee of the national associations, their agents and lobbyists, and their trade press. The immediate objective of the activities described here was to prevent the U.S. Forest Service from making certain reductions in the number of livestock permitted to graze on certain portions of the national forests.

That was the immediate objective but various long-term objectives must be borne in mind. Permits to graze stock in national forests are licenses, not rights, and are subject to regulation, modification, and revocation: for years the pressure group we deal with has been trying to vest the present holders of such permits with permanent rights. It has also been trying to secure such vested rights to present holders of grazing permits on other publicly owned ranges administered by the Bureau of Land Management. Associated with both efforts is a recurrent one to open both kinds of public land to private purchase and to give present holders of permits priority over other buyers, a long period to decide whether or not they want to buy, and the right to buy at the value of the grazing privilege alone, without regard to other uses of the land. In the background are still more astonishing aspirations. The pressure group has periodically undertaken to convert first to state and eventually to private ownership whatever land can be grazed now that belongs to other public reservations, for instance the national parks. It has thereby attracted the sympathy of more powerful interests whose ultimate hope is to destroy the established conservation policies of the United States.

That larger hope interests us here only indirectly. We deal with a small minority group of stockgrowers, with the Subcommittee on Public Lands, and with the hearings which that committee held in the West in August, September, and October 1947. The records of those hearings have been printed. I use ten volumes of them here, two being records of preliminary hearings in Washington in April and May of 1947. I can touch on only a small part of them: eight of the volumes contain more than twice as much reading matter apiece as is printed in an issue of *Harper's*. Some things that happened at the hearings were kept from print by the standard evidence of declaring them off the record. In addition I suspect that sometimes the printed record may not do the facts full justice. A witness at one of the hearings sent me the part of the typed transcript that contained his testimony: in some respects it differed from the corresponding passage in the printed record.

II

The pressure group dealt with here consists of only a small fraction of the Western livestock industry. For the most part it consists of large operators who hold government permits to graze cattle and sheep on publicly owned land. By no means all the large operators who hold such permits and only a small minority of the large operators in the Western industry belong to it. The group claims to speak for the industry as a whole but it does not. When you inquire what percentage of Western stockgrowers belong to the two national associations, for instance, you get not figures but polite evasions: it is a small percentage. Many local cattle and sheep associations have officially repudiated the objectives of the group, asserting that they were not consulted about the pressure campaign and have had no part in it. Since the ultimate objectives of the group were publicized in the early part of 1947, the number of stockgrowers who had opposed them has steadily increased.

The group claims that the entire livestock industry of the United States is in deadly peril because the Forest Service is reducing the number of stock grazed in national forests. Well, all told something more than a third of the sheep raised in the United States and about one-seventh of the cattle are raised in the West. Of these by far the greater part are not grazed in the forests at all: 91 per cent of the cattle and 73 per cent of the sheep. Those that are grazed there spend, on the average, less than four months of the year on forest ranges. In other words the national forests supply a little more than 2 per cent of the grazing for Western-owned cattle and a little less than 7 per cent of the grazing for Western-owned sheep. And of these small numbers only a microscopic fraction are affected by the Forest Service reductions that produced all the uproar.

Grazing in the national forests is wholly permissive. You and I as co-owners license stockmen, for ridiculously small fees, to graze their herds there subject to the regulations of the Forest Service. Moreover, grazing is a subsidiary use of the forests, which are dedicated by law primarily to the production of timber and the protection of watersheds. Timber production is much more important than grazing, especially in view of the growing timber famine, but watershed protection is more important still. The stock business of the West, its agriculture, its mining, its industry, and its community life all depend on the healthy condition of its watersheds.

The basic fact is that in many places the national forests have been dangerously overgrazed. Early practices of the Forest Service were in part to blame. Scientific range management has developed only in the twentieth century: the Service has had to learn from its own mistakes and in the beginning authorized more grazing than, as the outcome proved, the range could stand without deteriorating. More important, however, was the overstocking of the range during the First World War, when public demand for increased meat production forced the opening of the forests to much greater numbers of livestock than they had ever carried before. Widespread damage resulted, to the forest ranges, to the forests, to the vital watersheds they contain. Ever since then the Service has been working to repair the damage and to reduce grazing to a safe amount. It has not yet succeeded and many forest areas are still being overgrazed, with continuing damage to the range, the forests, and the watersheds. In some places this damage has become critical; in a few it has come close to the edge of disaster.

And there is another equally important fact. Some of the grazing ranges in the national forests had already been very seriously damaged by overgrazing when the forests were established. The pressure group has consistently opposed regulation of grazing by the Forest Service but most of all it has objected to the reduction of the number of cattle and sheep permitted in the forests. (There are still more cattle in them than there were in 1905.) Meanwhile unregulated grazing on other public lands has damaged them far worse. By 1926 the forage value of 84 per cent of the unreserved public domain had been cut in half. By 1932 further depletion of these ranges, plus the anarchy of the stock business, forced stockgrowers themselves to demand government regulation. Under the Taylor Act most of the remaining public domain was organized and turned over to a new agency, the Grazing Service. When the Grazing Service undertook to reduce overstocking of ranges and to raise grazing fees to a respectable fraction of what the grass was worth, it was marked for destruction. Senator Mc-Carran of Nevada obliged. After a three-year campaign he succeeded in getting the Grazing Service merged with the General Land Office to form the Bureau of Land Management. Then he got the agency's new appropriations reduced to the point where it was administratively impotent, a captive of the stockmen it was supposed to regulate.

It was during the final stages of the attack on the Grazing Service that plans for a similar attack on the Forest Service were matured. The Forest Service program for reducing the number of stock grazed in the forests was continuing. The need for it had become more urgent because in some places the deterioration of the range had become critical, because the wartime increase of population in the West necessitated a higher land-use policy, and because that increase also necessitated every possible measure that would develop, conserve, and protect the water supply which absolutely conditions Western life. The reductions in permitted grazing made by the Forest Service have been smaller than impersonal regard for public policy would require, they have been gradual, and except when an emergency situation called for drastic action they have been made with extreme consideration of the stockgrowers whose permits were being cut. They have been made only after discussion with the permit holders, usually after consultation with specialists and the local advisory boards, and always with complete freedom of appeal through the administrative channels of the Service up to the top. All these facts are brought out by the printed record.

Necessarily, however, some reductions bore severely on individual operators, and no stockman who does not see the wisdom of protecting the future of his own grazing can rejoice in any reduction of his permit. The pressure group, in whose eyes no land that can be grazed has any other value, was angered and alarmed. Something had to be done about the Forest Service. If the advisory boards which consulted with the Service could be given administrative power, then stockgrowers themselves could control grazing in the forests. If grazing permits could be given the status of legal rights, then reductions could not be made. Better still would be to get the grazing areas out of the jurisdiction of the Forest Service and into that of the Grazing Service. A number of bills providing for such measures were introduced or prepared for introduction in Congress and the propaganda arm set up a vociferous advocacy of them, or alternatively, for such as could be effected by executive order. But best of all would be to turn all publicly owned grazing lands in the United States over to state ownership, as a step toward private sale, or to open them directly to private sale.

It was here that the pressure group attracted the support of interests far more powerful. But it was here too that trouble began. Too many stockgrowers and their local associations were opposed to such a program. Too many other interests would suffer from it—agriculture, mining, industry, power, villages and towns and cities, hunters and fishermen, dude ranchers. Too many conservation organizations and too many newspapermen found out what was being planned. Too great a national interest was at stake.

A tentative formulation of plans was made in August 1946 at a meeting in Salt Lake City of the Joint Com-

mittee on Public Lands of the American National Livestock Association and the National Woolgrowers Association. In *Harper's* for January 1947 I described those
plans and during the next few months other writers described them in other magazines and other newspapers.
There has never been any refutation of what we said
about them. There never will be—stockgrowers who oppose the plans and conservation organizations have
transcripts of the Joint Committee's meeting. And in the
Denver Post for February 2, 1947, the Vice-Chairman of
the Joint Committee published an article which verified
what we had said.

This premature publicity stopped the program in its
tracks. Public opinion in the West was so instantly outraged, so many organizations began to protest, so many
Western newspapers lined up in opposition that the program had to be—temporarily—abandoned. Bills implementing it had been prepared for introduction in the
new Congress. They were never introduced—and various Congressmen hurried home to explain to angry con-
stituents that it was all a mistake, that they had been
cruelly misunderstood. There was no chance that, in the
immediate future, any effort will be made to open the
public lands to sale. The program has been laid away for
future use; at present the issue is too hot for anyone to
touch.

But, as the pressure-group press pointed out, there
are various ways of skinning a cat. There was the immediate problem of halting the Forest Service cuts in
grazing permits—it was too late to stop them for 1947
but how about 1948? There was the continuing problem
of bringing the Service to see things as the pressure
group wanted it to—by means of threat, by intimidation, by defamation. Stockgrowers' publications were
filled with denunciations of the reduction program as
unnecessary, unjust, and arbitrary. Stock associations
memorialized Congress, accusing the Forest Service of

despotic and illegal administrative policies, and demanding an investigation. The legislature of Wyoming demanded an investigation and suggested that it be made by the Public Lands Committee of the House or the Senate. The legislature also pointedly alluded to Forest Service appropriations, and this club—such a reduction of appropriations as had hamstrung the Grazing Service—began to be brandished in the trade journals with increasing frequency. Demands for the dismissal of forest rangers, forest supervisors, and regional foresters were made. A college professor who had discussed the proposed landgrab in a radio broadcast was prevented from repeating his talk. The mail of Congressmen was filled with complaints against the Forest Service, so similar in phraseology that a common source was indicated.

Seldom has so much noise been made about so small a matter. Remember that all told the forest ranges supply only two per cent of the grazing for Western cattle and only seven per cent of that for Western sheep. Consider too that the proposed cuts for 1948 would reduce sheep grazing in the forests by only two-tenths of one per cent and cattle grazing in them by only three one-hundredths of one per cent. It was in order to prevent this minute reduction that the pressure group organized its campaign. It concentrated on a proposal that no reductions in grazing permits be made for three years and that during this "test period" an investigation be made to determine whether any reductions whatever were needed.

This is the pressure to which Congress and its committees yielded. It yielded all the more rapidly because the election of 1946 had made Congress Republican and so had given the Republicans the chairmanships and the majority representations in congressional committees. On February 4, 1947, the House Committee on Public Lands resolved that its Subcommittee on Public Lands would hold public hearings on the grazing policies of the Forest Service. On April 17, 1947, the House of Representatives authorized such hearings with House Resolution 93.

Before the House resolution was passed the April issue of the *American Cattle Producer* published a "Notice to Forest Permittees," signed by the executive secretary of the American Livestock Association. The same "Notice" was published by the *Record Stockman* and the *New Mexico Stockman* and by other trade periodicals. It announced that hearings were to be held in the West and called for letters of complaint against the Forest Service, "in order to furnish this [the Congressional] committee with as much background material as possible." It listed seven kinds of complaint that would be most helpful to the committee. Its final paragraph thanked the prospective complainants for their help and remarked, "Generally speaking, it is the complaint of forest users that the Forest Service is judge, jury, and prosecuting attorney, all in one. In other words, it is a law unto itself." At the hearings so many witnesses faithfully parroted those words that they became embarrassing.

III

The House Committee on Public Lands, of which Congressman Richard J. Welch of California is chairman, consists of twenty-five members of Congress and the delegates from Hawaii, Alaska and Puerto Rico. Under the Reorganization Act it is charged with duties formerly distributed among six committees. Twenty-two of its members besides the three delegates compose the Subcommittee on Public Lands, of which Congressman Frank A. Barrett of Wyoming is chairman.[1] It was the Subcommittee that held the hearings. The number of its members who attended them varied; so far as I can make out from the record no more than nine were ever present at one time; ten signed the letter addressed to

Secretary Anderson when they were over. Since the touring Congressmen were members of other subcommittees that had work to do in the West, some of the hearings did not touch on the Forest Service.

The Subcommittee had already scheduled hearings on Congressman Barrett's annual attempt to abolish the Jackson Hole National Monument. They were held in Washington April 14–19, 1947, and the printed record contains some illuminating items. Mr. J. Byron Wilson, chairman of the legislative committee of the National Woolgrowers Association and a registered lobbyist for the industry, indeed one of the most skillful lobbyists who have ever worked in Washington, appeared as a witness favoring the abolition of the Monument. The testimony of such a person about such an issue would seem farfetched and irrelevant if it were not obviously part of a pattern. The pressure group is interested in undermining all federal authority over any part of the public lands, and to abolish one national monument would create precedent for further inroads. The same reason explains the appearance of the U.S. Chamber of Commerce. The manager of its Natural Resources Department testified in person and a telegram from a member of its Natural Resources Committee was entered in the record. They were speaking officially for one of the larger interests which I have said feel an affinity for the pressure group's ultimate aims. At that time it was standing on a platform for distributing the public lands to private ownership more extreme than any other that has been acknowledged in public. A year later, however, in May 1948, it retreated from that extreme and revised its statement of public lands policy, which is now rather mild.

Congressman Barrett's bill for abolishing the Jackson Hole Monument would have transferred some of the land in it from the National Park Service to the Forest Service. The record, therefore, strangely shows Mr. Wilson, the lobbyist, and Mr. J. Elmer Brock, the Vice-Chairman of the Joint Committee, praising the Forest Service for efficiency, co-operativeness, administrative skill, and expert knowledge. Other stockmen even praised its grazing policies. And with this praise Congressman Barrett found himself in generous agreement. Since he was harrying the Park Service, the Forest Service seemed to him, by comparison, a superb organization. The same oddity was to be repeated later in the year. When Mr. Barrett staged his production in Wyoming, Colorado, and Utah, the Forest Service was staffed with incompetents, petty tyrants, swivel-chair bureaucrats, and impractical theorists. But when the committee moved to Lake Crescent, Washington, where there was a proposal to detach a large tract of timber from the Olympic National Park and turn it over to the Forest Service, for two happy days the Service found itself admirable and expert again.

The committee held a preliminary hearing on Forest Service policy in Washington on May 12, 1947. The only witnesses were officials of the Service, who described the grazing policies and the multiple problems they involve. Chairman Barrett, a lawyer by profession, had prepared the pressure group's complaints with admirable thoroughness and put them on the record like a lawyer's brief and pleadings. The tone for the hearings that were to follow was set right there. Mr. Barrett's arraignment was hardly a foundation from which a fact-finding inquiry could be conducted. He was not going to be judicial; to use the language of the "Notice to Forest Permittees," he was going to act as prosecuting attorney on behalf of the pressure group and against the Forest Service. As such, he conducted this hearing very ably and with frequent cinematic effects.

Mr. Barrett is a very intelligent man. So are most of his fellow committeemen, though I confess that I cannot follow with full understanding the excursions of Mr.

Lemke's mind—present at only a couple of hearings, he seemed to be principally interested in providing booster advertising for the State of North Dakota. Both their impartiality and their competence to make such an investigation as they were about to embark on are, however, another matter. Chairman Barrett, Congressman Robert F. Rockwell of Colorado who played the second lead, and Congressman Wesley A. D'Ewart of Montana are all stockgrowers. The last two hold grazing permits on the national forests. Congressman A. L. Miller of Nebraska, who understudied Mr. Barrett and Mr. Rockwell, revealed at Lake Crescent that he could not recognize a burnt-over area in a forest. (He wondered if those blackened snags might not be the "over-mature" timber that lumbermen were so passionately eager to cut down for the common good.) Since no one who knows anything at all about forests can fail to identify the marks of a fire, a faint doubt of his qualifications for judgment rises in one's mind.

The record is upholstered with stately congressional courtesy, committeemen's ornate praise of one another as "your distinguished Representative," and topical references to "this great State." One who reads it comes to see that Congressman Peterson of Florida, who did not go West but attended the Washington hearings, wanted to bring out the facts. So did Congressman Crawford of Michigan, who attended in Washington and got back from an official trip to Alaska in time for some of the Western hearings. So especially did Congressman Fernandez of New Mexico, who frequently pinned down the outrageous statements by witnesses, forced equivocation into the open, and drew out facts that except for him would have been buried under abuse. Mr. Fernandez, in fact, is the only member of the committee who seems to have been actively interested in giving the Forest Service a hearing. But the necessity of all congressional committeemen to play ball on one another's home lots was dominant. This was Chairman Barrett's show and he must be allowed to stage it as he pleased. Mr. Rockwell supported him brilliantly. Dr. Miller (he is a Fellow of the College of Surgeons) backed them up well and, at Rawlins, went farther in attacking a witness than anyone else did anywhere. He was, however, obviously astonished to learn how small were the fees charged for grazing in the forests. His repeated elicitation from witnesses of the fact that they paid the Forest Service only about one-fourth of what grazing cost on the privately owned ranges of his home state was a discordant note.

The first hearing in the West was held at Glasgow, Montana, August 27, 1947. It was concerned with engineering projects and some public lands under the jurisdiction of the Soil Conservation Service; Forest Service matters were not mentioned. They were first taken up at Billings, Montana, on August 30. And here, if I read the script correctly, the performers went up in their lines. Mr. Barrett indulged in some of the blustering accusations of the Forest Service that he was to make much more prodigally later on, but the audience did not respond. For Montana was not answering the "Notice to Forest Permittees"; Montana was, on the whole, well satisfied with the Forest Service. A few officials of stock associations made complaints but they did not follow the outline of the "Notice" and seemed to be merely *pro forma*. A few individual stockmen expressed grievances, but these proved to be trivial and mostly irrelevant to the inquiry. Whereas a large number of individuals and associations, stockmen, chambers of commerce, veterans organizations, civic and sportsmen's societies, labor unions, and others had turned up to testify in favor of the Forest Service. The meeting had certainly not been planned as a vindication of the Service but it certainly turned into one. Moreover, as many as twenty-nine individuals (including the Governor of Montana) and organizations made it clear that they knew of plans to turn the grazing lands of the forest over to other agencies, to the states, or to private sale. They made it clear too that they were violently opposed. It was here that Chairman Barrett and Senator Edward V. Robertson of Wyoming—whose reason for sitting with a House committee and cross-examining witnesses is not clear—began to assert that they had never favored any such measures and in fact had never heard of any.

The assault on the Forest Service, then, made no headway at Billings. It is easy to see why. The Service completed its adjustments of permitted stock to the carrying capacity of its Montana ranges twenty years ago, and the stockmen are fully satisfied with them. Those ranges are now sound and healthy—the Montana forests are the only ones of which this is wholly true—and the resultant benefits to stockmen and public alike are fully evident. No one would dream of suggesting that greater numbers of stock be grazed on them. The Billings performance was a bust.

One September 2, however, the road company moved to Rawlins, Wyoming. This is Mr. Barrett's home state and in a couple of Wyoming forests the critical condition of watersheds had made some of the proposed cuts in grazing permits very large. "The hearing as I understand it is for the stockmen," a witness remarked. Though Mr. Barrett hastened to cover that break by pointing out that they were for the general public, the witness was telling the obvious truth. The hall was packed with an uproarious audience of stockmen, who had obviously assembled on call. They yelled, stamped, and applauded; the pressure group's witnesses and the active committeemen, the Chairman and Messrs. Rockwell and Miller, played up to them. Moreover, the oversight made at Billings was corrected. Forest Service witnesses, witnesses who wanted to testify in their behalf, and witnesses appearing for the conservation societies were held to very short periods, mostly at the end of the day. Most of their formal resolutions and statements were not read but only entered in the record for later publication. At the end of the day Congressman Miller spoke of the hearing as a "spanking" of the Forest Service and the word is mild. "I have sat through dreary hours," said Mr. Charles C. Moore, President of the Dude Rancher's Association, "listening to repetition, testimony of personal problems, testimony filled with useless verbiage; of the approximate fifteen hours of testimony, less than one hour and one-half was accorded our side for discussion of matters supposed to be taken up by [the] committee." Mr. Moore made a formal protest and added, "Never in all my experience have I attended a meeting so one-sided and unfair, so full of bias."

Mr. Moore's judgment must stand. Comparatively few specific complaints against the Forest Service were made. Some of them were quite footless, others consisted of accusations for which no supporting evidence was offered. For practically all the others the Forest Service had factual and unanswerable rebuttals in its records of the cases, which show misrepresentation by the complainants or completely just and judicial handling by the Service. Most of these case histories, however, were not entered in the record till later: the audience did not hear them and the committee could not have seen them when it made its recommendations.

The committee was willing to listen to wholly irresponsible accusations. Hostile witnesses, for instance, charged the Service with the intention of eventually eliminating all grazing of livestock from the forests. This is an accusation circulated by the pressure groups in order to arouse the fears of stockgrowers; it is untrue and absurd. The Service has invested fifteen million dollars in range improvements (on behalf of the very men who were lying about it), extensive programs of range development are under way, and the demands of witnesses that these programs be speeded up sufficiently revealed that they knew they were lying. Equally vicious was the repeated statement that the Forest Service had destroyed its own ranges. Again, one witness said, "The forests of the West furnish the major portion of the summer pasture used by its stock," and this clear falsification (I have given the true figures above) is typical of much reckless testimony. Its purpose must have been either to inflame public opinion or to set up a drawing account of propaganda to be used later on.

The intention to discredit the Forest Service showed clearly in the testimony of officers of state and national stock associations. What they had to say was extremely generalized. The proposed reductions in grazing permits, they said, were unfair, arbitrary, and quite unnecessary. There was no need for reduction. The ranges were not in bad shape. Forest Service scientists did not know what they were talking about, they did not know how to manage ranges, their researches and experiments were silly and their reports wrong. Besides, only stockgrowers understood range conditions and no stockgrower would ever overgraze a single acre. Again, the Service was heavily overstaffed—the threat to get its appropriations cut down glints here. Again, it was not spending enough money for range improvements. (It is spending all it can get from Congress. And the state of mind from which these complaints issued is revealed in the bellyache by one witness that the Service was heinously squandering public money in building forest roads for fire protection). Again, it was spending taxpayers' money for propaganda against stock interests. (This means that the Service, in its regular publications, has reported that some of its ranges are in bad shape and that there is opposition to its repairing them by reducing grazing. It is required by law to make such reports. In 1947 its total expenditure for education and information, including all bulletins and reports on all the manifold activities of forestry, was less than one-half of one per cent of its appropriation.) And, the accusation ran, the Service had incited attacks on the stock-growing industry by foreign, that is to say, Eastern, journalists. This also is entirely untrue; since it involves me I am discussing it in this month's Easy Chair.

The printed record shows Congressmen Barrett, Rockwell, and Miller acting as open partisans and shows their more than occasional belligerence toward Forest Service officials and witnesses who wanted to testify in the interest of conservation. At the end of the evening Mr. J. Byron Wilson, the lobbyist, made his inevitable appearance and got consent to enter a statement for the record. It skillfully summarized all the accusations that the hearing had produced and it ended by calling for a congressional investigation of the Forest Service. The Service, Mr. Wilson said, had grown so powerful that it was no longer accountable to Congress and an investigation would disclose that all the nonsense spouted about it at Rawlins was true. That demand for an investigation was not there idly or by chance: it was helping to lay some groundwork.

At Rawlins Chairman Barrett told the two highest Forest Service officials present that they were in for a tougher time at Grand Junction, Colorado, and he knew what he was talking about, he had advance information. A larger, more noisily contemptuous audience had been assembled there, and the "Notice of Forest Permittees" had been well implemented. A mimeographed broadside had been prepared and copies of it were distributed to everyone who entered the room. A quotation will be instructive.

> The Forest Service is a child of Congress, grown up without parental discipline or instruction, an arrogant, bigoted, tyrannical off-spring, the same as any off-spring reared in the same manner, void of respect of law or

customs of our land or the rights and feelings of other people.

We now demand the Congress to accept the responsibility of this outrageous off-spring and put the restraining hand of parenthood to guiding it in the straight and narrow way before it runs afoul of some sterner justice.

The reader will observe an interesting resemblance to Mr. Wilson's formal statement at Rawlins, though Mr. Wilson writes more suavely and grammatically. He will also observe the threat of mob violence in the second quoted sentence, another revelation of a state of mind. Let him remember that what the Forest Service is here accused of is action to protect the national forests from damage by improper grazing. Our forests and our children's.

The hearing at Grand Junction was better stacked than the one at Rawlins. Witnesses were required to sign cards and specify the subject they wanted to speak about. By a selective use of these cards, the testimony of conservationists, water users, city officials, and representatives of protesting organizations was kept to a minimum. (They were booed by the audience.) Almost all of them were limited to five minutes apiece, though there was as much time for complainants as they wanted. The Forest Service officials, who had been grouped together like prisoners, were not asked to make an answering statement until the evening session. Then Mr. Barrett announced, "I thought . . . we should give Mr. Watts and Mr. Dutton or any of their subordinates about fifteen minutes or more to answer any of the charges that were made here today."

So far as those charges were specific, they were practically all trivialities, distortions, or misrepresentations. The factual reports of the Forest Service disprove and dispose of them step by step—and reveal their reckless malice. But again those reports were entered in the record later on. They were not heard by the audience and could not have been consulted by the committee before it made its recommendations.

If the witnesses were out of bounds, so were the active committeemen. This is from the *Record Stockman,* which highly approves the behavior it is describing: "His [Chairman Barrett's] arms waved; he pointed an accusing finger at the Forest Service section of the huge, tense crowd. As he finished, his voice quaking with emotion, a large majority of the crowd rose to its feet, applauded, and hurrahed." This is from a report by the chairman of an Arizona conservation group: "Representative Barrett did all that he could to undermine the authority of the Forest Service, to belittle the scientific work that has been accomplished by some of the leading experts of our country, to discredit its employees from the Chief of the Forest Service ... down to the Supervisor and Rangers." This is from a report by a representative of the Izaak Walton League: "Rep. Frank A. Barrett ... launched into a shouting, fist-clenching outburst that was intemperate in language and at times reached screaming intensity." There are other eyewitnesses' descriptions of Mr. Barrett's passion and the record shows that Mr. Rockwell was not far behind him. It also shows that, almost at the end, a stockgrower from "the same [national forest] where Bob Rockwell runs cattle" testified that "we haven't much to complain about in our neighborhood and we are getting along all right with the Forest Service."

It was gaudy, gorgeous, and inflammatory. But it was a tactical mistake. Officials of cities whose water supply had been acutely endangered by overgrazing and especially a representative of the Colorado State Planning Commission got into the record factual descriptions that turned a bright light on the folly of the complainants. Other conservationists, among them cattlemen and sheepmen from the ranges under discussion, in the brief time allotted them controverted and rebutted much of the testimony that had been so nois-ily presented. A representative of the Farmers Union who had been gagged by the five-minute rule wired to Speaker Martin of the House that the committee's "fir-ing-squad hearings" were "a shocking exhibition" and "a reflection on the dignity and decency of the House of Representatives." And a large part of the Colorado press began to protest. The *Denver Post* spoke of "Stockman Barrett's Wild West Show." The *Gunnison Courier* used stronger language in editorials too long to be quoted here. The *Daily Sentinel* of Grand Junction, a town whose water supply was in danger, said in a blistering editorial that the committee was "weighted in favor of one side and presided over by a chairman, also a party to the controversy [he was not a party directly], miss-ing no opportunity to denounce the other party in the dispute, which was given limited opportunity to present its case." And so on—the surge of public opinion was like that which had followed exposure of the landgrab scheme earlier in the year.

There were prompt reactions. The committee called off the hearing it had scheduled for Phoenix, presum-ably because conservation societies in Arizona were or-ganizing to receive it. And when it moved to Salt Lake City, on September 8, things were different. The same kind of witnesses (sometimes the same witnesses, in fact) began the familiar act. But they ran into the mo-bilized opposition of a state which had been alarmed by repeated catastrophes resulting from overgrazing ranges, which understood that only by protecting its water supplies could it survive, and which knew that the one realistic hope of protecting them lay in the For-est Service and its co-operation with other government bureaus that direct conservation. Mayors of cities, rep-resentatives of many civic and labor and veterans or-ganizations, stockmen, sportsmen, farmers, engineers, plain citizens forced their protest into the record. The pressure group had run into the hard fact of higher land use and its spokesmen were stopped cold.

On September 20, after hearings elsewhere on other subjects, the committee was in Redding, California, dealing with the Forest Service again. The "Notice to Forest Permittees" was doing its stuff, and to a reader of the record the mob spirit makes the Redding hearing seem uglier, more reckless and sinister, than any other. But also the demonstration seems fantastic and it was certainly futile. Then, after hearings on unrelated subjects in California, the committee moved on October 4 to Ely, Nevada. Here something exploded in its face.

A member of the Joint Committee presented a long, well-argued, brilliantly written summary of the theses and arguments on which the pressure group stands, with their single-minded concentration on grazing interests to the exclusion of all others and their plain distortion of the realities. He was arguing for transfer of the forest grazing lands to the emasculated Grazing Service (now the Bureau of Land Management) which, as I have said, is helpless to oppose the will of stockgrowers. Also he permitted himself a kind of talk common among his colleagues but heretofore sagaciously kept out of their testimony before the committee. The power of the government to regulate grazing, he said, "seems nearly modeled on the Russian way of life" and though we are opposing Russian autocracy, in government regulation of the range we are building "that very same system." To protect the ranges, the forests, and the watersheds is communism.

But Nevada is a desert state and life there, even more straitly than elsewhere in the West, is a function of the water supply. So something like the breaking of a dam occurred. Beginning with the mining industry, the most important one in the state, and running through practically every other way of life, witness after witness repudiated as unsafe the proposed transfer of forest grazing lands, denounced proposals to sell the public lands, and backed the Forest Service to the hilt. As the flood rushed on, the congressional attorneys for the prosecution were uncharacteristically silent. The hearing turned into a rout, and a couple of days later the member of the Joint Committee who had testified was writing to Nevada newspapers, explaining that what he had said had been horribly misinterpreted.

IV

The Committee had visited only one of the forests whose condition it had undertaken to investigate. (That trip occupied only part of one day and the range visited was not one of those whose deterioration the Service wanted to offer in evidence.) It had not seen the reports of the Forest Service which replied to the complainants it had listened to. But, though it did not report to Congress under whose Resolution it was acting, it was willing to make recommendations. It made them in a letter to Clinton P. Anderson, the Secretary of Agriculture. That letter is dated October 8, 1947, four days after the Ely hearing, and it is signed by ten members of the committee. But by October 4 the committee had already begun to disperse and go home: the printed record and the local newspapers show that only five members were present at Ely. The letter must have been written in California before the hearings ended. What it said might just as well have been written in Washington in April.

The letter made six recommendations about Forest Service administration of grazing. Five of these recommendations were pure smoke screen—they dealt with practices effectively in operation already or with procedures which anyone would favor. The sixth recommendation, number two in the letter, was the payoff, the one for which the entire campaign had been conducted: "Effective immediately and extending for a three year 'test' period there shall be no reductions made in permits."

Conceivably pressure-group propaganda and the violent emotions encouraged at the hearing might have created a force which the Secretary would have found too great to resist. But the hearings had gone too far—their excesses, their partisanship, and the resulting misrepresentations were obvious—and so he was able to stand firm. In a letter to Congressman Barrett dated January 13, 1948, Mr. Anderson accepted the five immaterial recommendations but rejected the one on which everything pivoted. He accompanied his rejection with a detailed analysis that disposes of the charges so tiresomely repeated at the hearings. He demonstrated that the cuts made in grazing permits were not unnecessary or unduly large or arbitrarily imposed, that Forest Service administration is not capricious or biased, that its officials and representatives are not ignorant of the stock business but in the main know it through long experience, that its experts are not impractical theorists but scientists standing on the irrefutable findings of their science, that the Forest Service is doing justice to stockmen and protecting both their interests and those of the public. His letter makes mincemeat of the propaganda.

The Secretary's letter was just, courageous—and final. The hearings of the Subcommittee on Public Lands had failed of their immediate purpose. The three-year "moratorium" on cuts in grazing permits had been killed.

But those who watch over the interests of a pressure group neither slumber nor sleep. Though the hearings failed of their immediate purpose, they got said and printed a great deal of stuff that may be useful for the long haul. The demands for a congressional investigation of the Forest Service and other government bureaus that deal with the public lands, which were made repeatedly, were made with an eye to the future. They can be used in the effort to force the Forest Service to accept dictation from the pressure group: they add teeth to the threat to get its appropriations cut down. What is more important still, they are an open bid for the support of stronger and wealthier interests that would profit from any change in conservation policy, from any loosening of government regulation of the public lands, and especially from extinction of the public-lands reserves.

Such threats, always dangerous, are especially so in an election year. In March 1948, a pressure-group spokesman testifying before a subcommittee of the House Appropriations Committee proposed just such an investigation—and Congressman Barrett, appearing before the same committee, backed him up. Congressman Eagle, a member of Mr. Barrett's subcommittee, has called for "an impartial study"—and the phrase always means a study which will find that the ranges are not overgrazed. General Patrick J. Hurley, campaigning for the Republican senatorial nomination in New Mexico, has pledged his "support to a thorough investigation" of what he calls the Forest Service's "unreasonable domineering bureaucratic management" of "grazing rights." (Complete adoption of the propaganda: there are no grazing *rights* in the forest: there are only leasehold permits.) Mr. Harold E. Stassen has adopted not only the pressure group's position but that of the landgrabbers at large and has called for "a major revision of public-lands policy." No major revision of public-lands policy is possible except one that would put an end to the public lands. And though Governor Dewey promptly attacked Mr. Stassen's position, he did so in words that made conservationists shudder and suggest that the public lands would by no means be safe in his hands.

There are other straws in the wind. In the May Easy Chair I called attention to a resolution by the New Mexico Woolgrowers Association which demanded a reduction of Forest Service appropriations in order to bring the Service to heel. Since then the same resolution has been adopted by the cattlemen's association of the same state and equivalent ones have been adopted by other state associations. Both of the national associations and various of the state associations have increased their publicity funds and begun a campaign "to neutralize unfavorable publicity against the cattle [and sheep] industry"—that is, to neutralize such articles as this one. Pamphlets, canned news stories, and press releases carrying the pressure-group message are now in full production. Two weeks before this was written an article clearly inspired by the pressure group and packed with obvious untruths appeared in a magazine of national circulation. (Mr. Kenneth A. Reid has already exposed the misrepresentations it contains, but his detailed analysis is not likely to be circulated on the same scale.) Various professional writers have been approached about presenting "the stockgrowers' side." (None I know has yet accepted.) An earlier agitation by the national associations to present that "side" is shaping up as a guided tour for editors, reporters, and feature writers through the Western stock country.

Even the landgrab is stirring again, though, as I have said, there is at present no chance that it can get congressional support. Since the committee hearings, some of those who testified that they had never heard of it have come out in favor of part or all of it. At its annual convention in January 1948, the National Woolgrowers Association resolved that national parks and monuments (our wilderness and scenic reserves) ought to be opened to grazing and that "all lands not of timber value" (including watersheds) ought to be removed from the jurisdiction of the Forest Service. A month earlier the Secretary of the Wyoming Stockgrowers Association asked that those same lands be given "public domain status for ultimate State or private ownership," and he said the same thing more guardedly at the convention of the Izaak Walton League in February. In November 1947 the Farm Bureau Federation of Wyoming officially demanded that *all* the public lands except national parks and monuments eventually be turned over to private ownership. (There go the forests and, when someone remembers them, the graves of the Seventh Cavalry.) The pressure-group press alternates between declaring that no one has even made such proposals and demanding that they be put into effect at once.

By itself, the pressure group cannot succeed in any of these attempts. In a fighting speech Secretary Anderson asked the New Mexico Cattle Growers Association, "If there is going to be a battle, who has the most votes—the livestock ranchers or a combination of conservationists, game protective associations, public power enthusiasts, and the water users? Who is going to come out second best?" This small minority of Western stockgrowers, with their refusal to take into account any interests but their own immediate ones, their ignorant and arrogant rejection of scientific knowledge, their noisy but so far inept propaganda, will always lose out as long as they do not get allies.

But there are two dangers. The attack on the Forest Service is only one part of an unceasing, many-sided effort to discredit all conservation bureaus of the government, to discredit conservation itself. It is a stubborn effort to mislead the public. Conceivably it could succeed. And it could produce formidable combinations. Ever since the public lands were first withdrawn from private exploitation the natural resources they contain have been a challenge and a lodestar to interests that were frustrated when the reserves were made. Those interests are much more powerful now than they were then. The natural resources husbanded for the common good have enormously increased in value. The consumption of natural resources not publicly reserved has astronomically increased the lust to get at those that have been saved. If the interests that lust to get at them should form an effective combination they could bring the United States to the verge of catastrophe in a single generation.

The danger is not Western: it is national. Fifty percent more saw timber is cut every year than is grown to replace it—what would happen to our future wood supply if the national forests should be turned over to private ownership? The widespread impairment of range lands is a naked fact and our tariffs amount to a subsidy to stockgrowers to destroy them—what would happen if government regulation of the publicly owned ranges should be ended? East of the Sierra and the Cascades, Western agriculture is absolutely dependent on irrigation—can the United States at large afford to let dams and irrigation systems silt up and cropland deteriorate because of unwise grazing and lumbering that destroy watersheds? Business, industry, population growth, and life itself in the West are absolutely dependent on the fullest possible production of water—can the United States carry eleven states bankrupted by floods, a falling water table, and the destruction of land, business, and wealth that results from them?

These overwhelmingly important questions are given a sharp irony by the fact that they must be asked at a moment when a new era in conservation is beginning all over the world. Awareness of the necessity of protecting natural resources is now more widespread than it has ever been before, and in the United States, the first nation that ever made conservation a public policy, the happiest omen is that this awareness has spread not only among the public but among scores of nationally important businesses and industries as well. But at the same time the acknowledged goal of other businesses and industries is to put an end to conservation forever. That is what gives national significance to a minute fraction of the cattle and sheep growers of the West who are hammering away at the program here described. We must keep an eye on them, inconsiderable as they are. But it is infinitely more important to make sure that no support of their program by anyone else goes unobserved.

Statesmen on the Lam

Originally this essay was published simply as the 153rd edition of DeVoto's Easy Chair column in *Harper's*. It appeared concurrently with "Sacred Cows and Public Lands," the July 1948 issue, and afforded DeVoto additional space to continue his "Sacred Cows" argument. DeVoto assigned the title "Statesmen on the Lam" to this Easy Chair column when it was published in a collection of his columns for *Harper's* titled *The Easy Chair* and released shortly before DeVoto's death.

I want to treat at greater length several topics merely glanced at in my article about the hearings before the Subcommittee on Public Lands. The first of them is what Senator Robertson of Wyoming, at the Billings hearing, called "the biased and prejudiced articles which have been appearing in weekly papers and monthly magazines." He and Congressman Barrett, at Billings and again at Rawlins, were referring to articles by Mr. Arthur H. Carhart, Mr. William S. Voight, Mr. Kenneth A. Reid, Mr. Lester Velie, and me. The articles of Mr. Reid and Mr. Voight have appeared mostly in publications of the Izaak Walton League. Mr. Carhart, for years a specialist in wildlife management, has written for various magazines. Mr. Velie is an editor of *Collier's* and in the summer of 1947 published there two articles that dealt primarily with the efforts of the pressure group I have described to get hold of the public grazing lands. His articles and the one I published in *Harper's* for January 1947 were the ones most often referred to at the hearings.

Both Senator Robertson and Congressman Barrett accused the Forest Service of "collaborating" in articles with the attempted land grab. No, let's speak as cagily as a politician who is mending fences. They insinuated that the Forest Service had done so. Senator Robertson "came to the conclusion" that an Izaak Walton League pamphlet had been worked out in collaboration with the Forest Service and had been printed in the same shop as Agriculture and Interior Department pamphlets, which could only mean the Government Printing Office. (Whether he meant to imply that Forest Service funds had paid for it is anyone's guess.) Congressman Barrett said, "I don't know whether the Forest Service has collaborated with some of these writers in these magazines or not. I have reason to believe it has; I'll say that much, I'm not charging you with it but I really feel deep down in my heart that you have."

The Forest Service has never asked me to write anything, has never suggested that I write anything, has in no way collaborated with me in anything I have written. It has volunteered no information to me. It has given me no information except at my request and the information it has given me is only of the kind which it is required by law to give to anyone who asks for it. Senator Robertson's toes were pinched by my having published in *Harper's* the number of sheep for which he held grazing permits in a national forest. I knew that he held grazing permits, I had asked the Forest Service for the exact figures, and I had got them. At Rawlins he asked Mr. Lyle Watts, the Chief of the Forest Service, "Information as to individual permits of permittees, is that given out by the Forest Service to these writers?" Mr. Watts replied to the Senator that when anyone wants to know how many stock anyone runs on a forest under permit, the Forest Service would tell him. "That," Mr. Robertson said, "would be Mr. DeVoto as well as Mr. Velie." It would be Mr. DeVoto; by law it would be anyone who might ask. The privileges of a Senator do not extend to keeping his grazing permits secret.

More interesting are Senator Robertson's and Congressman Barrett's efforts to dissociate themselves from proposals to open the public lands to private purchase. At Rawlins Mr. Reynold A. Seaverson, the President of the Wyoming Woolgrowers Association, read a long statement. At the end of it Senator Robertson said, "I do not see any recommendation at all that the lands comprised in the national parks and monuments, the national forest lands, or the reclamation withdrawals should be sold to individual stockmen. You make no recommendation such as that, do you?" Mr. Seaverson said no. Mr. Robertson: "You never have?" Mr. Seaverson said no. Senator Robertson: "Speaking as president of the woolgrowers, you would definitely say that such a statement made by Mr. DeVoto, or Mr. Velie, or any of the Izaak Walton leagues, or any dude ranches in this country, to the effect woolgrowers advocate such a purchase by private individuals is absolutely without foundation, would you not?" Mr. Seaverson: "Yes, Senator, without foundation whatsoever."

The impression created here is that Senator Robertson had never heard of any such proposals, that none had ever been made, and that Mr. Velie, other writers, and I had malignantly invented the notion in what Mr. Barrett called our "scurrilous articles." Well, on March 14, 1946, Mr. Robertson had introduced into the Senate his bill S. 1945, which I described in one of my scurrilous articles. This bill, if it had passed, would have granted to the States all the organized Taylor Act grazing lands, lands to be eliminated from various other public reserves, and "all lands eliminated as hereinafter provided

from national forests, national parks or monuments. . ."
It would have made mandatory the creation of State
commissions and the elimination from national forests
of any lands which those commissions should find "to be
more valuable for grazing [in whose eyes?] or agriculture than for timber production." And it provided that
all these lands and all other lands which under its terms
were to be granted to the States, "shall be subject to
lease, sale, or other disposition as the legislature of such
State may determine."

At Rawlins, Senator Robertson was strikingly ignorant of the provisions of his own bill. True, he did not
write it but he must have read it and there can be no
doubt that he discussed every item in it many times
with many people. Moreover, in his official statement
Mr. Seaverson had recommended that lands "suitable
only for grazing" (who decides?) be eliminated from the
forests. This, of course, is not a recommendation that
they be sold, though such a recommendation usually accompanies that proposal. Conceivably neither Senator
Robertson nor the witness had heard of the many proposals to open Taylor Act land and forest grazing land to
sale that had appeared in the stockgrowers' press, or of
the twenty-nine protests against them made at Billings
three days before, though the Senator was present
there. Conceivably they had heard none of the reper-
cussions of the article by the Vice Chairman of the Joint
Committee in the Denver *Post* which said that "as a first
step toward acquiring ownership of the land they use"
the stockgrowers proposed that "the government be required to offer [the Taylor Act lands] for sale" and went
on to admit that "stockmen hope" eventually to get into
private ownership "some tracts now in national forests"
and others "which never should have been included in
national parks."

Conceivably. But the record shows that Senator
Robertson was present at the opening of the Rawlins

hearing at which he later questioned Mr. Seaverson. It seems odd that he did not hear the acting clerk of that hearing, at Mr. Barrett's direction, read a statement by the Governor of Wyoming, the Hon. Lester C. Hunt. Mr. Hunt's statement, so short that I think most people could keep it in mind, ended with several recommendations. The fourth one reads, "That the Federal Government either dispose of these forests *(a)* to private ownership, or *(b)* to the respective States in which they are located." For a few minutes, one would think, the Senator must have known about some of the proposals which his bill would have enacted, if only inadvertently, into law.

Congressman Barrett said at Glasgow, "So far as I know, no one in Congress ever advocated granting the forest or the timberlands to private ownership." At Rawlins he dissociated himself from such proposals and told a witness that Senator Robertson's bill, of which by then he *had* heard, was dead. Its spirit was not dead in November 1946, when a convention of the Wyoming Woolgrowers Association was discussing one of the bills which my articles mentions as having been in preparation when the land-grab scheme was publicized. The Casper, Wyoming, *Tribune-Herald* for November 14, 1946, reports Congressman Barrett's speech at that convention. It quotes him as saying that fifty-one per cent of the area of Wyoming belongs to the federal government and then going on, "We must work out a plan whereby the eleven public land States of the West can grow, develop and promote their own economy on a free and equal basis. The problem is to work out a plan for returning these millions of acres to the States. If such a plan is evolved, I believe we can sell the plan to the whole Congress."

Finally, it is worth noting that, after Mr. Velie's articles and mine had been thoroughly denounced by Mr. Barrett and Mr. Robertson at Rawlins, Mr. Charles C.

Moore asked that they be entered in the record. Page 219 of the record at Rawlins, Mr. Barrett speaking: "We will consider it; there has been objection by the committee; Dr. Miller has objected." They were not entered in the record.

Observe that Mr. Barrett speaks of "returning" the public lands to the States. The pressure-group press habitually speaks of "returning" them to the States or to private ownership. This is high-quality dust for throwing in the eyes—or should I say wool for pulling over them? True, the public lands contain some microscopic tracts that were once State land: mostly they represent either even-up exchanges or purchases of land that had been forfeited to the States for non-payment of taxes. There are also microscopic tracts which were once privately owned but for which the government exchanged equivalent tracts, usually agricultural, from public reserves. There are other tracts, agricultural land abandoned as submarginal or cutover forest land, which the federal government bought from private owners for purposes of conservation. The total area of all these tracts makes only an infinitesimal fraction of the public lands. Except for that minute fraction it would not be possible to "return" the public lands to State or private ownership. They never belonged to the States or to individuals. They have been publicly owned ever since their acquisition from France, Spain, Mexico, and Great Britain.

By the acts of admission the Western States were granted various tracts of the public land within their borders, to support education and for other purposes: these are the State lands. By their constitutions the States renounced forever all claim to the remaining public lands. These lands, the public domain of the United States, however, remained open for entry by individuals under the Homestead Act, various grazing and timber and irrigation acts, the malodorous Stone and Timber Act, and others. But from time to time parts of the public domain were closed to private entry and as "reserves" dedicated to the common good and benefit of the United States: the national forests are one such reserve. They are exactly what the term says and what they have been from the beginning, public lands. When the propaganda talks about "returning" them to the States it is talking nonsense. When it talks about "resuming the historic land-ownership policy of the United States," it is talking about a policy from which the public reserves were excepted, exempted, and withdrawn. (And one which failed tragically in the arid West.) When it draws analogies between these lands and lands in the East to which the original States had a more or less undefined claim, which they relinquished to the federal government, and which were then opened to private entry—it is perverting historical fact. But all this is grist to the mill. The idea is to set up a specious claim that the Western States have been robbed of their heritage. The further idea is to demand the Western public lands if Hawaii and Alaska are granted parts of the public reserves when they are admitted as States. But the basic idea is to get the forests and grazing lands of the West that are now a common possession of the American people into private hands.

The state of mind behind this agitation is sometimes grotesque. The Vice Chairman of the Joint Committee on Public Lands of the two national stockgrowers associations is testifying in favor of abolishing the Jackson Hole National Monument—now composed of land always under federal ownership to which Mr. John D. Rockefeller, Jr., has been trying to add as a gift land which he has bought. "First of all," he says, "I deny that the federal government has any right to that land. It has no right by its treaties of acquisition. It has no right for the proposed retention of those lands, which are now outside its constitutional limitations of land ownership. . . .

To me when you get a lot of federal bureaus operating and managing lands which are not the proper function of government provided in the Constitution, it is nothing more or less than a mild form of communism. And that malignant growth in the West is almost destroying the American form of government.... There is an arrangement [for?] taking our lands away from us, in violation of constitutional limitations and our act of admission as a State. Here the gentleman seems to be saying only that to reserve lands for national parks and monuments is communism. But in his article in the *Denver Post* two months earlier he had said flatly, "Federal ownership or control of land is a form of communism."

His constitutional argument is based on the clause in Section 8 of Article I of the Constitution, which confines to areas ten miles square the legislative authority of Congress over tracts granted by the States to the government for governmental use. Few constitutional ideas so absurd have been aired in public since 1787 but this sort of thing, if not accepted by his associates, is nevertheless useful to their purposes. The gentleman lives in Wyoming: one wonders what authority he accepts as guaranteeing his title to the land he owns there. And one is reminded of a suggestion made some years ago by a writer who had been studying the cattle-baron state of mind that germinates such arguments. Over its history, he said, under stockgrower control, Wyoming had failed to develop the mature responsibility for self-government that Statehood requires, and he saw no plausible evidence that it ever would develop it. He proposed that Wyoming be returned to territorial status so that it could be governed responsibly.

Such curiosa, however, are harmless. A really dangerous irresponsibility is the refusal of such stockgrowers as the Joint Committee represents to admit that overgrazing damages the forage, the land, or the watersheds. The record of the hearing is spotted with assertions that the results of overgrazing were in fact not due to it at all. The heaped-up, irrefutable findings of many sciences and many scientists—in various government bureaus that deal with land, in state and private universities, in private foundations, in experiment stations, in similar institutions all over the world are ignored, denied, or ridiculed. I have space to mention only one example, the common denial that natural processes of erosion are speeded up—and unnatural erosion caused—by the deterioration of plant cover which occurs when an area is grazed too heavily. No fact that science deals with is more firmly established, but the pressure group propaganda—and as I showed here last year, that of the U.S. Chamber of Commerce—challenges and denies it.

Some members of the Subcommittee were willing to support that denial. At Rawlins Mr. Barrett said, " . . . it seems to me that the Forest Service ought to make a little study of this thing [erosion—the Service has been studying it intensively from the beginning] and be a little honest about it, and say here 'This thing has been going on for centuries; it was going on before there was a cow in Wyoming; that it was going on before there was ever a white man in Wyoming. . . .' Why blame it on the poor sheepherder and the little old cowboy that's trying to make a living here on these hills?" There are places in Wyoming where the poor sheepherder and the little old cowboy have accelerated erosion several hundred thousand per cent and permanently impaired the range, but science does not impress Mr. Barrett. And the jocose Mr. Rockwell at Ely: "Geologists [scientists who apparently can be trusted about the condition of the land millions of years ago but not today] say the original height in my State of Colorado was 36,000 feet. It has now gone down to 10,000 feet. I wonder what the Forest Service would have done to prevent that loss, had they been in service at the time." An entire psychology is compressed in that arrogantly ignorant sneer. At Grand

Junction Mr. Rockwell had listened to scientific evidence which proved that the water supply of that and other Colorado towns had been endangered by erosion resulting from overgrazing. At Salt Lake City he had heard how erosion resulting from overgrazing had brought an entire Utah county to the brink of catastrophe—and how scientific measures to arrest erosion and repair the damage it had done had saved that county. But that was the talk of long-haired scientists and only a practical stockgrower, such a man as Mr. Rockwell, is qualified to judge the condition of a range.

Against such psychology as this only the force of the ballot can defend the public interest. Argument, demonstration, proof, considerations of higher land use, of long-term values, of any values except the immediate ones of the pressure group cannot alter it in the least. I come back to Secretary Anderson, asking a secessionist group of cattlemen who, if it should come to a battle, had the most votes. It may come to a battle—it could come as early as the appointment of Republican Secretaries of Agriculture and the Interior.

If the West cannot control the exceedingly small number of people whose program would destroy it, the rest of the country will have to control them for the West's sake and its own. Up to twenty Western votes in Congress might be swung to support that program, and such a bloc might be enough to hold the balance of power. But your Representative has a vote that counts as much as any other. Better make sure that he does not cast it on this issue in ignorance of what is at stake.

Two-Gun Desmond Is Back

The year of 1951 proved, for Bernard DeVoto, to be intensely focused on the writing of his National Book Award–winning classic, *The Course of Empire.* Though DeVoto primarily fixed his tunnel vision on the completion of *Empire,* he was not one to rest his sights on one simple and singular goal. DeVoto considered the workday to run from the completion of breakfast to the moment of sleep, and occupied all moments in between with the tasks at hand. His return to the conservation battlefield would, in typical DeVoto style, come with guns slinging and rhetoric firing. This March 1951 essay for *Harper's* found DeVoto addressing his old nemesis: the Landgrabbers. After losing their attempts to privatize grazing lands in national parks, the two major ranch organizations lining up against conservation formed a cohesive unit in the "Grazing Committee." Though most Westerners opposed their work, they found themselves unmotivated to fight. DeVoto once again exposed those individuals responsible for what he saw as a personal attack against the custodians of the public land: the American people. As the Grazing Committee drafted legislation to reduce the National Forest Service's control over the grazing rights, DeVoto once again stepped up to defend the West and its limited resources against those pioneers who lacked the vision of history.

The humble sheep-walker has come down from the rocks and the bronzed horseman rides again. They are after the national forests in thirteen Western states; they have been for years. They tried to steal them in 1947, together with all other public lands that could grow a little grass, but they got stopped. They decided that they had been trying to get away with too much at a time, so now they will settle temporarily for control of the forests, with some additional tricky stuff thrown in. Understanding that the methods they thought up for themselves in 1947 were too crude, they have hired some brains to brush a little suavity and finesse over the steal. You have got to know about it because it is your property they want to alienate.

As I said in *Harper's* at the time, if the 1947 effort had succeeded it would have been the biggest landgrab in American history. All the public lands that could be grazed at all were to undergo forced sale to stockmen. Those that were being grazed at the time were to be sold to the stockmen who were using them, sold at a rigged estimate of the grazing value alone without regard to other uses or values, and the happy beneficiaries of their own thrift were to have up to forty-five years to pay the gratuity. Any public land that wasn't being grazed but had some grass on it was to be sold on the same terms to the queue of stockmen lined up for it, and presumably anybody who could graze a cow in Yosemite Valley or on the lawn in front of headquarters at the Custer Battlefield could bid it in. The plan had the simplicity of the pastoral mind. But it was barefaced fraud and the pastoral mind did not get away with it. It endangered so many Western and national interests, private as well as public, that as soon as the light was turned on it public opinion killed it. The bills that had been written were never even introduced into Congress; as one of the Congressmen who had been detailed to smooth the way remarked out loud, once the public found out about them they became too hot to handle.

But, again as I pointed out in *Harper's,* there are many ways to skin a cat. The boys got out a different skinning knife and went to work on the Forest Service. The idea was to bring it into disrepute, undermine public confidence in it by every imaginable kind of accusation and propaganda, cut down its authority, and get out of its hands the power to regulate the grazing of stock in the national forests. The last has always been a major objective, not the ultimate objective but one that is a prerequisite for everything else in the plan. The Forest Service is the federal agency charged with administration of the national forests on behalf of the public. Grazing is only a minor, subsidiary, and contingent use of the forests, and the Service has to regulate it in accordance with a safe and equitable balance of all other uses. To regulate it, especially, to prevent stockmen from overgrazing the forest ranges, impairing or even destroying them, and gravely endangering other and more important forest values.

Precisely that is what the stockmen want to prevent. They want to get the power to regulate grazing taken away from the Forest Service and turned over to the stockmen who use the forest ranges. Everybody who has ever looked into the matter knows what that would mean.

Let's be clear about something else: this is not the Western stock business as a whole. About nine-tenths of the Western cattle business and about three-fourths of the Western sheep business never touch the national forests at all. The pressure campaign is conducted by a joint committee, now called the Grazing Committee, of the two big trade organizations, the American National Livestock Association and the National Wool Growers Association, working with various state organizations and a variegated assortment of other helpers. A good many of the small local stock associations and a good many Western stockgrowers as individuals oppose the campaign but they seem unable to make their opposition count. Don't ask me why the bulk of their Western colleagues simply stand by and let things slide; I have never understood why. One does not suspect them of undue saintliness and yet with amazing disregard of self they unprotestingly accept the handicap of the preferential treatment which their competitors who use the forest ranges get from the Forest Service and the public.

As taxpayers they help subsidize that preferential treatment—and so do you. For every dollar a stockman pays to graze his stock on national forest land, one who leases privately owned grazing land pays at least three dollars, sometimes as much as six dollars. The public, including you, pays the difference; it subsidizes the user of forest ranges by writing off two-thirds of his grazing fee. It then spends part of what it does get improving the range for him.

You and the lessee of privately owned grazing, however, take a worse beating than that. A lot of publicly owned land, the remnants of the Public Domain, was organized into grazing districts under what is known as the Taylor Act, districts which are administered by the Bureau of Land Management, Department of the Interior. (The Forest Service is a bureau of the Department of Agriculture.) For reasons and by methods which I have several times explained here, the local stockmen soon got effective control of the Taylor Act lands. So where a holder of a Forest Service permit pays a dollar for grazing, the Taylor Act licensee pays at most twenty-five cents. (Currently there is a move on—it probably originates in Moscow—to raise this to about twenty-nine cents.) The subsidy here is eleven-twelfths. You are paying it. The legislation which the Grazing Committee has worked up proposes a study of grazing fees on forest ranges with a view to revision. Guess what "revision" means.

As co-owners of both the Taylor Act lands and the national forests, you might require Congress to see to it that your licensees get their hands out of your pocket and pay the market rate for grazing, and I don't say that wouldn't be a good idea. Or if your heart bleeds for the sunburned supplicant for your bounty—how long since you could afford a sirloin?—you might at least require him to bid competitively for the privilege of using your ranges. When someone wants to cut timber in your forests he has to enter a sealed bid against all others who want to bid and can make the required guarantees. Not the cowboy and the shepherd, types who are always bellyaching about bureaucratic tyranny.

The national forests are the property of the American people. By far their greatest value, Western and national, is the preservation and protection of watersheds. The West is arid country; not only its solvency but its very survival depend on its water supply. On the safeguarding of that water supply and the utmost possible production of water the expansion of industry in the West depends, and the expansion of Western industry may be a matter of life and death to the United States if full-scale war comes. Any future expansion of Western agriculture also depends on water production. Vital parts of every important watershed in the West are in national forests—and stock grazing is a threat to a watershed the moment it becomes overgrazed. Many watersheds have been damaged by overgrazing, and the efforts of the Forest Service to reduce and repair the damage—in large part by reducing the number of stock grazed in areas that have deteriorated—have always been met with truculent opposition by the stockmen. A prime objective of this campaign, as of all its predecessors, is to end the power of the Forest Service to reduce the number of stock in overgrazed areas. To prevent a public agency, that is, from administering the public land for the public benefit.

There is no legal right to graze public land. The stockmen have long been trying to create such a right by legislation, to make it adverse to all other forest uses, and to vest it in the present holders of grazing permits—thus handing themselves a fine capital gain at public expense. Grazing on the public lands is a privilege and the man who holds a grazing permit is a licensee. In the forests, moreover, grazing is a subsidiary use, subsidiary not only to water production but to other uses which are worth more to the public and to the balance of properly managed land units as a whole. The forests are after all forests, not primarily grazing areas. They contain the only federally owned merchantable timber, federal reforestation is conducted on them, and they are the basis of the national forestry program. And they have many other uses. In the Western forests to which the proposed legislation is to apply there were just under 17,000 grazing permits last year. There were about 35,000 "special use" permits, ranging from private summer camps through commercial recreation enterprises and on up to prospecting and mining. There were 15,000 revenue-producing timber sales. And more than 16 million people used these same forests for recreation. The proposed legislation undertakes to subordinate all such uses to stock grazing and then to take the regulation of grazing away from the Forest Service.

I have space to mention only some of the proposals; I will return to the subject some months from now. Most of them are familiar and all of them are aimed at the constant objectives of the stock associations. They undertake to give local boards, composed of the stockmen who use the ranges they are to pass on, the administrative power that is now vested in the Forest Service, ultimately that of the Secretary of Agriculture. The regulation of grazing, that is, would be vested not in the representatives of the public but in the grazers. On their consent all other uses of grazing areas would depend. Any kind of emergency action in the public interest would be impossible. If drought, fire, flash floods, a bad winter, or one of the sudden lapses from productivity to which overgrazed land is subject should threaten the water supply of a Western town or irrigation district, no action could be taken unless the local board of licensed grazers should, as the proposed bill puts it, "concur."

Even if the board should concur, no holder of a permit could be required to make any changes in less than five years, by the end of which irreparable damage might be done to the range, to the public interests, and to other private interests.

The proposed bill provides that no holder of a grazing permit can have it canceled, or the number of stock it licenses him to graze reduced, if he has borrowed money on it. Nothing is specified about these immunity-producing loans except that they can be "bona fide." If I lease a store building from you, that is, I can force you to extend the lease indefinitely and on the original terms so long as I can get someone to lend me money on it. No amount or percentage specified; just legal tender.

The bill also provides that if land for which a grazing permit has been issued is turned to some other and higher use, or if the number of stock it licenses is reduced, then the holder of the permit shall be "compensated" to the extent of the "damage" he may suffer. Damage not to private property, that is, but to the subsidy he gets from the public. If you want to change the terms of the lease I hold for your store building when renewal time comes, you must pay me damages. Nice going. No miner, prospector, water user, timber cutter, or dude wrangler—no other user of the forests supposes he is entitled to a bonus.

These are some of the proposals the stockmen intend to make for getting administration of the national forests into their own hands and cutting themselves a melon. There are others, including a tricky one that would change the basis of investment in home property by which many grazing regulations are now scaled. They add up to the old game with a new backfield formation. But the proposed legislation contains a more dangerous threat to the national forests, the public lands in general, and the national stake in conservation. It is worded to take advantage of any possible change in public-lands administration and it seems to favor unification of land-management policy. That is a very pious idea— or would be if the plain intent of the whole game were not to bring the regulation of grazing in the national forests under the Taylor Act, and if this wording were not aimed to bring it under the Taylor Act if the Executive Departments of the government are reorganized.

The possibility that precisely this might be tried has kept a lot of conservationists from favoring the establishment of a Department of Natural Resources, as a task force and a minority report of the Hoover Commission proposed to do. We foresaw as all too easily possible what the stock associations are in fact now trying to bring about: the degradation, rather than the improvement, of public-lands management. Unification of grazing land under one bureau would indeed be desirable— if certain fundamental principles were applied to it and if certain fundamental values were safeguarded. One absolute consideration is this: the national forests are multiple-use lands and grazing in them will always be a minor use, whereas the Taylor Act lands are primarily grazing lands and have only minor value for other purposes. For reasons repeatedly explained here it will not do to concentrate the management of public grazing land under the Bureau of Land Management as it is now set up. The former is what the present stock-association campaign is trying to do immediately, and the latter is what the phrasing of its proposed legislation is designed to insure.

You had better watch this, now and from now on. The landgrabbers are on the loose again and they can be stopped only as they were before, by the effective marshaling of public opinion. Your property is in danger of being alienated, your interests and those of your children are threatened, and your money is to be used to subsidize a small percentage of the Western stock business while it makes further inroads on the public wealth. If the proposed legislation has not been introduced in Congress by the time this column is printed, it soon will be. The only question is whether the boys will try to do it by a series of first downs or with a touchdown pass that puts everything in one bill. You had better make sure that your Representatives and Senators understand quite clearly what is going on and where you stand. Then if you don't belong to one of the conservation societies, join one and keep in touch.

Another thing. The landgrabbers have a habit of talking loudly and indiscreetly. Loud talk in a hotel lobby in Salt Lake City, one summer evening in 1946, was what enabled a reporter to dig out the record of a secret meeting of the Joint Committee, publish the carefully guarded plans for the landgrab, and so touch off the public outcry that stopped it. Right now the stock associations are claiming out West that this time they have got the Department of the Interior on their side. They are saying that the Bureau of Land Management and the Bureau of Reclamation favor their proposed legislation.

This cannot possibly be true but the cowboys can gain a lot of ground merely by claiming that it is. For people remember occasions in the past when parts of Interior have lusted to get back jurisdiction over the lands that were withdrawn from it when the Forest Service was created. The plausibility thus traded on ought to draw a flat declaration from Director Clawson and Commissioner Straus that they do not favor the legislation and that no one under their authority will be permitted to assist it.

For there could be no better way to divide the forces of conservation than to let that old issue be revived even in appearance, and no better way of assuring the victory of anti-conservation forces than to increase or create rivalry among the federal bureaus that are charged with conservation. The public needs a solid front, absolute co-operation among those bureaus, and the bureaus need the united support of all conservationists. The brains the cowboys have hired are trying to serve their clients by the old and formidable game of dividing the opposition. We have all got to be on guard, to walk the bounds and keep our eyes peeled, and that goes for your representatives in Congress.

Billion Dollar Jackpot

In this February 1953 Easy Chair column for *Harper's* De-
Voto addresses the coming congressional session and the
new Eisenhower administration. DeVoto wasted no time in
invoking the sacred names of Theodore Roosevelt and Gifford Pinchot to prove to the current administration that Republican policy need not be synonymous with anti-conservation legislation.

Three weeks after the election the *Denver Post* ran
an editorial pointing out the necessity of maintaining "the public's right to protect its own land."
It did not know, the *Post* said, whether the incoming
Administration would retain or replace a U.S. district attorney who had filed suit against two Colorado ranchers
for grazing sheep on the public lands without a permit,
but in either event the suit must be fought through. For
its outcome might well determine whether the benefits
received from nearly half a billion acres of publicly
owned land "shall go to the people who own the land or
to those who, under any other name, may still be classified as trespassers."

In short, could the public continue to control the use
and prevent the abuse of its property? "We favor," said
the *Post,* which, I point out, is a soundly Republican
newspaper, "we favor the maximum beneficial use by
the people of the lands and forests they own, particu-

larly in the Western states, but we do not favor a few of the people being able to commit abuses or to establish a profitable monopoly in such lands under false pretenses or by absolute illegality." The land involved in this particular suit was grazing range administered by the Bureau of Land Management, but the principle supported by the *Post* applies to all categories of public land. The public lands policy which the editorial expresses is both typically Western and national as well.

A policy the exact opposite of this is the one expressed in some resolutions adopted by the Wyoming Farm Bureau Federation at about the same time. We are going to hear a lot of talk about the public lands from this and related points of view during the next few months, while alert special interests try to impose on a Republican Congress that will take a little time to learn its responsibilities. So the Federation's language is worth scrutinizing.

One of the whereases speaks of the public lands which are located in Wyoming as being "claimed by the federal government." Note: *claimed.* The notion that the United States never owned any land and has held the public lands unconstitutionally or illegally shows up in Wyoming now and then. Supporters of the idea cannot have reflected that their title to any land they may hold is no better than the "claim" of the United States. Title originates in a patent from the United States, whether direct to an original homesteader or purchaser, or at one remove through such a grantee as the state itself or a railroad company. If the United States did not own the land it granted, the present holders of it do not own it, and presumably they are liable to ejection, dispossession, alienation, and action for damage.

A related and more popular absurdity speaks of "returning" the public lands to the states in which they are situated. With the exception of a few minute areas which the government has acquired by exchange or purchase, it would be impossible to "return" any public land to the states, for it was never theirs. So long as it has been American it has belonged to the federal government, that is to the people of the United States.

Another of the Federation's whereases says that since the public lands are not on the Wyoming tax roll, land taxed by the state is under a double burden. This is a very ancient bouquet of horse feathers. Much of the public land in the West is desert that could never in any circumstances be taxed. As state officials well know, from practically all the rest of it, except the national parks, the Western states receive from the federal government payments in lieu of taxes at least as large as taxes would produce—greater, in fact, considering the additional benefits tied in with these payments.

The whereases lead to a thunderous conclusion. The Federation resolved "that all public lands and all minerals on or under said lands [oil rates as a mineral] claimed by the federal government should become the property of the State of Wyoming." It endorses "any steps necessary to attain this goal" and declares that legislation which will attain it should "be tied onto the Tide Lands Bills."

This is one version of a proposal that is going to be made in various forms and to various degrees, as desirous groups experiment to see how far they can get the new Congress to go. (The groups are numerically small but powerful, and after all there was that public-lands plank in the Republican platform; you will remember that I predicted just this in the October *Harper's*.) It is aimed at the most valuable publicly owned natural resources: oil and coal and natural gas reserves now worked under lease, other reserves such as phosphates and oil shale, power and irrigation sites, the mineral and water resources of the national parks, and the timber and grazing ranges of the national forests. It has some implications that should alarm all the West but the predatory groups.

Thus Montana would find itself the proprietor of the Custer Battlefield National Monument, including the national cemetery. The upkeep is considerable and the Montana taxpayer probably would not assume an expense that is now borne by the American at large. Unless some way of making it an amusement park for tourists could be found, it would have to be abandoned. (Leased for grazing, as the Wyoming cowboys have proposed, it might bring the state from $30 to $60 a year.) Wyoming could not possibly assume the expense of maintaining and operating Yellowstone and Grand Teton National Parks. The power potential of Jenny, Jackson, and Yellowstone Lakes is negligible but they could be sold to irrigation companies. (This one was actually tried in the nineteen-twenties.) The gold that is supposed to be "locked up" in Yellowstone Park could be sold, though only at a trivial price, for trying to find it would be a highly speculative enterprise. The timber in the parks could be sold and such scenery as might survive the construction of mining, dredging, and irrigation works could be sold to resort corporations.

Perhaps, once the foreground has been made hideous by irrigation developments, Wyoming would be willing to divert to the maintenance of Teton Park some of the money to be obtained by selling the national forests. But since they can be sold only once, the state must set up a trust fund and run the parks on the income from it. It won't be large: the idea is to dispose of the forests at fire-sale prices.

When the Western states get the forests they will be acquiring a big future expenditure. Once the grazing ranges have been worn out, as those now owned by the states mostly are, and once the timber has been clear-cut, silt from the resulting erosion will soon fill power dams, irrigation systems, and municipal reservoirs. The upstream states will find themselves defendants in damage suits brought by irrigators, cities, and factories and the corporations which by then will have bought the dams. Sometimes these suits will run to many millions of dollars, as when Los Angeles or the Pacific Gas & Electric Company sues Wyoming for loss of water and power caused by the destruction of Bridger National Forest. Since the forest will have ceased to be national, the damage can be assessed only against Wyoming taxpayers. If the Federation expects Vermont to pay damages, it had better inquire into the nature of Yankees.

The states are also going to lose a lot of income which they now get from the national treasury and only their own taxpayers can make good the deficit. They will have to build most of their own roads, for instance. Because they have got public lands within their borders, the federal government contributes considerably more for road construction than it does to states that haven't got them, and that benefaction will end. They will also have to raise their own tax funds for fire protection and fire control in the once national forests and for the 50 per cent cut that Treasury now pays for the same work in private and state forests. California might be able to do this, if its taxpayers should consent, but none of the other states could. Insect control, wild-game management, construction of recreation facilities and fire and access roads, and maintenance of roads and trails within the forests—these too will be a charge on the local taxpayer. So will reforestation and the reseeding of forest grazing ranges and those now under the Bureau of Land Management. Most research in forestry and related sciences, land management, power transmission, gas, petroleum, mining, and the like will have to be paid for by the states as soon as they and corporations get the public lands. The big-income states—New York, Pennsylvania, Massachusetts, Illinois, Texas—pay for

most of it now, and all the states pay their proportionate share, simply because these *are* public lands, the
property of all the people. But there is no reason why
Pennsylvania should pay a dime to maintain an Oregon
(or a Weyerhaeuser) forest, a Nevada (or P. G. & E.) dam,
or a Wyoming grazing range. And why should Pennsylvania pay for any of the other direct or indirect subsidies the West now receives because of the public lands?
Pennsylvania congressmen have to get re-elected and
will not appropriate federal funds for private profit or
state graft in the West.

Another gimmick is being hopefully set up because
of some incautious Republican speeches during the campaign. It will cost, say, three hundred million dollars and
upward to build a power project on any of the remaining sites. A percentage of this cost, under the present
system, is charged against reclamation (and ultimately
against the taxpayer by way of relief bills), and a larger
percentage is written off as "non-reimbursable" because
of flood protection, recreation, and native American
piety. Three hundred million dollars is a large sum for
even the biggest power company to raise by bonds. So
the hope is that Pennsylvania can be persuaded to build
the project, write off the percentages aforesaid, and either give it to Oregon (which pays 1 per cent of the federal income tax) or sell it at some agreeable valuation
to a public utility. Well, the Western bloc was able to put
over a series of silver-purchase acts but they were small
potatoes. A stop-the-music program with a billion Pennsylvania and New York dollars in the kitty would be different.

In connection with these grabs and giveaways we
are going to hear a lot about something else worth noting here, the wail that the Western states never got a
fair cut of the national domain and ought to be given
the public lands as an apologetic tip. This is simply a request that they be given free what everybody else had

to pay for. Connecticut and Virginia did indeed receive (from the area that is now Ohio) some land and some warrants to buy land, to satisfy bounties promised their Revolutionary veterans. (They got them in return for turning over to the national government their ancient grants of far larger areas.) All states carved out of the national domain received Section 16 of every unsold township for the support of public education. After the passage of the Morrill Act in 1862 additional small areas were given to the states for the support of agricultural and mechanical colleges, and those that had no national domain within their borders were allotted their proportionate share from the sale of the national domain. Payments to land-grant colleges ceased to be made from land sales in 1907 and they are now made direct from the Treasury. Last year they totaled $48,000,000. The West got its cut.

The total area of all these grants was infinitesimal compared to the portions of the public domain that were granted to the eleven Western states. They were given land for common schools, normal schools and colleges, internal improvements, various state institutions, state parks, and other purposes. Nevada, which received the smallest area, got just under three million acres—more than the total combined areas of Rhode Island and Delaware, neither of which ever got an acre of public domain, plus a third of Connecticut. New Mexico got most, just over ten million acres, almost twice the area of Massachusetts, more than twice that of New Jersey, neither of which, again, received any of the public domain. Eight Eastern states, in fact, are smaller than the area of public land granted New Mexico or that granted Arizona. California, Utah, and Oregon each got an area larger than Maryland; Montana an area larger than New Hampshire; Colorado, Idaho, and Wyoming each an area larger than Connecticut. Most of this land is still in the possession of the states. If, when the states ask for

Boulder Dam and Yellowstone Park, Congress will inquire into the condition, uses, finances, and management of these state lands, as the *Denver Post* did last
spring, it will find some shocking conditions. Montana
and Idaho have managed theirs with considerable wisdom, Washington and Oregon pretty well, and the others
with various degrees of venality, including the highest
possible degree. But I will discuss state lands at another
time.

The public lands are public property which Congress
long ago decided to preserve and develop in the common interest. The new Congress would be wise to recall
the reasons that made conservation a national policy.
The reservation of the public lands was the outcome of
the realization that much of our heritage of natural resources had been wasted, that much of what remained
was impaired, and that all of it was in grave danger of
being exhausted. The objectives were the controlled
use of non-renewable resources, the preservation and
scientific development and increase of renewable ones,
and the protection of watersheds, especially in the arid
West. The great achievements of our conservation policy
have been in the twentieth century but its roots go back
almost to the Civil War. One remembers the pioneers,
the prophetic genius John Wesley Powell, such scientists
as Charles Sargent and Nathaniel Shaler and Othniel
Marsh, such statesmen as Carl Schurz, many other scientists, public officials, industrialists, businessmen, and
the National Academy of Arts and Sciences and the Association for the Advancement of Science.

The new Congress will note that those I have named
were all Republicans; down to 1932 practically all the
achievements of conservation were the work of Republicans. The word "conservation" itself was given its present meaning by W. J. McGee, a Republican. The first
reservations of public land were made by President Benjamin Harrison and the biggest ones by Theodore Roo-

sevelt, who also established the Forest Service and procured the passage of the Reclamation Act. The Carey
Act, the Withdrawal Act, the Weeks Act were Republican measures. The Inland Waterways Commission was
a Republican creation and so were most of the national
parks, the mineral and oil and coal and water-power reserves, the licensing system under which they are used,
and the reservation of Mussel Shoals. If Franklin Roosevelt is one of the three greatest names in conservation, the other two, Theodore Roosevelt and Gifford Pinchot, are Republican. Finally, it was a Republican who
phrased the policy under which the public lands have
been administered: "the greatest good of the greatest
number over the longest time."

From this well-established point of view, safeguarding the future has always been more important than en-
riching small pressure groups at public expense, the
nation more important than 2 percent of the West, and
the public interest in publicly owned resources more important than the private interests that coveted them.
This view has always been under attack and will now
be under very hopeful attack by groups, hitherto frustrated, who hope they can induce Congress to undo the
great work that has been done. They are the same interests they have always been, and they constitute the
same threat to the future of the West and of the United
States. They are using the same pressures, arguments,
and fraud that they have been using for more than fifty
years. In the twentieth century they have won only one
victory, the annihilation of the Grazing Service expertly
perpetrated by Senator McCarran.

Senator McCarran's technique is in their minds as
they prepare now for what they hope will be the kill. As
I have been pointing out here at intervals ever since the
January 1947 issue of *Harper's,* their first objective will
be the Forest Service; if they cannot wreck it as completely as the Grazing Service was wrecked, depriving it

of its regulatory power would do almost as well. Beyond the Forest Service are oil and oil shale, phosphates, water power, and the hope that Massachusetts can be induced to build dams for Utah. They will be stopped again unless they carry it with the first rush, for Western and national public opinion will, as always, solidify against them. But there is that first rush. When it begins, Congress should remember three things: that the public lands belong to the citizens of forty-eight states and not to 2 per cent of eleven, that impairment of the public lands would arrest progress in the West and ultimately make the region a charge on the rest of the country, and that the public lands are the only responsibility of the government besides atomic energy about which Congress could make an irretrievable mistake, one that could not be corrected later on. For if the public lands are once relinquished, or even if any fundamental change is made in the present system, they will be gone for good.

The Sturdy Corporate Homesteader

Once again railing against the corporate landgrabbers from the East, DeVoto leaves no hypocrite unexposed in this May 1953 Easy Chair column for *Harper's*. He parallels the Eastern corporate establishment with the early Western settlers who could buy their slice of the American pie—160 acres—for $2.50 per acre. DeVoto gives the early Western settler his due, but refuses to accord the Eastern landgrabbers the same leeway. During this time DeVoto's fury was aimed also towards the W. Colston Leigh agency, with which he had contracted to coordinate lecture tours for him, since he was doubtful over his future as a freelance writer. Though he insisted the Leigh agency schedule around his Easy Chair writing assignments, they often overlooked his wishes.

In a happier time, so a U.S. Chamber of Commerce speaker tells us, the government used the public domain to "give every man a chance to earn land for himself through his own skill and hard work." This is the sturdy homemaker sob with which the air will presently resound when this gentleman's associates get to work on Congress. He may have been thinking of the California redwood forest. It was so attractive a part of the public domain that in this generation we have had to raise millions of dollars from rich men and school children to buy back a few acres of it here and there for the public.

Under a measure called the Timber and Stone Act, a homemaker who had his first citizenship papers could buy 160 acres of redwood forest from the government for $2.50 an acre, less than a panel for your living-room costs. Agents of a lumber company would go to a sailors' boarding house on the San Francisco waterfront. They would press a gang of homemakers and lead them to a Courthouse to take out first papers. Then they went to a land office and each filed claim to 160 acres of red-wood: a quarter-section whose number the lumber com-pany had supplied. At a lawyer's office they transferred to the lumber company the homesteads they had earned by skill and hard work, received $50 for services ren-dered, and could go back to the boarding house. "Fifty dollars was the usual fee," a historian says, "although the amount soon fell to $10 or $5 and eventually to the price of a glass of beer."

Under this Act four million acres of publicly owned timber passed into corporate ownership at a small frac-tion of its value, and 95 per cent of it by fraud. Under other Acts supposed to "give every man a chance to earn land for himself" enormously greater acreages came to the same end with the sturdy homemaker's help.

The laws stipulated that the homemaker must be in good faith. Erecting a "habitable dwelling" on his claim would prove that he was. Or if it was irrigable land, he had to "bring water" to it, for a homemaker would need water. Under a couple of dozen aliases apiece, employ-ees of land companies or cattle companies would file claim to as many quarter-sections or half-sections of the public domain and after six months would "commute" them, get title to them, at $1.25 per acre.

The sworn testimony of witnesses would prove that they had brought water to the claim; there was no rea-son for the witnesses to add they had brought it in a can. Or the witnesses swore that they had "seen water" on the homestead and so they had, having helped to throw it there cupful by cupful. Or to erect a "twelve by fourteen" cabin on a claim would prove good faith. Homemaker and witnesses neglected to mention that this "habitable dwelling" was twelve by fourteen inches, not feet. Alternatively, a "shingled residence" established that the homemaker intended to live on his claim; one could be created by fastening a couple of shingles to each side of a tent below the ridgepole. Sometimes a scrupulous corporation would build a genuine log cabin twelve by fourteen feet, mount it on wagon wheels, and have the boys drive it from claim to claim, getting the homemaker a lot of public domain in a few hours. In a celebrated instance in Utah the efficiency of this device was increased by always pushing the truck over the corner where four quarter-sections met.

In six months the homemakers, who meanwhile had been punching cows or clerking in town, commuted their two dozen parcels of the public domain. They transferred them to their employers and moved on to earn two dozen more quarter-sections apiece by their skill and hard work. Many millions of acres of publicly owned farmland and grazing land thus passed economically into the possession of corporate homemakers. If the corporation was a land company it might get half a million acres convenient to a railroad right-of-way or within a proposed irrigation district. Or a cattle company could thus acquire a hundred thousand acres that monopolized the water supply for miles and so graze a million acres of the public domain entirely free of charge.

Lumber companies could operate even more cheaply. Their employees need not pay $1.25 per acre or wait to commute their claims. They could pay a location fee, say $16 per 320 acres and the company could forthwith clear-cut the timber and let the claims lapse. At twenty cents an acre virgin stands of white or ponderosa pine, Douglas fir, or Norway or Colorado spruce were almost as good a buy as some of the dam-sites which, our propagandist hopes, will presently be offered to the power companies.

These are typical, routine, second-magnitude land frauds in the history of the public domain out West—to describe the bigger ones would require too much space. Enough that in the golden age of landgrabs, the total area of the public domain proved up and lived on by actual homesteaders amounted to only a trivial fraction of the area fraudulently acquired by land companies, cattle companies, and lumber companies. Among the compelling reasons why the present public-land reserves had to be set aside was the headlong monopolization of the public domain that was threatening the West with peonage. Those reserves were also made to halt the waste of natural resources which the United States has dissipated more prodigally than any other nation. They had to be made so that a useful part of our national wealth could be preserved, developed, wisely managed, and intelligently used in future times. They had to be made so that the watersheds which control the destiny of the West could be safeguarded. But no one should forget for a moment that they were, besides, necessary to prevent Eastern and foreign corporations from taking over the whole West by fraud, bribery, and engineered bankruptcy.

The land frauds and the landgrabs compose the shabbiest chapter in our history. We have had seventy-five years now of conservation as a government policy, of husbanding, developing, and using the publicly owned natural resources for the public benefit. So we have grown used to believing that such corruption, such raids on the treasury, such blind imbecility were ended for all time. But at this moment some powerful interests are preaching that what was intolerable corruption on a scale of half a million acres becomes wise public policy if you up the scale to half a billion acres. They are calling on Congress to legalize a final, conclusive raid on the publicly owned resources of the United States.

This one would be for keeps and it would put the government itself into the land-fraud racket. Officials of the government, true enough, were sometimes in that racket in the past, from two-dollar-a-day deputy clerks in the General Land Office on up to Senators and Secretaries of the Interior. Always before, however, the government regarded them as common criminals. It threw them out, sent to jail those it could get the goods on, and did what it could to repair the damage. Now Congress is asked to legitimatize and legalize what it used to make them felons for trying to do. It is asked, with an effrontery so great that it has not yet been widely perceived, to perpetrate by its own deliberate act a land fraud beside which any in our shameful period would appear insignificant.

As I write this, at mid-March, we have not learned by what means the citizens of forty-five states will have their property alienated on behalf of three states. Senator Holland's bill to convey to Texas, Louisiana, and California the publicly owned oil under the marginal sea has had slow going. The Attorney General has perceived some impairments of sovereignty and some administrative difficulties that were not visible when the tidelands were a bait for votes. There has arisen the interesting possibility that Rhode Island or some inland state which owns part of that oil may bring suit on the ground that Congress has no constitutional power to give it to any state. At least a part of the Administration is showing some regret for its campaign commitment. But it is committed and we may assume that the Supreme Court will find some opening through which it can follow the election returns.

So be it, but let's be clear about the tidelands episode. There has never been any doubt that the natural resources thus handed over to three states belong to the public, to the people of all the states. The Supreme Court has three times declared that they do; indeed in one of the cases which the Court was adjudicating, the State of Louisiana stipulated that they do. What we shall see, then, will be governmental conversion of public property. That the raiders were three states does not alter the fact that this is a successful raid on the public heritage.

So, with that precedent, what next? Senator Butler of Nebraska, the chairman of the Senate Committee on Interior and Insular Affairs, has announced that when the tidelands business is finished his committee will take up proposals for still more important attacks on our property. First the committee will deal with proposed measures to turn over the public lands to the states, then with similar measures to turn over the public power installations. This means, as the tidelands bills do not, the sale of public property to private corporations— the only reason for giving the public lands to the states is that the states will sell them. Unable to buy the public heritage from the federal government, corporations will be able to buy them at fire-sale prices from eleven Western states. They belong to the people of forty-eight states, the people of the eleven states have borne maybe 2 per cent of the cost of protecting and developing them, patriotic private enterprise can bid them in cheap, and everybody should be happy, more or less.

Among those who testified on the tidelands question before Senator Butler's committee was Mr. Oscar L. Chapman, lately Secretary of the Interior. He was afraid, he said, that the tidelands action would "establish the pattern for the greatest giveaway program in the history of the world." He added, "For years powerful pressure groups have been attempting to raid various parts of the public domain. They are now redoubling their efforts." Mr. Chapman was entirely right. He mentioned the U.S. Chamber of Commerce. In 1947 it supported the notorious effort of stockgrowing interests to grab (at a few cents an acre) large areas of the national forests, the national parks, and other public reservations. Public opinion stopped the stockmen cold and scared the Chamber into reversing its stand for a while. Now it is again agitating for the sale of public lands to private (that is, corporate) parties and is broadcasting remarkably misleading propaganda. The National Association of Manufacturers has lined up beside it, with propaganda equally mendacious and much subtler. For the first time in a generation big lumber interests are supporting the raid. As always the stockmen are out in front, happily carrying the ball for stronger and cannier groups that happily let them carry it. Previously circumspect power companies have come out from behind their public relations programs and various granges and farm bureaus have signed up.

In short, desirous ears have heard the sound of a great Perhaps which they hope they can convert to the great Amen. The day of jubilo may be about to dawn. The federal government's seventy-five years of fidelity to the public interest, the millions of dollars of public money spent to maintain and develop the public lands, the long husbanding and use of them for the benefit of all the people—this is acknowledged to have been a memorable and splendid thing. For lo, this policy has multiplied the value of the public assets a thousand-fold—and now the harvest can be reaped by those prepared to cash in on it. A business administration means business, doesn't it? Prolonging federal protection of this public interest would be bureaucratic tyranny and inefficiency, wouldn't it? There is so big a melon to be cut that not to cut it would be creeping socialism—let's go. Or, wheresoever the carcass is, there will the eagles be gathered together.

It is quite a carcass. Mr. Chapman told Senator Butler's committee that the public lands "contain an esti-

mated 4 billion barrels of oil, enough oil-shale to produce 130 billion barrels of crude oil, 111 trillion cubic
feet of gas, and 324 billion tons of coal." These are sam-
ple figures; Mr. Chapman said nothing about timber,
grass, electric power plants, sites for future ones, irrigation and other water potentials, precious metals, other
minerals, and the rest of the miscellany now owned by
the public—by everybody, including you. He said that a
rough estimate of their value in the United States, not
counting Alaska, made it "well over a trillion dollars."
Nobody can think of a trillion dollars; the sum is only a
symbol. But it gives the scale of the proposed operation
of transferring publicly owned property to the states, so
that whatever corporations may prove to be in the best
position can buy it for a fraction of what it is worth.
Every bill that Senator Butler's committee will proceed
to take up could be titled, An Act to Enrich Stockholders
at the Expense of Taxpayers.

In the cruder age there had to be a pretense that the
homemaker was to benefit but there can't be now, for no
land suitable for homesteading is left. Instead, the public
lands are to be disposed of on the sound business principle that they are a storehouse of raw materials of value
to corporations. The great stands of timber will go to Big
Lumber, oil and oil shale to Big Oil, minerals and chem-
icals to Big Mining, public power plants and sites for future ones to Big Power. Nor is there any pretense that the
desirous Western shibboleths will be regarded: the local
enterprise and home rule that were to emancipate the
plundered province from absentee ownership. The power
company that is prepared to build an installation in Hell's
Canyon which will generate 40 or maybe 60 per cent of
the power the government planned to is not an Idaho
corporation. It is not even a Western corporation: it is
chartered in Maine and owned by investment trusts.

The landgrabbers of the golden age were small time.
A cattle company's two hundred thousand acres of pub-

lic grazing land at a dollar-twenty-five, a lumber company's half-million acres of publicly owned Douglas fir
at two-fifty and a glass of beer—they are police court
stuff compared to a political job that undertakes to
knock off half a billion acres of public land in a single
session of Congress. This proposed steal is so large that
its size is counted on to conceal it—like ultraviolet light
and supersonic sound it is to escape attention. But it is
under way. The bills are drawn, Congressmen have been
found who will introduce them and direct their course,
and Senator Butler has agreed to clear the decks.

Mr. Chapman told the committee that the estimate
of a trillion dollars was only a rough guess, was in fact
much too low. And, he said, "if this Administration is intent upon following a giveaway policy, the people are at
least entitled to know what and how much is being
given away." So he proposed that a commission be established to inventory and appraise the public property
that is to become corporate assets. It is an excellent suggestion. We are being told every few minutes that business is on trial now, that this Administration will give
business its chance to prove itself, and everything ought
to be done on the best business principles. Establish the
commission and have it hire Price, Waterhouse.

The trouble is that such a study would put an end to
Operation Götterdämmerung on the public lands. Publication of its results would instantly blow this culminating land fraud sky high. As a matter of fact that is going
to happen anyway. The script is okay but the casting is
wrong: it calls for the public to be docile and for Congress to be fools.

A very distant association with the Credit Mobilier—
railroad-land fraud—kept James G. Blaine, and it may be
Schuyler Colfax too, out of the White House. There was
William Lorimer of Illinois: expelled from the Senate for
corrupt practices rooted in timber-land fraud. There was
Senator John Mitchell of Oregon: found guilty of timber-

land fraud but dying before he could serve his sentence. Albert B. Fall, Secretary of the Interior, went to jail—oil-land fraud. Richard A. Ballinger, Secretary of the Interior, left a blasted name to history—coal-land fraud. A lot of lesser names have disappeared from the newspapers but not from memory. When you hear them or look them up in books they give off, after all these years, the odor of corruption. Land fraud always did and it always will.

The redwood forest deals, the Oregon timber frauds, Teapot Dome—they were peanuts, birdseed, compared to what this crew of blue-sky pitchmen are asking Congress to slip over on us now. But the stench still rises from them and drifts down history and Capitol Hill. Congress will sit this one out, the carefully planned agenda notwithstanding.

Heading for the Last Roundup

In July 1953 DeVoto used this essay in *Harper's* to rebut the
U.S. Chamber of Commerce's March 10, 1953, broadcast of
their scripted weekly radio program "The Business Viewpoint: A Radio Report to the Community from its Business
Men." Once again, DeVoto exposes the hypocrisy and covert
tactics used by those opposed to the conservation of the
West. He exposes a former President of the Chamber of
Commerce, who regurgitated the propaganda lines provided
to him from the livestock lobbying organizations. DeVoto
further questions his allegiance by pointing out his Vice-
Presidency and Directorship of a large New Mexico stock
company with large public grazing permits. In addition, he
celebrates the Weeks Act and the Clark-McNary Act, which
provide the Forest Service authorization and resources to
purchase land for watershed protection and reforestation.
Throughout 1953 DeVoto continued to serve as an adviser to
the Secretary of the Interior, hoping to fend off the scrambling Landgrabbers. During this year he wrote four Easy
Chair columns relating to conservation. "Heading for the
Last Roundup" preceded his October column, "Close the National Parks," in which he advocated shutting down the national parks until the vultures backed off and Congress provided enough financial support to keep the parks running
effectively and free from molestation.

The most effective disseminator of propaganda is
the man who spreads it innocently. It is possible
that some of my readers took part in the radio
program which I proceed to describe. It is certain that

almost everyone who took part in it spoke the lines provided for him in good faith, trusting the organization which had provided them. He would not voluntarily have used his position as a leader in his community to support a series of misrepresentations and misstatements. But that is exactly what the organization in question beguiled him into doing.

That organization is the U.S. Chamber of Commerce. Its Radio-Television Section sends to local chambers scripts to be broadcast in a weekly program called "The Business Viewpoint: A Radio Report to the Community from its Business Men." On March 10, 1953, it thus sent out its Series A, Program 56, "The Public Lands." The program is in the form of a dialogue between two businessmen, and has blanks at the proper places so that the right local names and allusions can be inserted. Thus the local chambers would be led to co-operate in the campaign I have frequently described here: to turn over our publicly owned natural resources to exploitation by private parties.

A small but powerful group of Western stockmen have taken the lead in this campaign and their prime objective is the Forest Service. They hope, first, to deprive the Service of its power to regulate their use of the public grazing ranges and, ultimately, to buy at two cents on the dollar such national forest lands as they may want. This would so breach our long established conservation policy that private interests would forthwith be able to get hold of the far more valuable publicly owned timber, oil, minerals, and hydraulic power. And that shining vision explains why the U.S. Chamber of Commerce has put its power and prestige at the service of the stockmen's propaganda. It has elaborated and reissued the stockmen's misrepresentations in a series of press releases. It has produced them in an official pamphlet, "Policy Declaration on Natural Resources." They appeared in a much publicized speech by its president, from which I quoted when I discussed land frauds in the May *Harper's*. Observe that this speech was an official address by the President of the U.S. Chamber of Commerce—since then his term has expired—and that he was voicing the propaganda line of the livestock pressure group.

Perhaps he was voicing it not altogether altruistically: he is himself a stockgrower. He is Vice-President and Director, and his brother is President, of a large New Mexico stock company which uses public grazing ranges. His company holds grazing permits from the Bureau of Land Management for 3000 cattle, 10,000 sheep, 250 horses, and 165 goats. From the Forest Service it holds grazing permits for 180 sheep, and crossing permits, spring and fall, for 3000 cattle and 10,000 sheep. A big operator.

The canned radio speech is a rehash of these familiar distortions and misstatements. It is misleading throughout but for the most part too puerile to deceive anyone who has the slightest acquaintance with the facts—as of course neither the local speakers nor their audiences would be expected to have. I select from it a few statements that will be endlessly repeated in the developing, post-tidelands attack on the public lands. Remember that the operation against the Forest Service is the key to the whole campaign. If "a larger measure of local control" can be achieved by turning the national forests over to the states for private sale, then all the other public reserves will follow as a matter of course.

The voices of our radio dialogue open with a standard gambit. They were shocked by the large amount of land in the United States which is in federal ownership, and by the fact that the states in which that land is located collect no taxes on it. Revealing that their target is the Forest Service, they say that the federal government owns 91 million acres of timberland. They say that this amounts to 40 percent of all commercial standing timber. They compare this shocking figure with "a country where socialistic ideas are popular," Sweden: there, they say, in spite of socialistic ideas only 25 percent of the timber is publicly owned. Here one of the voices should be fed through a patch-board to the echo effect, so dire is its message: "Some of the Western states are owned almost lock, stock, and barrel by the government. . . . The national government owns 87 percent of all the land in Nevada."

Sensation! In Nevada, perceive, socialism has ceased to creep; it has broken into a gallop and will ride us down. The audience, its fear of Big Government aroused, is to envisage six-gun bureaucrats wrenching the state away from its citizens.

Thus an innocent local speaker is induced to mislead an uninformed audience, and we may call this lying by intimation. The basic reason why 87 percent of Nevada is in public ownership is that more than 70 percent of it is land which the government was unable to give away. When the national domain was virtually closed, in 1934, three-quarters of the state was still open to entry under the various Acts of Congress designed to give it to settlers. It had been thus open for many decades but no one had homesteaded it. It is the very dregs of the public domain, waterless and sterile. It could not be given away now, and if someone could be induced to take it, it could not pay a tax. Such land constitutes nine-tenths of the federal holding in Nevada. The Chamber's propagandists could hardly have avoided knowing as much. But Nevada's creosote-bush desert may serve to help them get a loop on publicly owned timber, oil, minerals, and power elsewhere.

Scrutinize the rest of that preamble. The Chamber plucks its statistics from the air and must be flunked in arithmetic: I can find no tables that give the areas it cites and its percentages are in error. Actually there are 74 million acres of commercial timberland in the national forests, 16 percent of the total in the United States. How did the Chamber arrive at its 91 million acres? Is it adding in timberland on Indian Reservations? That is private property. Is it including state, county, and municipal forests? They are publicly owned but not federally owned. And if the total is 91 million acres, however arrived at, then it constitutes 20 percent of our commercial timberland, not 40 percent. (Double by inadvertence?) And by the way, the less socialistic Sweden imposes government regulation of cutting and a good many other scientific forestry practices on private forests, none of which are enforced on private operators here.

When technicians of political distortion say that public lands pay no local taxes they are telling the truth, but not enough of it. This half-truth will be hurled at Congress innumerable times, as the technicians work to get the public storehouse of natural resources knocked down to desirous corporations. What the Chamber of Commerce neglected to mention to its uninformed audience was the payments made to states and counties by the federal government in lieu of taxes, and the revenue-sharing payments that are the same thing under another name. These payments vary from class to class of the public lands. The national forests pay 25 percent of their gross receipts to local communities. Lands under mineral lease pay $37\frac{1}{2}$ percent of royalties received. Land-utilization projects of the Soil Conservation Service pay 25 percent of net receipts. Federal Power Commission projects pay $37\frac{1}{2}$ percent of the license fees of power sites. Wildlife refuges pay 25 percent of net receipts. Grazing districts under the Bureau of Land Management pay $12\frac{1}{2}$ percent of gross receipts, lands under the same bureau not in grazing districts, 50 percent. There are some lump-sum payments, such as the $300,000 paid annually to Arizona and New Mexico by the Hoover Dam Project. Perhaps a few exceptions are theoretically conceivable, but a generalization will hold: if these properties were in private ownership they could not pay anywhere near so much in taxes to local governments.

In 1952 Forest Service payments to Idaho from timber sales were three-quarters of a million dollars, to Washington almost three million, to California more than three million, to Oregon more than four million. In 1951 Wyoming got four million dollars from mineral leases, Colorado nearly two million dollars, New Mexico one and three-quarters million.

There are also indirect benefits in cash. The federal government shares the expense of fire protection in state and privately owned forests. In 1951 the State of Washington received more than half a million dollars for this purpose, Oregon just less than three-quarters of a million. Federal highway aid is paid at a higher rate in the public-land states than in the others, and this too is in lieu of taxes. Mention of such facts, however, would have spoiled the propaganda effect.

Next the radio voices profess to be alarmed by the additions that are made to the public lands, purchases by a land-hungry, tax-obliterating centralized bureaucracy. One of them says with horror that since the turn of the century "the government has added 45 million acres to its holdings—and has consistently been trying to acquire more." You can see the Forest Service fairly pushing New York City into the Hudson.

Here are some classes of federal acquisitions: dustbowl and other submarginal land that had to be retired from cultivation; tax-delinquent lands bought in other forms of local relief; lands acquired by gift, such as the Rockefeller donations to the national parks; lands bought by towns to protect their water supply and given to the government for protection; similar tracts bought at the solicitation of threatened communities. The Chamber of Commerce also neglects to say that its total includes large areas bought for military and atomic installations—to mention them would have impaired the picture of the Forest Service as out of control and dangerously encroaching on our liberties. For the same reason it neglects to say that by far the largest part of its total actually attributable to the Forest Service consists of purchases made under two acts of soundly Republican Congresses, the Weeks Act and the Clark-McNary Act. One authorizes the Service to buy land for the protection of watersheds, the other to buy it for reforestation and the establishment of forests.

The Forest Service conducts this activity under the direction and supervision of a body set up by Congress, the National Forest Reservation Commission. It includes representatives of both houses of Congress and the Secretaries of the Army, Interior, and Agriculture. It has long been engaged in a scientific program which has given the South and the East the national forests they so greatly prize—before it there were national forests only in the West. Purchases under these Acts in the West have been negligible, 8000 acres in Nevada, 22,000 acres in Utah, and in most of the other states none at all. Whereas purchases amount to more than a million acres each in Arkansas, Michigan, Minnesota, Mississippi, Missouri, North Carolina, Virginia, and Wisconsin; to more than half a million acres each in Florida, Georgia, Louisiana, New Hampshire, South Carolina, Tennessee, Texas, and West Virginia. Weep for the disappearing West.

These forests are among the finest achievements of our conservation policy, a vital step toward reducing our serious scarcity of wood, invaluable for recreation in the heavily populated East and for the protection of its watersheds. Most of the land that was bought for them had been logged and was tax-delinquent; eroding, a fire hazard, it was a public danger; it was good for nothing except to grow trees. The Forest Service has changed it from a public liability to a public asset of constantly increasing value. And note this, which the Chamber of

Commerce fails to point out: every purchase was consented to by the state involved. Otherwise not an acre could have been bought.[1]

So far the program has confined itself to distortion and misrepresentation; now it experiments with falsification. One of the voices says that the government has its eyes on 35 million acres of private (it should have said, non-federal) timberland, which it wants to add to the national forests. That is true; the figure was proposed by a study of future needs and ways of meeting them. The voice goes on to imply, however, that the Forest Service is going to take this land by some kind of seizure, by somehow forcing it out of the hands of its helpless owners. The speaker describes the system by which the Service sometimes exchanges tracts of timber for other tracts of cutover land—but describes it with stark dishonesty. He intimates that the Service forces private owners to make exchanges, that it does so in avoidance or defiance of congressional intent, and that by doing so it defrauds the U.S. Treasury. And he says in a remarkable fabrication, "the idea has not been to save the taxpayers' money. It has been to increase the size of the United States forests and decrease the taxable lands from which they have been taken." The bureaucracy wants to bankrupt the states: I conclude that here one of the cowboys took over from the professional script writer.

What are the facts? Practically all the timber sales which the Forest Service makes are for cash, after competitive bidding. Sometimes, however, it exchanges mature timber for immature timber, which it will scientifically husband for future use, or tracts of timber for tracts of logged-out land which it will reforest.

These are comparatively small transactions, and *almost all of them are initiated by the timber operators who profit from them.* If there was no profit for the operator, there would be no exchange; no one is pointing a gun at him; usually, if he did not dispose of his land in this way, he would let his title lapse by nonpayment of taxes. Sometimes, however, there are value-for-value exchanges, from which the Forest Service profits directly as well as the operator. The Service makes an exchange to consolidate isolated small holdings or rationalize forest boundaries, to conserve scenic or recreational values, or to protect threatened portions of watersheds. No coercion is possible. No private owner is compelled to make an exchange and it is safe to say that none does unless he profits by it.

Look at the program's total, 35 million acres of contemplated future acquisitions. Of this, 23 million acres were long since approved for purchase—approved not by the ravenous Forest Service but by the body I have mentioned, the National Forest Reservation Commission—and this entire area is in the East. Not an acre is in the West which the Chamber of Commerce represents as being everywhere reduced to the helplessness of any clump of sagebrush in Nevada. The remaining 12 million acres are a small total, when you consider that they are spread over all the national forests, the forests which are and must always be the foundation of our entire conservation program, and when you consider what the future is going to demand of them. Sometime I will describe here the purpose of the contemplated acquisitions.

The rest of the Chamber's dialogue consists of repetitions of the stockmen's propaganda assertions, even more childish than the one I have just discussed. No one who knew anything about the subject could take it seriously. The point is, however, that it was written to be broadcast to a public which was assumed not to know anything about the subject and therefore, so the Chamber hoped, could be induced to support the attack on the public-lands system, the attack on the public's own property.

Just how does the U.S. Chamber of Commerce get that way? It is entitled to adopt any public-lands policy it may desire to and to advance that policy by any honest means. But it is not, I think, entitled to mislead and misinform its member chambers, the private persons whom it thus uses as stooges, and the public at large. The Chamber has lost status, it has become suspect.

This, however, is only a specimen of tactics that can currently be observed in many places. They are deliberately dishonest tactics. You will hear many repetitions of them; you will hear them, especially, repeated in Congress, as the bills to make corporate property of the public lands are taken up. See to it that no one is allowed to get away with them. See to it that no one imposes them on your Congressman.

Conservation: Down and on the Way Out

For DeVoto and other conservationists the Eisenhower administration ushered in a dismal time. In August 1954 DeVoto published this essay in *Harper's* thereby extending his gaze beyond the Landgrabbers of the West and turning toward the backroom energy brokers. The conservation of the West was not simply a land issue, but crossed over into the argument over public power, its distribution, and the other natural and exploited resources of the West. DeVoto again names the names of those faltering in the debate. As the country sank deeper into the Eisenhower administration, DeVoto's mood, too, grew drearier. In his remaining year DeVoto mustered the strength to compose two more Easy Chair columns dealing with the public lands debate, in addition to two other conservation essays that relocated the battle from the Western stage to the Northeast. DeVoto would—fifteen months after "Conservation: Down and on the Way Out" was published—die from a massive heart attack.

An aphorism of the Chinese philosopher Mencius declares that the problem of government presents no difficulties: it is only necessary to avoid offending the influential families. In January 1953 the Business Administration in Washington took off from a related premise: that it was only necessary to get along with the trade associations.

This article deals with public power and the public lands, other natural resources, and the national conservation policies which have been developing for three-quarters of a century. In dealing with them the Administration had to convert into concrete measures the generalizations of the Republican platform and campaign promises. It had no program when it took office. It was promptly handed one specific program, which the electric power companies had worked out in anticipation of a Republican victory in 1948. It has improvised several others, playing by ear. On several problems, it apparently is not concerned with programs; it has simply drifted downward.

Perhaps I can formulate the campaign generalities as working principles. In fields where private enterprise could operate at a profit, the Administration would try to reduce government operations. In fields where private enterprise could not make profits, it would maintain government operation up to the minimum political necessity. In both areas it would try to provide "a greater measure of local participation and control," greater cooperation between federal and local governments, and "a friendly partnership" with private business. It would try to "decentralize" federal administration, and it would—in an even more opaque phrase—"operate at the grass roots."

There was an inherent weakness in these working principles. They would throw the gates wide open to the boys in the back room unless the Administration could get in first with programs of its own. It did not and the boys—the trade associations, the lobbies, the special interest groups—rushed in with a loud whoop. During the campaign Mr. Eisenhower once remarked that he would not interpret his election as a mandate to preside over the liquidation of the publicly owned natural resources of the United States. Others *have* so interpreted it, however; a considerable liquidation has been effected already and much more is in the works. Eighteen months have made clear that the Executive departments and the independent agencies will go much farther than Congress in alienating public property—but not (except perhaps in the Department of the Interior) as far as the boys have in mind.

They pin their hopes to the new Hoover Commission. The first one worked out intelligent plans for reorganizing the Executive departments in the interests of efficiency and economy; but the second one is clearly intended to slay Mr. Hoover's white whale at last. It is to erase twenty years of infamy, root out all remnants of the New Deal, and turn the clock back to 1928. There are those who regard 1928 as practically a pinko compromise: the clock should be turned back somewhere beyond Theodore Roosevelt.

II

In the Departments of Agriculture and the Interior the businessman whom the Administration summoned to government promptly displayed the political ineptness visible in other departments. One reason may have been the sources of information which it was natural for them to rely on. A Congressman who wants a quick check on what the folks back home are thinking is apt to telephone to a local editor or political figure, or the head of some local labor or farm organization. From the top offices of Agriculture and Interior, however, the phone calls went instead to a chamber of commerce or the Washington office of a trade association. The information available there being of a radically different kind, there followed such miscues as Secretary McKay's nomination to be Director of the Bureau of Mines of an open and recorded enemy of the services he would have to direct.

Top officials were also unable to recognize public opinion as a political force. Congressmen saw a clear

portent in the widespread opposition to the Tidelands
Bill—and in the public outrage when the Assistant Secretary of Commerce tried to discharge the Director of
the Bureau of Standards for affirming that the addition
of a laxative to a storage battery would not improve it.
But to the Businessmen in Office these were unrelated
and meaningless phenomena, just one of those things.
The Department of Agriculture revealed this state of
mind in its handling of the reorganization of the Soil
Conservation Service. There could be no more local an
organization than a Soil Conservation District; more
than 2500 of them cover the country and they are literally of the grass roots. But they were not consulted
about the reorganization of SCS and indeed could not
find out what was going on till it was completed. In Administrative semantics, "local participation and control"
had become "fiat by Washington." The districts were en-
raged; they still are.

This reorganization, an aggrandizement of the land-
grant colleges and the Extension Service at the sacrifice
of conservation values, was typical of the new order in
several ways. SCS had originally been organized on the
basis of state units but had evolved a much more effective organization in a series of regions, each with its
own headquarters, specialists, and technicians. The reorganization plan proposed to dissolve the regions and
substitute state units for them. The heart of SCS assistance to farmers was its six technical services; four of
these were to be abandoned and the specialists of the
other two were to be distributed among the land-grant
colleges (so far as the colleges had jobs for them) and the
Washington headquarters. For the immensely successful program of SCS, forty-eight fractional and necessarily unharmonized programs were to be substituted; and
these were to be administered from Washington. Decen-
tralization had worked out in the semantics as greater
centralization. Incentive to local conservation practices

was to be provided by decreasing appropriations. And with technical service reduced, much research was to be abandoned.

But opposition to Tidelands and the firing of Dr. Astin had *not* been just one of those things, and nation-wide opposition to the new scheme forced the Department to reverse itself in midair. A new system of regional offices, under a different name and with headquarters in different cities, was extemporized. (In the semantics, A ceases to be A when you rename it B.) The technical services were retained, though in a more cumbersome and more expensive form.

As I write, SCS is half flux and half chaos. The technical teams have been broken up. Their invaluable pool of common experience at working together has been dissipated. This drastic impairment of professional skills is typical of the administration of public resources in the new order. So are the increased expense, delay, red tape, and inefficiency. So is the destruction of morale in a career service. Promising young men have left SCS in droves; promising young men who might have sought a career there are notably failing to join it. An Administration fetish whose name is Management-Practice Improvement has had its paper tribute, but a straitjacket of mediocrity has been forced on public administration. And a damaging blow has been struck at the conservation of American cropland and rangeland.

The Department of Agriculture, however, appears to have taken instruction from the public reaction. Evidently it has abandoned some reactionary changes which it had in mind a year ago and has narrowed the scope of some others. Not so the Department of the Interior. The boys have practically taken it over; the predicted giveaways are in progress. There is a cynicism in Interior which reminds observers of the aromatic days of the General Land Office. Yet some things that look like cynicism may be mere ineptness. Thus Secretary

McKay at a moment when all the conservation organizations in the country—national, nonpartisan, and representing hundreds of thousands of votes—were denouncing his recommendation of Echo Park Dam. Seeking for *le mot juste* to characterize conservationists, he came up with "punks."

III

The top officials of SCS have been put on Schedule C; so have those of all other conservation bureaus in Agriculture except (as yet, perhaps) the Forest Service, and all those in Interior except the Geological Survey. Schedule C is a classification withdrawn from Civil Service protection which permits discharge at the will of the Secretary, without regard to merit. It has a twofold purpose: (1) to provide jobs; (2) to substitute a pliable sycophancy for professional judgment in the making of policy. Promotion according to merit is abandoned for the spoils system, and career services become political footballs. The effect on the conservation agencies has been disastrous; it had not hitherto been supposed, and it cannot be supposed now, that the publicly owned resources could be administered on any basis except a purely professional one. These bureaus first introduced into the American government the concept of a professionally expert civil service. Staff them with spoilsmen, and the public resources must begin leaking away.

The Administrator of the Rural Electrification Administration is appointed to serve ten years. It was therefore a tip-off when the White House requested the resignation of Mr. Claude Wickard two and a half years before the end of his statutory term. Rural electrification and federal power can be treated together here, and several facts which are tirelessly misrepresented must be noted. The electric power generated at public installations runs between 13 and 16 percent of the national total, never more. In spite of nationwide propaganda by the utilities (paid for out of tax money and rate increase), unalterable natural circumstances make it certain that the percentage will decrease as time goes on. Furthermore, the consumer co-operatives which REA serves are strictly private enterprises, locally owned by their members and locally managed. They pay interest on the loans which REA makes them; they pay off the loans; they pay local taxes. They are "socialistic" only in the new semantics: in that they are not owned by the utility companies and they sell power to consumers so cheaply that their rates serve as a yardstick by which the rates of the utilities—a natural monopoly—can be regulated. Finally, most of the power they sell is bought from the utilities.

They constitute an area of private enterprise which the utilities had refused to pioneer or develop. In 1935 when REA was established, about 11 per cent of the farms in the United States had central-station power; in 1952 about 90 per cent had it. This constitutes an agricultural revolution even greater than that effected by SCS; it has transformed agricultural production, farm labor, and rural living. REA and the co-ops have greatly increased the business done by the utilities and very greatly increased that done by manufacturers of electrical equipment and appliances.

A multiple squeeze has been put on co-ops and REA. The Administration's first budget request drastically cut REA funds. Its power-generation program, and therefore its bargaining power with the utilities, would have been destroyed. Its ability to accommodate new co-ops and the ability of the co-ops to serve new customers would have been drastically reduced. Congress refused to go so far and saved much of the program by increasing the appropriation far above the request. But Congress did not vote an increase over the Budget's allotment for technical service. Thus the theme of SCS is repeated, for the abandonment or even any serious reduction of REA's technical service to the co-ops would be a serious blow, to some of them a fatal blow. Small co-ops, unable to afford such a technical staff as a utility company maintains, have been able to get their problems solved cheaply by REA. Moreover, the Power Use Section of REA was cut down, and the auditing services were abolished, thus increasing the financial hazards of the co-ops. A related but unsuccessful move was the attempt by Congressman Kit Clardy of Michigan—an old and dear friend of utility companies—to double the rate of interest which REA charges on loans to the co-ops.

Meanwhile what amounts to a rewriting of the Federal Power Act, supplementary acts, and even the Reclamation Act has been achieved by administrative action. The utilities would be glad to have the government build the large and expensive control dams—because they make private downstream dams efficient—provided they could buy the power generated at them on their own terms and could control its distribution. But they have always rebelled against the "preference clause." This clause—which in essence goes back to the earliest conception of public power in Theodore Roosevelt's first administration—is a provision that public bodies and co-operatives shall have first call on the power generated at public dams. ("Public bodies" means primarily municipally owned systems and such organizations as the power districts of Oregon and Washington.) The ordinary growth of such systems was provided for by selling the rest of the power to utilities on short-term contracts only. By abandoning this practice, the Administration is in effect discarding the preference clause.

In the Northwest, utility contracts, previously short-term, now run twenty years. This limits the growth of co-ops, denies them new customers, and rations the power used by their present customers. A similar change in the Missouri Valley has been held up till after the November election. The co-ops have been faced with an impossible choice. Either they must forfeit their preference privilege, thus arresting their own growth, or they must contract for power far in advance of their needs and so pay a ruinous bonus for power which they could not use and which would have to be resold to the utilities at dump prices.

The utilities have fought for the construction of steam-generating plants by REA to firm the power produced at government hydro-electric plants, a frequently necessary measure because of seasonal fluctuations in stream flow. And the low rates charged by the co-ops have always harrowed them, for the differential is all too visible. There would be no reason for co-ops if they could not pass on to their members the savings they effect, and Assistant Secretary of the Interior Aandahl announced the answer. Federal power rates, he said, would be raised to the point where there would be no incentive to continue REA or establish co-operatives. Here is one form of private business with which the Administration will not enter into a friendly partnership—and, as Senator Murray remarked, here is a negative yardstick for the power industry.

As for the generation of power, the Director of the Budget announced that there would be no "new starts"— no additional federal projects—till arrangements had been made with local (which here means large-scale and absentee) interests to install the generating facilities.

He thus proclaimed publicly a policy which some members of the Administration were simultaneously denying. It is significant that of the twenty-three new starts so far made by the Corps of Engineers, none are multiple purpose and none include power. And it seems likely that the Engineers will be favored over the Bureau of Reclamation in such new projects as are authorized. They are far friendlier to the utilities, they can legally assess against the taxpayers a larger percentage of the costs, and they are able to circumvent painful provisions of the Reclamation and Power Acts.

The program drawn up by the utilities in 1948 has not been carried out in full. But the process of strangulation that has been applied to REA should kill it in another two years. The co-ops will be withdrawn from competing with the utilities and furnishing data for the regulation of their rates. It would take considerably more than two years to get a wall round federal generation of power.

Secretary McKay's abandonment to the Idaho Power Company of the Hell's Canyon site—the greatest remaining one in the country—was geared to this policy. In the current semantics a consumer co-operative, owned and operated by farmers unable to get electricity except by their own efforts, would not be local enterprise; but Idaho Power is.

Idaho Power is a Maine corporation and holds its annual meetings across the continent from the Snake River. It is like any big utility company, which means that its policies are banker-directed, which means in turn that they are Wall Street policies. It belongs to all the institutes and associations, national and regional, that tie utility companies together. But its stock setup is such that statements about ownership have to be made with great care. A vigorous selling campaign in the last few years has distributed its preferred stock widely through the West; in fact 60 per cent of it is held in the intermountain West. Moreover, the preferred stock has voting rights and each share carries five votes whereas the common stock has only one vote per share. Yet the common stock has senior voting rights. And the thirty largest stockholders own 30 percent of the common stock; most of them hold large blocks of preferred stock as well. Of these thirty all, except Harvard University and the Commonwealth Fund, are insurance companies or security companies or investment trusts; all but two are east of the Mississippi and those two are insurance companies. The company is no more a local enterprise than Western Union or the New York Central is.

Secretary McKay also withdrew government opposition to the Pacific Gas & Electric Company's proposed developments on the North Fork of the King's River—developments made possible by existing facilities built at public expense. As I write, his assistants are constructing what they frankly call a "detour" round the basic Reclamation Law so that users of water from a federal project on the Kern River will not be subject to the 160-acre limitation. Bills to make the branch official in large areas have been introduced in Congress but are not likely to pass.

But as much as Eastern-owned Western utilities respect the spirit of private initiative, the West needs dams and wants payrolls. The relinquishment of federal reserved sites and the no-new-starts policy caused uneasiness, and there was November to think of. So the Upper Colorado Storage Project was taken out of mothballs and nearly a billion dollars' worth of construction was recommended. (It will cost at least twice that; for obvious reasons, Bureau of Reclamation estimates are poetic conventions.) Its political feasibility is obvious but its economic and social justification is open to the most serious doubt. Worse still, the plans for it are part fantasy and have been changed so often and so capriciously that no one knows to what extent its engineering is sound. But it satisfies the requirements. No corporation would ever want to build dams on this stretch of the Colorado, so there is no competition; but the promise of the Budget Director would attract corporate investment in the generating facilities, since the public would be paying all other costs.

The recommendation of this project breaches the basic national parks policy: one of the dams it includes, Echo Park, is to be built in Dinosaur National Monument.

(Later, another dam is to be built in the Monument.) The dam will destroy the beauty of spectacular canyons in the Yampa and Green Rivers. There was a peak of cynicism in Mr. McKay's promise to spend $21 million of Bureau of Reclamation funds to build the roads now denied the Monument and to construct "recreational" facilities at the fluctuating, unsightly reservoir which the dam would create. This sum is equal to four-fifths of the drastically cut 1955 appropriation for the entire National Park Service.

The progressive impairment of the parks by budgetary bloodletting is a national disgrace—but it is a smaller evil than Mr. McKay's approval of Echo Park Dam. Opening the parks to exploitation by the Bureau of Reclamation—which in the semantics is "co-operation between federal and state governments"—makes only a matter of time their exploitation by any corporations which may want their water, water power, timber, minerals, or grass, and which have sufficient capital to impress a businessman in office.

Many trial balloons about TVA have been sent up. The refusal to reappoint Mr. Gordon Clapp as its director made clear that career-service administration is not desired. His successor will need only a single qualification: a distaste for socialistically increasing private business in the Tennessee Valley by providing cheap power. Several other trial balloons from Interior are significant, such as suggestions that the tremendous Central Valley Project might be sold to the State of California. At the right price it would make a happy deal: the big corporate farms would get the water denied them by the 160-acre limitation they have been fighting since 1902 and P.G.& E. would get the power facilities. This clue is underscored by a recent announcement that the utility companies of the Northwest are forming a syndicate capable of taking over all the federal dams and power plants on the Columbia River, the projects that brought industry and boom times to the Northwest.

If the Central Valley and the Columbia Basin projects should be handed over to utility corporations, how will flood control, erosion control, and the other conservation functions of federal projects be carried on? The utilities could not possibly assume them. Indeed a corporation has no proper concern with them, and no state has ever done an even passable job at any of them. Nevertheless, the clues suggest that the groundwork is being laid for the property evaluators, rate specialists and constitutional lawyers of the new Hoover Commission to propose that all federal reclamation and power projects be sold.

IV

Both the platform and the campaign had promised to take care of the small but influential group of Western stockmen who ever since 1946 have been trying to gut the Forest Service and get hold of the grazing ranges in the national forests. A bill embodying as much of the malodorous "Stockmen's Proposal for an Act" as it seemed cagey to put in one package was sponsored by Senator Barrett of Wyoming—who as a Congressman had spearheaded the attempted landgrab of 1946–47. He has great parliamentary and backstage skill; but his sole victory with this bill was his success in keeping the Secretary of Agriculture's adverse report on it from reaching the House Subcommittee on Public Lands.

At the public hearing Western spokesmen—water users, sportsmen, wildlife specialists, hydrologists, city engineers, individual stockmen, small stock associations—ripped the bill to shreds. The Denver *Post* attacked it repeatedly; so did such other prominent papers as the Salt Lake *Tribune*, the Portland *Oregonian*, and the San Francisco *Chronicle*. More striking was the opposition of many small newspapers, even in Wyoming, which had always before supported the plans of the stockmen's lobby. Whereas the attempted landgrab of six years before had to be stopped by the East, this time the West itself prevented a shameful raid on the public resources. Senator Barrett—seeing that the bill would be defeated if it came to a vote—maneuvered to keep it in committee and to prevent publication of the testimony at the hearings.

But something had to be done for the stockmen and so the Hope-Thye-Aiken Bill was made an Administration measure. Bad to begin with, it was rendered truly vicious by amendment; it has been passed by the Senate but as I write has not yet been taken up by the House. That such sound conservationists as Senator Aiken and Congressman Hope have been lined up behind so reprehensible a measure shows the formidable pressure that the U.S. Chamber of Commerce and other allies of the stockmen's lobby have succeeded in bringing to bear on the White House. Long since, Senator Aiken should have been attacking his own bill.

The bill would achieve three major objectives of the landgrabbers. It would give present holders of grazing permits in the national forests two kinds of property rights in those forests, thus impairing the public title and in part alienating public property. It would enable the present permit holders to sell the permits at will and without reference to the Forest Service, closing the ranges to newcomers and making monopolization of them certain. It would permit them to construct permanent improvements on the public ranges, further alienating public property and enabling the permit holders to tie up the public lands indefinitely with lawsuits. Finally, it would cripple the regulatory power of the Forest Service by permitting appeal to the courts on various kinds of purely administrative decisions. It is a raid

on the public-lands system and its passage would seriously undermine our conservation policy.[1]

The House of Representatives stopped something
even worse, a bill by Representative Ellsworth of Oregon, long a congressional spokesman for big lumber interests. It provided that when the government acquired
privately owned timberland, as for the reservoir of a
dam, which a timber operator had under sustained yield
(that is, cutting only in step with replacement by natural growth), the operator would have the option of
being paid in cash or by the transfer to him of publicly
owned timberland of equivalent value. This meant the
national forests or the far smaller forests administered
by the Bureau of Land Management—and in committee
it was extended to include the forests in the national
parks. Proof of operation under sustained yield was not
stipulated and there was no guarantee that it would be
used on the land to be acquired. The government bureau which must provide the timberland was given no
control over its selection, and no power to require any
kind of protection or conservation.

Barefaced as these provisions were, however, they
were unimportant compared to the central fact: *ostensi-
bly a measure of relief for suffering corporations, the bill
provided for the direct transfer of portions of the permanently reserved public lands to private ownership.*
Enemies of the public-lands system have been trying to
achieve precisely that fundamental step ever since the
first reserves were made in Benjamin Harrison's time.
The Hope-Thye-Aiken Bill would open fissures in the
foundation of our national conservation policy—but the
Ellsworth Bill would have shattered it.

The Secretary of Agriculture drew up an adverse report and this time it reached the committee. Normally
this is enough to stop a bill. He was, however, prevailed
on to withdraw it. No notice of the public hearing was

given except the routine listing in the *Gazette;* conservation organizations and interested Congressmen did not know that it was to be held. It was attended only by representatives of the Department of the Interior, who had been instructed to think highly of the bill (one who wasn't thinking highly enough on the witness stand was called away by telephone), and of the Department of Agriculture, who had obviously been instructed not to think ill of it but to try to get it softened nevertheless. The committee reported it out and by a tricky lateral pass in the Rules Committee Mr. Ellsworth cleared the way for an attempt to slip it over on the House in the closing days of the session. Chance discovery at the last moment, however, scared him into holding it over till the next session.

By then the bill was in the open and it was murdered. The quarterbacking on the floor of the House was by Congressman Metcalf of Montana, who was making a distinguished record in his first term. His Democratic teammates were Madden of Indiana, Price of Illinois, and Brooks of Texas, with McCarthy of Minnesota, Magnuson of Washington, and Hays of Ohio assisting at critical junctures. A striking development, however, was the co-operation of four Pennsylvania Republicans who were well acquainted with the issues at stake—Messrs. Gavin, Saylor, Fulton, and Mumma. Mr. Gavin's role in the debate was especially informed and expert. This extemporized coalition drew the bill's teeth with amendments and then, when the strength of the opposition became manifest, Mr. Metcalf moved to recommit it. His motion carried on a roll-call vote of 226 yeas and 161 nays—a brilliant victory for the freshman Congressman, who is not even a member of the relevant committee.

Perhaps a few other Republican Congressmen, who were active in opposition to the grazing bill, can be added to what looks like a conservation bloc. If the Republican Party retains control of the House in November, this bloc will be important. For it is clear that if any of our historic conservation policy is to be saved, it must be saved in the House. Senator Langer opposed some anti-conservation measures but no other Republican Senator did. Senator Aiken, who devised the strategy for many earlier victories over anti-conservation forces, has now put his great prestige at the service of the attack on the Forest Service. The Independent Party, Senator Morse, has been magnificent, making an all-out fight against every anti-conservation move.

V

The Forest Service may also serve to illustrate dangers latent in other Administration fetishes—reorganization, consolidation, and that cant phrase from schools of business administration, "management-practice improvement." If consolidation and reorganization are the first recourse of a management engineer, they can serve more devious ends and become the last one of a lobby or a landgrabber.

The Forest Service has always been decentralized. It began with a regional organization, to prevent the delays and rigidities that half paralyzed the headquarters and specialist staffs. Differences in terrain, climate, forestation, methods of lumber operations, and other complex variables make this the only kind of organization that could conceivably be efficient. To consolidate the regions, reducing them to four or even two, as has been proposed, would greatly increase expense and greatly reduce efficiency. It would increase travel, paperwork, and red tape. It would slow up administration and all field operations. It would make the specialist and scientific activities of the Service more cumbersome and expensive. *In all these ways it would add to the costs of the private businesses that use the forests.* But the notion is attractive to the managerial mind. You consolidate the Omaha and Denver offices of Continental Gadgets; why not, then, consolidate Nebraska and Colorado?

There is a more sinister aspect. Weakening professional and administrative efficiency by such a consolidation of the regions would favor both the special-interest groups which want to exploit the national forests and those which want all federal regulation everywhere undermined. Also it would greatly reduce such ability as the Service now has to resist the attacks of its enemies. That is one of the ends in view.

All these hazards would be increased by the unbelievably idiotic plan, which has also been proposed, of abolishing the regional setup and achieving "local control" by grouping the national forests—which disregard state lines—in state units. Neither a forest stand nor the watershed of a river will stop short at a state boundary on Executive Order. But the thirty-eight miniature Forest Services thus created—in ten states there are no national forests—would be easy prey for the local special-interest groups. The Administration fetish which dreams of reorganizing federal conservation activities on a state-wide rather than a regional basis is a victory for the propaganda which represents issues as a conflict between one local interest and all the others; that is, between a special interest and the public interest. In every aspect of conservation this kind of "local control" must inevitably mean local vulnerability, local manipulation, and local intimidation.

All research in the Department of Agriculture except that of the Forest Service has been grouped under one bureau. In some respects the results have been of no particular importance, in some others they have reduced expense and increased efficiency. But also in some instances they have reduced efficiency and increased expense. It seems likely that the eye of the management-improver is on the Forest Service research, and that his table of organization calls for transferring it to the central bureau. To do so would be a truly stupendous blunder. Forest Service research created scientific forestry in the United States and is now the foremost in the world. It is so organically related to the field activities and daily jobs of the Forest Service that it could be dissected out only at the cost of permanent damage. The damage would increase geometrically in the future.

And one wonders. The Forest Service, always the cornerstone of our national conservation policy, is the most vigorous of the conservation bureaus. That is precisely what is wrong with it in the eyes of the landgrabbers, the cowboys, the U.S. Chamber of Commerce, and its other organized enemies. It is threefold: it consists of the national forests, its agencies which assist and supervise and co-operate with state forestry and private forestry, and its research programs and experiment stations. The effort by the Bureau of Budget to abolish two of its co-operative programs suggests an intention eventually to amputate one full third of the Service. Removing its research to another bureau would also lop off a third. Reduced by two-thirds, it would be weak, ineffective, easily preyed upon, immensely less valuable to the American future. Is that the end in view? At any rate, in their most arrogant moments the landgrabbers never dreamed up so promising a way to make it impotent.

VI

In a year and a half the businessmen in office have reversed the conservation policy by which the United States has been working for more than seventy years to substitute wise use of its natural resources in place of reckless destruction for the profit of special corporate interests. They have reversed most of the policy, weakened all of it, opened the way to complete destruction. Every move in regard to conservation that the Administration had made has been against the public interest—

which is to say against the future—and in favor of some special private interest. Most notably, too, every one has been in favor of some big special interest and against the local small ones. The friendly partnership with business has turned out to mean only some kinds of businesses, the bigger the better.

More important still is the appointment of officials friendly to the enemies of the public interest, for this is preparation for the future. Judicious selection of a director could doom TVA, for instance, and no doubt will. The utilities plan to "get the government out of the power business altogether," with all that that implies in destruction of resources and exploitation of consumers. Many other corporate plans look to getting hold of publicly owned resources and converting them to dividends. Under Secretary of Interior Tudor had announced that his legal staff is rewriting contracts for the water from federal dams in such a way that the 160-acre limitation can be "by-passed"—which means that the government will connive at breaking the fundamental Reclamation laws. Assistant Secretary Lewis has said that he looks forward to the time when there need be no federal forestry. Their chief, Secretary McKay, has repeatedly said that he favors the disposal to private hands of various classes of public lands.

We called it corruption in Harding's time. It is not corruption when it is Administration policy. But it does show an intent, or perhaps only a willingness, to turn the clock back beyond Hoover, beyond the first Roosevelt, to the Old Stone Age of Republican domination by those to whom the infinite wisdom of Providence had entrusted the property interests of the country. Meanwhile the future of the United States is caught between the inexorable millstones. Population pressure steadily increases. The rivers fill with silt, the water table drops, the rains run off as floods. In the West, booms end because there is neither enough water nor enough electricity. The West too has had four years of drought, parts of it five years. Two dustbowls have formed: "The best place to get a Colorado farm is eastern Kansas." And the best place to get anything else you may want is the Department of the Interior.

Indirect damage such as the sacrifice of professionalism in the public service is manifest. But consider something else. If, for instance, the Central Valley Project should be sold to California, doubtless Mr. Hoover's evaluators could work out a price. (California utilities and the Department of the Interior co-operating.) What would be entirely beyond computation is the loss to the public in past investment, future waste, and future expense. Similarly with every other aspect of conservation—erosion control, flood control, watershed management, forestry, range improvement. Whatever is lost or weakened now will mean pyramiding loss in the future.

For it is the nature of the problems of land and water that damage done to either is cumulative. And it is also their nature, as the entire American experience has shown, that they can be grappled with effectively only by federal action.

Soil conservation districts, REA co-operatives, conservation organizations, browned-out areas of power consumers, towns and counties apprehensive about dust and drought—here are a lot of voters. One obvious giveaway is the presentation to the Democratic Party of a shining issue for 1954 and 1956. And if Schedule C proved to be a fine means for a quick cleanup in top administrative offices, it will remain one after the elections.

In the early fall of 1953 Washington birdwalkers reported a phenomenon which their amiable hobby could not explain. The number of turkey buzzards resident in and near the city had increased remarkably. The buzzard population continued to grow through the winter and the following spring. By now it has created a sizable problem at feeding time at the zoo.

Western Paradox

Chapter One
To the Traveler's Eye

We may begin with what Lieutenant Zebulon Pike called "a small blue cloud." It is seen in eastern Colorado, somewhere in the valley of the Arkansas River, which hereabout looks like a flat plain but isn't. Just when it is seen and whether on the right hand or the left depend on what the weather has been like and on which particular hill or swell one has happened to ascend. I like it in the entry that appears in the journals of various travelers on the Santa Fe Trail in the 1840s. It is written two days or one day before the wagon reaches Bent's Old Fort, 530 miles out from Independence, or the day it arrives there, or the day it has taken to the trail again. Make it the last, which is to say that the event it records occurred a few miles west of La Junta, on what is now U.S. 350, which has turned south off U.S. 50.

If I may average out the temperaments of various diarists, the entry will read something like this. "Shortly before noon a cloud appeared above the western horizon. I was wondering whether it portended long-needed rain, when Wiggins and Bouvarde fired their rifles and galloped down the train, yelling like Comanches. The alarm they roused in me was heightened when most of our company joined in their fusillade. But I made out above their warcries the words, 'Las Montañas! The Mountains!' Instantly I was in the grip of an emotion so powerful that I was close to tears. My thoughts turned back to the lamplit kitchen last winter where we devoted so many evenings to planning this journey. I remembered too how often in boyhood my fancy had strained toward the very vision which I now beheld. For what I had mistaken for a cloud was the beginning of the great Rocky Mountains. The shining whiteness I had seen was the eternal snow on the summit of Pike's Peak. At last I had reached the West."

Thus the greenhorn, and the experience remains the same today. No matter how often you travel west, whether by car, train, or plane, you usually mistake for a cloud the first thrust of a peak above the western horizon. But observe that on the Santa Fe Trail, if you stick to the highway and don't go wandering off among the hills, that first materialization out of the gauze of distance is not Pike's Peak. It is the two almost identical summits, separated by a beautiful but here invisible cleft, that Lewis Garrard called Wah-To-Yah. The word is Ute and probably means "twins" but Garrard, a fervent traveler, made it "Breasts of the World." On our maps, the Spanish Peaks.

They are to the southwest and you first see them perhaps eight miles away. Pike's Peak is to the northwest and perhaps twenty miles farther away, so that the chances are our diarist did not see it till the next day. The maps of his time would not have helped him much but he didn't need a map. In the fancy of last winter only one Rocky Mountain peak had existence and a name. It was Lieutenant Pike's blue cloud, which Major Long had named James Peak but which the trappers renamed for its heroic and wandering discoverer. It had become a symbol in the literature of desire and the political advertising that had blended in the diarists' fancy to compose the West. The West was a single huge mountain, and now at last he had seen eternal snow like a cloud above the far horizon. It could only be Pike's Peak.

Experience of the West, then, begins with an illusion and a misconception.

And with something disregarded. For this jubilant moment did not actually mark the beginning of the West. That had come at least ten days before the gunfire that saluted the distant prospect of the Spanish Peaks. The greenhorn had been traveling the West for ten days, a West quivering with heat mirage and set in the bottom of a gigantic bowl. A plain so endlessly flat that "we could see the sky between their legs," a bowl whose sides rose high around you, and yet a succession of swells like those in midocean. Treeless, swept by winds that parched the skin and made the mind weary, a mind already oppressed by emptiness and enormousness. Without escape from the sun that is a tangible weight on one's soul, that threatens to obliterate personality, that creates a shapeless anxiety. . . . He had been crossing a portion of the West which comes to an end when that illusion of cloud appears on the horizon, the tragic area, the country for which, more than a century later, the American people have still failed to make a durable society. The high plains.

It is a poignant moment, the first sight of the Rockies on the way west, and it is best in Colorado. You are sure to see that cloud no matter by what route you travel, but I like best to send my greenhorn friends west on U.S. 40 or U.S. 50. North of them the mountains are lower and the approach is through the buttes and hills in which the northern plains break up during their last fifty miles, impressive for they are Creation's waste but a lesser spectacle. Whereas from the Colorado plains the

Front Range is an almost intolerable vertical thrust. Here the plains, there the awful wall—as if, a friend of mine in Pueblo said long ago, as if, señor, God had no care for time. As if God had no care for anything but drama.

We saw the cloud in May of 1940, a young historian and I.[1] A few years earlier he had been a student of mine at Harvard; now, each with a book in mind, we were following the Santa Fe Trail. Following it during the days when the Panzers rolled through the Low Countries and into France. The catastrophe had colored every day of our journey, but the day when we saw the cloud was depressing in its own right.

At any time the bottom of the bowl country, the swells of midocean country, creates that shapeless anxiety at some deep level of the mind. But this was 1940. There had been rain in some parts of the dustbowl in 1939 and in some other parts this year, but not in the part we crossed on May 26. Do not suppose it cannot be a beautiful country. In the haze and tempered sunlight of fall or when the grass lifts its head again after a spring rain, it is as beautiful as that mirage of Heaven farther west. But its loneliness is always on the edge of fear and this May loneliness had become desolation.

Cimarron, Garden City, Holcomb, Syracuse—the names of the towns do not matter, the towns do not matter, though they were apathy in clapboards. It was the fields that mattered, or what had been fields. A cemetery was ten inches deep in sand; half the headstones had toppled into it and been partly covered. Sagging shacks that had been farmhouses had their windows blown out and dust was two or four or six feet deep against their western walls and a foot deep against the far wall of every room. A repulsive dust as fine as sifted flour. The dust made an attenuated *V* to the leeward of every fence post. Corn had grown six inches above the dust that had wave marks on it like the ripple marks made by an ebbing tide, and then had been cured to straw, faintly yellow, faintly green, pockmarked, crackling when a breeze moved it. Or here, and we stopped the car to get out and see what it could be, here was a field of what had been, for God's sake!, wheat. It was a scale-model embryo of wheat, had leaved at eight inches and died. A further eight inches of matted roots were exposed; they looked like dried pinworms. The soil had blown down to what looked like hardpan. Little dust was blowing now; the breeze lifted a spray of it a few inches off the ground, shook it through a sifter, and scattered it a few yards farther on. Six years before, almost to the day, it had not been yards.

May 11, 1934. An editor was taking me to lunch and we came out of his office and got into one of the taxis of the period, which had tops the rear half of which you could fold back and so ride in open air and persuade yourself that you remembered a high heart in a younger time in Paris. The day had been meant to be one of those high blue days when New York is electric to the touch and a wind comes off the Jersey marshes and from farther away with a perfume of loam and tidal inlets. But it wasn't. Not much higher than the Fifth Avenue towers hung an impalpable gray curtain that was certainly not mist. What we smelled was not the moist Jersey grass or the Virginia loam. It was a smell that anyone would recognize as dust and with it there was a thinner, less intrusive smell, which any Westerner, however unbelieving on Fifth Avenue, would instantly identify as alkali. The eruption of a greater Krakatoa had reached New York. The editor scowled at a sky that would not be buoyant for him and wondered what for God's sake this was now. At long intervals some blandness by an Easterner wakes the expatriate Westerner in me, as at even longer ones a chance righteousness by a heretic wakes the apostate Catholic in me. "It is for God's sake Kansas," I told him, "and maybe it will annoy you

enough so that you'll let me write that piece about it."
He didn't commission the piece, as it turned out, but
one of his competitors did.[2]

But I rejoiced in the sight of that dust above New
York, tragic as it was, for I knew it would be a more powerful lobby in Washington than the desperate men who
were trying to get always more action against the black
rollers and the destruction of the high plains. Six years
later, in May 1940, crossing the blighted land, I could
not sound bottom in my gloom. In so much that at
lunchtime I phoned my wife in Cambridge. [Were there
troop transports in the Cape Cod Canal, had the Messer-
schmitts appeared over Boston? I wanted to know and]
What were Arthur and I doing on the Santa Fe Trail in
search of a vanished time when Western civilization was
vanishing in its own black roller? I wanted to know, had-
n't I, and this was the blasted earth urging me, [not my
nine-year-old son or the one who had been born four
months ago], hadn't I better turn round and come
home, to be with my family [when the invasion got
there]? My wife said Nuts, but she had not seen the
roots of wheat that were mummied pinworms.

We went on. Shortly after we crossed into Colorado
we reached a land that was convalescing and presently
the blight was behind us and this was just the high
plains country I had always known. East of La Junta we
turned off the highway to find the site of Bent's Old
Fort, merely some swales and hummocks now, and
traces of rubble. I made the notes I always make at such
sites. They convulse any friends who may be traveling
with me and they convince both my conscience and the
Bureau of Internal Revenue that the automobile trips I
take whenever I can are indispensable to the historian's
trade. The Bent's Fort notes fill nine pages in the notebook I have at hand now: compass bearings, distances to
various landmarks and to the Arkansas River, minute
descriptions of the entire landscape in view. They come

to five sentences in the book I was then preparing but there the five sentences are, and if I deduct travel expenses on April 15, why, the topographical descriptions in my book are eyewitness and no one has ever challenged my geography.

We got going again in late afternoon, I was on the alert but Arthur first saw what I was waiting for, and a few miles beyond La Junta he maintained the continuity of history by saying, "Storm coming up." "No," I said, with an old hand's smugness, "the Spanish Peaks." The sinking sun had turned their eternal snows crimson and the lower stratum black, and I thought that one should always reach the West at this hour. The plains grow vaster as darkness moves across them, seeming to come not down from the sky but out of the west, and the fading light takes the horizon from the land. It may be too that the edge of fear is withdrawn, or at least sheathed in mysteriousness, for even in the twentieth century as in the sixteenth, mystery opens up around the westering mind.

A mile or so short of Trinidad we pulled off the road in full dark, to listen to the President's fireside talk on defense. . . . We had left Cambridge on the day when Antwerp was abandoned, and all day long every day since then we had been turning on the radio every few minutes to make what our stunned minds could of the catastrophe. We were skirting Cleveland when the sepulchral voices said that Weygand had replaced Gamelin and would counter-attack. In East St. Louis we stopped at a roadside stand for "barbecued ribs" and a sound truck passed advertising a Nazarene revival and telling us that we must repent for the day of God's vengeance was at hand, and the radio said that the counter-attack was failing everywhere. (None was ever made.) St. Louis was where Boulogne and Calais fell. . . . Now in Colorado darkness we heard that well-remembered voice, the voice that the United States seems still to be listening for whenever the going gets hard. Some Hispanos—a loathsome and patronizing word, but I will not say "Mexicans" and they were not what the Southwest likes to call Anglos, a less likeable people—came out of an adobe house, smiling and bowing, and asked if they might listen with us. We exchanged cigarettes and the voice spoke about the sowers of discord, the growing navy, the mobilization of industry. In the darkness catastrophe had a bigger bulk than the mountains beyond Trinidad, among them the Spanish Peaks under near stars. "For more than three centuries we Americans have been building on this continent a free society, a society in which the promises of the human spirit may find fulfillment. . . . Your prayers join with mine that God will heal the wounds and the hearts of humanity."

Our guests gave us another cigarette. One of them said, "I guess maybe America declare war pretty soon now." We said we guessed so too. They thanked us and waved, and we went on into town. The only eating-place that was open was a Chinese restaurant, which in the interior West, as Arthur now learned, does not mean Mai Fong Lo's but only a short-order house, what Cambridge calls a "Mass. Avenue joint." We stood in the doorway of our motel, with the slant of a hogback in the dark above us. My serial lecture informed him that the penetrating cold showed we had got above the five-thousand foot contour today, and this was another monument for his orientation. He said, "The West has a different smell." There was no dust in the wind that was coming down to the Culebra foothills from Raton Pass. I pointed out that it was also a thinner air. We had reached the great Rocky Mountains, I said, that cloud was the eternal snow on Pike's Peak; this was, at last, the West. He insisted he could smell the pines too, though the leaves that rustled overhead were those of cottonwoods. There was still another smell, I told him, wondering whether anyone but Westerners can detect it. He could not and I said, water. Not damp vegetation, not mud, not sedge or swamp or marsh, but the smell of water. The river we had crossed outside of town was a hundred yards away here, running among cottonwoods and willows. It was the Picketwire, the Purgatoire, El Rio de las Animas Perdidas en Purgatorio. It was another landmark, an unmistakable landmark, I said; the West is where you can smell the water.

His mind went back to disasters of the radio, the ending that would not end. "Purgatorio," he said. "It's a fitting name."

For the West too, I thought, under the Spanish Peaks, and for how many greenhorns, winterers, native sons, and on down to now. Who traveled toward paradise and frequently arrived at inferno. A balance between them should be something other than purgatory but honest and scrupulous men have never found its name.

There is no West.

Mr. W. J. Cash wrote an illuminating book called *The Mind of the South*. He was able to define a pattern of thought and feeling, a social habit, a structure of tradition which we all can recognize and about which he could make many general statements that hold true. No matter how diverse the region and how different from one another are the people who live in it, no matter how demonstrable it is that there are many Souths, there is also one South. As Mr. Cash said, "A complex of established relationships and habits of thought, sentiments, prejudices, standards and values, and associations, which if it is not common strictly to every group of white people in the South, is still common in one appreciable measure or another, and in some part or another, to all but relatively negligible ones." But the people who live in the Western region do not have in common any such complex of established relationships, habits of thought, standards of value, and the rest. There are many Wests but there is no one West.

Mr. V. O. Key wrote an illuminating book called *Southern Politics*. He too defined and expounded a pattern. It would be possible to write a book called *Western Politics* which would uncover if not a pattern at least several characteristic patterns. But the first obligation of the writer would be to explain that the patterns do not originate in anything that can be called the Mind of the West.

The area we deal with here is thirty-nine percent of the area of the United States and it is a constant; the people we deal with compose about thirteen percent of the people of the United States, but that percentage is not a constant, it is increasing at a remarkable rate.[3] To generalize about the society of these people in this area is entirely feasible, but generalizations must be straitly limited and must be made tentatively and with wary caution, and they are in so grave a danger of being wrong that the writer who makes them must, as I do now, instruct the reader to suspect them all. That being declared, I repeat: it is possible to make usable general statements about the Westerners and their society. But it is not possible because they share traditions, habits of thoughts, ideas, and prejudices in such a measure as enabled Mr. Cash to generalize about the South. It is possible because of the geography, topography, and climate that they share.

A complex of sentiments and beliefs expediently called the myth of the Old South has played a part in our experience. It developed after the Civil War. It has little force outside the South and the force it has there is diminishing. A similar complex that can be called the myth of the Old West exists, but as soon as we begin to examine it we encounter dualities and paradoxes, and this is entirely appropriate for dualities and paradoxes abound throughout the West. The myth of the Old West was born less than seventy-five years ago, but also it is older than the United States. Its force is manifest in all parts of the United States and in all parts it is increasing in force. It was created by the East, not the West, and the West accepted it only belatedly, but its growing power is now felt even more strongly in the West than elsewhere.

This discourse will be unable to get away for very long at a time from Western topography, climate, and mythology. Frequently it will have to deal with dualities and paradoxes—and with illusions, misconceptions, contradictions, extremes, contrasts, and violence. For those qualities are characteristics of the West. Of the West's topography, climate, and sentiments. Of its history and of its society. But there is neither duality nor contradiction in its myth, there is the oneness of a romantic dream.

The West is plains, plateaus, and mountains. It is mountains and valleys, and it is therefore also foothills. It is mountains and deserts. It is, in fact, deserts where it is not mountains, in so much that the widest statement we could make is this: the West is a desert. Everything that follows in this book is related to that statement, and everything in Western history, Western life, and Western society is in some way referable to the desert. The West is a desert where life and society are made possible by the mountains. It follows that Western life and society are set in valleys. Valleys are a considerable distance apart and what lies between them is mountains and deserts. That is why the West is the wide-open spaces.

I use the word "desert" in various ways in this book, to mean somewhat different things. Over many years I have tried to find many ways round that awkward and relative but I believe not often ambiguous usage, but I have found no satisfactory ones. All the differences, however, are matters of degree and relate eventually to the amount of usable rainfall, and I believe that the reader will not be misled. Because it seems necessary to provide a fixed term among so many relativities, I employ another awkward phrase, "absolute desert." I mean a place where the average annual rainfall does not come to more than five inches.

We have no sand deserts, though there are areas of extensive dunes, some of which have been reserved as national monuments or state parks, I have never understood why. White Sands, New Mexico, has been forced on everyone's attention. It is part of the large Chihuahuan Desert that reaches up from Mexico. And indeed the deserts of the Southwest, especially those of California and Arizona, run more to sand than the other ones, and it is here that sandstorms are a common phenomenon. Where there are dunes, some have been fixed but others creep like glaciers. For reasons I will have to go into later, the dunes permit a sparse agriculture at times when drought snuffs it out in near-by regions, an Indian agriculture I mean. The Zunis, for instance, grow crops among them when their fields fail.

A pallid gray is the commonest desert color; it is the complexion of the weary earth showing through the spaced vegetation. It is the color too of the universal sagebrush, which runs through an extensive scale of tones. I do not know why the stretch of southern Wyoming between Rawlins and Rock Springs is called the Red Desert. Red is rather the color of the deserts of southern Utah and southwestern Colorado, where the various sandstones that date the geology are so visible, and the basic color in the chromatic luxuriance of the rock desert. But the tourist who crosses the Red Desert gets a lesson in monotony. U.S. 30 and the Union Pacific run side by side; there is nothing else there except railroad's telegraph line, nothing at all, no trees, no people, no buildings or structures of any kind except at long intervals where the railroad has erected a water tank, not even a hill. The tourist comes to welcoming the occasional warped and faded sign that says "Wonderful Wyoming," and I was gratified a few years ago by a melancholy gas station which had its two privies labeled "Cowboys" and "Cowgirls"—even here the myth makes itself felt—and which had set up another sign, "We haul water. It's free to customers only." (Elsewhere I have paid seventy-five cents a gallon to fill my radiator.) This melancholy, or if you like courageous, establishment was located where the Continental Divide, which is here an almost theoretical conception, crosses the highway and the railroad, and on an eminence not much higher than an automobile a monument has been set up to the promoter of the Lincoln Highway.

I talked there for a while with a Chicago lawyer who was making the grand tour of the West. His depressed glance swept the emptiness and he remarked that it was without inhabitants, without resources, and without value. Not quite. In parts of it, surface seepages permit the grazing of sheep even in summer and all of it is a winter range for sheep. Much of the Western desert is, for sheep can substitute snow for water, as cattle cannot. South of U.S. 40, say, all the deserts are a winter range except the absolute ones.

The desert becomes more hideous when its common gray tones are replaced by black. The black lava is not the only reason why Nevada is the ugliest state, but would in itself suffice. (It is also the most corrugated state, though it is seldom thought of as mountainous and indeed has no spectacular mountains, since it ends east of the tremendous Sierra.) It requires a careful weighing of values to decide which of the Nevada deserts is the most hideous. The one in which Las Vegas is set would win, I think, except for one burst of spectacle. Because of it, the superlative must go to the one north of Lovelock, whose principal area shows on maps as the Black Rock Desert.

There is lava throughout the West, but it is usually brown rather than coal black, and in most places it shows as an extrusion among other strata. The deserts east of the Cascade Mountains in the Northwest abound with it, and here it has a chocolate color that fills the afternoon shadows with purple. For the areas in which the ice cap bulldozed the later soil off it, geologists have the striking term "scabland." The word is precise; the exposed lava looks like a scab.

In the deserts the Western sun is even more overwhelming than it is elsewhere. But everywhere east of the Sierra-Cascade massif that sun is so intense that it adds to the uneasiness at the margin of the newcomer's mind. Light seems to have weight and pressure, even in high mountain meadows where a cold wind is blowing. "You told me the sun was hot and the shade cool," a friend of mine said, joining me out west; "what you didn't tell me was that there isn't any shade to hide in." The verb "hide" seems to be inevitable; I have heard Easterners use it many times and it occurs often in the journals of emigrant trains.

Motorists see the road ahead of them flowing blue water. This simple reflection of the sky is the embryo of mirage. Heat mirage develops it farther with an overlay that looks like a membrane. There is a drifting shimmer which blurs outlines, magnifies and distorts shapes, and falsifies distances. On the road, straight lines may seem to rise and drift sideward; across a sagebrush flat the spatial relationship of objects gets out of true. An antelope or even a jackrabbit near at hand may seem to be a horse in the middle distance, as in the emigrant journals a herd of elk sometimes becomes a horde of galloping Indians. Objects approaching each other in the distance, two cars or trucks, say, or a couple of grazing steers, may be unidentifiable and the angle and even the direction of their movement may be beyond determination. The sides of hills belly out and flow; cliffs lose their edge. A brown or black fluidity washes across whatever the eye tries to come to rest on, translating known things to rumor.

The horizon landscapes, always with groves, that mean mirage to Easterners, who know them most familiarly at the edge of lakes, usually come at sunset, though I have seen them at midday. I have not often seen the "false ponds" that so impressed the early desert travelers but the travelers' astonishment was just. In a landscape breathless with heat and so flattened by the intense light that colors have no middle tones and space lacks the dimension of depth, with the shadow of your horse or car or of the sagebrush thinned to transparency—in such a landscape you see, some miles beyond you, just such a body of blue rippling water as Winnepesaukee or Winnebago. How severe the lack has been is instantly apparent in the longing that gushes up in you. You are aware that your eyes have been overstrained and now demand to be satisfied with seeing, that your very capillaries have shrunk, that if you waded into it you could take in water through your skin. The moment has stampeded many a mind but your horse does not raise his head.

In the desert, during the summer months at least, all these effects are intensified and to them is added the further disorientation of heat. I do not know what, physically and psychologically, the critical temperature is. At a reading of 100 degrees one may not even be aware of heat but thousands of visitors to Las Vegas and Hoover Dam learn every summer that 120 degrees is almost intolerable. My references say that temperatures above 136 degrees have never been recorded and I have not myself seen a thermometer that had managed to reach 130 degrees. Yet in guts of naked rock, arroyos, depressions at the foot of cliffs, and other places where the heat is multiply reflected it must go considerably higher. Desert animals stay hidden, desert workers are subject to fixed notions bordering on delusion and in extremity develop hallucinations, and the intelligent tourist not only supplies himself with gallons of drinking water but sticks to the roads.

The enchantment that the desert works on many people seems to be very difficult to explain. No one has explained it convincingly to me, and I do not understand it. Certainly all the hideousness I have mentioned, and I could itemize it for many additional pages, can be counterbalanced by as much beauty, majesty, and sublimity. The rock deserts, those chromatic ecstasies, have been painted with brushes of comet's hair. The great chasms not only produce the awe which I think the saints and mystics feel but overwhelm one with magnificence of color and light and change. Death Valley is only one of many areas where time has been frozen in geology, where mesas and mountains have been riven and scattered as if, señor, God were a child petulant with His building blocks, and where consciousness angles down a very strange dimension. The desert silence is a blessed healing. Above all, the desert is where one sees the stars. It is the nighttime splendor that I seem always to forget, for it is a discovery whenever I come back to it. I have landed at sundown in small planes on the dry beds of lakes, and after the curt twilight of the desert found myself looking at the sky as children look at fireworks for the first time.

Yet I do not understand the desert-dweller, whether the aimless wanderer typified in my boyhood by the prospector, the marginal rancher, the escapee, or the artists and literary persons who have been attracted in such quantity and who have depicted it so voluminously. Whenever journalism or scholarship takes me to the desert, I always find that I am glad to leave, that I have been under some tension to skimp the job and get away. Santa Fe is a fascinating town and a beautiful one too; though well supplied with phonies, it has more than its fair share of interesting people; and the sound of its waters is musical in the morning air. Yet I never lose the feeling that it is an oasis in an immense desert and I had better be getting on. Driving north toward Colorado, the road leads up into the Carson National Forest. There are stands of ponderosa, the Western yellow pine, to my mind the loveliest of trees and to anyone's mind one of the emblems of the West. There are little streams that in the East would be brooks but are creeks here. They flow through grasses and I have lately grown used to a miscellaneous chaparral. Suddenly, as the psalm says, my heart leaps, whatever strain or uneasiness has been oppressing me is gone, and I have reached my own place.

I said as much to Sam, in a similar place not far from the Carson. I will need Sam from time to time here, so he must have a word. He is a novelist good enough to have several times roused the envious defensiveness of Ernest Hemingway that produces those snide critical asides which are not so droll as Mr. Hemingway appears to think they are. And his novels sell in such carload lots that Sam is able to loaf around Europe and Africa and as much of Asia as is still open, devoting an eager curiosity to the restaurants and beer halls and wine cellars of the world. He charms me by having resisted education more successfully than anyone else I have ever known, in so much that he will marvel to hear how many planets there are or that a Congressman serves a two-year term. So that to his agile and inquisitive mind any casual conversation, any walk down a street, is an experience of bounty and absorption. Moreover, he thinks of no writer as a rival and respects the profession's skill whenever it is manifested.

I had often challenged Sam to explore the mysteries of his own continent, not supposing he would ever take me up. He finally felt the impulse when I was preparing to go west on the most strenuous assignment I have ever had. At midsummer we drove across Montana, quartered across Idaho (whose Snake River desert is one of the most dreary), and got to San Francisco in time to revive his faith in American culture, for God knows the West, at least the roadside West, is no place for gastronomes.

(His mind was as tireless as a woodpecker at dawn and he had a sunny faith in my omniscience. If that was not a road coming out of the canyon and running along the mountainside, if it was as I said an acequia madre, a "high-line ditch," then did I mean to sit there and tell him that water flowed uphill? No, I said, he was experiencing one of the tenderfoot's common illusions. The canal was almost level, it was flowing downhill but not more than five or six feet a mile; what made it appear to angle uphill was that the land below the mouth of the canyon sloped downward.... what did the wisecrack mean that in the West you dug for wood and climbed for water? As for wood it was easy: the roots of sagebrush and creosote bush and dwarf mahogany were excellent fuel and often the only one you could find. As for water, he could take his choice. Some of the larger cacti had reservoirs of drinkable fluid, though I would not care to climb for it. More to the point, if you saw on a bare mountainside some outcrop of green, then the chances were that if you went uphill from it you would find a little seepage or perhaps even a spring or fifty yards of trickle. In an arroyo or the dry bed of a creek, if you went upstream you might find pools and eventually something like a stream.... What was a stope? How did loco weed act? Were mountain oysters still obtained in the historical way? Why did I call the cottonwood the exile's nostalgia? Would the corn found in the kivas of the cliff-dwellers sprout? Where had they used camels? ...)

We headed toward Flagstaff from Bakersfield. In August the lower end of the San Joaquin Valley is wrapped in a brown heat-haze which I have never fully understood, for assuredly there is no water vapor in it. A reek of crude oil goes with it; the sky is a steel-white; one does not rest a forearm on the car door. Presently Sam stripped and he remained naked, talking busily, till evening except when he pulled his trousers on for a stop. There was some moderation in Tehachapi Pass, but it climbs to only four thousand feet. Beyond it is the California desert, true desert heat, the incandescence of desert light, both tangible, white, quivering, inconceivable until experienced. Look at a road map. You come to Mojave, Muroc, Barstow, Soda Lake, similar places. It is a hideous stretch, without interest; the rock formations are well to the north, the giant cacti well to the south. Desert after desert, playas, fissured mud flats baked to macadam, salt and alkali flats blindingly white, dunes, mirages, sand devils, creosote bush, at long intervals a hundred-foot oasis with a filling station and five sick palms. It badly needs Technicolor, Sam kept saying, and he was outraged by small sandstorms we had to drive through. He saw Technicolor a day or so later, in the country of peeled mesas and mountains which the wide screen has commended to horse opera. We doubled back to Phoenix, which Sam thought both depressing and ugly—he had not seen Las Vegas—and then went on to Santa Fe.

There and at Taos we spent about ten days. While I worked at my trade Sam pursued his avocation as a tourist in foreign parts. He met the notables, the writers, the artists, the anthropologists. He visited the museums and galleries and pueblos; he made the several obligatory pilgrimages. Evenings we spent with our kind and our colleagues, most hospitable, of extensive acquaintance, and clustered thickly round with satellites. I am able, though sometimes only just, to receive gravely the discourse on white inferiority and the all-worldliness of the Pueblo metaphysics to which the perceptions of Jesus and the Buddha are but the stumbling first steps along the Way—to remember that it is no funnier than the chatter of a Cambridge cocktail party when my hostess takes off her shoes, shakes her hair down over her forehead, picks up her drum, and, swaying in the breeze like ripe corn, sings the chant that old Gregorio taught her, her alone, a few months before he took the road to the otherwhere.

I finished my job and we headed north from Taos toward Denver. We reached ponderosa forest, there was a tone poem of flowing water, the world was as beautiful as paradise, my exasperations vanished, and I was impelled to discourse on the symbolism and paradox of the desert. Sam might if he liked, I said, interpret my desert-depression as a distaste for death that hardly bothered to pull a veil over fear, but I was also fascinated by the obvious lust for death to be observed in the Southwest. I would like sometime to bring one of my friends among the Boston psychoanalysts out here to study the death-wish as evidenced by the migration, now more than a century old, of the disaffected, the withdrawers, and especially their literary analogue. The sands, the chromatic rock, the skinned landscape, the universal drought—these, I said, were symbols of sterility, of lifelessness, of the ending not only of struggle and hope but of life itself. They were death symbols. It was not by chance that the extinction of matter had been localized at such places as Los Alamos, White Sands, the farthest flats in the Mojave and the Great Salt Desert. Of the several hundred paintings Sam had lately seen he must have observed that singularly few by the really good painters dealt with the desert itself—they wrought instead with its alleviations and had made what amounted to clichés of corn and waterholes. For myself, I had a particular admiration for the photographs of

Ansel Adams but it struck you with force that the Adams landscape was sterile, a human figure in it would have been discordant to the point of sacrilege—say as much as you pleased about the landscape of time beginning, or of the world before time, the more accurate remark was that it was the landscape before life, without life, the landscape of death.

Sam said it was an absolute necessity to make a sharp differentiation. He had been struck by the number of pros. In Sam's vocabulary the term is equivalent to the saved, the fecund, or the genuine; pros are writers and apart from them there are only dilettanti and amateurs, for whom God will not provide even hell-room. Frankly, he had been surprised by the number of writers and painters who knew and did their jobs and by the excellence of the job they did—here in what from the point of view of Westport or Bucks County was an outpost station somewhere beyond Somaliland. It does not surprise me; New Mexico and California are the two Western states where there is a topsoil of acquaintance with the usages of art, of custom and tradition, of scholarship, of real as distinct from literary folklore, of legend. It strikes you that they are also the places with a Spanish subsoil, though this remark may represent my own literary romanticism.

The pros, Sam said, were like any pros anywhere. But what hit you in the eye was the extraordinary number of ritualists—that wasn't the term but nobody had invented an exact term. He meant the people who went through the motions, who acted out an intricate drama of what they clearly were not, and he must say that out here they certainly costumed the part. They were not writers, they were not painters, they were not ethnologists or archeologists, but they spent their lives, their waking lives and he suspected their dream life too, as if they were writers, painters, and anthropologists. They were damn well going to *seem* to be, to behave and order their lives as if they were. On a per capita basis there must be far more of them in Santa Fe, Taos, and the tributary ranchos than in Bloomsbury or Paris. He suggested that they might be the key to what I was saying and he seemed to remember that I had somewhere called their kind *castrati*.

I hadn't, I said, though I might steal the word now, and I would add that they set the drama in a frame, in a fantasy of the West. A lot of them too were damn well going to be Pueblos, or preferably Hopis. He himself had chanced on the exact term and I thought it significant that Helene Deutsch had used it before he did, in psychoanalytic treatises. Dr. Deutsch had observed a type whom she called the "as-if people." They had only the most shadowy personalities, in fact they had not proper and active personality at all. So they identified themselves with persons who had positive personalities and substituted the identification for what they lacked.[4] I agreed with Sam that there were a lot of them hereabout but the label did not explain why they came here. Perhaps you could be an as-if Indian only in Indian country but I had not known any as-if Mashpees, Mohawks, or Sioux. Why were they Pueblos? And why did the as-if writers and painters swarm in the desert? The more as-if you were, the more scrupulously and complexly you were a symbolist; and I insisted, the tropism that had brought them here was clearly the tug of the death symbols.

Hell, Sam said, if he read history right (I cannot imagine him reading at all), then going west had always been a form of psychic suicide. In our war the euphemism for being killed was "he's gone west." The dead god was always carried westward. From Egypt on, the soul released from its tenement winged toward the house of the dying sun. I myself had written thousands of pages which asserted that the Fortunate Isles, all of them, lay west of the western hills.

That, I said, was the West as such, not its deserts, but the interesting thing was the paradox. Actually, the deserts are not lifeless at all. It would be possible to say that they symbolize rather the tenacity of life. The arroyos round Santa Fe which contain the ranchos that roused Sam's admiration are oases but their positively explosive fecundity shows what the desert can do. You drop down to them from the gray and searing plain and you are in a tangle of vegetation that almost shocks you and is the most violent and exhilarating contrast with what you have been seeing. But the desert itself is crowded with specific adaptations. The vegetation telescopes a growth cycle into a few weeks following the spring or summer rains. See a desert then and it is a flower garden. For the rest, the plants, like all Western things, hang on for rain. Their privates are deeply hidden from the sun. Their thorns, spines, and hairy coats, their tough leaves, the waxy substances that cover their leaves and stems, are all devices to conserve moisture. Their roots go deep to reach moisture as the deep earth may have, the root systems spread widely to catch the thin moisture of microscopic dews and rains. (That is why the creosote bush, which is the most repulsive of shrubs and inhabits the most complete deserts, is spaced so widely.) They are Western boomers in that they expend the rains drunkenly when they come, but between rains they are mechanisms for getting along without any water at all. Wilting does not damage them and in periods of extreme drought they simply omit to put forth leaves and flowers. They sit back and wait.

And the deserts are crowded with animal and insect life. It is not visible to the casual passerby because it hides out by day. At sunset it comes awake and the night is populous.

On the roads the desert-dwellers and the tourists also make the deserts populous at night. The typical roadside oasis, a gas-station with lunchroom (and in

Nevada a bleary dealer at a baize-covered table taking
quarters from casuals) is much livelier than by day.
There are night mirages on the roads, too. The headlights of approaching cars will be reflected triply or
quadruply by the road, so that one car will seem to be a
caravan of four or five. And when they are some miles
away they seem to be almost at hand, so that a driver
will hug the side of the road for minutes at a time waiting for them to reach him. The traffic is thicker than by
day and yet so vast is the emptiness that the momentary passage is at once lost in nothingness and you seem
to travel in a vacant world. With our younger son, then
six, my wife and I once drove by night from Carson
City to Salt Lake City. I know no other way to find
Nevada pleasing, to find it anything but a waste that
lies between Utah and California. It was the night of the
full moon and we saw moonrise half a dozen times as
the road curved in close to ranges of the shapeless
hills. The water smell was strong in the valley of the
Humboldt. The casuals kept appearing in our headlights, thirty or forty miles from a gas station or the
turnoff for a ranch, thumbs up, suitcases beside them,
sometimes young couples who were careful to hold an
infant up to the light, more than one solitary woman
with just such a pack as bindle stiffs used to carry in
boxcars.

We had reached the Salt Desert when the dawn exploded in color. It is a plain of salt so flat and packed so
tight, though a foul brine underlies it some inches
down, that a stretch of it is the track where automobile
speed records are set. By day it is a blinding white but
some minutes before sunrise it was a child's kaleido-
scope grown sidereal. I can say pink, green, or blue but
there were a hundred shades and tones of each; they
sparkled and shone and flowed into and through each
other with the angle of the road. Each of three quarters
of the world was a different color, with mile-long arrows

of gold shooting across it. A wheel or a lighthouse beam revolved over it and the pink turned crimson, the opal became prussian blue, or pale green vibrated to the moving beam like the throb of an organ pipe. Chaos may have been such an interflow of color before Creation. Sometimes a wind lifted a column of salt dust high in the air and striped and dotted it with all the colors and set them to whirling through one another.

A few miles to our right, granted the ability to get there, we could have found fragments of wagons that had belonged to the Donner Party, who came to disaster on this cosmic palette. I have crossed the waste only by car and plane. Men who have explored it tell me that no description ever written comes close to rendering its strain. The columns of salt we saw lifted by the wind become clouds and they fill the throat with strangling dust. The distance is crowded with monstrous mirages. It is no place for the withdrawing or the maladjusted mind, and the military have found it, like White Sands, a fit place for the rehearsal of war.

The colors lasted but a few minutes and then we were crossing a world of flameless fire. By six A.M. it had drained us to a sullen apathy; we were as exhausted as if we had walked for a week without sleep. At the eastern edge there is a transition zone of gray earth and repulsive salt shrub and stinking mire. Then comes the black desert, merely dead rather than poisoned land, but with the same heat that presses down on you with the weight of the sky. Then there are hills of black and brown rock. The stench of brine persists and the sulphur of thermal springs is added to it. At intervals a cluster of sheds stands in a tentative green patch where a Mormon pioneer found a spring; they are two-dimensional, shapeless with mirage. Then the road skirts Great Salt Lake, for which Dale Morgan found the just phrase, a desert of water. It is foul and a lie; it derides thirst, water that is dead.

Suddenly one has crossed an absolute boundary, coming to irrigated fields, and soon there is the heart-wrenching emotion that the approach to nearly any Western town creates with a magnificence of trees planted for the soul to hide in from the sun. A small irrigation ditch flows beside the road; small seepage pools reflect the sky. Cattle lie in the shade of box elders and the east is the green of the Wasatch peaks. The tongue of the dumb sings for in the wilderness have waters broken out and streams in the desert.

Each of the great river valleys of the West has a unique topographical pattern. If a man were set down unknowing anywhere in the valley of the Missouri, Yellowstone, Big Horn, Green, Yampa, Grand (which in the texts is the Colorado), or the Snake, the shape of the bluffs would tell him where he was. Turn now to the upper valley of the Seedskadee Agie or Sagehen River, Father Escalante's San Buenaventura, because of Escalante the Spanish River to the generation of the Rocky Mountain trappers. It is the Green River and if the federal government had followed the logic of geography it would be the Colorado.

A tourist who drives north from U.S. 30 toward Grand Teton or Yellowstone National Park has the Wind River Mountains in sight for some hours. We are not now concerned with them as scenery, though one wonders why of the hundreds of cars that every summer day hurry up U.S. 189 and 187, so few turn off into them. These two highways join near a hamlet called Daniel, whose site was important in the 1830s but has not been since and never will be again. Here a stream called Horse Creek which flows down from the low Wyoming Range reaches Green River. Its meadows and cottonwood groves made it a favorite place for the trappers' summer rendezvous. A couple of miles up Horse Creek Captain Bonneville built his trading place with the imperatives of continental strategy in mind, for it commanded not only South Pass but the portals to the western ranges through which troops would have to move to or from Oregon and California.

The tourist who reaches Daniel on 189 has been traveling along the floor of the desert valley of Green River, whose pink and pale green bluffs are as unmistakable as the terraced yellow bluffs of the Yellowstone Valley. At the road junction, Daniel, he is some ten miles west of Pinedale, which the traveler on 187 passed through seven or eight minutes ago. Pinedale has erected signs proclaiming, whether in pride or grief I do not know, that it is farther from a railroad than any other town in the United States. (The claim will not stand examination.) A historian will erect a different marker, one that would hymn the persistence of the Old West mentality among Pinedale's stock associations. I suppose that as many bands of bronzed horsemen set out from Pinedale as from any other jumping-off place to hold the trade festival known as a sheepkillin'. You wanted to get the God-damned sheepmen off your range, which incidentally did not belong to you. There would be only one sheepherder at a camp, or at most two or three, and a dozen drunk and masked caballeros would be enough. They burned the wagon, bedding, and supplies. Whether they killed the herders, beat them up, or merely set them afoot and told them to get going depended on whose herders they were, how drunk the caballeros were, or perhaps how recently one of them had come from Texas. Then they set about killing the sheep. They clubbed them to death—who in the hell would waste two thousand cartridges? A dozen cowpokes could kill a couple of thousand of sheep in three or four hours, and an enjoyable day's work at that.

(Understand, sheep ruined the range, smelled bad, and fouled the water supply. Till cattlemen went into the sheep business.)

From Pinedale the motorist can drive into the Wind River Mountains in half an hour, on roads which the U.S. Forest Service (here the Bridger National Forest) has somehow scraped up the money to build. Or in the same length of time he can reach starting places where by foot trail or on horseback he can head into primitive, exceedingly rugged wilderness. Both Yellowstone and Teton Parks have more grandeur than anyone can ever know in its entirety. Yellowstone is infinitely fascinating, the most popular and the most variegated of the National Parks. The wonder of Teton is its verticals. The range is gothic, the most dramatic of our mountains. There are no foothills, the peaks thrust straight up from the plain, and the climactic Three Tetons rise more than seven thousand feet above it. Yet the high country of the Wind Rivers, which few people visit, is in its different but unique way, fully as spectacular. If it were not inclosed in national forests, we would have to make it a national park.

There are massive peaks, ice fields and glaciers, fragmented crags, subarctic meadows, canyons so narrow that the wind is always noisy in them, high flats forlorn with the debris of creation. Marvelously beautiful lakes such as Fremont and Crescent can be reached by car in a few minutes from the valley floor; the Green River Lakes are almost as accessible. Higher and deeper in the ridge are many smaller lakes that only wilderness men ever see; except in the High Sierra this is the only place where I have felt the force of the word "tarn." From the long irregular ridge and the peaks that jut above it, the whole world falls away at your feet.

It really is the whole world, or at least North America. For the ridge is the Continental Divide and this is one of the few places where it has the propriety to look like what one thinks it ought to be. Elsewhere it tends to be deceptive, disguised, or improbable. In the great

Colorado ranges it usually is not the ridge it obviously must be but a lesser one, lower and at an unlikely angle. It can be a kind of camber in a flat or a hairline to be located only with instruments. In many places people will argue heatedly when told that they are at the parting of the waters, for to any eye the Divide is certainly that mile-high ridge to the east or west of where they stand.

The southern end of the Wind Rivers is a series of diminishing pyramids above the thirty-mile-wide plain of South Pass. Here for forty years of exploration, trade, and emigration westering Americans felt, as our diarist did, that they had reached the West. Laboring up the Platte and the Sweetwater, across sagebrush or rock deserts, they had not seen the full magnificence of the Wind Rivers for they had been diminished in scale by lesser ranges constantly in sight. Here was the Divide at last, however, though none knew exactly where. (You have to hunt carefully to be sure that Wyoming knows today, or the Geological Survey or the Coast and Geodetic Survey either.) The United States ended here, Oregon began, and on the southwestern horizon a small blue cloud that was the as yet unnamed Uinta Mountains told the better informed among the travelers that they were near Mexico as well. Above the ascending pyramids of the Wind Rivers at the right was a stationary cloud that seldom lifted and there were apt to be snow flurries in the Pass.

My trade has often taken me to South Pass. A good many times, the job finished, I have sat for some hours at a stretch in the shade of my car or of an inconsiderable clump of people, smelled the clean wind, and watched the heat mirage flow like a sluggish flood across the sage. Or watched that cloud above the Wind Rivers swell and contract, build itself higher, topple into brown and black and pure white fragments, and methodically reassemble them. The wind in the Pass is usu-

ally moderate and silent but one knows that it is an avalanche down the eastern gulches of the range. And
once I inspected the Wind Rivers from the air.

I was on a junket that lasted three weeks and cost
the taxpayer God knows how much. I do not apologize;
the junket was offered to me and to A. B. Guthrie without solicitation by either of us and we would have been
fools to decline. The Air Force flew us in some general's
converted R-25 up the Platte and the Sweetwater and
into and through the Pass. So fair and foul a day I have
not seen. All four houses of the sky were flawed with
rain. A dozen separate showers hung curtains of black,
gray, brown, or green gauze round us, drifted away, left
us dazzled by sudden sunlight and long vistas which
were stereoscopic through the proscenium of the Pass.
The Wind River cloud dropped down below the waistline
of the peaks, rose up and cleared them, settled back,
and blotted out cliffs, boiled down the canyons that
creased the mountainsides, swirled up and towered.
From 12,000 feet—for our pilots were reluctant to fly so
delicate an instrument lower and climbed fast after
they had taken us down to circle landmarks—from such
a height rock walls burst through the gauze curtains,
stood erect in the sun, were erased. A peak would be
alone, its neighbors hidden, the creases of its canyons
flowing like foam. . . . We reached the Green, turned
back through the Pass, and headed northeastward with
the Wind Rivers on our left. The flawed showers ended
and the clouds went nowhither till the whole range
shone in the sun, immense, of an overwhelming mas-
siveness, the backbone of the continent. Yet it was a
painted diorama unrolling northward at our side, as our
few feet of silver with the child's pinwheels hung motionless in space and a minute drawing of it in shadow
was pinned to the ground thousands of feet down.

We arrive at a crux of geography, and a maze. I need
a clear day in the Wind Rivers, and a position motionless

in space far higher above them than we were above South Pass. Their axis is northwest-southeast, or close to that, and they are more than a hundred miles long. Our high platform in space may be above their mid-point. From here the architecture of the West is visible, and the leverage of its waters.

Below us is a peak that from the plane looks like a mesa set on top of a massive dike; it is long and broad, not sharp, its sides seem to be vertical and its top flat. It is Fremont Peak, named for John Charles Fremont, the Byronic press agent, who thought it was the highest of the Wind River peaks. He was wrong only by fifty feet and the sharper and slenderer peak that tops it is Gannett, five miles farther north. At the foot of the range, somewhere to the west of Gannett Peak is the source of the Green River.

What is the source of a river? Snow becomes water and (this is a natural law of which nearly everyone is ignorant, especially Westerners) water runs downhill. Contour levels bring trickles together, other trickles join them, and at some point enough of them have joined so that they may be designated by any of several nouns ending in *-let*. A rill becomes a brook and grows to be, shall we say, a creek. The people of Green River Valley tell you that the source of their river is the smaller of the two silver-blue ponds called the Green River Lakes. That would be a close enough approximation for my purpose but an official adjudication by the Geological Survey gives it six or seven miles more length. The Green begins where two creeks called Wells and Trail come together.

It flows north and northwest, then west through the foothills of the Wind Rivers and turns south down the valley named for it. Creeks keep joining it and by the time it reaches the road-junction at Daniel it is big enough to be called a river. Also it has acquired the faint green tint that christened it, limpid and transparent, not the opaque green that means glacial till. It keeps flowing south till it reaches the Uinta Mountains, high, massive, and mostly red. It turns east along the badlands at their foot, then trends south through those badlands and reaches the first of Major John Wesley Powell's canyons, Flaming Gorge. From here on it is violent and tortuous and it comes into spectacle at Red Canyon. From here on too, flouting the official ruling which says otherwise, it is by nature the Colorado River. It is the Colorado by length, by volume, but most of all by its specific features, its violence, its protean changeability, the canyons it flows through. All these make it sharply different from the river which is officially called the Colorado and which, when the two streams meet, has come down from the high Colorado ranges along the western boundary of Rocky Mountain National Park. At this junction the Green has traveled 730 miles from its source.

The Colorado will keep recurring here, or rather the Colorado from the mouth of the Green on. It is a desert river, the River of the American Desert. Troublesome, antic, violent, the smallest in volume of the West's principal rivers, it is nevertheless a great one. It is a century-old despair and a great hope; it is as important to the West as his aorta is to a man.

Back to the Continental Divide at the ridge of the Wind Rivers east of the source of the Green. Let this knife-edge split a falling snowflake and let the eastern half of it flow straight down the eastern slope till it reaches the stream called Wind River. Here the beds of Wind River and Green River are, in an east-west air-line, less than twenty-five miles apart, with the massif between them. But at the point where the snowflake reaches it, Wind River has been flowing about fifty miles as an identifiable stream. Its "source" is some forty miles north of the source of the Green and, because of the direction the Divide takes, actually west of it. Thus their headwaters are nearly fifty miles apart. (But water flows downhill and the distance between their watersheds is the width of that knife-edge.) Wind River flows southeastward through its mountains, coming down from just below Togwotee Pass, and out into the mingling hills and plains. Here it is some 125 miles long and here it meets a smaller stream that has been flowing northeast, the Popo Agie. (A Crow name, Reed River or Rye-Grass River or Wickiup River.)

The Popo Agie has also come down the eastern slope of the Wind River range but it originates ninety miles south of the Wind River, which at the junction makes a right-angle turn and begins to flow north. From there on, however, the merged streams are called the Big Horn River, and this time it is common usage, not official decree, that has changed the name. The Big Horn, a clear mountain stream when Antoine LeRocque and William Clark first saw it in 1805 and 1806 but now the most silt-laden member of a heavily silted system, flows north and east of north through a series of canyons, of which two are famous and one among the most spectacular in the Rockies. At the mouth of the latter canyon it emerges into the Montana plains, the country where one of its affluents, the Little Big Horn, witnessed the massacre of our stupidest general and his command. It traverses nearly a hundred miles of Montana and then empties into a great river, the Yellowstone. It has come 336 miles from the Popo Agie and, all told, 461 miles from the source of the Wind River. To scan the relief of this geography from our high platform in space would be, as to work it out on a map is, an instructive lesson in the flow of water, all the more so because at the mouth of the Big Horn the Yellowstone has traveled 280 miles from its source. Having reached the Yellowstone, our bisected snowflake goes on to the Missouri, the Mississippi, the Gulf of Mexico, and the Atlantic.

The geography seen from our fixed point is a stirred chaos of peaks, ridges, plateaus, and high basins. Routes through and out of it have only such logic as water flow-

ing downhill gives them and there is no reason to state
the details here. North of it is a range of savagely precipitous mountains called the Absarokas. They form
the eastern boundary of Yellowstone National Park. The
brooks that flow down their eastern slopes become
creeks that find their way to the Yellowstone River directly or are affluents of the Big Horn and so reach the
Yellowstone farther east. But west of the Absarokas the
Yellowstone itself, receiving affluents from their western slopes, is flowing north.

The source of the Yellowstone is about twenty-five
miles from that of the Wind River and nearly fifty miles
from that of the Green. Fifty miles is a considerable and
unusual distance for this Place Where Rivers Are Born.
It is explained by the fact that here a third great river
system intervenes between the other two. Here, in fact,
we could split the snowflake into three parts and take
its third fraction on an amazing journey, but two at a
time are enough.

The Yellowstone, which here is north as well as east
of the Continental Divide, rises southeast of Yellowstone
Park and has already flowed nearly forty miles when it
reaches the lakes from which it plunges into its Grand
Canyon. It has crossed Montana and is 671 miles long
when it reaches the Missouri River, practically at the
North Dakota line. Here the Missouri is 784 miles below
its beginning, the Three Forks. But at the point where
the Yellowstone leaves the Park it is distant from the
Gallatin River, which is the eastern Fork, only about
nineteen miles and is only ten miles from a headwater
tributary of the Gallatin; a little farther on, the two
rivers are within sixteen miles of each other.

The middle fork of the Missouri is the Madison River
and its head is the junction of the Firehole and the Gibbon Rivers, inside Yellowstone Park. This junction is
about fifteen miles from waters of the Yellowstone
drainage big enough to be recognized as a stream.

Headwater streams of the Gibbon do not approach the Gallatin closer than about twelve miles, but Grayling Creek, which flows into the Madison, the river formed by the Firehole and Gibbon, runs only half a mile from the source of the Gallatin. Almost the knife-edge.

(Some of this geographical scrambling is geologically recent. At the end of the last ice age Yellowstone lake, which is now drained by the Yellowstone River, found its way to the Snake River and so to the Pacific. It was then, that is to say, west and south of the Continental Divide. At an earlier time the Yellowstone River too was Pacific drainage, though it had found its present course—east and north of the Park at last—by the first ice age. A species of rainbow trout was found in the Atlantic drainage only in the Yellowstone River, till game departments planted it elsewhere.... All this will be much clearer than words can make it if the reader will observe on the map the course of the Continental Divide into, across, and out of Yellowstone National Park and on to the Wind River Mountains.)

It is time to trisect the snowflake. One part of it started for the Gulf of California by way of the Green, above whose headwaters our space platform is centered. The second part started for the Gulf of Mexico by way of the Yellowstone but might just as easily have started by way of the Wind River. The third part will reach the Pacific by way of the Snake River, and a beautiful river it is too.

As the Yellowstone, flowing north, crosses the boundary into Yellowstone Park, it receives the negligible waters of Falcon Creek, which has come down from the Continental Divide. (Here the Divide has taken a north-south route, as in decency it ought to.) An even more negligible stream begins on a plateau that lies a couple of miles west of the Divide. When it becomes large enough to be noticed it is perhaps four miles from the Yellowstone, at the boundary of the Park, and per-

haps three miles from the head of Falcon Creek. It is
the Snake. It twists through three-quarters of a circle,
crosses into the Park, wanders generally westward,
turns south, and leaves the Park about nineteen miles
west of where it entered.[5] Just before it makes its exit it
receives the waters of a river that comes down from the
north through a rugged canyon which the tourist sees
only from the rim.

This affluent is the only part of the Snake system
that retains the name given to the parent stream by
William Clark in 1868: it is the Lewis River. Only twenty
miles long, it is the outlet of a handsome body of water
called Shoshone Lake. At the other, the western, end of
the lake a small stream called Shoshone Creek enters it.
The mouth of this creek (near Shoshone Geyser Basin)
is a little over four miles due east of the smaller, marshy
Madison Lake, and in its short course the creek comes
two miles nearer it. Madison Lake is the source of the
Firehole River, which when the Gibbon River joins it becomes the Madison, which at the Three Forks become
the Missouri.

. . . Here is one of several places where traveling companions of mine who do not share my warm tenderness
for the Continental Divide have thrown in their hands,
declaring that geography does not make sense. For, no
question about it, to the eye and on the map Shoshone
Lake is east of the Divide and Madison Lake west of it,
and the Pacific-bound waters flow east whereas those
bound for the Atlantic flow west. No difficulty: an illusion of inattention. The parting of the waters is not
east-west but north-south. The Lewis originates east of
the Firehole, it is true, but its flow is, from the Divide,
southward. . . .

Follow the Snake for a while. It flows south through
Grand Teton National Park and Jackson Hole. Before
leaving the latter it receives the waters of two creeks

that must be noted. Pacific Creek rises in Two Ocean Pass and at its source is only half a dozen miles from the source of the Snake. It is separated only by the summit of the Pass from Atlantic Creek, which flows into the Yellowstone, a separation so slight that Two Ocean Lake is popularly, though erroneously, supposed to empty into both drainages. The other creek is Buffalo Fork and it has several forks. One of them comes within five miles of Pacific Creek (Snake River drainage) and within five miles of the Yellowstone (east of the Divide). A second fork heads less than three miles from a creek that joins the Shoshone River, one called the Stinkingwater, which flows into the Big Horn. A third fork, heading near Togwotee Pass, is hardly more than two miles from headwaters of Wind River.

Somewhere hereabout, in fact, we might locate a prime point. Come four miles south of this affluent of Buffalo Fork is Moccasin Creek and this too, with the high range in between, is within three or four air-line miles of Wind River. It becomes a fork of the Gros Ventre River, which reaches the Snake in Jackson Hole, and southern affluents of the Gros Ventre come almost as close to the Green as Moccasin Creek comes to the Wind River. South of the Gros Ventre another river, the Hoback (down whose pleasant canyon our tourist bound for the national parks will travel), flows toward the Snake, which it reaches at the lower end of Jackson Hole. A good many small creeks join it from the south and southwest; they are separated by divides, most of which are low and trivial, from similar ones that flow into the Green. The Green itself is some fourteen miles east of the Hoback and about thirty-five miles from the nearest point of the Snake.

This is enough. (And will be clear, and I trust more vivid, if the reader will look at the map again.) From the space platform over Fremont Peak, the three great river basins of the West, the Colorado, the Columbia, and the Missouri, and all in sight—by means of the principal tributaries.

I will not so painfully examine the details of a comparable though much more extended spawning bed of rivers in the Colorado ranges, though I ought to do so and have supplied a map. But the outline is required.

We have seen the Green River enter the Uinta Mountains and reach Red Canyon. Through melodramatic canyons that occasionally widen to valleys or basins, as at Brown's Park,[6] it flows out of Utah into Colorado and through the sublimities of Dinosaur National Monument into Utah again. In the Monument it is joined, at the immense cliff called Steamboat Rock, by the Yampa River. The Yampa, reaching this junction through a terraced canyon, has come down, past Steamboat Springs and Craig, Colorado, from the western slope of the Park Mountains.

The Green emerges from Dinosaur Monument through Split Mountain Gorge, a postscript to the violent Split Mountain Canyon. It is joined by White River, from another mingling of Colorado ranges, and heads across the first of the chromatic high plateaus of Utah, the Tavaputs, with its spectacular line of Brown (or Roan) Cliffs. We have no present need of it after, at the Utah village called Green River, it reaches the Colorado River. Which up to here, if there were logic or justice in nomenclature, would be called what it used to be called, the Grand River.

On its way to this meeting the Colorado has at one stretch wandered to within twenty miles of the Yampa, but it rises well to the east of it, in Grand Lake at the western boundary of Rocky Mountain National Park. This is Middle Park, one of four great high basins in Colorado, and we are now in a jackstraw pile of mountain ranges, all huge, many of them higher and more rugged and forbidding than the Wind Rivers. The names of two ranges are commendable, the Rabbit Ears and the Never Summer Mountains. The latter is the translation of a Ute phrase which, so a learned friend tells me, has a double negative in it, so that properly they are the Never No Summer Mountains. Their high country seems infinitely desolate; no mountains were ever better named.

To the mouth of Grand Lake the Park Range, whose crest is here the Continental Divide, has changed its axis to east-west, almost ninety degrees from what it is above the source of the Yampa. At its northern foot is North Park. Near its western edge two creeks come together and from there on are the North Platte River. It flows north into Wyoming and where the Sweetwater River joins it, its valley comes into the main stream of Western history for it was the route of the Oregon Trail. (We have all but touched the Sweetwater before; gathering brooks from the southern end of the Wind River Mountains, it flows eastward from South Pass.) The North Platte makes the long angle cursed by innumerable drivers of emigrant wagons, northeast to Casper, Wyoming, southeast to Torrington, and on into Nebraska. Just below the Nebraska town that bears its name it is joined by the South Platte. It has come 660 miles from its source. As the Platte River, the merged streams flow 310 miles farther and reach the Missouri. This junction, the Equator of the Missouri in fur-trade days, is 1042 miles below the mouth of the Yellowstone and 1830 miles from the Three Forks.

The South Platte is 442 miles long; shorter than the North Platte, it has had a more tortuous course. The largest and most beautiful of the high Colorado basins is South Park, the Bayou Salado of the trappers. Its tremendous western wall is the Park Range, here on a north-south axis again but no longer carrying the Continental Divide.[7] Near it, on a line northeast of Leadville, three creeks form the South Platte. It flows southeast and then, with the vast bulk of Pike's Peak due east, it turns northward and finds the lowest level through the Front Range. The long course brings it out to the foothills south of Denver and then to the plains. It is an edge-of-the-plains river to Greeley and a plains river from there on.

Leadville is 10,000 feet high on the western slope of the Parks, which contain a number of the fifty-one Colorado peaks that rise above 14,000 feet. Farther west are the Sawatch, which has the highest average elevation of all the Colorado ranges, the highest peak (Mt. Elbert), and the tremendous monoliths called the Collegiate Peaks. This highest ridge carries the Continental Divide. In the valley between these ramparts, to the northwest of Leadville, is the head of the Arkansas River. It flows southeastward through an intricacy of valleys and canyons, of which the Royal Gorge is the most celebrated but not the most spectacular, and comes out of the Front Range between Cañon City and Pueblo. All this distance it is a notably beautiful mountain river; here it becomes one of the most bedraggled of plains rivers. It crosses the rest of Colorado and most of Kansas (in this stretch it was the route of the Santa Fe Trail and the southern boundary of the United States till our war of conquest) and then heads southeastward across a corner of Oklahoma and the whole width of Arkansas. It is 1450 miles from its source when it empties into the Mississippi.

One principal river system remains, that of the Rio Grande. Its source is far from the central meeting place of the waters I have been describing, 120 miles southwest of Leadville, in one of the most beautiful of all mountain ranges, the San Juans. (A few miles west and northwest of here are mountains and waters we must deal with later, particularly the Uncompahgre peaks and the Gunnison River, which flows into the Colorado.) It flows between its parent range and the La Garita peaks eastward into the fourth of the great parks, the San Luis Valley. It crosses this southward and bisects New Mexico, becoming a Texas river at El Paso, beyond which I need not trace it.

This summary panorama has been confined to the belt of ranges called the Rocky Mountains that traverses the United States from north to south with only inconsiderable ellipses. They are the dominant mountains and the principal conditioner of the West.

The West has, however, two other belts of mountains that are fundamental in its conditioning. One of these stretches along the eastern border of California and bisects Oregon and Washington, the Sierra Nevada plus the Cascades. Topographically continuous, they are geologically as different as it is possible to be. The Sierra is not a system but a single range, incomparably the biggest one in the United States. It has much more and on the whole better literary celebration than any other. In some ways—I risk assault from the California outdoorsman by thus limiting the statement—it seems to a casual traveler the most imposing.[8] Along the Pacific coast, in some places at the water's edge, there is a third series of mountains, collectively called the Coast Range, though they are a number of separate ranges. They vary considerably in size, height, and importance. Some of them, though of only moderate height, are among the most rugged on the continent; some are hardly more than hills.

But the Rockies are the principal determinant of the West, where everything is determined by mountains. We may some day think of all the West that lies east of the Sierra-Cascade system as, economically and even socially, an appendage to the part that lies west of it. But the fundamentals of geography are what counts and the trans-Sierran west will always be, geo-biologically, an appendage to the Rockies.

The traveler, the successor of Lieutenant Pike and the greenhorn with the wagon train, sees them first as a cloud and then as an impassable barrier. Both impressions are just. The importance of the ever-present illusion will, I trust, become evident as this treatise goes on. And as the traveler himself goes on, he finds that there are ways through and across the barrier. We have seen South Pass, which historically was the most important of them, though comparatively few travelers (none who go by rail) see it today and hardly any cross all of it. Historically, one went from here on to cross the Cascade barrier, most often, by the Columbia River canyons, and the Sierra, most often, by Donner Pass. There was a southern route across the Rockies but it was rather around than through them for in New Mexico the diminishing ranges are widely spaced. Proceeding down the valley of the Gila River, this route turned the southern end of the Sierra. There was another natural and comparatively easy route through the Rockies far to the north, by Marias Pass, at the southern boundary of Glacier National Park. Though the trappers used it and the rumor of its existence stayed alive, it was not discovered for practical use till 1889. Till the railroad age it would have had little use, anyway.

These are the "natural," which is to say the easiest, routes across the Continental Divide and the Rockies. All but one of the railroads and all the main highways cross the great wall by other routes. The discovery of suitable passes was exceedingly difficult; the construction of routes to and through them required technological developments not achieved till well past the Civil War. The foolhardy Fremont precipitated a disaster by trying to discover a route through the San Juans; the motorist who crosses the Divide by Berthoud Pass on U.S. 40 is the indifferent heir of the first revolution in American engineering.

Like the desert, the mountains are uninhabitable. Yet the West lives because and by means of them.

"Be fruitful and multiply and replenish the earth and subdue it." Unlike his kindred creatures man can subdue the earth, within limits and terms set by nature. History is a record of his efforts to determine the limits and find out what the terms are. A favorable natural environment is one where the limits are wide apart and the terms flexible; here populations cluster and societies develop complex organization. In other places the limits are close together. The play permitted human action is slight; the terms granted it are strait and inflexible. In such areas populations are meager and society but simply organized, if at all: the jungles of the Amazon, the subarctic lands. There are also places where the limits approach each other so closely that, though man may maintain himself in them, he cannot inhabit them. It may be well to keep the continent of Antarctica in mind and to recall the American pioneer.

When he got here from Europe in the sixteenth century he found a richness of which the wonder has not yet ceased to dazzle the race. It put a slowly incrementing but not excessive strain on his intelligence and ways of life. He met extremes of heat and cold and a variation and variability of climate beyond what he was used to. There were diseases to which he had inherited no immunity. Differences of flora, soil, weather, and growing seasons required him to modify his agriculture and his handicrafts and other skills. Similar, slowly developing adjustments of his political and societal techniques necessarily followed. He had to learn wilderness and crafts and skills from the primitives he found here and to modify them too so that he could use them for his purposes. All this was a job rather of adjusting known methods to unfamiliar circumstances than of developing new methods to meet new circumstances. In the end he had made so many adjustments that the result was something truly new under the sun, but he had made them gradually, over a long time, and by small individual adaptations. And this was true alike of individuals and of their societies.

Those who turned northward found out soon enough that there were areas where nature had said No Farther. It was a long time, however, before those who moved westward found that there were areas where nature had said Farther Only Whereas and If. And most of us moved to the west; the design of the continent made the sun's course the direction of our wayfaring. The great interior valley of the United States, which we had traversed by the middle of the nineteenth century, was a favorable habitat; the limits were wide and the terms flexible; it required only such adjustments in already mastered techniques as the carburetor of a car may require when autumn mornings turn from cool to cold. They were within the competence of anyone who could use a wrench; we made them so easily, adding them to so great and so long-familiar a store of inherited ways, that it became impossible to believe that more thoroughgoing or more difficult adjustments would ever be required of us. But crossing into the West, we reached an area where the limits set by nature to man's activity were narrow and the terms rigid. Radical adjustments were necessary but customary experience had so shared our methods and so conditioned our thinking that we could barely be brought to accept the proof. Western history is the record at once of the proof and of our reluctance to accept it. Neither the West nor the United States at large has yet entirely understood it or entirely accepted it. Neither, it is safe to guess, ever will.

The terms began to change at the place where the prairies became the plains and change became radical at the place where the plains became the high plains. Where, if you like, the tall grass ended and the short grass began. It did not help that the physical boundaries of these regions were both invisible and somewhat variable in space and time: that there was here a desert not recognizable as such and shifting, more or less cyclically, much as dunes of a sand desert shift. Beyond the high plains were the unmistakable deserts and the mountains, separate, successive, alternating, mingling, or jumbled together. The sum of them is the West. And the wilderness techniques which the Americans had so superbly developed while occupying the eastern half of the continent shattered against the West—against the geography, topography, and climates of the West. New techniques for subduing the earth had to be developed. This made certain that many social, political, and legal institutions which had been developed to the eastward would have to be so modified that they might as well be called new. Here was an imperative, a fiat, a *must*. We have been forced to act on it but we do not altogether believe it.

All this can be said more simply. The limits which nature sets to life and society are narrower in the West than elsewhere in the United States. Nature's terms are more rigid. The penalty for violating the terms or trying to widen the limits is more prompt and more drastic.

The West, thirty-nine percent of the area of the United States, must be seen as a society narrowly constrained by nature's absolutes. It exists under sanctions far more rigid than those which govern life and society elsewhere. It exists in, so to speak, a very narrow life zone; and this metaphor corresponds closely to one of the actual life zones that anybody may see governing the societies of plants as he travels up a mountain. Beyond either boundary of that zone human society is impossible and though man may maintain himself in the area, he may not inhabit it. Moreover, the terms are so rigid that even within the life zone of the West disaster to society on a varying scale is always possible. Indeed, that is one of the terms: disaster is a constant possibility and the West must live with it as it does with the local weather. But there is something else as well: if the possibility of disaster is constant, so is the possibility of natural catastrophe. Disaster, let us say, may destroy a crop or a town or a valley. Catastrophe might destroy half the West.

It is deserts and mountains; it is desert where it is not mountains. Desert and mountains are both uninhabitable, but the West's life zone is a desert where society exists by means of the mountains. It exists, in fact, by means of a perfectly visible, tangible, and even measurable vertical zone—a zone not of life but of snow. The West is the garden of the world but if it did not have a snow-pack line which may be averaged at 7,000 feet of altitude, it would be as empty and as meaningless for mankind as the Sahara.

The Westerner is a man who perforce lifts up his eyes to the hills. From them cometh not his strength alone but his life. And from them, at any time, may come his destruction.

Chapter Two
Damnedest Country
Under the Sun

We must now make a more precise determination but can get no help with it out west. For the West has come to think of itself as a small blue cloud.

You can buy the whole cloud for five cents at any drugstore, cigar counter, or newsstand in the West. Where does the West begin? Out where the skies are a trifle bluer. The sun is a little brighter there, the snows a trifle whiter, the breeze fresher. These meteorological observations, which correspond more or less to the facts, are less specific, however, than the poem's sentiments. The West begins, it says, out where the handclasp's a little stronger, where the smile dwells a little longer. The bonds of home are a wee bit tighter, fewer hearts in despair are aching, there's laughter in every streamlet flowing, there's more of singing and less of sighing, more of giving and less of buying, and a man makes friends without half trying.

This definition was composed by a Chicago newspaperman who went west and worked for a time in Denver, then got out and, after a spell on the New York *Tri-bune,* devoted himself to writing books about the region he had abandoned. That personal history is appropriate, and it is to the point that the date of the poem, so far as I can learn, is 1916. This fantasy, which is Eastern and literary, began to be popular about 1890 when a new style of magazine writing developed, but it is only one of a sequence of fantasies that the East has cherished about the West over a period of more than three centuries. The significance of the date is that the twentieth century was well along before the West began to accept the Eastern-made fantasies and to elaborate them. I find it a happy coincidence that dude ranching, theretofore a small and informal business, began to expand at about the same time. The date has great cultural importance. The West was substituting for its established, corrosively disenchanted images of itself the romantic nonsense of the Old West myth. A decisive point has been reached when a culture begins to believe its own advertising copy.

I have amused myself constructing tenable alternatives to the criteria stated by the poem and picking up other, locally held ones as I go about the West. The foremost literary man in the West is forced to make a couple of trips to New York every year. His father, a native of the disenchanted West, looked forward to such journeys as a respite from fried potatoes for breakfast, but he does not because he always develops what appears to be influenza. He takes a plane or train home and presently the virus leaves him; at that point the West begins. All along the fringe country you can get local determinations: Ogallala, Nebraska, you are told, is West but North Platte is Middle West. The increased circulation of the *Ladies Home Journal* has destroyed one that was pretty reliable, the components of the salad served you. All others, and this is revealing, relate to horse opera clothes, whether worn or offered for sale. A few big hats may not be altogether convincing, but if at a Kiwanis luncheon the checkroom is full of them, you may be sure. Similarly if there is a store called, approximately, Western Outfitters, you have crossed over into camp ground.

But we can be a good deal more precise than that. The West begins out where the average rainfall drops below twenty inches.

As always with the West, there is variability here, and contrast, unpredictability, and illusion. There is a zone of varying width and shape and it is not square with the compass. Its boundary shifts east and west as much as three hundred miles—meaning the line west of which twenty inches of rain falls in a year. Nor is "twenty inches" an absolute; it is an expedient generalization. We are dealing with the amount of rainfall that enables agriculture to be conducted without irrigation and there are modifying factors—season of greatest precipitation, altitude, wind, rate of evaporation—and these necessitate the concept of "equivalent rainfall." Equivalent rainfall makes the eastern boundary of the West not a straight north-south line but an irregular curve. In the southeastern corner of Texas, the West begins not far inland from the Gulf of Mexico. In Kansas the line of twenty inches is four-fifths of the way to the Colorado line but the West begins long before you get there. The Ninety-eighth Meridian of west longitude corresponds fairly well to the line of twenty inches. The Hundredth Meridian corresponds somewhat less closely, but well enough, to the line established by the modifying factors and equivalent rainfall. Geographical convention has established the Hundredth Meridian as the beginning of the West; it is an expedient convention and will be adhered to here.

The Hundredth Meridian divides the Dakotas in tolerably equal halves. It crosses the Missouri River half-way between the Grand Detour and Pierre. Rather more than half of Nebraska, including the town of North Platte, is west of it. Only a third of Kansas is west of it; it misses Dodge City by a little more than a hoot and less than a holler. It is the boundary of the Texas panhandle and may serve here as the boundary of West Texas.

However, climate may shift the boundary three degrees east or west and in extremity even farther. Human folly and one of the most abiding of the West's illusions have repeatedly moved it much farther west. Divide North Dakota into three zones of equal width. Normally, if that word has meaning in this context, the central zone, which the Hundredth Meridian bisects, would be the marginal one. Normally, agriculture would be stable in the eastern zone because there is sufficient rainfall there, and stable in the western zone because irrigation is always necessary there. This central zone, in fact, was the one which John Wesley Powell, the great prophet of the West, said must forever exist on the knife edge— since in some years there would be enough water for crops and in other years there wouldn't be.

But in reality the uncertain zone is much wider than that central third, wider in human folly, illusion, and tragedy, and wider in the variability of rainfall. And let me say at once that though we may speak with acceptable accuracy of a wet and dry cycle, it is not symmetrical; it is an uneven and unpredictable oscillation.

This chapter is written in December 1954. Last year the dry half of the cycle pushed the line of insufficient rain all the way across the Dakotas to the Red River and, south of that river, well into Minnesota. This year the pattern was different and the Dakotas were normal, as that word applies here, and some portions of New Mexico and Arizona that had been drought-bound for five successive years were approaching normality again, but in Kansas the line of insufficient rainfall pushed east of

Topeka, almost within sight of Kansas City. Similarly, in the wet half of the cycle years of abundant rain have swung the line westward to the Montana and Colorado lines. At such times hope and illusion have pushed it much farther west.

The West, then, is the United States west of the Hundredth Meridian. It is a country without rain enough to grow crops. A country with a deficit rainfall. A country which has crops and towns because it also has mountains, and because snow falls on the mountains in the winter and melts in the spring and summer, and flows down the rivers as water that can be taken to fields and town reservoirs.

Snow courses have been laid out in all mountain ranges. They are measured expanses, reasonably level and reasonably open, sited so that they will not lie in snow shadows or be unduly windswept. At stated intervals throughout the winter representatives of various federal and state bureaus, universities, and private businesses visit them to measure the snow pack. To measure its depth and the rate at which it is accumulating or diminishing, and to take core-boring just as geologists do when prospecting for oil or probing for bedrock. When these observations have been correlated with various others, the Bureau of Reclamation will predict—with reliable accuracy—how much water its dams must release to irrigation systems next summer, at what rates, and even in what weeks. Power companies will predict whether and when they will have to call on stand-by steam generating plants to firm up their power. Crop yields, crop loans, car loading, sugar and wine production, meat prices, hotel receipts, gasoline taxes, bank deposits—to some degree all these and many other matters can be forecast. Almost, the graph of the snow pack could tell a rural social worker how much bastardy she will report next year, or a priest how many marriages he will perform.

The altitude at which the useful snow deposits occur varies. In the mountains of northern Idaho it may be less than two thousand feet, in Arizona above eight thousand feet. Mainly it is high and I have already stated the generalized line of critical snow: it is seven thousand feet. In the West life, society, agriculture, business, and industry depend on the snow that falls at and above seven thousand feet.

A light winter means a hard summer. If the line withdraws to eight thousand feet, or as it sometimes does in the Sierra to ten thousand, we are in for trouble. The pressure of the snow drought on marginal agricultural lands, those on the fringes of irrigation systems which cannot be assured their full allotment, becomes ominously severe. Crops dwindle. Stockgrowers can move their herds only to certain summer ranges and keep them there only for a short season, and must sell in a falling market. Municipalities know that they will have to restrict the sprinkling of lawns. The anxiety that underlies and encloses the Western consciousness tightens toward dread.

It is an immemorial and unchanged dread. Purified by continence and emetics and prayer, the priests scatter the sacred corn meal to make roads for their chants and the supernaturals to travel. Yucca roots form soapy clouds in bowls of spring water. Snakes slither in zigzag paths, the gods are told that clouds and rivers and the breasts of women are sinuous, and the drums make the sound of the thunderbird's obsidian wings. A forest ranger thrusts a hollow rod into the snow. That thy people may have corn. The earth is the Pimas' sleeping nude who will conceive if a raindrop falls in her navel. Not when: *if.*

The tremendous exception must be noted, and then some contrasts.

West of the Cascade Mountains, Washington and Oregon are regions of abundant, and in one area extreme, rainfall. The abundance extends southward into California west of the Sierra, the average dropping as it goes. The line of twenty inches strikes the California coast near Monterey. South of it along the coast, including the city of San Diego, rainfall dwindles to ten inches. Inland from the coast, and this is important, the critical line is farther north.[1]

The Sierra creates the most extensive rain shadow. The line that marks a maximum of five inches circumscribes a huge irregularly shaped area, all of it called absolute desert here. It includes southeastern California, most of the narrow part of Nevada and half of western Nevada, almost as far north as the Idaho line, and a southwestern corner of Arizona. (The line of ten inches outside it circumscribes an area not only much larger but more significant.)

Well, absolute desert. The western edge of Yuma County, Arizona, gets some four inches of rain a year, the town of Yuma half an inch less. Most of the Nevada portion of this dry world is between three and four inches. So, out from the mountains, are the California counties of Inyo (the Panamint country), San Bernardino, and Riverside. (A hamlet in Inyo County which is named Bishop Creek has the lowest average rainfall of all recording weather stations in the United States, 1.49 inches.) The parade ground of movie stars and oil googolionaires, Palm Springs (in Riverside County), gets five inches. Imperial County averages the lowest rainfall of all counties in the country. The four recording stations show 2.8, 2.4, 3.1, and 3.3 inches.

Imperial County is thus absolute desert throughout— and it concentrates the West in a single vivid symbol. Scores, even hundreds of men and many thousands of horses, cattle, sheep, and swine have died of thirst here. But that was before the sleeping nude conceived. By artificial insemination.

This is Imperial Valley, the most productive farmland

in the world. Water that fell as snow in the Wind Rivers, the Uintas, the Uncompahgres, that has come down Flaming Gorge and the Black Canyon of the Gunnison, that has lain for some years reflecting the sky in Lake Mead above Hoover Dam—Colorado River water is brought to this mirage-swept hell, forsaken of all vegetation but creosote bush, and makes it the innermost garden-close of the Garden of the World. There are no frosts here and crops grow twelve months a year, some of them twelve times a year. Agriculture has ceased to be farming, it has become industrial production. Vegetables, melons, fruits are factory products, their growing season constantly shortened by selective crossing in the experiment stations and not infrequently by exposing them in the ground to some of the component rays of light. Their size is regulated to fit graded containers, the refrigerators from which they will be taken to the breakfast table, and the machines that pick some of them—for the fumbling human hand slows down the belt line. In 1900 there were only sidewinders here to watch the mirages.

And something else, the ever-present West, the omen of what may be. In geological times this was the valley of the Colorado River, and for a brief and terrible time in 1905 and 1906 it reverted. In fact, it was created by the river, which extended its mouth ever southward, dropping the silt collected from what are now the high plateaus, till that mouth got to where it is now, the Gulf of California. Between the lettuce fields and the great bore that rushes upriver at the mouth there is only a delta, and now the Colorado River silt is stopped by Hoover Dam. So year by year the river mouth that once built out to sea is eating farther upstream. There are those, exceedingly respectable geologists and hydrologists among them, who believe that nothing effective can be done to prevent it from ultimately taking over

Imperial Valley again. . . . Moreover, two or three hundred years from now Lake Mead will be solid silt.

But this is any part of the West speeded up in time-lapse movies. The cotton fields along the Gila and its inconsiderable affluents nowhere get as much as ten inches of rain and in places get as little as five inches. The world's largest and by far its greatest farm is the Central Valley of California, fifty thousand square miles (including its tributary valleys) of practically continuous gardens and orchards. Eighty percent of the world's dried-fruit pack is produced here; the Californians claim that half the fruit of the whole world is. Along its northwestern edge Central Valley does get the twenty inches of rain that will grow crops, though it does not get them in the growing season. Everywhere else, however, the rainfall of the Valley is less than the critical amount, and it progressively diminishes southward, so that the heart of the area gets less than ten inches. Almost all the Los Angeles Basin gets less than ten too. All the statistics of California agriculture are fabulous; even the Californians cannot easily push them farther than the facts. The state is second in the production of cotton and third in the production of rice—and first in that of twenty-five field, garden, and orchard crops. The bulk of two of them, lettuce and artichokes, is grown in regions of less than twenty inches of rain, and mostly in regions of less than ten. The industrial concentration of Southern California is set in the same aridity.

There is a true rain forest in Olympic National Park in Washington. Much of this coast gets 120 inches of rain, part of it more, some seaward islands a lot more, and the line of 110 inches extends well inland. In the Olympic Mountains and along the crest of the Cascades, those achingly beautiful cones, the snowpack is the equivalent of 140 inches of rain, twice what it is in the Sierra. Pierce County, Washington, lies at the western foot of the Cascades. Its lowland areas get 45 inches of rain. Travel east toward the high ridge; here a typical weather station gets an average 99 inches. Now cross the divide to Kittitas County and start down. At a station called Cle Elum the average has dwindled to 23 inches. Twenty-five miles farther east is Ellensburg and you have descended a thousand feet getting to it; Ellensburg gets nine inches of rain. You have come into another rain shadow and into the Washington desert. Ephrata, where the idea of the Grand Coulee Dam was born, gets 7.7 inches; Richland, which houses atomic secrets, gets 6 inches. At Richland you are 250 miles from the Olympic Mountains, which get our maximum average rainfall, 140 inches, and from the station that has the highest recorded, 146 inches.

Utah, which in everything except its society is the most dramatic Western state, simplifies the principle even more starkly. Salt Lake City, at the western foot of the Wasatch Mountains, gets 16 inches of rain a year. Travel forty miles due west from the Temple and you reach absolute desert. But just above the city, five thousand feet higher and less than three miles east, the Wasatch crest gets 43 inches. Forty-three less 16 equals 27, produced in a snow pack between 7000 and 9000 feet, above town—equals Salt Lake City.

The West is a desert. Its mountains are the oases that make its society possible. A phrase of Reed W. Bailey's, Director of the Intermountain Forest and Range Experiment Station of the Forest Service, exactly describes them. Mr. Bailey calls the mountains humid islands.

Desert and mountains have exerted an absolute determinism. Every generation has to learn that it is subject to no exception. Observe how it affected the exploration and occupation of the West.

East of the Mississippi movement westward followed the rivers not because they were drinking water but because they were roadways; you could travel more expeditiously by boat than by horse. Two centuries of wilderness culture made the Missouri River the inevitable route for the penetration of the West. It did serve as a route of exploration. It took the predecessors of Lewis and Clark to the mouth of the Platte and on to the mouth of the Yellowstone. It took Lewis and Clark to within a few miles of the Continental Divide (in Lemhi Pass, through the Bitterroot Mountains) by boat, though with infinite difficulty. Everywhere else penetration was on land, not by boat, but it nevertheless had to be by river valley, for men and horses had to have water. The Americans got to Santa Fe by the valley of the Arkansas River. They got to the interior west by the valley of the Platte, to the Columbia by the valley of the Snake, to transmontane Oregon (usually) by the valley of the Columbia, to California by the valleys of the Humboldt and the Gila.

I have already mentioned the circuitous route of the Great Medicine Road to South Pass. From eastern Nebraska to the Wyoming line it made a long, gently curving loop southward and then northward. From the Wyoming line it traced two sides of a right triangle, first northwest, then southwest. It followed the valleys of the Platte, the North Platte, and the Sweetwater. It had to follow them. Only here was there grass in sufficient supply for so many horses and oxen and grass grows so thickly only where there is so much water. But the absolute determinant of the Oregon Trail was this: only here was there water for men and stock to drink.

Butte is where it is because that is where "the richest hill of earth" is—but also because water could be brought to that hill from canyons and peaks near at hand. Butte has advertised itself as the toughest town on earth. In its past there was enough liquor, vice, eye-gouging, gang-fighting and murder to give it at least a fair claim to that much-converted championship, though it came

late. There may be hills far richer than Butte in the
Western areas now being prospected for uranium, where
the old booms are on again and some of the old fairy-tale
bonanzas are being repeated as I write, together with
the old wholesale slaughter of the lambs who buy stock.
But there will never be midways there, no Little Egypts
on "Rues de la Pay," no Hell on Wheels, no block-long
bars with costumed miners swigging champagne under
murals brought from Paris bordellos. It will be possible
to bring water to the mines and shipping points to sustain the labor done at them. But it will not be possible
to bring water for the Bucket of Blood and its tinhorns,
whores, and bouncers—water costs too much, there is
too little of it, it is too far away. Even at survival prices
it will not be possible to bring water enough to work the
ore. Which is to say that, though there may be a richest
hill on earth (or a number of them) and so a Butte, there
will never be an Anaconda in the rock deserts. It is incomparably cheaper to transport ore than to amass and
transport water in quantity. The ore will be taken to
places nearer the snow pack.

Thus simply the West has arisen as a valley civilization and will remain one. On the valley fringes, which is
to say peripherally, it is also a piedmont civilization, and
a later chapter will show that the foothills are an area
as tragic as the high plains.

A creek comes out of a canyon. The firstcomers
dammed it at the mouth of the canyon and conducted
its water over the alluvial fan, over such portions of the
foothills as were at a lower level than the mouth of the
canyon, along the sides of the valley that were at similar levels, and out over the valley floor. The main irrigation ditch, the acequia madre, ran at that primary level
and smaller ditches took its water to the fields. So there
were valley farms, a village or two, a church, a shipping
corral, eventually a station when the railroad built a
branch up the valley from the larger one at its mouth.

Sometime later a cooperative association which the farmers had organized went some miles farther up the canyon and at that higher elevation built a larger (and costlier) dam. So from such a flume or canal as my friend Sam observed, higher above the mouth of the canyon, water could be taken to fields at higher levels of foothills, farther up the sides of the valley, farther down the valley. Later a Water Company went still farther up the canyon and did the same thing on a larger scale. But everything about that Water Company, as indeed with most cooperatives, was misconceived and fated. All of them were financed speculatively, almost all of them were underfinanced, most of them envisaged creating a monopoly of water, and none of them came anywhere near a correct estimate of maintenance costs. The underestimates need not have been fatal but speculation and the dream of monopoly were—there was more water in their sock than in their reservoirs. Only the most miniature ones survive and these met the receiver long ago and will soon meet their angry God.

But there were and are the creeks. The soil of the desert was infinitely rich; in an arid country rain has not leached the minerals away. So, as the brooks that are so musical in the forests and so healing to the soul of industrial man—as the brooks were brought to the arid soil, Western civilization was established. Its history, violent throughout, has been most violent in contention over water, and of its innumerable bankruptcies most have been directly related to water.

On July 24, 1847, Brigham Young's party of seers and pioneers came through the Wasatch by the canyon ever since called Emigration. They emerged in Salt Lake Valley at the site now marked by the most beautiful monumental sculpture an American has ever produced. A small advance party which had preceded him by two days had already laid out some fields, not far from where a statue of him now stands at the corner of Main and

South Temple. ("That's Brigham all right," old Gentiles used to say, "with his back to the Temple and his hand stretched toward the bank.") They were bringing water to their planting from City Creek, whose canyon debouches just a little to the east. City Creek Canyon, Red Canyon, Emigration Canyon, Parley's Canyon, Mill Creek Canyon, Little Cottonwood Canyon, Cottonwood Canyon—they are why Salt Lake City exists.

There was a scattering of gold in the gravel bars of Cherry Creek but the disappointed miners who learned how thin it was washed their socks in what gave its valley incalculable value. Later on when the mountains farther on proved to hold a bonanza, there had to be a city. Cherry Creek and the fortunately convenient South Platte—that is Denver. And now Denver is getting water by tunnel through the Continental Divide, by engineering works that will eventually cost many hundreds of millions of dollars as they go farther and, from additional dams, get more water to be pumped through even more fantastic works. . . . Los Angeles crossed the Sierra to bring water from Owens Lake by an aqueduct 240 miles long. Then it brought water from the Colorado River by an aqueduct of the same length, across a desert which I have already described. And water from this aqueduct flows another hundred miles to supply cities that have joined Los Angeles in its gigantic enterprise.

But this is anywhere in the West. El Paso and Albuquerque are the Rio Grande Valley. Idaho spuds and sugar are the valleys of Henry's Fork, the Snake, the Boise, and the Payette. Montana is the valleys of the Missouri, the Yellowstone, and the multiply named Clark's Fork.

Into the desert as far as water can be taken, water that originated as snow at an altitude of 7000 feet.

Bring a main irrigation canal out of a canyon and lead it along one of the hillsides that are the valley walls. Twenty or thirty feet wide, flowing clear mountain water, its concrete sides sloping outward, it follows the contour line. Merely to watch it flow is soothing and from a plane its curves have the calm beauty of engineering. Sagebrush grows at its uphill bank, or rabbit bush, greasewood, the squat cactus called prickly pear. (We may be sure of the sage; the others will depend on the altitude and the degree of the alkalinity of the soil.) Downhill from it are truck gardens, orchards, fields of alfalfa, of sugar beets, Brigham City peaches, Wenatchee apples, Rocky Ford cantaloupes. Where a bridge crosses it you may with ten paces step from desolation to the Garden of the World, from death to life.

It is a violent contrast, a dramatic contrast, and it is ever-present, but it is only one of many. The West is drama, contrast, and violence. The wide-open spaces are vast distances: so great that necessarily the Westerners have evolved a sense of the relationships between space and time different from that of the other Americans. But vastness is never uniform.

Your road drops down less than two hundred feet vertically from the habitation of the owl and the bittern, from a sagebrush plain crawling with heat mirage, into the sunken canyon of the Snake River—and among cottonwood groves you buy at a farmer's roadside stand a watermelon that has been chilled by the Thousand Springs. Tioga Pass plunges from the alpine meadows of Yosemite to the stinking brim of Mono Lake. With the land an unbroken plain before your eyes you stroll through sagebrush so sparsely spaced that you observe the tint of rose-pink in the clay, and Bryce Canyon opens up at your feet. Or through a grove of ponderosa and what drops away at your feet is Red Canyon. An hour in a car will take you from piñon and juniper to lichens, from sand dunes to glaciers. An hour in a plane will take you across a red-rock desert, a blue and roan plateau, three mountain ranges, a metropolis, a herd of wild horses, and fifty ghost towns. Cross Nevada by car and the desert hypnotism will present it to you as a series of plains with can-can ruffles of hills along the hem; cross it by plane and you see that it is the most corrugated and crenelated of all landscapes, a vertigo of changing relief. Montana has both the highest and the lowest of temperatures on record.[2] Jim Bridger was not lying when he said that he had caught fish in Yellowstone Lake, which is too cold to swim in, and without taking a step cooked them in a boiling spring. The highest point in the United States is Mount Whitney, 14,495 feet; the lowest point is at its eastern foot, Bennett Wells in Death Valley, 276 feet below sea level. Pioneer wives made bread and pie of the blue-flowered camass, a food staple of the Northwest Indians; its near relative with a white flower is quite properly called the Death Camass for it is fatal.

One of these alternations needs some development here. To climb a mountain, or to drive up one, is to travel not only through altitude but through latitude. Several passes in Colorado that take highways across the Continental Divide are above 11,000 feet at the summit. Start, then, at Colorado Springs, whose altitude is 5900 feet. Just to the east are the plains and there is no need to specify the grasses. We are just too high, or alternatively just too far north, to see in quantity the characteristic association of piñons and junipers. There is an abundance of sagebrush and saltbrush. Wherever there is water there are cottonwoods, wherever there are streams there are willows. Box elders are common, oak brush fairly common. This is typical plains vegetation and at this latitude it extends to about 6000 feet. The next two thousand feet may be called the foothills zone; at this latitude it is 6000–8000 feet but in some places it is much lower. Oak brush is almost universal in its lower stratum, willow, alder, and birch common though diminishing. We have reached the evergreens and this is pre-eminently the altitude of ponderosa pine, blue spruce, and Douglas fir. The next zone, 8,000–10,000, is montane. Douglas fir is still common here and so is ponderosa but the principal pine is lodgepole. We have also reached aspen, and at the upper edge come Engelmann spruce and alpine fir. The next zone is the sub-alpine and it ends at timberline, in this latitude about 11,500 feet. Here the principal species are Engelmann spruce, alpine fir, and limber pine; they have shrunk much, the growth is so slow that you cannot differentiate the annual rings, and as they approach timberline they are dwarfs. The lesser vegetation too has fallen off sharply from the scores of species of shrubs and hundreds of grasses and flowering plants in the lower zones. Above timberline is the alpine zone: lichens, mosses, small tundra plants, an Arctic vegetation. A two-hour drive from the Broadmoor Hotel, a little more than a vertical mile, has taken you two thousand miles north.

It can be done gigantically in time. At the bottom of the Grand Canyon the Colorado River has cut deep into the earth's oldest rock, the schists and gneisses and granites of the Archeozoic Era. Ascend Bright Angel Trail and you will rise through the Archeozoic and Paleozoic to the Kaibab Limestone of the Permian Period at the rim, and you will have crossed the deposits of every geological period except two in this history of creation. From this display case the Ordovician and Silurian are omitted, for reasons given in Schuchert and Dunbar, *Outline of Historical Geology*.[3] Now cross the Painted Desert to Zion National Park and, period by period, you will traverse the Mesozoic; go on to the Cenozoic at Bryce Canyon and you will have seen all Time. Mr. Edwin Corle puts it more succinctly than Schuchert and Dunbar: "[The visitor] will have run the gamut of geological history; he will have passed through every phase of the earth's development; he will have seen the home of every species of life since the first algae swam in the primordial sea; and he will have done it all in the space

of one day."[4] Two billion, three hundred million years.
Such matters as majesty and sublimity in the Western
landscape and the awe and related emotions which they
evoke in an attuned beholder are not within the compass of this book, which has a pedestrian purpose. But
this theme of Time and its derivation from Chaos, which
I mentioned in the preceding chapter, must be cited in
relation to the Western psyche. I have already said that
the Tetons are a gothic range. The Lewis Mountains are
the principal justification of Glacier National Park; the
peaks are not remarkable enough for height but they
have been shattered, crushed, sheared off, folded, and
piled on one another. (The Lewis Overthrust of the textbooks has piled the oldest strata on top of the more recent ones.) All that makes the Grand Canyon assimila-
ble is the perception, far off and long delayed, that there
are bounds to space; its perspectives are finite, if only
just. The line of the Grand Mesa is half the diameter of
sight. If the Front Range is thrown across the visible
world as if, señor, God had no care for time, the amazed
mind gradually becomes aware that time has brought
them into meaning. The Sangre de Cristo, the Uncompahgres and Sawatch, the Sawtooths, the Uintas are the
Grand Canyon inverted; the Sierra is a tilted block four
hundred miles long; and for such as these there is no
scale but their own—and the awareness that time is beginning with them or at least beginning to begin. This
is the architecture of earth's travail, of fire, ice, and
melting snow—and it is the landscape of time beginning
to impose order. It is a landscape where, if there are
algae, there will eventually be society; the world is beginning to be. Out of Time, time; out of Chaos, order. In
a way. Of a kind.

There is much-repeated architecture of wind and
rain; its landscape is outside time, it is almost outside
space, it has no omen of man or society. The badlands,
malpais in the Southwest and there usually of lava, are

unearthly. They are a landscape of the moon, in fact of the dark side of the moon, a fantasy of outer space. They are chaos. To a colorblind man they would be anti-human; with color they remain inhuman, lifeless; they are unearthly but they are absolute spectacle. No mind can bring them into time.

The weather is as violent as the landscape.

The big snows get featured by the wire services. Fifty automobiles, or five hundred, are stalled below a pass: the number is imposing and human-interest stuff can be written by the long ton. (Lovers on their way to be married will be delayed.) A freeze follows prolonged snows and some cattle are said to be dying. (Usually, they are only suffering a slight weight loss and if post-Judean methods had affected the Western range-stock business they would not be where they are anyway.) The Air Force dispatches squadrons of planes to drop baled hay to a few of them and public relations officers paste up scrapbooks of clippings for the Old Man; the stockmen's lobby gets, or thinks it gets, a powerful as-sist in its efforts to raise tariffs and steal the nation's forests. A school bus slithers to a stop in a drift and the rescue is a combined operation: highway department, state police, a battery of bulldozers and scrapers from a construction camp, another battery from a federal agency or an army base, and fifty reporters coming in by plane to make sure that the kiddies, who are on a main highway ten miles from help, first break and then heal the great heart of America.

The most spectacular heart interest in recent years came in January of 1951, when the Southern Pacific streamliner, the City of San Francisco, was stuck in the Sierra snow just below Donner Summit, and passengers and crew could not be taken out until the third day. The railroad mobilized its full resources, part of the Sixth Army and several regiments of volunteer skiers and snowshoers joined them, there were dog sleds, snow tractors, and a helicopter—the last an inspiration, for the Summit is more than 7,000 feet high and at such an altitude current helicopters could be little more than stage properties. It was drama and for five days newspapers and radio stations got out of it all that was in it and a good deal more. The publicity was a useful reminder that there are big storms. The drama of threat and deliverance was intensified by the memory of the emigrant party whose name the Pass preserves, who died or fed on the bodies of those who died at Donner Lake, two miles down from the Summit.

This is news but the big snows keep on occurring unnoticed by the wire services. Nobody died in the streamliner, nobody was more than moderately uncomfortable, and yet I saw no census of how many Californians and Nevadans had died of premature heart attacks on their way to town through that same storm, how many ranchers had frozen to death trying to do something for stock that the Air Force was not summoned to, how many watchmen and trackwalkers and linemen had been buried under slides. A busful of school kids stalled on U.S. 40 a few miles from town is news, but not the rancher who froze to death with his wife and infant child when they got stalled on a back road some miles from home, nor the road crew or trailer combine buried under an avalanche in the line of duty. It is not news that the work has to be done, the goods kept moving, the roads kept open, the stock fed, the deliveries made, the wires and dams and rails and beacons inspected.

Worse still when the blizzard has the full sweep of the plains. This is the real mankiller, cattle-killer, even tree-killer. It blows the snow in laterals, parallel with the ground, and turns it to razor-edged particles of ice. Men die on the way back from the barn. The blizzard is a north wind and it does not last as long as a colder gale that comes straight out of the north, "with nothing but a barbed wire fence this side of the Pole." Even if you do not hear the radio warnings you are supposed to know the signs of its coming and so not get caught in it. But what if you do? What if you get caught in your car or on foot or horseback with only the lee of a bluff for shelter? The gale may blow for three days, or five days, with the thermometer below zero. When it blows out at last, the mercury may drop to forty or fifty below. Smoke from a ranch house chimney rises a hundred feet straight up, or three hundred feet. The blue arch of the sky glistens black. The temperature may not rise to minus 20 degrees for a week, or to zero for a month.

You are not supposed to get caught in a blizzard. Range cattle must, and the most careful and intelligent rancher will lose a few and the slipshod rancher may lose many. Men and women do get caught, more every year than make the papers. In the back country and the range country, you must run your chances, which are not good. Elsewhere highway patrols and good communications, state and county acceptance of responsibility, and the improved machinery developed by the Arctic war have reduced the hazard. The Montana Highway Commission has abolished most of the little shacks it used to maintain, where the stormbound wayfarer could get shelter. . . . There was one near a historical marker—Montana has the best markers in the country—somewhere out in the eastern plains. Nothing else was in sight, north, south, east, or west, not so much as a shed or a gravel pile this side of any horizon. ("Damnedest country under the sun. You can look farther and see less than anywhere else on earth.") The shack pleased some touring school teachers who stopped to read the marker while I was photographing it. Montana had been pleasing them quite a lot, I gathered, and now this. How thoughtful of the state to provide toilet facilities so far from town.

More damn winds. The plains wind that is never still and drove the pioneer farmwife mad because it never was; it can burn the crops up in the summer and in the dry years it multiplies the drought. The Washoe Zephyr which Mark Twain had so much fun with; it has parallels in many places; a minor one that unpredictably and always for exactly twenty minutes at a time howls symphonies silent at Denver's Red Rocks Theater. The beloved Chinook, the "black wind" of the Indians for it comes when a bank of black clouds rears up in the west. It turns midwinter to late spring in fifteen minutes, melts snow like a blowtorch, uncovers grass for stock, is a perfume in the nostrils and a smile in the heart. (And like many Western joys it is dangerous; if it ends too soon and is followed by a quick freeze, it may cover the grass with ice instead of uncovering it. Just such a climax was the final and most destructive part of the Big Freeze of 1886–1887 that finished off the Cattle Kingdom.) The steady updraft on the western slope of all ranges is in some places, and unpredictably in others, a roaring gale; on eastern slopes its analogous downdraft can drop an airline faster than its instruments can record it and so bring the plane crashing into a mountain which the flight deck thinks it is clearing by a couple of thousand feet. Through some passes the wind surges unceasingly. It is always a hard wind through San Gorgonio Pass, for instance, and in April or May it roars into a steady gale. It is literally a sand blast, its abrasion as sharp as the norther's ice particles, and when it gets down to the Colorado Desert it becomes a violent sandstorm. Throughout the desert country there are frequent sandstorms; they can come at any time but are direly repeated in the summer. They drive people indoors, those who can go indoors, are deeply depressing, rasp the nerves worse than the skin. Usually they are short, up to a few hours at most.

But the duststorm is man-made, made by the stockman and the wheat farmer, and it is far worse.

You can see miniature duststorms on plowed land at nearly any time. A wind lifts dust from fields of sugar beets or new wheat thirty or forty feet into the air, and a Colorado plain will look like a misty autumn morning in New England. Intensify this and spread it over a larger area and you get the ordinary duststorm. It lifts the soil a couple of hundred feet, carries it half a mile or a mile or two miles, and lets it fall. It gets into the table of statistics only if visibility falls below a mile. Behind it the sun is a bronze moon. It may end in twenty minutes or it may last an hour. A worse one will reduce visibility three-quarters and turn the sun a sick green. These, however, are local phenomena. They distribute some of Bill's topsoil over Joe's fields; he may get it back next month, though in a less useful form. They are the more enraging if Joe has been applying all the principles expounded by the Soil Conservation Service, so that his soil stays put. Bill's topsoil then falls on Joe's crops.

The refusal of the West to learn from its own bankruptcies is obdurate in direct proportion to the richness of its possessions. Large areas of eastern Washington wheatland have soil deep enough to evoke envy in Iowa—most of them steeply slanting and ready to blow at a mere sneeze. SCS has made less progress here than anywhere else in the United States. "Let it blow," a good many Washington wheat ranchers have said to me, "there's no end to it." From his Cadillac such an honest husbandman sniffs at my old Chevrolet, and I remember that there never has been an end of anything in the West till the end came. My taxes bring water to his land now and will support his family when the next drought strikes, but the idea is, clean up big now and get out.

The big duststorms are phenomena of drought. Crop failures leave the ground bare over green areas and now the long, hard winds have something to work with. A "black roller" lifts a solid bank of soil a mile, or up to three and a half miles, into the air and takes off eastward with it. This is not mist but midnight; the sun is not bronze or green, it is invisible. In the 1930s in an area of 51 million drought-stricken acres in the southern plains 9 million acres blew out to form the dustbowl. There were twenty-two regional duststorms in the first year of the big blowout, 1934, among them the one I mentioned in the first chapter. There were forty in 1935, sixty-eight in 1936, seventy-two in 1937, sixty-one in 1938, thirty in 1939. In the northern plains the blowout was much less severe but more extensive, totaling 175 million acres.

Wheat and corn and, farther south, cotton. Science had developed varieties that flourished in the sparse rainfall of the high plains—which should not grow crops but remain grazing range. Technology had put tractors and combines within reach of the farmer's purse. Through the first war and on through the 1920s rain had been, on the whole, abundant. War and the later famine so raised the price of wheat that millions of acres were brought under the plow for the first time. When the market broke millions of additional acres were plowed, because a man had to raise a bigger crop. West of the plow there were always additional millions of acres. These had been dangerously impaired by the stockmen's universal practice of overgrazing. They ought to have been put under stringent regulation and brought back to health. Instead the high price of beef followed by the break in the market put more stock on them. All agricultural scientists, all meteorologists, all historians, all Westerners of middle age knew what would happen when the wet years should end. It had happened twice before on a big scale, repeatedly on a local scale. But now the area involved was far larger.

There followed the dustbowls and the "okies," the desperate people who left the plains in a mass migration, the third big one that the plains had seen. "It takes three bankruptcies to make a farm." It also takes a destruction of the local tax structure and sustained relief measures. The federal government had been periodically bailing out the plains ever since the 1870s; by now it had assumed the full responsibility for them the West had always demanded. Also the science of land management had by now progressed to the point where it knew how to control plains land in accord with natural law. So the government bought many millions of acres, primarily as a measure of relief, so that the owners would have a few dollars for a new start, but also to institute on it intelligent measures of land management. (This is the Bankhead-Jones land, so named for the act that authorized the purchase; it is also called the LU land for the Land Utilization Board that administered it.) Restorative measures were applied to it. A system of agriculture proper to the region was applied: land classification, cooperative grazing, diversified planting, contour plowing and related practices. Basically the plains would have a grazing economy, with crops grown only where it was safe to grow them and grown as an agreeable supplement to the raising of beef. Also, individual farms would be associated in cooperative efforts in districts large enough to make both planning and soil-control possible.

The Soil Conservation Service won a very great victory during the years between the dustbowl and the second war. The purchased lands were leased to individuals and corporations on terms that required intelligent land management. (And on terms much below their actual value.) By a series of rewards, of cash bonuses, farmers who had not been bought out but only supported during the bad years were induced to adopt the

same practices, form soil conservation districts, secure
their future, and develop a stable society in an area that
had never had one.

The West had learned its lesson. Quite certainly another drought would come but now the plains knew how
to survive it. An outsider who strayed into a grange or
farm bureau meeting in, say, 1939, as I sometimes did,
might have thought for a while that he was attending a
revival. The West had come to Jesus in a big way.

War came before drought did. Wheat was a bigger
bonanza than it had ever been. The dustbowl could not
be plowed up for it was organized in soil-conservation
districts and the law forbade. . . . Let's make one thing
entirely clear right now. It was not the tyrannical, com-
munistic federal government that forbade, not the long-
haired swivel-chair bureaucrat in Washington, but the
farmer himself. Not federal regulations but *state* laws
which the farmer had demanded that his own legislature
pass. . . . In central and south-central Colorado, well to
the west of the original dustbowl, was a large area that
had never been plowed; it was a grazing range somewhat impaired by overgrazing, as all Western ranges
are, but not dangerously so. Into this area rushed the
speculator, the boomer, the suitcase farmer, which is to
say the Westerner with a bonanza in his eye. He plowed
it up, got his investment back the first year, doubled it
the second year, would get out before the crash, and to
hell with blowouts. In the dustbowl area the sacred
rights of individual initiative and enterprise were hog-
tied by the despotic fiats of wide-eyed theorists. (Kissing
kin of those who, in other areas of our economy, had
never met a payroll.) The farmers descended on the legislatures again. The laws that gave soil conservation districts regulatory power over the agricultural practices of
their members were repealed.

"I can't tell you when the next dustbowl will come,"
an SCS drought specialist said to me in Washington in

the fall of 1947, "but I can tell you where it will come."
He crossed to a wall map, put one forefinger on a Colorado county, and with his other forefinger sketched an
irregular outline round it. In June of 1953, on assignment from a magazine, I arrived in that county on the
day when, at the demand of the Governor of Colorado,
the President of the United States declared it a disaster
area eligible for relief. We would bail out the sacred principle of land destruction once more.

That county was the center of a widening dustbowl.
There was another dustbowl in Texas and it too was
widening. Parts of the West were in their third year of
drought, parts in their fourth year. I crossed the same
area of Kansas that the young historian and I had crossed
in May 1940; it was baked brown and beginning to pul-
verize but it was not, as yet, blowing. As far east as
Lawrence I saw fissures and crevices in fields and private gardens which had, so the owners told me, no bottom. There was, however, sufficient water in the storage
dams and quite a bit in the rivers—as yet. It went on. In
February of 1954 Colorado saw something new, a black
blizzard. Gales brought snow roaring out of the north,
lifted the dust, mixed dust and snow together, and went
on. "The best place to get a Colorado farm," they were
saying, "is eastern Kansas." In Arizona, which to support its war boom had been living on its water capital
even in the pre-drought years, artesian wells had been
driven as deep as they could go. A belatedly desperate
legislature was on the verge of passing a long-needed
statute to control the drilling of new wells, to bring this
kind of water use into some kind of balance with supply.
In February large parts of Arizona had three days of
pounding rain, the storm went on to create floods in
Texas and was not followed by another; the statute was
dropped, Arizona would have no more drought. That
winter there was a snow drought in Colorado, with
roses blooming in Denver in February and the snow

pack retreating far up the Front Range. I was sent west again in May to take another look at the drought. The Colorado rivers were now down to one-fourth their normal flow. Just below the border, in New Mexico, there were areas on which no rain at all had fallen for thirty months. Thirty months, I remind you, are two and a half years.

Interpreting my assignment perhaps too scrupulously, when a black roller blew up I chartered a plane and set out to fly along its edge. I did not fly along its edge and I do not commend the attempt to lovers of serenity. But in retrospect I enjoy the symbolism: a historian of the West bumped about in the green twilight of the zone of whirlwinds that run ahead, and back there to the westward a solid blackness more than a mile high, the soil that is richer than gold.

In the desert, especially in the rock desert, in places where the pair of tracks that mark a road cross an arroyo, there is likely to be a sign warning you to be careful in wet weather. What wet weather? The tourist wonders. Well, half a dozen times a summer, or it may be once every third year. The sign is talking about the cloudburst storm. It may come in June or September but is more likely to come in July and August. Most Western weather comes from farther west, but this storm comes northward from the Gulf of Mexico and is bent westward. Thunder runs furiously along its edge. Lightning may strike the plain, raising a puff of dust like a shellburst; later you find the sand fused into glass for some yards around. An inch of rain, perhaps a tenth of the year's total, may fall in an hour, or in half an hour. But that statement gives no measure of the storm's violence, for most of that inch may fall practically at once. Five-minute downpours at the rate of five inches an hour are common, rates of more than eight inches an hour have been recorded.

In the rock deserts and the deserts of sagebrush and creosote bush, there is nothing to hold the rain. It finds the little gullies, which run into the larger gullies, which run into the arroyos—a natural system of catch-basins and drainage channels. So down the big ones comes a wall of water ten feet high, or twenty feet, carrying assorted jetsam with it, brush, dead piñon or juniper logs, corral posts, some drowned sheep or steers. It is so heavy with silt, gravel, and small boulders that it scours the arroyo deeper. . . . The Southwestern Indians planted crops where the arroyo widened at its lower end—indeed this area is the flood plain of a dry stream—and first learned irrigation by conducting flood water to a wider expanse of fields.

This is the flash flood. It occurs in many parts of the West and always has. Captain William Clark and Sacajawea, for example, came close to drowning in a dry wash downstream from the Great Falls of the Missouri. Anyone drowns today who cannot get out of its path—which is why the warning sign is set up in emptiness. For the cloudburst may have occurred so far away that you did not see the sky darken or hear the thunder. Half the explanation of the badlands is the cloudburst. But it appears here for use in a later chapter. For the West has constructed its own system of man-made catch-basins and drainage channels and put them to work efficiently destroying the most valuable areas of Western farmland.

Other storms are on the same scale. Tornadoes, not unknown in the mountains, are routine on the plains, but do comparatively little damage for they are short-lived and these are the wide-open spaces. The sand-devil of the desert is a miniature tornado; on a hot day fifty or two hundred of them may be in sight at once, some rising as high as five hundred feet. The plains hailstorm is as violent as a tornado and far more destructive; its opening barrage is comparable to that of a cloudburst.

It comes most commonly in the season when spring and winter wheat are most vulnerable, and it may destroy a crop in ten minutes.

On a cool, clear morning my wife and I were driving toward Williston. Easterners do not think of North Dakota as a beautiful country but it can be, especially when the slow, gigantic plains are a swirl of new wheat. The car skidded a little and when I looked back—my wife was driving—I saw a wide damp stripe across the highway, though there had been no rain. A few miles farther on we crossed another stripe, with another slight skid. At the third one we stopped and, getting out to look, encountered a stench indescribably foul. The stripe—rather it was like a rash of individual liver spots—was composed of crushed and matted grasshoppers. Marching in close order across the road, they had been made blacktop by the far from heavy traffic. We saw now that on a front perhaps two hundred feet wide there was no wheat on either side of the road, only stems curiously short and bent over as if by hail, naked white but beginning to turn brown. We went on and the fresh wind of early summer stiffened. I was driving half an hour later when it brought out of the southwest a small, low-drifting cloud that looked like a capful of mist coming in from the sea along the Maine coast. Then we were in a whirring fog and before I could close the left-hand windows at least a thousand grasshoppers had been blown into the car. We did our best to clear them out but before we could, most of the upholstery was devoured; close up, the stench was nauseating. The wind-driven swarm bumped on over the slopes to the north and disappeared. That night the Williston paper, estimating crop damage and uttering the routine Western curse about the weather, had a story of Northern Pacific trains stalled by columns of grasshoppers so wide and deep that the wheels could not get traction on the rails.

They have a malignant voracity. They eat, the saying is, everything but shingles and the poisons that are spread for them. They are especially fond of silk. The first Forest Service smoke-jumpers found that their parachutes had been devoured by the time a packer could get to them, and shifted to unappetizing nylon. A woman who hangs a silk slip on a clothesline won't have a slip if the grasshoppers come by. I believe it is not true that they eat leather but you cannot tell wheat ranchers that they don't, and tales spread of saddles eaten off horses' backs and cowpokes finding themselves bootless when they wake.

The grasshoppers, which do about a quarter of a billion dollars' annual damage to Western agriculture, travel by flight when not wind-borne, if flight is the word for their obscene hedgehopping. *Anabius simplex,* which is less well publicized because more localized, is wingless and therefore infantry. Acre for acre, it does more damage and is far more repulsive. It lives in rangeland, particularly in the foothills, and there it stays till it has bred itself up to a population explosion, whereupon in brown, undulant columns up to three miles wide it marches on the cropland. Because it marched thus on the first plantings of 1848 in the Salt Lake Valley, it has ever since been called the Mormon cricket. God vouchsafed his Saints deliverance. Seagulls came in flocks so large they darkened the sky, or so the holy writers say. They gorged on the crickets—which neither trenches nor fires nor the labor of the entire Church had been able to halt—and then flew to Great Salt Lake, cast up their food so that the devoured crickets were (I am still quoting the Talmud) washed in mile-long windrows up that hideous shore, and went back to gorge again and again. So the crops were saved. The seagull has been a sacred bird in Utah ever since; a person who kills one is liable to a fine of five hundred dollars. Mahonri

Young has a remarkable sculpture in Temple Square, commemorating the miracle.

Having only semi-miraculous powers, the Department of Agriculture does what it can by scattering from planes dusts of sodium arsenate and fluosilicate and spreading baits of toxaphene. But the columns still come marching from time to time in the mountain West, especially in Nevada, and especially in drought years, when all plagues are intensified. I have seen them only by hundreds, and confess that I prefer the company of rattlesnakes. A scientist who has seen many of the columns tells me that they look like rivers of syrup, thinks lava must flow in just the same way, and has left a remark in my memory, "I was afraid I might faint and fall in them." They settle on cropland several hundred thousand to an acre. (Take seventy steps north and seventy more east; you have described two sides of a square that covers an acre.) The smell is of decay and excretion. There is a whirring sound as of several reapers, for though you cannot hear one cricket masticating you can hear several hundred thousand. No crop is left on that acre. Presently there are fewer crickets, for they devour one another.

But the violence that makes all others seem unimportant by comparison is the gradual one, the drought. The West spells and pronounces it *drouth*.

Droughts are not exclusively or even specifically Western; they occur from time to time in all sections and in all states. It is only that in a deficit water-economy they are disastrous almost to the point of catastrophe. By rule of thumb it is a drought year if the total rainfall drops below eighty-five percent of the average, but the rule must be qualified a little. Crop yield has to be taken into account too, and the harvest may be satisfactory in a year of deficient rainfall if enough of the rain that does fall comes in the growing season. Moreover, drought affects cities and industry as well as agriculture, and a deficient rainfall that produces a satisfactory harvest may restrict and grievously damage other portions of society.[5]

An absolute fact, an unalterable fact, is that there will be discrete drought years and there will be successions of drought years. I repeat what I have said before: there is not a symmetrical or a predictable wet-dry cycle but there is an irregular alternation. Nevertheless, it happens that for nearly a century the even-numbered decades have been considerably wetter than the odd-numbered ones; a gambler would be justified in making book on this form of cycle. The house percentage would be highly favorable if he bet that any given locality in the West would get one dry year out of five even in the wet end of the curve. But it is not the local drought that counts, except for the localities that suffer from it, or the single drought year, except for those whom it bankrupts. What counts is the widespread drought, the one that extends across several states, and the dry end of the curve, the succession of drought years. In the twentieth century so far we have had the great droughts of 1910–1914, 1931–1938, and 1950–1954.

The first to fail are the marginal farmers and ranchers, those who have been but precariously financed, whose mortgages one crop failure will foreclose. Banks get a lot of real estate they don't want and marginal money-lenders, with whom the West has always been overstocked, go broke. This is enough to initiate a rural depression of the familiar kind, with its concentric widening through the interknit economy. But the big trouble begins when a second drought year follows the first one.

The earliest failures now are not farmers but farms, the marginal farms, those which have an insufficient supply of irrigation water—the ones high on the uplands, far down the valleys, out in the desert, the ones which are sound only in the wet years, land to which water ought not have been brought in the first place. Irrigation is the most stable and dependable form of agriculture, for it is entirely independent of the vagaries of rainfall, but it does need water. That is why there are storage dams.

The reservoirs behind those dams drop farther down the gauge boards. The rivers contract, not only because there is less water but because only the minimum contractual amounts are allowed to flow down the spillways: pools contract and fish die. Tanks cannot be filled, springs go dry, the water table sinks, artesian wells are driven always deeper to reach it. Farmers and stockmen get religion and begin to employ, precisely and economically, the methods they have been disregarding while drawing federal payments for employing them. The bureaucracy of starry-eyed, long-haired, swivel-chair theorists that has been paying the benefits is metamorphosed into a ministering angel. The provisions for credit extension and crop relief painfully built into our political structure during the 1930s come automatically into operation. Washington fills with delegations demanding that they be extended and increased. Rainmakers of all kinds strike gold, the heat goes on for enormously larger reclamation projects than any the most mystical engineers have yet envisaged, and Arizona demands that the United States spend upward of two billion dollars to make good the speculation of some five hundred individual flyers in marginal farmland.

Towns and cities restrict the water that may be used for gardens, then forbid its use at all; lawns are parched as brown as the foothills. Desert communities haul in water by tank truck. Stock ranges are exhausted by midsummer and cattle have to be shipped to distant ones that are not burned, or else thrown on a falling market to depress it further. Grass fires and forest fires increase. . . . It has become a major drought when the big dust storms start to blow and bankrupted farmers begin, like the Okies, to move out. Now it has become a national problem. The West can only hold on, one way or another, and watch the clouds.

Nature's hostility toward the activities of man, passive elsewhere, is dynamic in the West; a drought gives a curiously vengeful quality to its automatisms. Desert plants wait out the drought, suspending the processes of germination and seed-bearing. In the somewhat less arid ranges native plants have an analogous ability—notably the famous buffalo grass, which man brought so close to extinction—but as the dry years lengthen out they die widely. And now because such forage plants reproduce themselves less plentifully, noxious ones increase. Starving cattle feed on them and starve faster or die of poison; the decline of the range accelerates as the proportion of worthless and baneful plants increases and as the bare spots widen. The land has a multiple and manifold toxicity, as if in the crisis of a fever. Vermin increase too. There are more jackrabbits, prairie dogs, gophers, coyotes. The grasshopper and cricket populations leap up from an endemic to an epidemic phase.

Perhaps it was true that mankind and society could not exist in the West at all. There is an essential truth in the fable of the Mormons, which hold that God's Church exists in the West as a miracle of His providence. At any rate there *is* a tinge of the miraculous, or at least of implausible achievement against impossible odds. Look, there she is, a beet field, a factory, a supermarket, a golf course in the wasteland of the Grand Canyon, Death Valley, and the Craters of the Moon. It is impossible, it is even preposterous. Therefore understand in the complex Western consciousness one element which is awareness of achievement.

Perhaps it remains true that mankind and society cannot exist in the West. The answer, we must remember, is not yet in. Therefore understand another element in that consciousness which I have had to mention several times already, the anxiety that is as deep as the pride. In fact, deeper.

It rests on orderly strata of simplicities. You must get to the water hole or you will die, but the water hole may be dry when you get there. Your crops must get water or you will be bankrupted, but the rains may come at the wrong time or may not come at all. Snowslide, blizzard, norther, hailstorm, flash flood—no one can say when they will come, no one can secure himself against their coming, everyone knows they will come. The crickets march out of the hills, the budworm settles in the stand of Douglas fir, halogeton appears in the sheep range. The earth stirs in its sleep and the flume that brings water to a town breaks, or the main canal is ruptured and bent back on itself. A hot wind blows throughout July. Brine starts flowing in your well.

There was just so much dust in the gravel at Bonanza Bar, and just so much more in the hillsides above it. When the bar had been panned and the hillsides sluiced down—finish. In hard rock the vein pinched out or the shaft got down to a point beyond which the pumps could not keep even with the water—the end. So a thousand ghost towns. And fifty times as many traces of color, from two hundred feet below sea level in Death Valley to 14,000 feet above in Uncompahgres—they were just color, not ore. Or the irrigation system for which we mortgaged our fields and bonded our future brought a fine yield for a few years and then the fields were waterlogged or alkalied—and that was that. Or we built the system and there was simply not enough yield from the fields it fructified. The water that failed and the crop that failed are each a typical Western story. No less typical is the boom that failed because the stuff ran out—metal, timber, gas, oil, cropland, rangeland. Always across that bright sky falls the shadow which never withdraws or lessens; there may be an end to our venture too.

This is the accepted risk of disaster from natural circumstance. Part of the drama of the West, it has worked into the Western metabolism. Western society has—more or less—come to terms with the hostile environment, has produced something like an equilibrium, is able to hold it off but only just. And only in a way. And perhaps only for a time.

There is an even more basic drama, the perpetual risk of destruction by catastrophe, by natural cataclysm. Have engineers built anything more triumphant, or for that matter more beautiful, than the Golden Gate Bridge? There are learned men who say that the abutments from which those great towers rise are square on a fault line, a kind of terrestrial quicksand, and will some day slip and plunge the towers into the Gate. On April 18, 1906 that fault line shuddered and San Francisco crumbled and began to burn. Every year hundreds of quivers stir along it and along others like it; in the city built upon a hill the watchman may yet wake in vain. In the spring of the year before the great earthquake, the flood I have already mentioned took the Colorado River out of its channels and back to an older one, part of which is the defiance of nature called Imperial Valley. That flood created the Salton Sea in what had been the Salton Sink. Only by an eyelash was the river stopped from permanently occupying its older bed. Who says that it has been stopped permanently? No one dares who knows the Colorado. And there is that ravenous river-mouth eating its way back up the delta which it built. And Lake Mead fills passionlessly with silt.

These are specimen *if's* of moderate size, not small but not enormous either. The scale is much smaller when we glance at villages depopulated by the failure of grazing ranges or irrigation systems, specimens of which abound. It increases considerably when we glance at dustbowls or 7,000,000 acres of LU lands. Or, as we are presently going to, at Davis County. But the scale can be increased to useful size, and foreshortened too. We may now turn to Pueblo III.

Mesa Verde: the green table. The road climbs toward it from a valley that irrigation has made greener than nature had, and comes out on that flat magnificence in the aromatic greenness of piñon and juniper. Canyons are gashed deep into the sides of the tableland. As the road twists along the saddles between them there comes a moment when through the shining desert air you catch a glimpse, far off to the southward, of as strange and stirring a sight as any the desert has. "Look!" my wife said in astonishment. "A mesa that looks like a ship!" Like a ship in full sail, and therefore called Ship Rock. Presently the road comes to the headquarters of the National Park. From here you can stroll out and see the uncovered ground plans and kivas of the houses built by the people who the anthropologists have designated Pueblo III. Or you can go down into the canyons and see the only partially ruined houses themselves, the houses that have given those people their popular name, the Cliff Dwellers. . . . We have attached our own futile names to the ruins: Cliff Palace, Spruce Tree House, Long House, Square Tower House, and the like.

They are impressive and endlessly fascinating, these stone and stone-faced structures built long ago under the cave-like overthrust of eroded cliffs, and preserved almost intact through centuries of desert dryness. They were built in these caves for a combination of reasons, among which were certainly the beauty of the sites, the accessibility of springs, and the ease with which they could be defended from marauders. They are built too in caves that face south, so that they got sun in winter and shade in summer; they were sheltered from northers, snow, and the cloudbursts. They are apartment houses with setbacks and terraces; some of them have more than a hundred flats. They were built in the twelfth and thirteenth centuries. By no mean people.

They were people of the culture called by scholars the Anasazi. Considering the nature of the Four Corners country, they were a dense population; their center was the San Juan Valley. Many of their dwellings have survived at other places besides Mesa Verde; many more than are known by the whites are kept secret by the Utes, whose country this was and who feel that they were twice defrauded, and by their friends, when the national park was created; doubtless many others have been destroyed and no trace left.

In the canyons the Pueblo III people had large fields of corn, squash, beans, pumpkins, cotton; sometimes on the mesa tops too, though these were harder to water. They kept flocks of turkeys and hunted the abundant game. They were skilled weavers, leather-workers, potters, jewelers. Their period, so the scholars say, began about A.D. 1050. It brought the Pueblo culture to its finest flowering and is called the Golden Age, the Great Period. It may have been beginning to decline, sometime after 1250. Social friction may have been manifesting itself. There may have been ceremonial decay or perhaps religious schism. Or restlessness or quarrelsomeness may have increased. Maybe, in short, the inexplicable but unmistakable falling-off in vigor that all peoples come to had set in.

A lot of maybes. But there is no doubt at all when it ended.

There is a tool called a core-borer. It is sheathed in a hollow, sharpened rod through which it can be screwed into a tree like an auger. It brings out a boring that is a complete, unaltered section of the tree from bark to heartwood. It has various uses for lumbermen and foresters but basically it is an instrument that enables anyone to tell the age of the tree by counting the rings of annual growth. Leonardo da Vinci suggested that the rings might be a historical record of climate and hardly four and a half centuries later, shortly after 1900, Dr. Andrew Ellicott Douglass of the University of Arizona began to use them as one. He created the exquisite science of investigation called dendrochronology. He and many others, including by now practitioners of a dozen different sciences, have extended their inquiries across the Southwest, well to the north, and far out into the plains. There is, you see, less growth, and therefore a narrower tree ring, in a dry year than in a wet one. From living trees the record is carried back by a series of overlapping matched sections of logs—logs uncovered in river deltas and alluvial fans, beams of buildings and charred brands of cooking fires which archeologists find by excavating prehistoric sites, and the beams in structures that still stand such as those at Mesa Verde. In some areas the record has been extended back before the time of Christ. (California sequoias take it back more than a thousand years further.)

Core borings have thus revealed and documented the Great Drought of the San Juan valley and the surrounding zone in the states which meet at the Four Corners. The record has been read in piñon, ponderosa, and Douglas fir.

The drought began in 1276 and that was the worst year, though "worst" does not mean much when we deal with twenty-four successive years and with moisture so sparse that tenths of an inch are helpful units of measure. The people of Mesa Verde built their last cliff house the year before, 1275, and no doubt consecrated it with proper observances and sacrifice. Unhappily there is a gap in the chronology so far worked out for exactly that area. It will be closed some day and there are unbroken chronologies for a number of other places well within the stricken zone. So it is established that 1279 and 1283 were almost as bad as 1276, 1280 and 1295 only minutely better, and 1299, the twenty-fourth year, a climax just less arid than the overture. By then the Pueblo III people had moved out of their homeland, whose now barren ground had become as fatal as if it had been saturated with the poisons of atomic fission.

The springs slackened and dried up. The little creeks sank out of sight. Corn and beans pushed a few inches out of the ground, stopped growing, turned brown and rattled in the wind. Many hundreds of storage pits had been filled with corn because centuries of living in the desert had taught the Pueblo people till their very bloodstream knew that summers were certain to come when the supernaturals would be angry and the clouds would bring no rain. But how many winters could the people live on it, how many years would it provide seed for the spring planting and cornmeal for the roads the supernaturals would walk again if their anger could be appeased? Two or three at most, and each year the quail and rabbits and deer were fewer. Every year the people would have to trudge farther to bring back water in pottery jars (perhaps very beautiful, "black on white" with designs that symbolized the sacred rain) on their shoulders. Each year there would be fewer skins for clothing and footwear, less cotton for blankets, fewer feathers for robes.

Man's understanding of the universe rested on a solid base. If you performed the right purifications, sang the right chants, went through the right rituals in the order taught by the fathers, then the clouds would come, the thunderbird would shake his wings, and the earth would conceive and bring forth. It did not happen and no doubt the failure of the gods to turn again intensified the theological divisions. No doubt families

and clans came to killing one another for water, as Westerners with paler skins would some seven hundred years
later. So the people, like the animals they hunted, began
to leave their stricken land. The most terrified first, or the
most skeptical, or the most vigorous and courageous? By
families, by groups or clans, taking their infirm and aged
with them? We do not know, but we know that the
Pueblo Okies went. They went out into the desert, seeking beyond it a land which had not been cursed, a land
where virtue and sacrifice and prayer would be acceptable to the spirits of sky and earth and the creeks would
have water. The distances were great, but somewhere,
they hoped, there was water. In many valleys that channel the desert they found it—the Little Colorado, the
Gila, the Salt, the Verde, most of all the Rio Grande. In
the southern faces of the abandoned cliffs the big
dwellings with their ramparts and kivas and old fields
were silent. Empty, without cook fires, without the
voices of priests and children, under the desert sun, lifeless before 1300.

Thus the twenty-four years of the Great Drought of
the thirteenth century in the Four Corners country. The
tree rings show that there has been nothing like it since.
The Great Drought of the 1930s, the first dustbowl era,
lasted seven years. That was on the margin of the West,
the high plains, an area but thinly populated, with few
towns, no cities, and no industry. In the interior West,
at least since it has been United States territory and
records have been kept, the longest period of drought is
the one that began in 1950 and may be over by the time
this page is printed. That is, it may not last more than
five years.

The Colorado Aqueduct crosses a desert to deliver to
the desert city of Los Angeles water from the Colorado
River, the great river of the American desert. The Aqueduct is two hundred and forty miles of canals, siphons,
and tunnels, from Parker Dam to Riverside. In 1950 there

were in Los Angeles two million people and there are
many more now, people whose culture is more complexly vulnerable than that of Pueblo III. What happens
to them through the twenty-four years of some Great
Drought that may begin any New Year's Day?

But they are any part of the West, or all of it.

Chapter Three
Emptiness Can Affect the Unwary

The Spanish reached the Rio Grande Valley in the sixteenth century. They found the Pueblos there, and elsewhere in New Mexico they found other sedentary tribes—in valleys. They made no effort to occupy the plains beyond; they lacked wealth, military power, and most of all technology. They had large numbers of cattle and far larger numbers of sheep when the American conquest reached New Mexico in 1846. But their herds grazed on valley, foothill, and upland ranges. By the Americans' second generation technology had advanced sufficiently for them to spread a grazing economy across the plains, great areas of which were magnificent grasslands. They got windmills to lift groundwater from shallow wells. Later they got deeper borings and power to pump the water so tapped. Finally, after the turn of the century, they got complex systems of dams, canals, flumes, siphons, and pumping works.

Any grazing economy is a thin settlement; that of New Mexico, besides being half-ruined now, is deceptive. The map of the state is freckled with towns but outside the valleys they are only freckles, hamlets straitly limited in size by the local water. Population-density figures show that the state has 5.6 inhabitants per square mile; this number too is misleading. Of the 680,000 people who live in New Mexico, almost a third live in one city, Albuquerque (96,000) and four towns, Santa Fe, Roswell, Carlsbad, and Clovis (which with 17,000 is just smaller than Carlsbad.)[1] Of the rest, more than half live in the same river valleys that contain these towns and all but a handful in other, smaller valleys. Outside the valleys the population density is much less than one per square mile.

Nevada has an area of 110,000 square miles and a population of 160,000;[2] that is, a density of 1.5 persons per square mile. Just less than half of them are in five towns, of which one is a politically differentiated portion of Las Vegas and another one, Sparks, has attained the metropolitan eminence of something over 3,000. At mid-decade the booster clubs are claiming that the state is growing more rapidly than any other and has 40,000 more inhabitants than it had in 1950. The figure is magnified by Western illusion, but whatever the true figure may be, most of the increase has been at Las Vegas and practically all the rest of it in the portion of Washoe County that includes Reno and its satellite divorce ranches. Not much more can happen; there are plenty of square miles but there are no more water sources.[3] Outside the present centers the population density cannot increase more than microscopically. Nevada will remain the least populous state and the one with the widest-open spaces. It will be the first Western state to attain a stable equilibrium with the desert.

As usual, Utah illustrates the conditions most vividly. Its area is 84,916 square miles. Its 1950 population was 688,862. Of these people 293,000 lived in two cities and three towns; four of these centers are in Salt Lake Valley and one in Cache Valley. They and the remaining

arable portions of the two valleys in which they are situated compose the area of greatest population density.
It is a zone at the foot of the mountains, a zone which
varies in width from two to ten miles and is about 160
miles long. It amounts to 1.2 percent of the area of Utah.
In 1950 it held about 385,000 people, fifty-six percent of
the population. Of the remaining forty-four percent all
live in valley settlements smaller in area but almost
equal in density, mile for mile; these smaller centers
add up to just less than 1.8 percent of the state's area.
That is to say: not quite three percent of Utah, less than
2500 square miles, is inhabited. The rest is mountains
and desert.

Plans exist for the development of the unused water
resources of the upper Colorado, to whose basin Utah
belongs. The master plan is currently called the Upper
Colorado Storage Project; its name has changed before
this and may well change again. No one can say just
what it consists of, for it changes according to political
opportunism and what looks like bureaucratic caprice.
(I will examine it later on.) To whatever extent the plan
is sound and to whatever extent it may eventually be
acted on, it is to some extent also unsound and certain
not to be acted on. It is in part mythical, in part mystical, in part impossible—engineering extrapolated beyond
conceivability. I wish I could predict here how much of
the master plan and associated plans will be completed,
but I am even less qualified as a prophet, though perhaps not much less, than the Bureau of Reclamation,
which made them.

An associated plan, a "participating project," is called
the General Utah Project. It is designated to make available to Utah considerably more water from the Colorado
watershed (including the main stem of the river) than
is now being used. The people of Utah have come to
think of it as their brightest hope for the future. Doubtless they are right, though to what degree no one can

say, and they are caught in the mass-illusion of the West, unable to perceive that some part, possibly the greatest part, of their hope is mirage. The Central Utah Project is a mystic's trance-vision. It too will change as the rainbow does, but in the current revelation it is to have 37 dams (up to 440 feet high), 188 miles of tunnels (up to 16 feet in diameter), 470 miles of canals, 106 miles of aqueduct (up to 17 feet in diameter), and a poetic lace-work of siphons, pumping plants, power plants, drainage systems, and the proper appurtenances.

This dream is supposed to be realized in two stages. Not even its imaginers have set a date for the completion of its second, inclusive phase. Nor can any useful estimate of its ultimate cost be made in terms of the current dollar or any other dollar. Bureau of Reclamation estimates are poetic and political fantasies which have no bearings on realities. (One doubles them as a first step and proceeds from there according to one's persuasion.) Three things are certain: that portions of the Central Utah Project as it is now planned will not be built; that, whatever may be substituted for these portions, the ultimate phase as built will fall short of the present plans; that corresponding portions of the purposes it envisages will never be fulfilled. Utah will get less water from the Colorado watershed than the plans say it will.

It may get much less. It may get none at all; none, I mean, except what it is now getting.

But accept the fantasy as the mystics have created it. Their figures, which are as optimistic as the advertising of a uranium stock, contemplate that when the second and post-hashish phase is completed, water will be brought to 313 square miles of Utah that have not got water now. Or: the utmost the mystics can envisage is that another four-tenths of one percent of Utah will be made habitable.

Note this: of the 313 additional square miles (200,000 acres) which compose the mystics' vision, all would be contiguous to lands that are now irrigated. Indeed most of them consist of land that is higher up the valley sides or farther out in the desert (here the plateaus) beyond the mouths of valleys. Most of it too is at such high altitudes that it will be useful only for growing hay.[4]

The head mystic, the author of the plans for the Central Utah Project, who is not a man to err on the side of caution, sets a limit to vision. Grant that all now undeveloped water sources in Utah (besides the Colorado watershed) will some day be developed and with maximum efficiency. This is inconceivable but if the miracle should occur, the mystic says, then the state could support twice as many people as it had in 1950.

Here is a measurable quantity as one emerges on the far side of the trance. In the most favorable terms conceivable, Utah will achieve equilibrium with the desert at a population of one and a third million people. Who will live in 3.4 percent of the area of the state. But most of whom will be in the 1.2 percent, the less than twelve hundred square miles, where most people live now.

Similar though necessarily looser computations could be made for the remainder of the West, always excepting the portion that gets abundant rain. The limits vary from a large potential increase in the population of Colorado east of the mountains to the fair certainty that no sizable portions of Idaho now uninhabited ever will be inhabited.

Idaho brings in another consideration. The wide southern third of the state is desert. Some of it could be reclaimed by water from the Snake River which crosses it, through sunken canyons most of the way, and from its principal tributaries. The most formidable proposal is the Mountain Home Project, which has been incorporated in various sweeping plans for Columbia basin development, abandoned as impractical or prohibitive in cost, and advanced again in new adaptations. The Mountain Home area is sagebrush desert north of the Snake and south of the Boise River. (The Boise Valley is the richest farming area of Idaho and one of the most remarkable triumphs of irrigation in the West.) As I write, this project is tied in with the bill for a federal dam at Hell's Canyon introduced in the Senate by Wayne Morse and in the House by Mrs. Gracie Pfost in March 1955. It is intended to reclaim 192,000 acres.

North of the desert the state is all mountains. The great snow pack, however, will always be used farther west, outside of Idaho. The valleys that contain the state's wealth and population are narrower and less favorable than the principal Utah valleys; their limits will be reached much earlier. In the northern part of the state, the panhandle, the expanses are wider. Here the abundant water could be put to use if the climate and the distances did not introduce other prohibitions. The panhandle is so far from everywhere that transportation costs will always be prohibitive. This factor will always operate, even if portions of the electric power certain to be developed in this region are sequestered there for local use at preferential rates. Moreover, the winter of the region is both mountain and northern. It has a forest economy now; no change in it can be foreseen.

The bearing of these facts is obvious. Take Chicago. Theoretically, there is no topographic, climatic, or meteorological reason why it should not continue to expand till a solid metropolitan and industrial unit extends from, say, South Bend in the east to Milwaukee in the north and Rock Island in the west. (Disregarding the social and economic changes such a development might produce internally and its effects on the rest of Illinois.) But in the arid West the population pattern must always remain what it now is.

Cities and towns will grow in population but those that do so will have the same proportionate relationship toward one another that they have now. They will become more disproportionate than they now are to the thinly populated areas of their states. With only negligible exceptions, additional agriculture will develop in or along the margins of the areas now irrigated: no more deserts are going to be made fertile. So far as the Western dream of industrialization may come true, it will come true in the areas now most densely populated. There may be one considerable exception to that last statement: the Columbia Valley below Grand Coulee Dam but upstream from existing industry. A long stretch of this valley that does not have industry now, that is, may eventually be industrialized. But the statement does hold true of the Columbia Valley above Grand Coulee. In any event, the Columbia Valley is a valley.

I am saying that not only will the West always be a valley civilization, it will always be a civilization of the valleys that are now developed.

The jubilant Mormons told the world as early as 1849 that they had made the desert blossom as the rose and, being the most vociferous of Western braggarts, have so incorporated the phrase in their daily talk that you get it as small change when you buy a pack of cigarettes they disapprove but profit from. They gave the biblical phrase to the West at large; it has long been a stereotype. The West, understand, has made the desert blossom as the rose. The stereotype happens not to be true. The West has not made the desert blossom. By means of the most formidable engineering works man has ever constructed, it has transferred portions of the mountain snow pack to minute areas that lie along the edge of the desert.

Between the valleys is wilderness, little changed by all that has happened in more than a century. It exerts a continuous influence on the society of the West and the occupations and personal lives of Westerners.

Here is a siding on the Great Northern in western Montana, southeast of Browning, the Blackfoot Agency town. There will be a small grain elevator; perhaps two, one of them a cooperative. There will be a loading pen for cattle and the railroad maintains a couple of sheds for equipment and tools. There will be a small general store, a filling station, a garage, and a sign painted with the name of the siding. Two or three or four houses. That is all. The economy has required this cluster to exist; the ranches that create the requirement are distant and hidden from the view of the passersby in folds of the land.

If it is a siding on the Burlington east of Sheridan, Wyoming, there will be no elevator. The loading pen will be larger and there may be some collapsing structures where the bituminous coal of the vicinity was once loaded. Perhaps there is a small mill that chops alfalfa. On the Santa Fe, say somewhere near the Wagon Mound, the siding will be dominated by a big water tank, less used now than in the days before diesel power, very costly when erected. On the Union Pacific in Nevada or the Western Pacific in the Utah desert the cluster will have shrunk some.

Treeless, its paint cracking in the turbulence of sun, this dot in space overwhelms a traveler with loneliness. He wonders about the loneliness of those who live here, and his mind darkens when he remembers winter. If he is traveling by train, he will see nothing but cattle for thirty miles. If by car, he will in thirty miles meet or overtake six other cars, three of them from out of state. By such long stitches is the West sewed together.

But we have faced away from the mountains, which are also wilderness. From any town or city the wilderness can be reached in a drive of a few hours, frequently of a few miles. The town's main street may become a

road that leads to the edge of wilderness. The om-
nipresence and the accessibility of wilderness multiply
the Western paradoxes.

In the contemporary West none of them is more arresting than what I have elsewhere called the Desert
Yacht Club. I grew up in Ogden, which has two rivers of
a size that would make them creeks in Indiana. My generation learned to swim in their "holes," occasionally
stretched a hundred feet long and from three to an extremity of six feet deep. Disregarding Great Salt Lake,
where swimming is a stunt for tourists and which could
not be reached from Ogden anyway, the only other
places where you could swim were an old mill pond in
town and the small reservoir of a power dam in a canyon
eight or ten miles above town.[5] At this dam a microscopic resort had half a dozen rowboats for hire; you
could row upstream for perhaps a mile.

Half-way to Salt Lake City there was (and still is) a
resort called "Lagoon" because it had dammed a creek. It
had a large swimming pool, which was almost inexpress-
ibly attractive to the desert-born, and a pond for rowboats. There was no indoor swimming pool of standard
size, or as I remember it of any other size, in Utah till
the Mormon Church built a gymnasium in Salt Lake City
about 1914. (My memory may be doing an injustice to
the University of Utah and the Agricultural College.) At
Bear Lake on the Idaho border and at Utah Lake, which
is just outside Provo, there were of course swimming
beaches and some elementary rowing about. These lakes
may have seen their first canoes about 1920 and by that
time roads were sufficiently improved so that Bear Lake,
which is not near any town, was easily accessible. I
doubt if either lake had known sailing before 1920. The
beautiful lakes in the Wasatch, the Uintas, and the High
Plateaus could not be reached by automobile.

In that period Nevada, Arizona, and the Western
Slope of Colorado were even worse off for water sports.

Wyoming was somewhat different. The lakes in its mountains, like those of Utah, were inaccessible by car, and as late as 1920 getting to Yellowstone Lake or the beautiful lakes in Grand Teton Park was a hard chore, one best left to motor-stage companies that had recently replaced horse express. (In the summer of 1920, just out of Harvard, I refused a job as superintendent of schools and principal of the high school at Jackson, because in winter the town was cut off from the outside world unless you snowshoed over Teton Pass to the railhead at Victor, Idaho.) Where there were big lakes outside the national parks, such as Coeur d'Alene and Pend Oreille in Idaho and Flathead in Montana, there were some boating and primordial water sports—for those who could travel long distances to get to them. So far as the interior West was concerned, that summed it up.

Two things have happened. Roads have provided access to the mountain lakes and the big dams, private and federal, have made big artificial lakes. The Westerners have taken to water sports with a vehemence that says much about their country; nature lovers will hear no protest from me because deep in national forests the primeval silence has been shattered by outboards. There are scheduled sailing races in many places, foldboat races down the canyons of the Arkansas, hair-raising voyages in queer craft down such rivers as the Green and Salmon and San Juan, and "aquacades" practically everywhere. Lake Roosevelt in the Washington desert or Lake Mead in the Nevada desert is a stirring sight but it has a pang of heartbreak too. As an ex-Westerner, returning at intervals, I am invariably moved to marvel when I see sails in Ogden Valley. When I see, on any highway, all day long, scores of cars making for the mountains with a small boat lashed to the top or pulling a longer one on a trailer.

Quite apart from boating, the Westerners, who live much more in the open than the people of other sections, are much more given to outdoor recreations. Sometimes the phenomena are, to a philistine, inscrutable—fishing for instance. At such a place as the Fishing Bridge in Yellowstone Park, they are a mob; on any stream near a city they are likely to be spotted every few yards. Nature gave up long ago. The fry and fingerlings that hatcheries used to plant did not multiply so successfully as had been counted on; nowadays the trout an angler takes on Saturday was probably dumped in the stream on Thursday. I have seen city slickers actually following the tank truck, and I have been told that Colorado has spent something like four dollars on every trout caught by its licensees. Some trout streams are nationally famous, the Gunnison, the Madison where I have sometimes seen San Franciscans who had driven there for the weekend, the Rogue, the John Day, the Mackenzie (in Oregon). More appealing are the secret places of the heart, the fantasies of desire, where there has never been any stocking, where the rainbows or the cutthroats or the steelheads are native and naive. Such unfished streams are known only to believers and are protected by an oath. In the secrecy of old friendship the location of at least fifty such paradises has been imparted to me over the years; I dare say that of some of them the fantasy is true.

A game warden in South Dakota told me that during the previous hunting season three million pheasants had been shot in his state. I do not guarantee the statistic—he may have been playing me for a greenhorn—but it suggests the scale. On the opening day of the season in 1953, fourteen thousand deer hunters registered at the checking station of the Stanislaus National Forest, which is on the western slope of the Sierra. (No mortality figures at hand.) Even more than the Southern farmer, the Westerner is habitually a hunter. A startling number of families depend on game as part of their food supply; the man who hunts only for sport often expects to get a moose, an elk, a deer, and an antelope every fall.

More important is the great number of Westerners who own shacks or cabins in the mountains and use them for weekends and vacations most of the year, in many places all year. They range upward from the inexpensive one-room structure that is generally called a "camp." Typically they are log cabins and as such have developed one of the two indigenous styles of Western domestic architecture.[6] The cabin has genuine distinction and merit; it is harmonious with its surroundings, weather-wise, cool in hot weather, warm in winter. It is made of whatever timber may be at hand but best made of some medium-sized pine such as lodgepole, and is finished with a dark stain or clear shellac. (The style is not suit-able for the monumental; some of the most hideous buildings in the West are at resorts, big hotels with steel frames and an exterior of enormous logs.) The roads that have made it accessible permit it to be luxurious. It may have a gasoline-powered water system and electric-lighting system, and a cookstove and refrigerator that burn propane or butane. Such incongruity with the wilderness setting long ago ceased to be noticeable.

The wilderness may come down to the sides of the rutted road that leads to such a cabin and may lap it round for many miles. The same Stanislaus Forest that drew fourteen thousand deer hunters in a single day contains a large area of primitive wilderness. The back country and the high country are but little different today from what they were before the white man. Like the absolute desert in summer, the high country can be perilous to the unwary. Therefore much of the wilder-ness craft that was once the common American heritage is still a living skill in the West. Most Westerners who practice it do so for sport, but a large number of them still practice it professionally.

Not that the average camper needs more mountain craft than a city park calls for, and not that the average outdoorsman is anything but a ritualist. There would be no pretence that craftsmanship was needed on the first day of deer-season in the Stanislaus; a red coat and a pinch of gambler's luck would be more useful. But any who went on to the primitive area or the higher slope would have been wise to go in pairs. Every year people die within a mile or two of continental highways traveled by hundreds of cars a day. A fall that breaks a hip or any similar accident could do the job if one had not left a trail that could be followed. The disaster stories in the Western press usually relate to newcomers, people who ought not to enter even a national forest unaccompanied, still less take an icy trail between cliffs.

I touched the edges of two typical stories in the summer of 1953. I spent a week at the Priest River Experiment Station, in the Kaniksu National Forest near the Canadian border. Several miles away there was a camp of young men, mostly college undergraduates, who were working on a project to eradicate the blister rust that afflicts white pine. A camp regulation forbade them to go hiking alone but one boy was superior to it. An experienced mountain climber, he made a map of some high country he wanted to explore by himself. One Sunday, when out with the group, he fell behind them and then angled off alone, intending to return to camp by his own route. The party that began to search for him the next day numbered nearly a hundred, most of them necessarily experts. His body was not found for a week. He had started to cross a narrow cove of Priest Lake on a fallen log—these are big trees, larches, cedars, fir, that may be a hundred and fifty feet high—and had slipped and fallen into the water. The water was choked with weeds that held him under and drowned him. If he had a companion, the story would have been one merely of a wetting.

During the same month while I was in the Bridger National Forest, on the western slope of the Wind River Mountains, a man and his two sons, thirteen and eight years old, got lost. Boulder Lake is about two miles from Pinedale. They had packed in from it some eight miles, through a canyon to a cluster of smaller lakes—along well-marked horse-trails all the way. They made a camp on one of these lakes and one day went fishing on another one, less than two miles away. The lunch they took with them was the only food they were to eat for six days, except for three fish. When they started back to their camp they missed their trail, and presently followed another one till the father knew they were lost.

What followed is standard. A person who realizes he is lost usually loses his capacity to think logically. First it goes out of orientation; then it panics. Fears rise out of the unconscious; frequently hallucinations follow. When experienced searchers locate a lost person, they spread out and surround him before making their presence known, for at sight of them he is likely to bolt away in terror. Or they may find that he is serenely and courageously following a logical plan that is entirely hallucinatory, based on the belief that the compass has broken down and the cardinal points are reversed, the creeks are flowing uphill, and unmistakable landmarks are in some other country. When taken back to his camp, he may vehemently deny that the tent and equipment are his or that the name-tapes on his spare shirt bears his name. This fisherman was never more than five miles from heavily traversed areas at night and could see the lights of Pinedale and those of automobiles on the main highway. If at any time he had followed any course for a mile and a half he would have reached a trail that would have soon taken him to safety. His commonest direction of travel was the only one that could have taken him to rougher country than that which he was in. He cooked the three fish they had caught, but he didn't remember to catch any more, though it was spawning season and trout could have been caught by hand along the edge of either a lake or creek. He made a small fire on an out-crop of rock, from sticks so dry that the smoke was not visible at a quarter of a mile. If he had set fire to a snag, if he had even put some green branches on his own fire, he would have been located at once, but he was afraid of starting a forest fire and getting killed.

The search for him, which was directed by a forest ranger whom I know well, was typical. He was an im-portant man back home and the governor of his state or-dered out thirty national guard planes to search for him—military planes incapable of flying low enough or slow enough to be of any use, as helpful as so many canal boats. They were joined by others—so many all told that the ranger was worried lest there would be an air crash that would require another rescue party—but, till the search was over, not by any planes fitted for mountain flying. All that the searching parties knew was that their quarry was in an area of about twenty-five square miles, which had to be gridded till a trail was found. One was found on the sixth day and it led to the man and his sons within an hour. So they were found by means of a skill of Jim Bridger's, practiced in the forest that bears his name.

The ranger in charge has spent his life in the wilder-ness and made his living there from boyhood on. But most young men who enter the Forest Service are West-erners who, if only as sportsmen, that is as amateurs, have always practiced wilderness crafts. Those from Eastern schools of forestry learn them promptly.

These men are trained, sometimes self-trained, tech-nologists or scientists. They belong to an extensive caste: national park rangers, state and private as well as fed-eral foresters, many kinds of engineers in federal or pri-vate employ, power men, water men, prospectors of oil and metals, practitioners of pure research sciences. Apart from the professional level there are the working stiffs who live in the same way by means of the same skills. There is no difference in wilderness competence between the men who chart the route along a mountainside of an aqueduct or a pipeline and the men who operate the fantastic machines that construct it.

They are fascinating people; I find them the most likable of Westerners. They have poise and serenity, they are unhurried, most of them are remarkably soft-spoken. Their casual talk reveals the delights and incidental dangers of the wilderness. The stories they tell with such easy zest are set, unregardfully, in the matrix of the violent and hostile West. But you feel it most directly in the talk of their wives. A woman is in town, at the station, at the trailer. Her husband is out where the forest fires are, the snowslides, the sudden floods, the avalanches, the bulldozers that slide off cliffs, the senseless fall of a tall tree or the washout of a trail or the caving of a cut-bank. A wife is a woman who is listening for the telephone bell.

Not only wilderness but emptiness can affect the unwary. Let a moment come when it turns strange and at once it evokes the same anxiety the historian finds in the behavior of the emigrant trains.

Right after the war I spent a summer driving about the West. Besides the objectives of my notebooks, which were now shaping toward the last volume of my trilogy, I had half a dozen magazine assignments. So that a chart of my travels would have resembled a series of figure 8s; this was the summer when I seemed to be going through Three Forks. It was in Colorado that I first saw a syndicated newspaper column by a man who was touring the West and writing his impressions, in admitted imitation of Ernie Pyle. Any Western editor would kill the flash on the assassination of a President of the United States to make room for a later one on the birth

of twins at Nine Mile, and so a lot of local papers were
carrying his column. Filing it from the field, he seemed
to be only a couple weeks ahead of me. On this his first
experience of the West he had an engaging omniscience.
I could divine that he had bought a hat with a six-inch
brim at Miles City if not Rapid City, and with it he had
acquired Western savvy and Western lingo. A worker in
the same vineyard, I could picture him listening hard in
bars, stopping to talk to irrigators and road foremen and
bridge-tenders, staying up late to sweat out his geography and statistics. He had an edifying virginity and when
I reached an area where the papers were not running
him, I missed him.

Presently I made a long detour in order to spend
some hours in South Pass, as I always do. I stayed too
long revisiting the sacred ruts and landmarks and it was
close to sunset when I turned back toward Rock Springs,
where I intended to spend the night. It is one of the ugliest towns in the West, but it has a good restaurant and
there are not eight others in all Wyoming. Full dark
had come up when I turned off the highway down a
road, a kind of road, that bypasses Farson and satisfies
a tourist's ritual by saving him seven or eight miles,
though it probably adds half an hour to his running
time. I had gone half a dozen miles down this devious,
upended pair of ruts when my headlights picked up a
man who was waving his arm out furiously.

When I got out of my car he scared me by gripping
my arm with both hands and uttering gasps that
sounded epileptic, though they meant only that he was
breathing too hard to speak. In a moment I saw that he
was, in the idiom, spooked. The indicated treatment
was a drink. I took him into my car and gave him a big
one, then got out my flashlight and looked at his car. I
am no more a mechanic than you are but I could see
that it was through for the day. At a climactic lurch on
this rollercoaster, his water-pump had torn loose from

its base, severed the fan belt, and chewed up the radiator. I would have to take him to Farson, whence a wrecker could be sent for his car tomorrow. We exchanged names and he proved to be the touring columnist.

We shared a motel and a bad dinner and he polished off my rye while telling me his adventure. I am not clear why he turned down that abominable road in the first place, but he did. Almost at once the swells that look so flat from the highway shut out such slight evidence of mankind's existence as there were and he was alone in the waste of sagebrush. This he was prepared for; he had written a column on the therapeutic emptiness of similar country west of Craig, Colorado—country which, however, had a highway across it. When with a clatter like the crumpling of a tin roof his car notified him that he was in trouble, he was rather pleased. He knew that the frontier was always near at hand, and this breakdown linked its interpreter with the pioneers. While he waited for a car to come, he could make notes for a column about his adventures. And the silence was a superb experience.

No car came; he had brought neither lunch nor drinking water. As the afternoon waned he began to feel uneasy and by sunset he was scared. Panic must have hit him before dark. With reality back on its hinges and a large if overcooked T-bone and plenty of rye inside him, he was abysmally ashamed. A newspaperman, a sophisticate, an interviewer of celebrities, a familiar of name cafes—to be overcome by jitters like a child who has heard a ghost downstairs! There was no reason to be ashamed: the country had gone strange on him.

He could not understand why, all afternoon, he had not gone as much as a hundred feet from his car. (Not even to the shade of some popple and his face was badly burned.) A moment came when he knew that he had damned well better get into his car and stay there; also that he had better make sure that no rattlesnakes had got into it first. As darkness came up over the plain, it concealed a lot of movement and it had noises. Every few minutes something kept shaking itself. (Hallucination: if it was a sheep you wouldn't hear it.) Things thrashed about and ran. He knew that the barking he heard was a coyote (but it could have been a dog at a sheep wagon hidden in a swale) and that coyotes were harmless. But they reminded him of wolves, about which he was not sure, and of cougars. By now he could neither stay in the car nor stay out of it and kept changing about. He kept remembering that this was a country where people die of thirst and starvation. He told me that he kept seeing a famous FSA drought photograph, the bleached skull of a steer lying on sun-cracked hardpan. It must be many miles to help and just as dangerous to set out on foot as to stay where he was. Shortly before he saw my headlights swaying over the sagebrush, he found himself wondering about drunken renegades from the Shoshone reservation.

He was only a few miles from a highway where the traffic of a sovereign state had been passing all day and all evening. There may have been that sheep wagon within half a mile; there must have been a ranch house within three or four miles. Only chance had delayed help so long; worthless as the road was, several cars should normally have come down it before mine did. He was as safe as he would have been at the Waldorf. He was altogether safe from Indians, cougars, wolves, rattlesnakes, thirst, and starvation. But though his phantasmagoria may make an amusing anecdote it is not a silly one. The country had gone strange in daylight, then mysterious in darkness. If the gentleman ever wrote a column about his kinship with pioneers, I missed it. But a sentence in a later column which I did read told the essential truth about the episode. "Get off a main road," it said, "and you find out that the West is a big country."

History and literature have both typed the man ahead of the sheriff, the latter so monotonously that one is disposed to forget that sometimes still he finds sanctuary in the wilderness. One of several I have known will do for a specimen. He is wanted in a Southern state for a murder which he certainly committed. The crime dates back more than twenty years; he has spent those years in one of the wildest areas of Idaho, along one of the most turbulent rivers. He sometimes pans a little gold,[7] works at times for dude wranglers, goes out to little towns on errands for isolated ranches, signs on for a while with the work parties of construction firms or federal bureaus. He has a "spread" of his own, a cabin, a corral, some horses, a boat. Who he is and what he is wanted for are known throughout the big area he works. Just as in horse opera, no one gives a damn. But, in bitter violation of the horse opera code, everyone talks about him.

This type, if there are enough to constitute a type, has no significance but there is another one that has a great deal. He is to be found in or on the edge of every Western wilderness; he is almost certain to be called "the Professor." Frequently he used to be a professor.

His cabin is hidden in deep forest, or occasionally at some trickle of water far from a road in the desert. It may be strongly built and kept clean and neat with the outdoorsman's fanaticism for order, which is more obsessive than any housewife's. It may be a half-weather-tight shack, filthy and stinking, the bedding lousy, an inch of grease on the rattletrap stove, an inch of grime on the walls. It is likely to be crammed like the Collyer brothers' house . . . with learned books and periodicals, or with heaps of newspapers picked up from old camps, or with a rubble of objects that have no value and no conceivable use.

Very occasionally the Professor is, in a way, gregarious; if so, his cabin is a rendezvous for the thinly spaced residents of a big area, but he never goes out of the forest. Almost always it is only a few of his neighbors who ever see him, and they only at long intervals and never for long. A stranger who comes into his range will never see him, but the Professor will hide out spying on the stranger. If you should catch a glimpse of him bolting into the undergrowth, he will be dressed in just such patched, cast-off clothes as hobos used to wear in the comic sections. Sometimes he has acquired the skills he needs: shoots a lot of game, cuts and stacks his firewood, winterproofs his cabin, searches out wilderness delicacies. Sometimes he has got hold, God knows how, of some money. The nearest rancher, or the mail rider, or a ranger or engineer will find hung in the trail or tied to his saddle a paper bag with some greasy bills in it and a list of supplies which he will be so good as to bring back the next time he makes a trip out.

Sometimes, however, the Professor is unable to live by his own labor. It is the neighbors—if the word can be widened to the proper scale—who keep him alive. The rancher leaves a sack of flour and a side of bacon at the place where the path to the cabin joins the trail. The district ranger periodically brings to the empty cabin a grainsack full of groceries and canned stuff. The mail rider brings tobacco, some fruit, an armful of old shirts and levis. During hunting season all of them drop by with a rib-roast of elk, and I have known more than one game warden to let an out-of-season hunter go free on condition that he leave his deer for the Professor. One or another of them chops the firewood, mends the roof, banks the cabin with evergreens as winter comes on, sometimes delouses the quilts.

The Professor may be gentle, cantankerous, or truculent. He may be a monomaniac who, by mathematical calculations of great brilliance and complexity, has established that on a given date mankind will enter some new phase or that at precisely this spot the mystical forces of the universe come together in harmony. Or he may be a genius who is devoting his gift to some set of observations or computations that are sane in every respect except that they are wholly futile. Or to some manic study of immense size and vagueness that will still have thousands of pages to go when, some day, the ranger finds him dead and gnawed by rodents. Just as often, he has put learning behind him altogether, and a career that may once have promised great achievement ends in the compulsive gathering of oddly shaped peb-bles, to be heaped in front of a cabin that is rank with excrement of squirrels.

The common element is feral. This is a man in terror and in flight. His reflexes are sharper than Leather-stocking's. They have been honed by the fear that he may encounter some ordinary need of mankind, indeed that he may encounter mankind; while he slips through the brush, nerved to bolt from your malevolence if you should look over your shoulder, his mind is vertiginous with fear. It seems obvious that his fear masks a basic hostility. I have seen in his eyes a rage like that of a cor-nered eagle with a broken wing.

One reads too often that our culture has crippled men like the Professor. We are all born into a world we never made and cannot master, and tragic as he is, he is nevertheless just another of us for whom the hazard proved too much. Not civilization or learning or the us-ages of the mind broke his wing but something not tran-scended in himself. I have been accepted by a few of his species and have heard in full about many more; I would guess that what he most commonly walled himself away from is the existence of women. Many a man who fears women feels safe with a whore, who is felt to be differ-ent in kind from a woman. But I have never heard of a professor who sought out a whore or any other woman, or was known to live with a woman, or was ever seen talking to a woman.

This is another species of the genus that includes the *castrati* whom Dr. Deutsch and my friend Sam called the as-if people. He has come to the wilderness because it is his safety. He is in direct succession from the frontier, one of whose many functions was to provide sanctuary for the maladjusted. It is historically true that happy, satisfied people have been the least likely to go west.

Broad characterizations of the Westerners are not feasible. When I read the books they have been writing about themselves of late years, and especially when I read books by converts who have gone west, I find much that does not square with experience. Most of this literature must be regarded as an exhibit of illusion. It issues from the myth of the Old West.

Thus the variations of Mr. Chapman's verses about the handclasp and the smile are simply not true. Westerners are no friendlier, no more kindly or generous or outgoing, than anyone else. It is true that in many circumstances small formalities long part of the folkways elsewhere are dispensed with in the West. This sometimes pleasant fact is due to the fluidity of Western society and the rapidity with which it changes—economic forces, not wellsprings of character. The shirtsleeves cycle was always likely to be repeated three times in a career, instead of once in three generations. Your waiter at a country club may be the chairman of its membership committee a few years from now. The attendant at a gas station may own it and a dozen others soon. The cashier at a restaurant may hold the mortgage or be lording it over the proprietor's wife at the Sons and Daughters of the Pioneers. The servitor has never felt a need to curtsy or touch a forelock, and it behooves the client or customer to use his first name. In return the hotel clerk will use your first name, a waitress will call you and your wife "honey," the universal assent is "sure," not "yes, sir," and no introductions are required.

In many circumstances this easiness of manner becomes pleasing manners. But "Come in just as you are," is economic.

Hospitality was a historical reality; it has bequeathed modulations to this age. It was not Western but frontier; as common, because as necessary, on the Connecticut or the Kanawha as on the stream that flowed through the roseate fantasy of my friend and ally Struthers Burt and was called there Powder River. (She's a mile wide and an inch deep and she runs uphills; let her buck. But this began as the slogan of a commercial entertainment.) On every frontier the arriving stranger had to be fed and sheltered from the weather. But he might be anyone, he might be a feudist or a cop or a Texan, and the writer of horse opera forgets that if he was treated as a guest he was watched as a potential assassin. In the contemporary West this has worked out as a notable xenophobia.

Distinguish between the rural westerner, who has never been a yokel, and the westerner who lives in a city or one of the dreambound towns which believe that Western enterprise and the manifest favor of God will make it a city by quitting time on Friday. To a high degree the rural westerner has qualities of poise, self-containment, skepticism, and unhurriedness of thought and habit comparable to those I have noted in the wilderness men. So very often, except during Old West week, has the ordinary citizen of a town that has not eaten the loco of the Coming Boom. The breeziness you read about is abundant in the cities. The booster-club vociferousness, the Chamber of Commerce blatancy, are reflexes of commerce and illusion, and they are louder in the West today than they have ever been anywhere else. It is as if Henry Mencken and Sinclair Lewis had never lived, as if the acids of the depression had never worked on Kiwanis, as if urbanity had never leavened our time. And this in the section that, historically, was urbane and sophisticated from the beginning.

Some time back I was travelling on a journalistic errand with an ally in the fight to preserve the public-power program. He is an educated and cultivated man, one who had had a distinguished role in that long war. We came at noon to a little town where he was known, which indeed he had helped to create, since it was a product of a reclamation project that was turning desert into cropland. Rotary was meeting. So we had to go to Rotary and we had to speak.

I cannot love group singing that is not on the one hand formal or on the other spontaneous; Rotary singing is a sleazy self-hypnotism. The machine-made fellowship of Call me Scotty and the pumped-up solicitude for the Boy Scout picnic offend me. The prayer, I am sure, offends God. Here the man who made it was both the pastor of the town's lone church and the president of Rotary. In a lubricated voice he tabulated the local assets for God's closing bid. Then several members and my friend and I made speeches. We created here a new Chicago, a greater Seattle. We annexed subdivisions till the horizon shut them out, built colleges and skyscrapers, and erected along the railroad spur such miles of Kaiser, Ford, Alcoa, and Inland Steel as you could not count unaided. No later than November 1.

All this magnificence in a wretched little dump, hideous beyond expression, and of no future except as a crossroads market where wheat-ranchers would drive in on Saturday for supplies. Doubtless in time there would be lawns here and a gymnasium for the parson's YPS but never, throughout eternity, an instance of double parking on the main stem.

Inevitably, the hamlet was threatened by local and migratory communists. The orators told us they were resolved to die, if need be, hazing them out of the cactus. (A few months later, one of them flew east to tell a Congressional committee of the plots that had made the alkali quiver.) And of course all New Deal tyrannies were defied, the bureaucracy was ridden out of town on a rail—here in this mote in a desert, which existed only because the Bureau of Reclamation had brought water here. And had arranged the financing so that six-sevenths of its cost would be paid by the taxpayers back east. These villagers were six-sevenths pensioners of the bureaucracy.

I cannot account for the moment of the West I grew up in that succeeded in breaking through this sweat-stained illusion. The speaker who provided it must have been a red, for he told about a man whom Rotary had induced to settle here by promising him that the town teemed with beautiful and complaisant women, an over-supply of women; he would find a woman behind every tree. The trouble was, he learned on arrival, that there were no trees. Thus the West used to laugh at its own mirages. The core of the Western humor used to be dis-enchantment, self-derision. Its corrosiveness was sanity. Predestinate suckers defrauded by the climate, the ge-ography, the minerals, the land, and the booms that always turned into busts, the Westerners took solace in calling themselves the come-ons of the world. But not today. DuPont and Dow would have this crossroads a metropolis by Friday.

We must also differentiate the Western rich. I do not mean such a large-scale spectacle of fear, cruelty, and swinishness as Texas has accustomed us to. I do not mean that there is a clue in the fact that, as a class, the rich are the unhappiest Westerners, and the most vul-gar. (Again allow the widest exceptions for California, which has its own culture.) Part of their fretfulness is due to their serf-like status in an economy which they neither control nor direct, though they profit from it. But they exhibit in a pure state another aspect of the anxiety that is basic in the West.

So many of their ways, fears, embarrassments, and illusions are so boundlessly silly. Here once more the

Westerner is the fall guy of the world, and his wife and daughter more conspicuously so. The engaging inno-cence the type had when Harry Leon Wilson sketched it, and Mark Twain before him, is gone now; there is only a timorous arrogance. The West skins them at the sucker traps it has built for Eastern vulgarians on tour: Las Vegas, Palm Springs, the false fronts of Hollywood. Even as they swarm there they are fretful because, and here is the heart of it, this is not New York; it is, alas, the provinces, a one-night-stand Babylon, a bush-league Paris. What the space writers call café society does not begin to be thought of as existing till one reaches the Hundredth Meridian. At that line its clip joints become a precious paradise, but a paradise in which the rich Westerner can be at best only a second-class angel since he is just a sojourner.

No novelist has yet described the anguish of a Den-ver millionaire's wife who, superbly aware that she has on a ninety-dollar corset from Bergdorf-Goodman, never-theless perceives that Sherman Billingsley has not rec-ognized her, though he returns her greeting most cor-dially. Nor has any shown us a band of Western first vice-presidents joyfully following some Judas goat with a by-line into night clubs that feed on their fat, where the very waiters sneer at them in what they take to be acknowledgment of their status.

The obverse of this used to be the Western con man. Of his two functions, east and west, the first has pretty well disappeared. The professional Westerner has joined the dinosaur. He frequently looked like Albert B. Fall. In a frock coat, big hat, immaculate linen, and a string tie, of courtly manners and slow speech carefully orna-mented with Southern slurs and elisions, he frequented Wall Street offices and the clubs their proprietors intro-duced him to. He moved with the same authenticity in Paris, London, Edinburgh, and the clubs, chateaus, and country houses thereby opened to him. His job was to get the capital which the West intended should not pay out. The function remains but has been corporately systematized, and he does not. But nothing has changed the boom or its bust. No element of mirage in the Western consciousness is more fundamental than the big cleanup that is to come.

If we must have a symbolic image of the Pioneer, it should not be the Homesteader or the Cowboy, it should be the Boomer. Settling the West was an inflationary movement; developing it has remained one. Gold, silver, copper, cattle, oil, timber, real estate. The Mother Lode, Paradise Flat, Little Los Angeles—you would make your stake, you would get the fillings in Jim Hill's teeth, you would cash in. Ten thousand ghost towns, millions of acres of now sterile wheat land, a hundred thousand surveyors' plots of subdivisions never built, five hundred thousand boomers going back to my wife's folks, busted by God—they have never made any difference. You are still going to shoot the moon and get out in time.

Anyone interested in seeing history replayed should visit a bucket shop where millions of uranium shares, quoted at a quarter of a cent, change hands every day. He cannot see a uranium boom town for, of the two capitals, Moab is in a desert and Grand Junction a long way from the deposits. An oil town will be provided for him every little while, however, and it differs from Bonanza Bar only in the style of boots. Or the same thing is on view whenever construction work is about to begin on a big dam. . . . So I saw the North Dakota plain in 1946 when, the war over, they were going to start the Garrison Dam. Scores of shacks left untenanted by the northern dustbowl were being hauled there on rollers; so were hundreds of wooden and metal corn cribs that would be housing soon.

Here is another set of plots and plans but they are different in that they are being acted on. The plain is mapped off in fifty-foot lots. Small signs say "Store,"

"Bar," "Cocktail Lounge," "Hotel." On the other bank of
the river there is order, for Reclamation or the Engineers will build substantial houses for the executive and
engineering caste, hoping to sell them to the citizens or
speculators of a permanent town when the dam is finished. Meanwhile they righteously turn back from the
border not only crime but sin too, and incidentally suf-
frage and citizen participation in schools, government,
and the police department.[8] But this side of the river is
Frontier, the contractor's town, and whatever it is able
to attract. The signs should say, "Fifty feet for fifty dollars yesterday, a thousand bucks today, five thousand if
you can get out in time." They should also read "Bucket
of Blood," "Lil's Cribhouse," "Madam Billygoat's Parlor
House," and "Rattlesnake Bill's Faro Palace." Production
is by belt line but the stuff fabricated is the same.

Remember, however, that in all booms someone does
clean up, someone always did. And sometimes when the
waters recede it is found that organism has somehow
attached itself to organism till something like a coral
reef will remain permanently. When the survivors look
at it, they see the cathedral towers that Kennecott or
Reynolds will have built there by tomorrow night. As
they look, the outlines blur and belly out and flow into
one another and drift off above the ground.

I have said that Denver is hardly a Western town.
Perhaps it is Western only in that it is not Midwestern
and that it is sure it will be the metropolis of the continent before the year is out. Otherwise it is the frontier
outpost of Eastern finance. That fact went to shape it
very early, and another force, felt in various other
Western localities, has been felt most strongly here.
Denver became a haven for the tubercular. How mistaken they may have been does not matter, nor how
many died. (Though the sanitariums were mostly at
Colorado Springs, a town built altogether of fantasy but

now being transformed by military secrecies.) An extraordinary number of lungers, or people who thought they were lungers, found the disease arrested and themselves invigorated, and so stayed on. The type gave the University of Colorado an early lead over other Western colleges and became prominent on later Colorado faculties. Also in Colorado businesses and professions and as a perky, eccentric and mannered leisure class that always had brilliance. They have given Denver its individuality and an intellectual and artistic life that is only tinged, not colored, by the West.

Few people have been able to write unemotionally about San Francisco. It is the most beautiful American city, and the whitest and most shining city. Only two American cities, I think, are truly loved. And whereas New York's lovers are shamefaced, suspecting that their love is neurotic, San Francisco is loved as naturally and passionately as a woman is. It is, in fact, our one city that is naturally referred to with the feminine pronoun. She is beautiful as a woman is beautiful, and gay, melancholy, capricious, generous, cruel, delightful, and appalling as a beloved woman is.

You may see her truly in trivial things. Often I arrive at San Francisco preoccupied, absorbed in whatever errand has taken me west, hardly aware of where I am except as a stop on an itinerary I laid out some weeks ago. What brings me awake may be only a sandwich or the sauce on a roast or the dressing in a salad, and this in some commonplace, anonymous restaurant. Even a lunchroom respects food. I suppose there are thousands of Italian bootblacks in the United States, and that San Francisco bootblacks are no more fortunate economically than any others. But you hear bootblacks singing in San Francisco, and you don't anywhere else. Is the day clear? I taxi out to where I can get a glimpse of the Farallones. Or stroll casually and gaze at the towers that crown the hills. You can see no such composition, no

such variations, in any other city. Even the architect-
engineers of our Bauhaus culture have departed from
type; their euclidean blocks are not technocratic. Find
some steep cove where remnants of the old city are left;
even the Grant Age gingerbread is droll.

I have dinner with a friend, any friend, any San Franciscan. We must choose a restaurant where he can show
me the lights shining in the Bay, his cloth of gold spread
on the water. Later on we must go to the Russian Hill
and see Jacob's Ladder pitched betwixt Sausalito and
the Top of the Mark. We must go to Telegraph Hill, to
Point Diablo, to Wolfback Ridge with the wind you can
lean against and the black water crawling in from Asia.
Surely there is time to drive to Point Lobos and then
back toward the Bridge. And tomorrow night we must
dine at Julian's Castle. Over the weekend he must show
me delights of his mistress I could not possibly perceive
myself—the ferries for instance, there are ferries on the
water and beached forever on the shore, and they are
San Franciscan ferries. He will show me how the fog
rolls over the Marin Peninsula at 4 P.M. and blots out the
Bridge. As reverently he will take me to some crumbling
Benicia wharf and satiate the seeing eye with a film of
oil on the water. . . .

Seattle has had no such impact on the national
awareness. It has lacked expositors and still does. Its
setting is hardly less beautiful than San Francisco's,
though wholly different. At the far corner of the continent, it is a city of mountains and wilderness with the
frontier near at hand, and it is also a seaport opening on
the Orient and the North, and a kind of Venice as well.
Rich, powerful, violent, it is yet self-contained and con-
trives to mask the strife beneath its surface with an admirable suavity. It will be the principal determinant of
the future in the Northwest, a region more seismic with
change than even California. But, most curiously, it is
not Northwestern in the sense that, for instance, Port-

land is. It is comparable to St. Louis, in the heart of the Middle West but not a Midwestern city, sharply integrated in its separation from the Midwestern culture. St. Louis has its own personality, its own characteristic life and feeling; whether Seattle has I have never been able to make out.

If Seattle is St. Louis, then assuredly Spokane is Kansas City, though it is trying to be Chicago. In fact, it is Kansas City's twin, with the family characteristics magnified and intensified. It expresses well the area it likes to call the Inland Empire, which is the Northwest between the Rockies and the Cascades. A hard, half-frontier, vociferous, boomer-ridden country, where the harshness of our business culture and the hysterias and delusions of our advertising-agency religion have reached their maximum, or their maximum so far. In a region thus saturated with Cro-Magnon political convictions, it has inevitably developed its Chicago *Tribune*. Here in a region that tells you, with much reason, that it is bringing in the future (and with the speed of an avalanche), there is the *Spokesman-Review* to articulate and systematize the phobias and fantasies of two generations ago.

. . . What about the West's newspapers? The Portland *Oregonian* was long the best of them and it still is a good newspaper, though editorially it has badly regressed. The Denver *Post* is by a good deal the best of them now; a fine paper from any point of view and with the staunchest, most independent, most liberal editorial voice the West has. The Salt Lake *Tribune* is a good newspaper and the San Francisco *Chronicle* a better one, though it too has regressed. Name the Sacramento *Bee* and you have finished with the metropolitan press. In a million square miles there are enough good small newspapers to count on the fingers of one hand. Of these, one is the *Tribune* at Lewiston, Idaho. The people of Spokane must read that one if they are interested in finding out what has been happening in the United States or the world at large, or in reading editorial opinion whose orientation is of the present century. The *Spokesman-Review* is the biggest whistle-stop daily in the United States. Two or four enormous sections will tabulate the calf-drop of every county in the Inland Empire, mention every church social, and name every farmer who drives to town for a pound of nails. The domestic news of the United States will add up to a column and a half, and the visitor will be lucky if he finds any foreign news at all. The editorials might as well be boiler plate from NAM.

In fact, outside the radius of the papers I have mentioned and perhaps a few more I am momentarily forgetting, the ordinary usages of journalism are much better served by radio than by the press, and the West is the only American region where the observation can be made. The broadcasters and commentators are not, God knows, in general fixed stars of liberal enlightenment— California has more carbon copies of Fulton Lewis than Texas, and most other states have front runners too. But every local station does at intervals put on the air five minutes of the stuff that the wire services carry, which is much more than the local paper prints, and without them the West would have no way of knowing what is going on. My trade requires me to keep abreast of the news and when I am in the West I can do so only by invading telegraph rooms and digging out the wastebaskets. During the last two weeks of the 83d Congress I was making my way from Spokane to Denver by one-night stands. I was interested in the outcome of several Congressional wrangles and the fate of several bills. Of these bills three directly and fundamentally affected the West. But there was never a word of the wrangles or the bills in any of the local papers. Frequently, I could not find anyone who knew about them when I phoned the local city room. So I would go over to the plant, present myself as a working member of the craft as I am entitled to do, and read the day's accumulation of teletype copy that the city desk had not bothered to read. It is true to the region that, as a result, I usually had to submit to an interview on the tremendous future of Nine Mile. . . .

And the Inland Empire is scared. The Western anxieties rise to a high pitch here, and with them Western xenophobia, suspicion, and the hallelujah-shouting of the vigilantes. It is repressive; it beats down dissent more brutally than ever the San Joaquin farm associations clubbed Okies or wetbacks. And there is that most reliable of indicators, the splinter evangelical sects. Popular belief is correct in holding that Los Angeles is the capital of millennarians, perfectionists, revelationists, and the other crackpots of our day and our past, but outside Los Angeles they are nowhere near so uniform a rash as they are in the Northwest and especially the Inland Empire. . . . The Inland Empire culture is not what one hopes to see prevail in the Northwest. The hope is that Seattle and the lower Columbia Valley can leaven it.

Is the Northwest a *pays* within region? I don't think so; it is only more virulently afflicted with the boomer inheritance than the rest of the West.

Utah is a *pays*. Or rather, not Utah, which is the political unit, but the Mormons' lovely Deseret where the Saints of God are met, which is the society. It is the harmonious society of a staid and stolid people. Let no one tell you that the Mormons are the Prophet Joseph's people, they are Brigham Young's people. Their religion does not concern us here—I find it supremely dull—but their society does. It has proved to be the most successful adaptation, so far and with the ultimate verdict not in, of man's institutions to the desert. It is a fruitful way of life for those who compose it: they are happier and more contented than most people, they are members one of another, and they have an infinite hierarchy of worldly

as well as heavenly obligations to work through. They
are a highly cooperative society. If this indicates that
the desert is best to be mastered by the usages of cooperation—and considerable Western evidence apart from
Deseret points in the same direction—then, embar-
rassingly, more inquiry should be made into dictatorship.

For if the Mormons are a cooperative society, they are
also one ruled by an oligarchy, and ruled more absolutely
than any other Americans, now or in the past. A puritanical people, they are also a genial, industrious, and
happy people—and an entirely submissive people. The
originally Icarian beehive which they have adopted as
their symbol is entirely appropriate; they are not, and
have never wanted to be, individuals. It does not matter
to them that their institutions faithfully parallel those
of the police state. It does not matter to a historian, either, but it does to the inquirer into cultures. Pleasantly
leavened by some of the communal arts, Deseret is a society without intellectual life, socially conservative to an
extreme, anachronistic in idea, verbosely moralistic, un-
stimulating, uniform. In Utah you can live the outdoor
phases of Western life to the full; no one except the Mormons finds much that is interesting in the rest of the
culture.

New Mexico is also an autochthonous culture, an incomparably deeper and more pleasing one than that of
Deseret. Against the formidable odds of three nations
and a self-constituted master race, the New Mexicans
have contrived to learn how to live with one another, to
learn from one another, and to incorporate rather than
destroy traditions. No claim could be made that the
frauds and injustices perpetrated through a century on
Indians and Spanish-Americans have been resolved. But
to perceive how strikingly they have been reduced you
need only cross the border north, west, or east. . . . The
truth is that you do not need to cross the eastern border.
The eastern counties are heavily tinctured with Texas,

and Texas has always been the curse put on New Mexico. In the old days it was violence and mobbing and feuding and a threefold Jim Crowism; today it is Jim Crowism and the superstitions and compulsions of a spiritually squalid evangelism.

New Mexico is the least Western of Western states, in that it is the weakest Rotary. It has no vision of becoming an Inland Empire or Gary, Indiana. It is at peace with the desert, mature as the West at large is not. It has absorbed some of the tranquility of the Indians and the Hispanos. There is a living awareness of the past here and an acceptance of the present; the youngest of states, it has the oldest consciousness. And that this is New Mexico, not the Southwest at large, is clear when you cross into Arizona. Each state thanks God, fervently and with reason, that it is not the other one.

New Mexico is limited by the desert, is self-limited. California is not. This is the fabulous country. How fabulous it is there is an overabundant literature to tell you, and I have no intention of adding to it. Violence, precariousness, illusion, paradox, and absurdity have no doubt reached their peak here. But the state has evolved its own way of living, its own society, and it increasingly diverges. It may very well come to imprison the rest of the West; it is certain to shift the center of gravity of the United States. The thing rushes on; if it has its indecencies, and on its own scale, it has its grandeur too. It will continue to rush and diverge till the migrations, the population explosion, and the manswarm have filled it up. Or till the water runs out.

Deseret, New Mexico, and California are the autochthonous cultures—they have form, pattern, symmetry, as the remainder of the West has not. The generalization about deserts and mountains which I have been making and will shortly resume apply to it, but nothing differentiated takes shape. If the manswarm goes on multiplying the population of Colorado east of the mountains, nothing

specifically Colorado will emerge. How distinguish Idaho
from Montana? What separates, except superficially,
Great Falls from Greeley, Portland from Tacoma, Boise
from Tucson? Culturally, not enough to count.

We must note a couple of arrests. Two Western states
exercise sovereignty without having reached the social
maturity that should justify it. It is evident that one
never will reach it; I am entirely skeptical about the other
one too.

Lincoln needed another state to ratify the Thirteenth
Amendment and two more Senators who could be
counted on to stand beside him against the Radicals in
Congress when the time came for reconstruction. So
110,000 square miles of desert became the thirty-sixth
state and were named Nevada. Lincoln did not live long
enough to use the Senators but the new sovereignty
voted for the Amendment. It was a notable service to
the United States and would justify maintaining the
area as a National Historical Park on the same basis as
Jamestown Island or Washington's headquarters at
Morristown. What other benefit has the United States
had from Nevada in ninety years?

The state is an evolutionary product of its poverty,
which is to say of its desert. Of the eleven Western
states, it has the smallest agricultural production, the
smallest livestock production, the smallest number of
farms, acreage of cropland, and acreage of pasture. It is
the last in cattle, sheep, and all crops except hay and potatoes, in which it ranks above New Mexico. It grows so
little fruit that the *Statistical Abstract* of the Department of Commerce sees no reason to list it.

Nearly 79,000 square miles of Nevada are under the
jurisdiction of the Bureau of Land Management. Practically all of this that is usable at all is desert rangeland,
and degraded by overgrazing below its original sparse
productivity. It is the dregs of the public domain, the

land that the government could not give away. (Much of it is still open to homesteading but no one files on it.) Another 9,000 square miles are held by the Department of Defense and the Forest Service. There is no secret about the military uses. Most of the national forest area is held for watershed protection and has little value as timber.

Nevada's great wealth was the Comstock Lode. It ran out long ago and mineral production today is not impressive. Of Western states it is fourth in gold, fifth in copper, sixth in zinc, and seventh in lead and silver. The only new development has come with the refinement of magnesium near Las Vegas with power from Hoover Dam.

One hundred and sixty thousand people live in 110,000 square miles. A small population bound firmly to an exploitive economy, they have always been manageable and have always been managed. Nevada has always been the private fief of a small group of managers representing mine-owners, railroads, the largest cattle interests, and of late years the quasi-financiers who own the gambling. In the flush times of the Comstock Lode the legislature was openly on sale and was bought as a matter of course. Such wasteful expenditure has been obviated; there is no need to buy what you control. There have been periods when no more than three men have managed a sovereign state, and I doubt if vice-presidents have numbered more than two dozen at any time. The late Pat McCarran acted as if he personally operated the state. He didn't. He operated some of it but he answered to tiller ropes that were in the hands of a small financial oligarchy. New Mexico sent to the United States Senate one of the biggest scoundrels ever to sit there. Even so, New Mexico since 1912 has sent more good men to Congress, or lower the sights and make it merely decent men, than Nevada has sent since 1864.

Of productive pursuits, Western history has shown that a mining economy makes for bad government and "big" (as distinguished from "little") stockgrowing for worse government. But much of Nevada's economy can never be productive at all, it is parasitical. The great blight is the gambling, with some assistance from the organized divorce traffic. (The latter is important to the state but is not large comparatively—Florida grants twice as many divorces a year, most of them to temporary residents.)

Gambling is a business but it creates no wealth. Except for a handful of professionals, the people who gamble are transients. They have no stake in Nevada; they come, spend their money, and get out. A fair percentage of them are the hoodlums attracted by all crowds and all chances for a quick buck. They are noticeably restrained from crime, on main streets and in the towns anyway, by one of the most efficient police systems in the country. But their language, their behavior, their very presence make honky-tonks of the oppressively luxurious resorts whose business it is to rob the rich. And the proprietors of the honky-tonks are necessarily in a managerial alliance with the racketeers turned technically respectable businessmen. The biggest business in Nevada has tie-ins with the foulest elements of American society. No matter how burnished a casino, filled with millionaires, movie gals, and the most highly paid of entertainers, there is always a reek of the underworld.

The grotesque structures at Las Vegas and the Strip have nothing to sell except luxury and gambling. Those at Reno, mostly, have not got even genuine luxury but sell excitement to the middle-middle class. There is nothing else, not even scenery, not even climate. This is an ordered amusement system; it has no other social importance and no economic function at all; it is a fungus. Its basis is the simple fact that the kind of amusement it sells is illegal elsewhere. It is politically vulnerable in the highest degree. So there has been nothing for its owners to do but become political managers.

For another aspect of the fungus look at gambling not in the movie-fantasy casinos and hotels but in its truly squalid sets. Take the room just off (or in the corner of) the bus station, the lunch counter, or the corrugated-iron hotel in any highway hamlet. There may be two tables and dealers, more often there is only one. Spend late afternoon and evening there and watch the transients of the road, the hobos, the local mechanics and cowboys and high-school teachers and high-school students make their four-bit or four-dollar flyers at the slot machines, craps or twenty-one. There is no splendor here, there is not even excitement. Nor are these people tourists who can afford, or almost afford, their losses; the truth is, they are not even people running the gambler's race against chance. They are simply local victims of a slight, endemic poison, as if they had adjusted to a tincture of arsenic in the artesian well—people who have grown up with a contained infection of social rot. And one wonders where the dealers come from, gross and fisheyed, character extras in some gangland movie made on Hollywood's back streets.

Nevada has as many votes in the Senate as New York, Pennsylvania, Massachusetts, or California. No Senator from any of those states, in many years, has had so much power to use nationally as McCarran had, and in all our history few Senators have used power so harmfully. Nothing is likely to change in Nevada. The business community, the middle class, the farmers, the small stockgrowers, the labor unions, the University—they are too weak to break the system. The United States is stuck with it and the West may live to regret that it is too.

Wyoming was erected into a Territory in order to reduce the political jurisdiction of the Mormon Church, and to put the approaches to the Mormon citadel in the hands of a Protestant government. That was in 1868.

The territory became a state in 1890. At the time it had neither an economy nor a society. It did have a number of what used to be called cattle barons and some Gentleman Ranchers. The barons were of the second and lesser degree—successors to the real barons of the previous decade. They had got their start as foremen of the real barons, stealing their employers' cows, and then had been able to buy up what was left of their herds when the inflation called the Cattle Kingdom collapsed and the Big Freeze finished the job. They were in temporary alliance with the Gentleman Ranchers, whom they were preparing to bankrupt presently but meanwhile had a use for. There was a job to be done, a slight job of massacring the competition. It could be done most handily under state government, that is by formally endowing the Wyoming Stock Growers Association with the sovereign powers it was illegally exercising. The notion, ridiculous a year or so back, made sense to a Congress which foresaw that the Republican hegemony, briefly overthrown by the Cleveland victory of 1884, might suffer the same inconvenience in 1892. So the Association became the State of Wyoming. There was nothing to make a state out of but nothing was required. The Association needed the police power, the militia, and the courts.

The stage coach era was over and there was no such emergency as the one that justified Nevada. The Union Pacific and Kansas Pacific had been operating in the Territory for twenty years; the Burlington was on its way there. Telegraph lines joined the principal villages. There were telephones and electric light. There was everything except a logical reason to make a state.

The Stock Growers Association eventually became bicameral, for there came a time when you had to stop shooting sheepmen and either raise sheep yourself or make an alliance with those who did. It has always been the state government. It has managed the state on the principles of the most primitive, most parochial, and most massively inert of human occupations. In sixty-five years it has shown no sign that it could develop the adult political responsibility that self-government requires.

This is not to say that it exhibits either the political or the social decay that Nevada does. It is merely arrested in its political adolescence and should have its governors and judiciary appointed in Washington and its legislative powers subjected to review till it matures. Oil, labor unions, and the dude-ranch business may eventually make a state of it.

It has oil, as Nevada has not. It has no other minerals worth mentioning, except such deposits of bituminous and lignite coal as eternity could hardly exhaust if an economic use for them could be found. It has more agriculture than Nevada but this is only a comparative, for mostly it is too high to grow in quantity anything except forage. It is more exclusively a grazing economy than any other state.

Two other considerations. Wyoming also has scenery, as again Nevada has not. And it is the center of the Old West myth, the stage on which the myth is principally dramatized, its capital, its spiritual home. That the scenery, which is to say the tourist business and the recreation business, has not broken the stockgrowers' hegemony is another paradox. The dude ranchers provide the most powerful opposition to the bronzed horseman mentality. But their stock in trade is the Old West, which provides the strongest defense of the bronzed horsemen. They have sometimes allied themselves against the Association with the labor unions which supply the state's principal drive toward political maturity. (The unions are weak as compared with those in Montana and Colorado but much stronger than those in Nevada.) If the alliance becomes permanent and the rest of the recreation business joins it Wyoming will achieve statehood.

Under Section 3, Article IV, of the Constitution of the United States, a state can join with another one as a single sovereignty. That none ever has means nothing; all that is necessary is the consent of the two legislatures and that of Congress. The provision licenses us to hope that Nevada may yet become an extension of California. The event would require the purchase of the Nevada legislature, on historical lines. No doubt the price of a permanent rather than a temporary sale would be high, but California has the money.

The hope does not hold for Wyoming. The legislature would not sell, Colorado would not buy, no other state could afford to. The Constitution provides no way by which state sovereignty can be nullified and Territorial status restored. Permanent martial law is not feasible, and civil war seems to be out of the question. It looks as if the West is stuck with the 44th state.

Chapter Four

Unregarded Inheritance from the Frontier

The longest narrative in American history is the one covered in the texts by a chapter called "the Westward Movement." The local library has a lot of books—I myself have written four of them—explaining what it was. Here it is accepted as given. I will merely allude to the portions of it that scan "the West" in popular thinking, and to them only by way of certain symbolic images or emblems that stand for them. Such images as: the Mountain Man, the Covered Wagon, the Gold Rush (to California, and hence also the Forty-Niner, but by extension to later bonanzas and hence the Miner), the Plains Indians and the Indian Wars, the Stage Coach and the Pony Express, the Pacific Railroad, the Long Trail and the Cattle Kingdom and the Cowboy.

From here on iconography grows more reticent. We have constructed few images for a period of the West that begins just as those I have listed peter out. It has proved possible to make a hero out of a crook who is a psychopathic murderer but not out of one who steals timber. Not even the West does. A pioneer grandfather who shot a rustler is to be bragged about; one who got rich by promoting a phantom water-company gets no schools named for him.

The common use of such symbolic images is inevitable and on the whole they are satisfactory. We have to be satisfied with them, in fact, for they constitute all the Western history most people will ever know. The job of the historian is to separate the historical experience in them from what has been added to it. Others besides the historian have the same job.

The people of "the Westward movement" were heterogeneous. Every kind of person went west, all our types and categories. But the kinds went in different proportions. I have remarked that the impulse was weakest among the well-heeled and the well-adjusted. The well-heeled were likely to stay put. And well-adjusted people who undertook the tremendous and pattern-shattering step of moving out were likely to be young. They were likely to be broke, poor, or of humble station. They were likely to go west in the hope of bettering their estate; Americans had always grown up to believe that they would do better in a new country. They would get a farm out west and prosper either from "the richest soil in the world" or from the rise in the value of land—they would farm or sell or speculate. Or they would find an infinite number of opportunities to make a living, "to grow up with the country," to rise in the world.

These people are the stabilizing force on the Western frontier. They are "bringing the country in." They are creating an agriculture, towns, business, trade, transportation. They are making the settlements and we are on their side here. For it is from the settlements, the permanent residents with a stake in the country, that civilization is to come.

The fact is that farmers, ranchers, the wilderness technicians, and townsmen are the West and always have been. Nothing is more curious about the contemporary West than its inability to get this fact through its head.

A habit-shattering and pattern-shattering experience. When a person headed west, he broke the bonds and constraints of the culture he had grown up in. There was a chance that the severed strands of personality, behavior, and value might knit together in a different pattern when he reached his destination. There was a chance that they might not knit together at all. A migrating people took their social institutions with them as they took garden seed, and they labored to erect them unchanged in the new country. But there was a chance that those who took the institutions and garden seed with them might not be, when they got there, the same people they were when they started out. Nothing is commoner than to find that the pioneer was a changed person. He might be an enhanced person but he might be a stripped man by his own act.

He might be stripped, too, by this migration. At best crossing the plains was an exhausting labor; many died on it and many more went to pieces. To the strain of labor, with extremities of cold and heat and storm, might be added fear, accident, crippling, disease. There was also a forced acquaintance with the brutalities of mere existence in a hard and hideous country and with the brutalities, miseries, truculence, injustice, cowardice, bullying, weakness, and dishonesty of those you traveled with. The sum might be too great to be withstood. If some people mastered the experience and may be said to have been developed by it, to have the integrity of personality enhanced, others crumbled under it.

Bringing in a country a thousand miles not only from one's roots but from everything else is a severity that has been taken for granted but not much understood. It would help to think of the pioneer as a man or woman who smelled high. Personal cleanliness did not become

a widespread American ideal even in long-settled portions of the country till toward the middle of the nineteenth century—most Indian tribes were habitually
cleaner than the white stock. But on the frontier even
those who held the ideal found it hard to live by. Many
settlers might not bathe at all during the winter
months. Many did not bathe at all for periods considerably longer.

For a considerable time children might have no
shoes. They might grow into the family pair as their
brothers and sisters grew out of it, and it was too precious a possession to be used much. Meanwhile they
went barefoot except in winter, when their feet might
be wrapped in rabbit skins or gunnysacking. Pa might
not know how to cobble shoes out of home-tanned hides,
or he might have no truck with such fanciness. There
might be no cobbler for a distance that was not to be
traveled lightly. The value of a hide might be so great
that it was to be bartered not for shoes but for necessities. Throughout childhood there might be no under-
wear. Girls wore one garment and boys wore two; in
winter other layers were added outside, not under-
neath. Hair lice and body lice were so commonplace as
to be expected—the frontier mother is a woman fanatical, and frequently unable, to delouse her children.

What of a family of four, eight, or twelve living in a
twelve-by-fourteen log cabin, with later on a lean-to and
a summer kitchen added? Well, for one thing, millions
of American children, pretending to be asleep or peer-
ing through the cracks in the loft floor, watched the
begetting of their younger brothers. It was almost impossible to keep a cabin clean or smelling sweet, but a
cabin was far superior to any other frontier dwelling.
Take the soddy of the plains or the pole-roofed dugout
built into a hillside or a cut bank. During dry weather
dust and pulverized earth sifted into everything, and
when there was rain your house was mud, rivulets, and

drip. For years after one drove one's stake the bacon, mush, bread, and bedclothes might be full of grit. And I might raise the question of toilet paper.

In the beginning there was nothing except what you had brought with you and what you could make out of the material at hand. Then for a period the amelioration of discomfort depended on the slow production of a little wealth and on the conquest of distance. You could get shoes for the children when you could barter produce or exchange labor for them—and when you could travel, or have them brought, the equivalent of what today might be three thousand miles. As for health—and disregarding a diet without vitamins in the winter and always limited and monotonous—you survived by virtue of the fact that no one has more than one fatal illness.

Medicine was folk medicine, which meant that there were specifics for a few ailments, charms and spells and amulets for many, and nursing that was on the whole sound. For systemic, chronic, deficiency, and metabolic distempers there was no treatment at all. Up to the Civil War this did not much differentiate frontier life from life in the medical centers of the East—but thereafter it did, and increasingly. There was little dentistry and less surgery. What of a broken hip, or for that matter a broken collar bone, which the doctor might not get to for five days, or ten days? What of a man gored by an ox, chewed by a bear, crushed by a falling tree, or shattered by any other accident? The pioneer at forty is often a man who needs spectacles he cannot get and so perhaps cannot read print or do fine craftsmanship. Half his teeth may be gone; those that remain may be snags, frequently painful, often infected. He may have a twisted leg or arm. A "gathering" may have cost him the hearing of one ear. His wife's scrawniness may be due not to his having worn her out with childbearing but to the fact that after childbirth there was no one to do trivial surgical repair.

Bear constantly in mind the sharp deviation between town, even a crossroads hamlet, and the farm or ranch country. A village that is on a freight road or has a dock where a river steamer ties up is a paradise of goods, services, and social health. Here there are nails, pants, safety pins. I suppose that, next to the church and the saloon, the barber shop was the most vivid emblem of civilization: you could get a hot bath. As rare but more often beyond one's reach would be the shack where some widow made hats for women and calico dresses for nubile girls.

This disparity continued into the twentieth century, in fact till its first quarter was ending, and during most of this time it actually increased. Until there is a kind of road into the back country, a hundred miles is a hundred miles—ninety minutes nowadays but three or four days by horseback and a week or ten days by wagon. By 1850 eastern America had achieved a very widespread comfort, much of which was available to rural populations. But in the West there were long-established frontiers, and new ones opening up, till Model T.

None of this is to impugn the satisfactions, pleasures, or happiness of life in the frontier West. It is merely to mention some of the forces that affected people who, severed from cultural continuity and sometimes impaired in personality, arrived at a country that imposed straight and narrow terms for human survival. And who had to build a culture in such a country from the ground up. See such forces in relation to the establishment of a commonwealth in a place where next door is three or ten days away. In relation to habits of worship. Or to the establishment of a legal system or of schools. Or to the exchange of friendly visits, the talk of neighbors, the development of ideas. . . . There was the culture one had left behind, to be reconstituted so far as possible. There was the strongest of all drives, to make a community, to facilitate intercourse, to ordain government. But the forces

I have alluded to interfered. In varying degrees, but
everywhere to a considerable degree, the first generation on any Western frontier was a regression.

The next step may be conveniently examined at a
mining camp, preferably a rich one. Nobody has come
here to erect a community. Bring water to an acre on
cropland and you have built for eternity, or at least for
humanity's portion of it. But take an ounce of gold or silver from the ground and you have brought the end of
the local society that much nearer. (Even if hardrock
mining comes and the veins prove profitable into a second generation, they will run out.) You have come in a
monomaniac, mirage-bound passion to get rich. Or you
have come to live by means of people whom that passion
has brought here, or to prey on them. There is no need
to call the passion greed and occasionally it is not illusory, but it is powerful beyond expression and it is anarchic. Human culture will evolve at Nine Mile; it will
not even begin at Nine Mile Gulch.

Most of these camps are in the mountains, many of
them very high up. Since we have stipulated a bonanza,
they are prosperous. They are hard to build and hard to
supply. The surrounding forest is flattened to build
shacks and to timber the shafts of mines or extend the
flumes of placers. Much business is done in structures
that are part canvas. Half of the population, or more,
lives in tents, huts made of packing cases, dugouts,
caves. Banks, hotels, saloons, whorehouses will come to
clapboards and brick before other structures, but for a
time they too will be a composite of logs, plankings, canvas, and dirt. There is no problem of money—no problem, that is, for those who have it, and they may be as
much as twenty or at times forty percent of the popu-
lace. Presently money will buy quite a bit, will buy some
of the most fantastic and hilarious paradoxes in this
country of paradox. Presently, that is, it will buy cham-

pagne (where there is no uncontaminated drinking water), and plate-glass mirrors and nudes from Paris for the saloons, and gold-plated fire-axes for the politicians, and gold doorknobs for the offices of nabobs. Almost from the beginning it will buy whiskey of a kind, whores, and an evening with the tinhorns. But for a period it will buy, quite literally, nothing else. A long time will pass before it will buy comfort, however elementary, for anyone at all.

Amusement may be extemporized in some form of personal combat or the baiting of animals, but only whiskey, whores, and gambling can be counted on. There is no other form of relaxation. Five thousand men, or it may be twenty thousand, have swarmed in a gulch on a mountainside. They exhaust themselves by brutal labor, in conditions that increase its brutality. They are afflicted by brutal weather, against which most have little protection and none adequate protection. They live in constant danger of accidental death. They are driven by the oestrus of gold, made delirious by fantasy, racked by fear of failure and of one another. . . . At the end of the day there is nothing else to do. A farmer can talk to his children and sleep with his wife. His son can ride a few miles and spark a girl. His young daughter can borrow the grain-scoop and slide down the hill in it. But at Bonanza Bar there is no escaping frenzy or desperation except by getting drunk, spending ten minutes with a whore (in a parlor house, up to half an hour), and backing the delusion of your luck against the gamblers.

Except in war, and Southern prison stockades, Americans have never lived so vilely and degradingly as in the mining camps. All the barbarities of other frontiers, diet for instance, must be thought of as greatly magnified here. The Boot Hills so objectionably advertised by chambers of commerce today are to be brought into perspective not by Chuckwalla Pete whom the marshal shot after a Hollywood walkdown, but by the injured laborer whose gangrene the maggots in his wound could not take care of, and by the frozen corpses of starved bums and beggars that were found half-devoured by rats when the snow melted. . . . This was not a society, it was the atomization of society. No form of wider human association existed till the stabilization of hard-rock mining came, when Bonanza Bar could have a Masonic lodge, some fire companies, rudimentary labor unions, and far from rudimentary organizations of finks and scabs. The annals of murder appall one not by their brutality but by their triviality. Life has become so cheap that it is barely worth saving—or even taking.

Three successive entries in an old notebook of mine (which was devoted to minerals, not crime) will give the idea. A drunk invites a bystander to have a drink and is refused; he lifts the bystander by the hair, holds a revolver to his ear, and blows his brains out. In the street someone objects to a freighter's bringing his team up the wrong side, and disembowels the freighter with a butcher knife. Not liking a stranger's stutter, someone empties a shotgun into his belly. Or take a few items from a recent book whose author makes etchings of ghost towns in Colorado. At Rosita two drunks kill the bouncers who have thrown them out of a dance hall. At Creede drunks empty their six-guns into people's legs for fun, and Bob Ford, the dirty little coward who shot Mr. Howard, is killed in a quarrel with a tinhorn. At Silverton two men are killed for associating with a sheriff, so the camp lynches a Negro who wasn't there at the time. At Lake City, which is well along in civilization, school is dismissed so that the children can see two bodies hanging from trees. At Buena Vista "Men were killed every day and the killer simply went before the judge, pleaded guilty, and paid a ten-dollar fine." Ten dollars was an exorbitant license fee, representing an advanced stage of civilization. Commonly a life was worth less than a slug of a red-eye, which cost a long bit if unadulterated, a short bit if rectified on the premises.

If casual murder is revealing, incidental murder is still more so. On all frontiers it is basic that life is less valuable than property, any property. Whatever you may have, someone else wants. He will take it by murder if he must; you will retain it by murder if you can. What the mining camp focuses more sharply than other frontiers is the growth of organization. Two men can rob better than one, a dozen better than two, an organized lodge better than an extemporized gang. Most camps soon came to be dominated by a ring of thugs, who increased their wealth by robbery, terrorism, and murder. When instruments of local government were provided, the ring took them over for its own use.

Organization to resist such organized robbery is the next step. The citizens' committee develops to safeguard ownership, the fruit of a man's labor, his claim or his dust or the contents of his safe. Only incidentally does it protect life. Once it has taken the instruments of local government away from the thugs, it devotes them to its own end, the protection of property; a considerable time must pass before personal murder as distinguished from murder in the line of business becomes reprehensible. By that time something of a governmental system beyond the locality has usually developed, and the next stage is for the vigilantes to go into politics. They now formalize, for control of a Territory and eventually of a State means power and wealth. Their non-political functions are separated out and come into the keeping of the stockgrowers' association, the territorial or state commissions of mining and lands, the chamber of commerce, the corporate alliances, and the university trustees. Throughout the evolution of the West the vigilantes survive under other names. Their power fluctuates but they are always there.

Lawlessness is a function of solitude, that is of the wilderness, and of distance, that is of the wide open spaces. Anarchy and outlawry *as such* diminish in exact proportion to the improvement of communication. The agent of the law, whom I want to differentiate specifically from the agent of the courts, has the problem of distance, which is his enemy as it is the friend of his quarry. His is the same dilemma as that expressed by one of the West's stories about the Indian wars. There came a moment when a captain of cavalry at some small post rebelled against the conditions in which he was required to practice his futile and always maligned skill. Fifty or a hundred miles away the Sioux or the Cheyennes or the Comanches had raided one more ranch or stage station, and a telegram arrived from the commanding general, conceivably Phil Sheridan, ordering him to take the field—to get there, he knew, with the corpses scalped, the buildings burned, the Indians long since dissolved in space. It directed him to ride forthwith, locate the Indians, and surround them. He wired back, asking for instruction in tactics. How, he inquired, did one cavalryman surround twenty Sioux?

So with the marshal or the sheriff setting out to take Laredo Bob who has robbed the bank at Mesquite. Bob disappears into the illimitable country and there is no way of taking him unless he commits some flagrant indiscretion or someone turns stool pigeon. A rival thug is less likely to give him away than some legitimate business associate. Tradition and literature are full of tales of relentless, long drawn out pursuit of outlaws through manifold risks and hardships, by trailers who in the end get their man. Down to the construction of railroad and telegraph lines practically all of them—all that are not in fact stories of commercial rivalry—are myths.

I have differentiated the agent of the courts. Politics begins when government widens beyond the local community. "Law and order" is a phrase. To the citizen of a settlement—the farmer, the small stockman, the burgher—it means something entirely different from what it means to those following the big opportunity. Legislatures and courts are instruments of power infinitely more important than the six-gun and the vigilance committee. The citizen wanted community orderliness. The agent of the big shot wanted the natural wealth of the West. Hence the violence of Western politics. It was facilitated by Territorial government, the most efficient device for corrupt political control in our history. And the use of this instrument was facilitated by the process of history itself. The Territory of Illinois filled up with inhabitants so rapidly that the anarchic stage of politics could be ended in a few years. New Mexico Territory or Wyoming Territory must string out this stage over more than a generation.

The division already noted is fully evident here. On one side are the interests of those who are "growing up with the country." The ordinary citizen stood to gain from a stable and peaceable society: the security of person and property, the proliferation of trade, the growth of schools and hospitals and similar institutions, the assistance of local undertakings by the greater power and wealth of Territory or State. The implicit enemies of the ordinary citizen were the big stockgrowers (individual or corporate), the mineowners, the speculators, and as it soon turned out the bankers who were either the creatures or the owners of all these. All these too began in natural alliance with those who very soon owned them, the Easterners who had or could get the capital that the West had to have. Money in unflagging streams was essential to development, inflation, and speculation. The individual absentee capitalist yielded to the corporation, and here a process that was gradual elsewhere, and was modified by many divergences and competitions, was in the West swift and without effective opposition. The land, the water, the minerals, the grass, the oil, production and supply—there the vast wealth was. The local big shot lined up voluntarily with the outsider, or the outsider cracked the whip and he came in.

The history of Western politics is a story of recurrent uprisings by the exploited local interests against a master class that was always rich and always either aligned with or owned by aliens. The instruments of government were for sale and they were bought. It does not matter much who bought them, a stock association, a railroad, a land company, a mining combine, a mortgage company, or a syndicate composed of them all. The point is, government was subverted for use. It was, I believe, in Carson City before the nabobs of the Comstock Lode had mastered the principle that rich men ought not to fight one another—it was at this time that an agent of one faction gave Western politics a definition which has endured, "An honest man is a son of a bitch who will stay bought."

Courts, sheriffs, legislatures were devices to be employed against the builders of the commonwealth precisely as mortgages, freight rates, and rigged markets were employed. The periodic rebellions of the exploited, more or less successful, more or less temporary, were as Grangerites, Populists, Progressives, the sons of the wild jackass, soft-dollar men and anti's of every possible combination. But from the beginning those in revolt could oppose their masters and make genuine gains for themselves only when they could bring against the Territorial and State systems owned by their masters the force that remains the only really effective one today. The federal government.

We need some paragraphs here about whores, badmen, and Texans.

The sexual folkways of the pioneer West will never get into history books. So far as I know only one historian (whom I am about to quote) has ever perceived that they were a part of Western culture. What prevented him from analyzing them will stop anyone else who may try: there are no documents. But anyone who lived in the West early enough to have known pioneers knows of one specifically Western quality in prostitution. Even in the notably puritanical society of Utah, as a boy and adolescent I became fully aware of it. From a great many witnesses I heard testimony to a great deal whose cultural significance I was not to understand till many years later. In particular I heard one ancient whom I will not name since he was a friend of my father's and in a way of mine. Students of Western history would recognize his name for he eventually felt an urge to write his memoirs, and with a local hack ghosting them he did. Worthless as literature, the book has proved useful to historians for it deals with a couple of subjects I am discussing now, for its author respected the literary taboo. Whereas he talked for hours at a time, and in my memory over a good many years, about the whorehouses he had known across a million square miles.

The specific aspect of prostitution I refer to is the brutality that harmonizes with so much else of the West. I do not mean the coarseness and forthright violence of men in crowds who need women when there are few women. That is to be expected and in that respect Western honky-tonks did not differ from honky-tonks anywhere else; the behavior of cowboys or miners on a bust was no different from that of anyone else on a bust, including college boys.

But quite apart from this, an unmistakable strain of cruelty runs through Western prostitution. Literature and horse opera have completely disregarded it. Of the two stock types of prostitutes they deal with, one can be accepted as valid, the madam or the parlor-house girl who married the man on his way up. It happened as a matter of course because society was in flux—and why not? But horse opera's other figurine, whom it casts as the dance-hall girl, is preposterous She is presented as the feminine principle with bruised petals, one more tear-jerker. In the actuality, however, she was often a female dehumanized by the manic cruelty of her customers.

The frontier whore, that is, was often so degraded that it is futile to look for the equivalent in the waterfront dives of far ports. She was an old bag for whom her profession could provide no employment in any place where the first steps toward social stratification had been taken. Or, very often, she was a child who had become physiologically a woman within the year. Or she was any other female whom circumstances had exposed to the utmost conceivable debasement and depravity. This fact goes without mention in the literature, which also fails to mention on the one hand her pimps and on the other her mercilessness in robbing and on occasion murdering her clients. The clients were made triply helpless by lust, drunkenness, and their compulsive needs, but she supplied an additional element. The stories I head from oldtimers detailed violences she inflicted that would not bear print. They were only a weak reflex of the vileness repeatedly inflicted on her.

We arrive again at several kinds of frontiersmen I have mentioned before, who had in common the need to escape from civilization. It will be shortest to quote Mr. George F. Willison, whose judgement is supported by all I have heard. Speaking of those whom he calls "lone wolves," Mr. Willison says that he thinks a lot of them were schizophrenics who went west "driven to desperate adventure and often bloody violence by their own difficulties and deep-seated emotional conflicts." As for women, these invalids had "a sort of virginity complex in reverse." They "could not associate sex with a 'decent' woman." They were in fact terrified.

So, Mr. Willison says, "the obverse of this was that as no 'good' woman had anything to do with sex, those

who frankly did—the women of the town—were scarcely
women; indeed were lower than animals and to be
treated accordingly, with all manner of brutality and
perversion. Anyone who knows the mountains is well
aware that the traditional old sourdough was celibate
only in terms of respectable society, and those who have
listened to his stories also know that the most blood-cur-
dling tales of violence and sadism on the frontier have
never been printed, and never will be."

I have heard the stories and I agree. The loungers at
the Red Front Livery Stable would roar with laughter,
recounting the West's traditional and largely fictitious
yarns about the sexual behavior of sheepherders with
their sheep. Then with a gusto that was unmistakably
autobiographical they would tell you about much more
revolting vileness which it had pleased them to inflict
on the girls in the cribs. This has to be added without af-
fidavit to the frontier heritage, but it has to be added.

I am less interested in the "badmen" than in the
place they occupy in the myth of the Old West. Two observations must be made here, however. First, they
were psychopaths. It is self-evident that those recognized in the myths as the patricians were: the repulsive
moron Anderson, alias Bonney, alias Billy the Kid, for instance, or Doc Holliday, or Tom Horn. Is it possible, outside a romantic fantasy, to see a professional murderer,
whether an agent of Murder, Inc., one of Al Capone's
hoods, or the hero of Lincoln County—is it possible to
see him as anything but a disease? And I doubt if there
was any difference worth measuring between Billy the
Kid and his extinguisher Pat Garrett, the overgrown
playboy who was an admiration of Theodore Roosevelt's, an associate of Albert B. Fall, and a friend of
John Nance Garner. Hickok, Masterson, the Earps[1]
were, from time to time, allied with what for want of a
better term may be called the law. But what is to be said

of any man who takes pleasure in killing? Or, alternatively, who is proud of his reputation as a killer? We need not wait for psychiatry to answer.

Precisely there is the important clue. The "peace officer" was in the employ of the local ring, or the business combine that had broken it. The ring wanted to be protected from competition and challenge. Its successors wanted the customers and their money to be safe during business hours. They hired a murderer and gave his murders legal sanction. The badman must be understood as an employee, and the killing he did as a business method. The conduct of commerce required intimidation and murder as it required ledgers and bank loans. It happens that, during one of the phases of the stockgrowing business, conditions required the services of a killer more commonly than other Western businesses did. When you think of Billy the Kid, or any other knight in high-heeled boots striding out in what horse opera calls the walkdown, you think of him as you would of an inspector, an insurance adjuster, or a file clerk. He killed to keep his employer in the black, and when the books were balanced at the end of the year they were likely to show that he was worth what he had cost. He did not cost much.

Why was this psychopathic thug so often a Texan? For one thing, as Texas society began to grow out of its primitive stage, it chased him out in impressive numbers. An official publication of the State of Texas in 1878 ran to 226 pages and, acknowledging that it was incomplete because forty counties had not reported in time, listed 4,402 names wanted by the Texas law.[2] Most of them had gone over the line into New Mexico—the line that was the boundary of Lincoln County—and a lot of them stayed right there, though a lot followed their star toward other opportunities. This was the peak of a process that had been going on for some years, during which there was a steady drift toward the safer and freer areas.

But the basic reasons are to be sought in the history of Texas. It was an earlier West, almost as big as the West, subject to most of the same conditions, and with unique conditions of its own that reinforced them. It existed as a frontier society much longer than any other state did, and its frontier period dated back to a much earlier time. The process of stripping I have described—social regression and the dissolution of personality—were therefore more complete than anywhere else. In those enormous areas (which, besides, were populated mainly from the South), the institutions of society were harder to establish and maintain. As an example, schools: frequently the Texan as a Wyoming Lancelot was illiterate. Again, the church: the religion commonly taken into Texas was from the shrieking evangelisms of the backwoods South. It was degrading in itself and the stripping process left only its most repulsive portions. Lancelot was irreligious but his mind fermented with tag-ends of terrors, compulsions, manias and superstitions as powerful as those of voodoo and less rational.

The South also endowed Texas and the émigrés that went west from it with the blood feud and the habit of personal vengeance. And during the long frontier stage of Texas warfare was continuous—war with Indians, with Mexicans, with the Mexicans who became New Mexicans. It had given Texans a consciousness that can be recognized as that of a Master Race. The concept of the Negro as subhuman had been widened to include Mexicans and New Mexicans. It was no more unethical to murder any of the three animals than it was to flog a slave you owned. And to this had been added the social annihilation of the Civil War, defeat in it, and Reconstruction. Add the postwar bankruptcy, which was an induction coil that raised the voltage of fear, resentment, and vengefulness. Finally, the Texan who went into the West went as a cattleman or a cowpoke. It is, as I have remarked, the most primitive of occupations.

This then is the Texan in the West immediately after the Civil War. As a generalization, he was a rudimentary consciousness, exceedingly emotional, preyed on by terrors and passionate vengeances, a man at once feudal and feral. He was a nervous system whose reflexes were compulsive violence. He long antedates the modern orchitic myth of Texas, and yet there is visible in him some of the same doubt of his maleness that has produced it. All this made him, merely as a Texan, raw material for the murder business; he was from a culture that closed its arguments, points of honor, and commercial transactions with gunfire. If he was already on the lam, an outlaw from a society beginning to proliferate, he was by so much the more available for hire as a thug. It is striking how much more commonly he was for hire than cowpokes like him from the ranges of Oregon and California, who were infiltrating the interior West at the same time.

Turn now to the cattle business which the nation at large, and the West itself, belatedly adopting the general view, have come to regard as the most culturally beneficent portion of the Western frontier. Some of its benevolence I have already alluded to and others will be noted further on. Here we may observe how it fits into the pattern.

To get the necessary acknowledgements out of the way, let me say forthwith that, like all frontier occupations, it was hard, dangerous, and skilled. The cowpoke did not need the complex and extreme skill of the mountain trapper of a generation before his time, but he was much more a craftsman than a miner, say, or a pony express rider. He lived at the mercy of the Western weather and the daily circumstances of his work seldom rose above hardship. His life was rough, comfortless, monotonous, in a dangerous country, and in association with cows.

His employer was at the mercy of many things besides weather. The cattle business has always had to be conducted on a basis of quicksand, on paradoxes that could not be resolved. One constant is that it was always being pushed back by the advance of settlement to less productive lands. Another is that this least controllable kind of agricultural production was always to be conducted more efficiently in large operations, and yet the larger the operation was the more vulnerable it became. Yet another is that it was the Western business most subject to fluctuations and the most easily dominated by financial concentrations—by people outside the business who had capital.

Its base was competition for the public range. It never made a satisfactory adaptation to this necessity; its organization was at best little above anarchy. In competition for the range the odds favored those who had power and sometimes capital. This created and maintained the division I have noted, the big operator as against the little one. And yet the bigshots had to compete with one another. It was never possible for them to do so in socially acceptable ways or with reasonably constant profits. The romances, many of which are called histories, speak of a convention or conception called "range rights." According to this theory, in a given region there were recognized and respected boundaries to the area which a given grower's stock could graze. At a particular line, that is, the Hashknife range ended and the Bar-K range began. It was never very true anywhere and never true at all for very long. Cattlemen had to invent the stock association in order to safeguard their hierarchy and to maintain the advantages of the bigshots against small cattlemen, sheepmen, homesteaders, and rustlers. (Rustler: a person who was in the cattle business or the employee of such a person.) But there was an earlier and even greater necessity to invent the stock association in order to maintain a species of peace and a means of arbitration among bigshots.

The bigger the operation, the more profitable. And it is the nature of herds to increase. And there is nowhere more than just so much grass. Whatever their will was, and though always caste-conscious it was seldom fraternal, the bigshots could not help encroaching on one another's range. There were only two ways of meeting this competition; both undermined the business. You could hold your own range, or enlarge it, by force—in the end by terrorism and gunfire. Or, since grass your cows eat will not feed someone else's cows, you could overstock your range. Both solutions made trouble and pointed toward bankruptcy, but the second was an economic catastrophe. Overgrazing rapidly cut down the productiveness of the range, which meant that a given area supported fewer cows, which meant in turn that the cattleman's costs rose and his capital assets shrank. (In the era called the Cattle Kingdom, cost-finding was so sloppy that this fundamental fact was only infrequently perceived in time.) But what is worse, overgrazing produced deterioration of the land.

Within a very few years after the opening of any new Western range there are complaints about overgrazing, complaints made by the men who did it. Overgrazing and the destruction it has caused are one of the most formidable problems of the West today, but they always have been. I may point out that the buffalo were brighter than the cattle barons. The now eroded ranges of the plains were never at any time grazed by half as many cows, perhaps never by a fifth or a tenth as many cows, as by the buffalo whose uncountable herds damaged no land. The buffalo were migrants; they kept going. The cattlemen concentrated their herds, held them in place, and increased them.

Competition for the range meant vigilance committees, range detectives, hired thugs. Thus the range war,
the standard theme of horse opera. It was in fact standard and standardized. It was of three principal varieties. The big operators undertook to scare or murder
the small operators off the range. Later, cattlemen made
war on sheepmen. Eventually sheepmen combined with
cattlemen to make war on the homesteaders, whom the
cattlemen had been shooting up all along. The second of
these business practices, the "sheepkillin'," introduces
another variety of Western violence.

(Theme for meditation. Why has romantic fantasy,
which glorifies the trailing of cattle, especially of longhorns to the railroad, entirely ignored the trailing of
sheep? It is as striking and picturesque as the Long
Trail. The era in which it was standard procedure lasted
much longer—roughly the last forty years of the nineteenth century—and the areas it was practiced in were
more numerous and extensive. It was at least as important economically to the West. It was quite as dangerous
and on the whole more difficult, for the sheep trails led
across deserts and mountains, as the cattle trails did
only seldom and then only for short distances. It produced more incident, excitement, rage, and hazard, and
if its spectacles were on a smaller scale they were more
diversified. It required as much skill and produced as
much hardship.

There were memorable sheep drives before the Civil
War, to California from New Mexico. But the important
trailing of sheep was postwar and in the opposite direction. It was from the ranges of California and the Northwest that those of the interior West were filled. Longer
drives from these areas to St. Paul, Omaha, Kansas City,
and other markets are on record but were uncommon.
Similar drives northward from New Mexico were routine. But the established eastward trails give the idea
best. One led from the Willamette Valley to the Grand

Ronde, to the Snake River, and across Idaho to the valley of Green River. A glance at the map will show that it was strenuous. Still more so was one that led from the Sacramento Valley across the Sierra and the northern Nevada desert to southern Idaho and on to Wyoming. Even that one was mild compared to the trail that crossed the Sierra from the San Joaquin and traversed Nevada diagonally to Utah. But sheep trailing has not interested horse opera.)

Well, the grass was in the public domain. That phrase is specific; it means the public lands. The open range was part of the common wealth of the American people. It no more belonged to the cattle barons—only in Texas and the Southwest did they choose to speak of themselves as kings—than it did to you or Joe DiMaggio. There was no pre-emption or homesteading, which were the two legal methods (apart from the earlier land auction) by which title to the public domain passed to private ownership. The barons were accustomed to assert that they held title by conquest, "We took it from the Indians," but outside of Texas this was in general not true. Nobody was using the range when the barons reached it. But because they did reach it, it was theirs. No statute forbade anyone else to use it—quite the contrary, legal procedures for its acquisition in due form by anyone were established—but God's law did. So it was not only illegal but blasphemous for someone else to try. When the sheepmen arrived, you ran them out.

There were fewer sheepkillings in Utah than in any other state, the Mormons being peaceable and orderly folk and, because of the desert, very often sheepmen. They were commonest in Colorado and Wyoming, with New Mexico and Arizona making a creditable run, there are instances everywhere, and the most systematic campaign was in Oregon.

The barons, or rather their cowpokes, were killing sheep as early as 1870 and as late as 1920. The methods were inexpensive and, of course, safe. (For horse opera's Lancelots did not needlessly expose themselves to risk.) Sometimes they notified all comers not to bring bands on the ranges they said were theirs.[3] Sometimes they warned interlopers off "their" ranges, or off ranges they proposed to add to theirs. Sometimes, though this was late historically, they posted "deadlines," on one side of which it was OK for sheep to use the public's range. Usually, however, nobody bothered to send cards. And very often a killin' was without previous plan; it was a high-spirited romp thought up at a saloon.

The waddies assembled in sufficient force to make opposition even more unlikely than it would be in natural course. (Except there would be only one herder, or at most two, at a sheep camp. As a caste, herders were unwarlike—not being Texans—and usually they were foreigners.) If society had developed to the stage which insisted on protocol, they wore masks. They rode to the interloper's camp and burned the sheep wagon, bedding, supplies, and outfit and killed the horses, though elevated sentiment sometimes kept them from killing the dogs. They headed the herders out of the country on foot, sometimes beating them up to give them the idea. If the waddies were carrying a load of redeye or included Texas Lancelots, or if the herders showed fight, the herders got killed. Then the formal ceremonies began.

Sheep are even dumber than cows and horses; they are the stupidest of animals. They are also the most easily frightened. Ammunition being expensive, usually they were not shot. (Besides, who would carry five thousand rounds on a summer holiday?) The most expeditious method was to drive them over a cliff, if any were at hand, or even a cut bank, where they would smother one another. Dynamite would be used sometimes, and oftener than you would think their throats were cut, by the hundreds. Most often, however, they were clubbed, and it got to be hard work. A dozen cowpokes would require several hours to beat two or three thousand sheep to death and would be bushed after the eighteenth hole. But there were ingenuities. Once in the San Francisco Mountains of Arizona a herd of mustangs turned up and were chased back and forth through the bands of sheep under attack. (In bands numbering 25,000.) On the Little Colorado a stretch of quicksand was at hand and four thousand sheep were driven into it. Fire was highly effective but hard to control; you seldom got such a break as some waddies of Carbon County, Wyoming, did in 1887, when they found 2600 sheep in shipping corrals at a desert siding, sprayed them with kerosene, and touched them off. The widespread practice of scattering poison on the range was abandoned, for though there were selective poisons they sometimes did not work selectively and some of the barons' cows died. Besides, poison provided no sport for Lancelot.

There is no census of sheep killed or sheepherders murdered. Over the decades, the former must be numbered by the hundred thousand, many hundred thousand, and the latter by the score, many score. Such murder was punished only occasionally, and only nominally. A few fines are recorded and a few jail sentences, all of them short. The death sentence was passed once in Idaho but it was immediately commuted and the outraged victim was soon pardoned. Disturbances preceding or following a sheepkilling sometimes became so widespread that social action was required. The Utah-Colorado border was sometimes patrolled in force. The Wyoming-Colorado border was even more troublesome, for the country round Craig had ranchers tough even for the Master class and the southern Green River Valley (across the center of which ran the most famous deadline) insisted on producing tough sheepmen. When the Colorado militia were used they made it, for a space, safe for cattlemen. But there arrived a period in Colorado, Wyoming, and New Mexico when sheepmen (most of whom had begun as cattlemen) got rich enough to hire Texans, legislatures, and the militia.

The record is copious and I see no reason to elaborate. I simply invite the reader to picture this blend of business transaction and fiesta in detail, casting Gary Cooper or John Wayne in the lead. Ten or fifteen cowpokes are clubbing two or three thousand sheep to death. What are the sights, sounds, and smells? What, especially, are the emotions? For that matter, what are the men and the culture?

The practice fell off after the Forest Service was established and Theodore Roosevelt—a traitor to his class, by God, for he had been a cattle rancher—made fully evident that he would support its policy of admitting sheep as well as cattle to its ranges. And as the twentieth century came into its second decade there were moments of public disapproval, even in Colorado, indeed even in Wyoming. In 1909 the "Big Horn Basin War"—Western sentiment insists on elevating murder to war—developed out of a sheepkilling that was bungled, no doubt because the knights errant got too drunk, and the "Tensleep Murders" followed. Three sheepherders were killed and northern Wyoming found itself a little shocked. The unprecedented followed. One murderer was sentenced to death; naturally, sentence was commuted but this time he stayed in jail for thirty-five years. Four of his colleagues were convicted and they too served prison terms, though shorter ones. Unfavorable publicity had as much to do with this happy outcome as public conscience, for one of the murdered men was a French citizen and his government obstinately insisted on punishment and indemnification. Still, with this incident an era may be said to have ended or at least begun to end.

The texts say that the last sheepkilling in Wyoming occurred only three years later, in 1912. Men now living in Wyoming have told me otherwise and have described their participation in later ones. I see no reason to doubt their word but these killings were on a much smaller scale than those of the golden age. The last of public record in Colorado was in the Gunnison National Forest in 1917, at a place aptly named Oh Be Joyful Gulch, where two thousand sheep were driven over a cliff and their herder tossed off it too. Again I have heard stories of later killings, in the vicinity of Craig, Creede, and Gunnison. In the summer of 1954 I heard that there had been a small killing the previous year in the Arizona Strip, but it is sagacious to believe no story that is attributed to the Strip.

In the desperate 1930s, when drought and the depression were forcing the organization of the remaining public domain under the Grazing Service, a lot of sheep and a number of herders were killed. But these involved "outlaw" or wildcat sheep outfits—wholly migratory outfits without home ranches—and established sheep outfits whose parched and eroded ranges they were further destroying. That is, they were intramural and don't count.

Fraud in the acquisition of the public domain, and with it the corruption of government officials, began when the public domain did, that is when the United States was governed by the Articles of Confederation. From then on it was constant, and it is still with us today. So widespread and commonplace has land fraud been throughout our history that our historians appear to accept it as a given. There is no inclusive study of it and the monographic literature is astonishingly sparse. In most general histories it appears only in footnotes, and those are usually devoted to the land companies of the eighteenth century. A student can become a professor and retire after a lifetime of instructing students without becoming aware that one of the fundamental forces in the westward movement was the theft of public lands. Or that, in order to make methods of theft more efficient, the government found it desirable to convert one of its own bureaus, the General Land Office, into an official clearing house for fraud. Or that land fraud has been endemic in the Department of the Interior since its foundation, like the riverside yellow fever of a century ago, at times receding to covert and localized graft, at times exploding into an epidemic that seemed to make corruption the official policy of the United States. But all we need here is a recognition that Western land frauds were on a Western scale.

Such historians as Walter Webb and Wallace Stegner have pointed out that the all but universal small-scale land fraud in the West was necessitated by a combination of American mysticism and the ignorance of the Congresses which drew up the land laws. In the arid country an honest man had to commit fraud in order to support a family. I add that that ignorance of Eastern Congressmen, who did not know the conditions imposed by Western geography and climate, was not noticeably diminished by their colleagues from the West who refused to recognize those conditions. And this: since it was necessary for Westerners to commit fraud against the people of the United States, it became natural for them to expect to commit it.

And Western Congressmen had a conclusive reason to perpetuate, so far as they could, the ignorance of the East: ignorance provided magnificent business opportunities in large-scale fraud. As would be expected, the opportunities were in the interests of big operators and against those of local communities. In fact, some of the Acts of Congress under which big frauds were perpetrated were passed on the explicit ground that under the existing laws opportunities for fraud were too limited.

My topic here is the theft of the public domain under the land laws.[4] This excludes many other kinds of land fraud, by collusion, by terrorism, by systematic gang action, and by private swindling, some of them of heroic size. So it excludes some fascinating stories, notably the fabulous effort of one James A. Reavis to acquire a strip of Arizona seventy-five miles wide and some two hundred miles long, which included most of the arable land and much of the mineral wealth in the state—or rather to acquire acknowledged title to it, for much of it consisted of towns, cities, ranches, farms, and railroad rights of way already in existence. Reavis was a genius and he forged historical documents in three nations, probably more of them than any other American has ever done. He was working a rich vein, Spanish land grants existing before the American conquest of California and the Southwest, title to which was accepted and ratified by the peace treaty and, later, by the treaty that confirmed the Gadsden Purchase.

Reavis created his claim by forgery and so did many another operator, though none on anywhere near so large a scale. But there were plenty of unforged claims under Spanish grants that were vague, ambiguous, contradictory, or merely perjured and they were a rich field for monopolists and crooked lawyers. In California it was possible to form partnerships between millionaires and lawyers at the very beginning, and the resulting efficiency brought the era to a comparatively early end. But in the Southwest and particularly in New Mexico, where there was an illiterate and intimidated feudal population (as well as both genuine and phony grandees at its top level), lawyers could become millionaires on their own and the era was prolonged for more than fifty years. Enormous injustices were done, and though some of them were no doubt the inevitable outcome of con-

quest, illiteracy, and the feudal organization of the conquered society, others were made possible only by enormous corruption.

(I exclude also the far from picturesque thefts of
state lands, those portions of the public domain that
were granted to the states by the United States for the
support of schools and other social purposes.)

The social and political theory of the Homestead Act
and the Acts that supplemented it was simple enough.
A citizen of the United States or a resident who was becoming a citizen was entitled to a portion of the public
domain large enough to support his family by farming.
Many reasons, of which the weightiest were romantic or
illusory or mystical, led to the stipulation that a family-
size farm was a quarter of a section, 160 acres. The
United States, then, would grant 160 acres of the undis-
tributed public domain to any citizen who would manifest his bona fide intention by living on it for five years
(later, three years) or any portion of five successive
years that would permit him to farm it, and by "improving" it, that is building a dwelling house on it and
bringing portions of it under cultivation. The cost to the
citizen was only that of filing his claim at the proper office and of certain surveying services. After six months
he could "commute" his claim. That is, he could obtain
full title (called a patent) to his quarter-section at once,
without completing his five or three years, by paying
cash for it at the standard price, which was arrived at by
the process of history, of $1.25 per acre.

There were ways of adding to a homestead claim the
kind of claim, a "pre-emption," possessed by a bona fide
settler who had located on the public domain before the
government survey was made. When this combination
was possible, the citizen could acquire title to a family-
size farm of up to 320 acres. Then when the agricultural
frontier reached the arid West, almost universal failure
and bankruptcy made slowly manifest even to Congress

that, though 160 acres of Iowa or Wisconsin cropland would support a family, 160 acres of western Kansas or Dakota grazing land unquestionably would not. There followed a series of Acts that enlarged the homestead claim to 320 acres and in some circumstances 640 acres. The major prophet John Wesley Powell had decided that the permissible minimum for a family-size farm in the arid country was four sections, 2540 acres. . . . Clearly not only the bona fide settler, denied irrigation, had to commit fraud to get land to support a family, but also what we may call the bona fide speculator, the man who intended to sell his land after legally acquiring title to it.

We must take note of various kinds of "script" which entitled the holder to 160- or 320-acre units of the public domain as a reward for military services or as compensation for various personal or legal injuries. (States also issued script for their lands.) Script-certificates were negotiable, they could be bought and sold, and their use in the West continued an honorable tradition of fraud and corruption that had begun with the Revolution.

The basis of large-scale land fraud was the entry of fraudulent homestead claims. A speculator, a bigshot, or a corporation hired people to file location claims to quarter-sections of the public domain, or the larger units permitted by later Acts of Congress, and to transfer to their employers the rights so acquired. In some circumstances it was desirable to commute the claims, that is to pay for the land. In other circumstances to establish the right by legally entering the claim sufficed. An employer sometimes hired false locators by the score, even the hundred. An employee sometimes filed dozens of claims, using aliases.

If the claim went through to patent, that is to actual transfer of title by the United States, sound business practice demanded that costs be kept low. Therefore to fraudulent entry was added fraudulent "proof." The claimant made oath, and brought witnesses who made oath, that he had spent the required length of time on his claim, that he had built a substantial dwelling house on it, that he had constructed irrigation ditches, or sowed and harvested crops, or made whatever other improvement the law required to establish good faith. Hence the devices that amuse students and gave the West a standard joke. A claimant of arid land established by sworn testimony that he had "brought water" to his claim and so he had, in a can, though the law intended canals. Or that he had built a substantial "twelve by fourteen dwelling"—actually twelve by fourteen inches. Or a "shingled dwelling"—a tent with a couple of shingles fastened to the ridge pole. Or he had made a crop by cutting an armful of wild hay. Certain operators built a shack or cabin that actually measured twelve by fourteen feet, mounted it on wheels and moved it from quarter-section to quarter-section, in each of which a different alias would own it but the same witnesses could truthfully swear they had seen it. Efficiency was increased by setting it up on a corner where four quarters met.

Fraud so open and extensive could not occur without the connivance of federal officials, officials of the General Land Office. The local officials were paid a private fee, recognized as a species of commission and most welcome, considering the size of their salaries. An honest one was powerless not only because the system gave him few effective measures to use against fraud but because the superior next above him was not honest. If he made trouble he was fired. All the way to the top he was fired; that was what Senators were for. Complaints and shocked protests are common in the annual reports of Commissioners of the General Land Office and Secretaries of the Interior. No estimate is made here of how many of them were honest; the system had been developed in order to work as it did, and few Commissioners or Secretaries tried to take action. Most of them were personally honest; all of them accepted the system as given. Such action as was taken, such reforms as were made, originated outside the system.

The usefulness of this tool to the cattle barons is self-evident. In truly vast areas of New Mexico and Arizona the only water sources are springs. By filing on them a baron or corporation could control the whole vastness, closing it to all others. A few thousand acres patented, or merely filed on, by the outfit's cowpokes could and did secure the exclusive use of a million acres of range, sometimes more. Some of the most notable feuds in the Southwest originated in this practice. It created patterns which may still be traced today in the cattle business and the politics of New Mexico.

Farther north it was the streams that must be controlled, which meant that an outfit had to spend more and got smaller, if still large, areas for its money. Here the tool was used mostly against "nesters," the pioneers of the advancing farm frontier.[5] By controlling the banks of a creek you could prevent the construction of irrigation works and so could control the whole drainage by owning a hundredth of it. But in the northern ranges the period of its usefulness was short. The back of the system was broken by the deflation of the late 1880s and the remnants perished in the droughts of the next two decades. There are areas in Wyoming where upward of three-quarters of the land-titles go back to patents fraudulently acquired. But, in varying degree, that is true of land title all over the West.

Fraudulent land-entry played a minor role in the creation of Henry Miller's truly imperial domination of the Central Valley of California. But there were other frauds, many kinds, and the empire must be mentioned because it is a classic illustration of land monopoly. Miller acquired solid blocks of land along the Kern and San Joaquin Rivers and so was able absolutely to dominate the south-

ern half of the Central Valley. More than that, his holdings are the reason why riparian rights are still the basis
of water law in California, as they are not elsewhere in
the West. They created what is now a monstrous, probably indestructible anachronism. It has resulted in incalculable loss and injustice, has been responsible for
much social anarchy, and has sometimes seemed likely
to produce a kind of civil war. Civil war of a local kind it
may yet produce, and it is certain to produce gigantic
corruption as the contradictions of Central Valley come
at last to the stage where they must be resolved somehow. Or anyhow.

Land companies and especially water companies also
procured false entries in wholesale quantities. But the
ends in view were speculative and inflationary, that is to
say normal for the West, and we may get on to the truly
spectacular land frauds. The timber frauds.

The West and the United States at large were resolved that the land composing the public domain should
not be classified according to its nature. It should all be
officially considered arable farmland capable of comfortably supporting one family per quarter-section. For
this infrangible resolution two motives were responsible: the illusion which experience had nowhere succeeded in altering, the myth of immeasurable fertility,[6]
and the empirical fact that there was profit in keeping
it unclassified.

It was primarily the illusion that kept deserts from
being classified as range land and so put the United
States in the position of saying that a family could be
supported by a quarter-section which could graze no
more than eight cows, sometimes four. But it was the
chance to clean up that kept the timberlands of the
West from being classified as timberlands and so kept
the United States in the position of saying that you
could farm a forest.[7] You couldn't. Only very occasion-

ally, in fact, could you farm the land where a forest had been, and from Maine to Puget Sound we have submarginal populations living on slablands and stumplands to this day. But from Maine to Puget Sound the timber operators cleaned up.

They always had practiced land fraud and by the time the industry headed west they had perfected their methods. A new kind of entrepreneur developed. He was a man with enough liquid capital to finance timberland fraud on a large scale. His operations were extensive and required him to hire specialists in the appraisal of timber and the bribery of public officials. He procured homestead claims on the forested public domain. He procured them for chickenfeed.

He may have benefited the United States in the end for, more than any other cause, his operations brought the Federal government to establish the Forest Reserves which withdrew large areas of Western forests from entry. At last, that is, there were land frauds so shocking that they turned a majority of the stomachs in Congress. So shocking that even some Western Senators changed sides.

I need mention only two species of timber frauds. The most valuable timber in the United States—in dollars per acre—was the redwoods that grew in a narrow coastal belt of northern California. In the last generation the state of California, wealthy philanthropists, private foundations, and organizations which raised funds by public subscription have spent a good many million dollars buying back for public preservation and enjoyment small groves of *Sequoia sempervirens* that passed out of public ownership at $2.50 per acre. Note that the price has doubled. In the Timber Culture Act and the Timber and Stone Act which extended it to the West, a step toward land classification had been made—in order to facilitate theft, if at a higher price. The Timber and Stone

Act bade the lumber business enter and feed. Nine-
tenths of the redwoods that came into private hands did
so by fraud; in Humboldt County, practically all of them.

The entrepreneurs were able to buy at forty cents an
acre and some land script that was redeemable in redwoods, but mostly they had to pay through the nose,
$2.50 an acre plus operating expenses. It was the finest
bargain in the history of our public lands.[8]

Enterprise was most picturesque in Humboldt
County. As soon as the government survey was finished
the entrepreneur, or the lumber company that dispensed with the middleman, was provided with a plot
which showed the sections duly marked and numbered.
The County seaport, Eureka, used principally by lumber
schooners, had the usual institutions of ports. An agent
of the entrepreneurs would appear at the sailors' boarding house in Eureka and draft a ship's crew for temporary duty. He marched them to the office of a U.S. commissioner, where those of them who were not citizens
made application for first papers; then to the land office, where each of them filed a homestead claim on 160
acres of redwood; and finally to a lawyer's or notary's office, where they signed blank deeds which would later
be filled out with the description of the individual quarter-sections filed on. The fee for service, fifty dollars a
head, was good considering what sea wages were. The
profit to the entrepreneur or the lumber company was
also good. And the fee declined from its early high to a
few dollars and eventually to what one writer calls "the
price of a glass of beer."

The redwoods came into the system of enlightened
private enterprise in the 1880s and under an Act of Congress which, according to one Commissioner of Public
Lands, was applied fraudulently in 95 percent of the entries made under it. (Another and later one estimated
that up to 90 percent of *all* private holdings of Western
timberland had been acquired by fraud.) A decade later

the Forest Lieu Act was passed in order to create another kind of land fraud. This was after the Forest Reserves had been established. The area within the boundaries of a Forest Reserve when it was set aside usually included certain private, state, and land-grant railroad holdings. The Lieu Act gave the owners or claimants—for many of them were mere pre-emptions—the right to exchange the land they held within the reserve for lands outside it.

Rich thefts were thus set up. A corporation which had acquired timberland under the Timber and Stone Act—that is, by fraud 95 percent of the time—could cut the timber and then exchange the stumpland for virgin white pine or Douglas fir. An owner or claimant of timberless and perhaps worthless land (high on a mountainside, say) could exchange it for an equivalent acreage of the finest forest remaining in the United States. If the holder was a railroad or a toll-road company whose land grant intersected the Reserve, the take could be spectacular. And most spectacular of all was the Northern Pacific's take. Its original grant from the public domain was more than three times as large as the Union Pacific's and four times as large as the Santa Fe's, which ran second and third. All told it received just less than 39,000,000 acres of the public domain—61,000 square miles, an area larger than Michigan. By special amendment of the Lieu Act, it was enabled to exchange worthless, bad, or merely fair land included in its original grant for some of the best forests in Oregon.

This last was before the forests of the Northwest had been surveyed. Presently they were surveyed and the fragrance known in the books as "the Oregon Timber frauds" followed—under the thoughtfully drawn provisions of the Forest Lieu Act. There was a miscellaneous rush, not unlike a mining stampede. The basis of the new operation was to acquire state-owned land that lay inside Forest Reserve boundaries or to file homestead claims on timberland likely to be reserved (advance information on sale in Congress). This is the period when the entrepreneurs or their principals ran holiday specials for Minnesota schoolteachers and got their locations in return—when dummy entries were sold on the open market—when the price of federal land agents and inspectors could be quoted on the curb—when a United States Senator received $25 apiece for the fraudulently acquired land patents he expedited. The Senator got higher fees for more important assistance to fraud but eventually he and an Oregon Congressman were jailed.

Here we can examine actual market figures, thanks to Mr. S. A. D. Puter, who occupied his time in jail writing his reminiscences as a specialist in timber fraud. Like other commodities, fraudulent timber claims fluctuated in price. One of Puter's employers paid $750 for a half-interest in 160 acres or 320 acres of prime timber—the other half-interest went to Puter and his partner. On this working capital of $750, the partners, after paying location and commutation fees and other expenses of $235 to $430, could turn over $320 to $515 to the dummy locator as his fee for service. Twenty or thirty such locators, some of whom might be repeaters using aliases, would go through the legal ritual and turn over up to 9600 acres of forest to the partnership. The partners might eventually sell their half to a lumber company for $30 an acre, $5120 a quarter. Again a nice profit from the public domain for the entrepreneur but a nicer one for the lumber company. The public has got $1.25 an acre for its timber. Or sometimes twenty-five cents—for there were acres which would be logged on location papers only. You claimed them as homesteads, clear-cut them, and let the claim return to the people.

Puter's prose is made of ferro-concrete but if you labor with it you can work out the details of much larger deals and even more generous profits. It was a blow, he says, when the cost rose to ten dollars an acre, that is $1600 a quarter-section, but they stayed in business.

A big mining corporation, for that matter any corporation that used land, could not stay in business, or at least could not do so at minimum cost, without practicing land fraud. At minimum cost, that is the point; it was much cheaper to defraud the people of the United States than to pay for value received and used. And if this was true of the West's basic legitimate businesses there was no point at all in reckless expenditure by businesses which dealt solely in inflationary finance. No venture in counterfeit land values, such as those which dreamed up gaudy irrigation schemes (I clerked for one in 1920), would think of paying the government price for the worthless lands it dealt in.

I have entered land fraud among the less commonly specified bequests to the modern West from its frontier past because of the state of mind it has begotten. I have pointed out that the West's only effective measure against exploitation by absentee finance that has always drained its wealth eastward has been to call on the Federal government. But if you rob the government privately as a matter of habit, you develop a kind of schizophrenia. It is the state of mind that enabled Senator McCarran to destroy the Grazing Service when it showed signs of intending to serve the public owner against the interest of the private leaseholder—all the while demanding that the leaseholder be given bigger cash gratuities from the public purse.[9] It sends a Western Congressional delegation boiling to the White House to demand a five-year payroll for a dam that will destroy the public's national park—at the same time demanding free land, cheap power, direct subsidy of wool, a larger percentage of the highway fund, direct payments for soil conservation, larger benefits for cattle and lumber, and half a dozen other tips and gratuities which it is the

God-given right of free Western enterprise to receive
from the U.S. Treasury. It sanctions the two stock associations to demand in the same breath that the national
forests be turned over to them and that larger federal
funds be spent on improving the grazing ranges in the
national forests. It enables the State of California to
argue simultaneously that the United States must build
the Central Valley Project because the State cannot afford to and that of right the United States can have no
voice in the regulation of its use. It is the simple basis of
the common argument about Grand Coulee Dam, the
brilliant theft that pays zinc and copper mining companies a magnificent tip for recovering their own silver as
a by-product of smelting their own ores, the assault on
the 160-acre limitation of the Reclamation laws, the sui-
cidal but constant attempt to overturn the Power Acts,
the endless attack on the Forest Service—the entire uproar.

It is a simple ambivalence: defend us against everyone but ourselves, pay us more money and get out, give
but for God's sake don't regulate. We took the country
from the Indians, didn't we?

When you come down to it, no. That was the U.S.
Army.

These usually unmentioned testamentary bequests
are like the loam and humus of a forcing bed. And sometimes there is harvested a perfect expression of them all
in a single set of circumstances or the career of one man.

The good that servants of the Republic do lives after
them but their names are oft interred with their bones.
It may be that the name of Henry Slattery will mean
nothing to the reader who comes on it here. Mr. Slattery
served the Republic magnificently throughout a long
and distinguished career. More than anyone else, for instance, he was responsible for uncovering the Alaskan
coal-land frauds that permanently blackened in history

the name of one Secretary of the Interior, Richard H. Ballinger. He had a long career of public service ahead of him still when, in July 1932, friends and associates of his met at the Cosmos Club in Washington to tender him a dinner in honor of the twenty-five years of such service he had already completed.

One of the speakers at the dinner harked back reminiscently to Mr. Slattery's part in the exposure of Secretary Ballinger's conversion of his high office to the profit of his well-heeled friends. Probably this reminiscence was what led Mr. Slattery, when he spoke, to recall similar investigations he had made which had led to the exposure of the shocking land frauds perpetrated, for cash in hand, by another and later Secretary of the Interior. That had been a tense time, he said, and the Secretary did not take kindly to having anyone, Mr. Slattery least of all, question his official activities. "He had a two-gun man named Baracca who had passed several men over the Great Divide." So, Mr. Slattery said, "The Secretary sent him around to see me, with a threat. I kicked him out of my office."

The person whom Mr. Slattery here describes as employing a gunman and practicing terrorism on a public official was the Secretary of the Interior, a member of the President's Cabinet, on the highest level of official life short of the Presidency itself and the Supreme Court. He was speaking of a Westerner who had got as far as he could go, as far as he wanted to go. He was speaking of Albert Bacon Fall.

In New Mexico you hear that Fall had a commanding presence, that a kind of magnetism and command radiated from him. They say that he had an "aquiline eye" and that something imperious in his being frightened those whom it did not win to happy subjection. I cannot say for I never saw him; in his photographs he is only a heavily mustached man dressed in the costume of a Western Senator or of the Western confidence man whom I have described as frequenting New York clubs (and London restaurants) in an earlier age of splendor. He looked still more specific to one of the sharpest observers of his own age, William Allen White. "The man's face, figure, and mien were a shock to me," Mr. White wrote, "that such a man could be in a President's Cabinet: a tall, gaunt, unkempt, ill-visaged face that showed a disheveled spirit behind restless eyes. He looked like the patent medicine vendor of my childhood days who used to stand, with long hair falling upon a long coat under a wide hat, with military goatee and mustache, at the back of a wagon selling Wizard Oil—a cheap, obvious faker."[10] Not faker, thief.

An excellent way to get yourself maligned, or it may be shot, is to say publicly or privately in certain circles of New Mexico today that Albert B. Fall was anything but a man of the most sensitive conscience and highest honor, whose motives were always pure throughout a lifetime of self-sacrificing service to the Territory and the State and to the United States. New Mexico has many legends and will do battle for them. There are also circles in New Mexico where you can bring the same bee-swarm round your head by seeming to disparage the courtliness of the depraved juvenile delinquent called Billy the Kid. And circles where you can produce the same result by denying, or in other circles affirming, that Pat Garrett who murdered the Kid was a coward and a cur because he did not identify himself before he shot.

Pat Garrett. New Mexico has legends—and keeps its secrets inviolate except in all bars and living rooms. A time came when Garrett was murdered too. In New Mexico it is a universally inviolate secret that his murder was procured—bought and paid for; that, by plan, a man who didn't do it was tried for it and found not guilty; and that he had to be murdered for the simple business reason that he knew too much and his knowledge was costing others too much. That is the secret but it is only legend which whispers the name of a lawyer who was to be Secretary of the Interior. The legend says that Albert B. Fall knew more than most men about the actual reasons behind the killing of Pat Garrett and knew more than he ever revealed about how the killing was accomplished.

He was a product of his time, place, and opportunities. It is also mere legend that whispers his name in connection with the barroom murder of one Clements. Among the most loathsome of gunmen was John Wesley Hardin, who when his career had run its course was murdered by John Selman, a better if not immaculate man. Fall represented Selman in the subsequent formalities and there were those, Clements among them, who believed he manipulated the evidence—a wholly unnecessary labor if he did, for in such murders a plea of self-defense always sufficed. Clements proclaimed over a wide area his intention of killing Fall, and legend says that this was the reason why he was presently killed in a saloon crowded with spectators, none of whom claimed to observe who fired the shot. The legend does not, quite, say that Fall knew.

Legend bestows on this Senator and Secretary of the Interior a variable number of brawls, canings, public fistfights, and knife-and-gun-wounds both suffered and inflicted. Some of them are by no means legends. "He quarreled in court with some of the witnesses," Dee Harkey says of his defense of another murderer, "and would have been in a duel or shot on the courthouse steps, if I had not arranged apologies." The careful William A. Keleher speaks of his "carrying a cane on his arm, with the ever-present possibility that he might use it vigorously if occasion requires," and says that "his greatest ambition in life" was to be a crack shot. It is Mr. Keleher who relates the shooting, not fatal, of one Bill Williams, "a tough fighter and a good shot of the old days."... A tough fighter and a good shot of the old days. It is certain that Mr. Keleher was unaware of the suffusion of his phrase by cultural values.

This Williams was on his way home one night, in Las Cruces. Fall and his brother-in-law, Joseph Morgan, a deputy U.S. marshal, met him and started shooting at him. Morgan hit him in the head; Fall, who never did realize his greatest ambition, merely winged him. It ended there, for a crowd rushed up in time to prevent a leading citizen from shooting when his man was, as the code is supposed to put it, down. Enemies of Fall said that the gunfire resulted from an effort by Williams, also a deputy marshal, to have Morgan extradited to Texas to face a murder charge. Friends claimed that Williams started the shooting himself, at the instigation of the local Republicans—it happened a couple of months before Fall switched parties. Note the values in Mr. Keleher's further report: "Fall himself said the shooting had no political significance; that he had seen Williams coming along the street and suddenly decided to take a shot at him; that he didn't like Williams anyway, and that the dislike had recently been intensified because Williams had shot and dangerously wounded a sheepherder from Mexico without just cause." If so, the man must have been one of Fall's sheepherders.

Fall went to New Mexico from Kentucky, a young man who had thought of entering the ministry but instead had decided to read law. He became a cowpoke, a cook for a cow outfit, a hardrock miner. But the opportunities his talents fitted him to use were at a different level; he began to practice law and went into politics. He developed the skills of both trades but in both his greatest skill was for pressure and manipulation. And, when it was required, terrorism. Mr. Keleher describes how he controlled one election by stealing a ballot box and another one by providing an armed gang. He describes a murder trial—the most famous one in the history of New

Mexico—that Fall won, or at least climaxed, by an address to the jury which accused the judge of conspiracy
against the defendant and defied the judge to interrupt
his contempt.

What Mr. Keleher does not describe is the progress of
opportunity. You could use with rich men and with the
dispossessed Spanish-Americans the same manipulation, pressure, leverage, terrorism, and six-gun menace
that paid off in court and at the polls. There were vast
riches in land, cattle, sheep, and minerals; there was a
big take for those who could bring power to bear on any
of them. Nothing is alleged against Fall here except that
he acquired power and used it. That was the way fortunes were made in the Southwest of his time. You could
hold up (or defend from hold-up) a mining company, a
land company, a railroad company, a street-car company, a cattle company. Or any of its component parts or
its owners. You could use your legislature, your voters,
your cowpokes, your allies. There was money in small
hold-ups too. You could levy a tax or tribute on the humble. There was the Territorial government, there were
the political parties and alliances, there were courts.
There were the fiscal agents of the master class, whom
the poetry calls gunmen.[11]

No one has charted this course in detail. This was an
age and a place where fortunes were lost even more easily than they were made, because of the inflationary factor in speculation. Fall was repeatedly a rich man—who
consorted with and was used by richer men. The opportunity that will go down in history appears to have been
a side issue but made Fall a cattle baron. They say in
New Mexico that he loved the land he worked, and that
may well be true. Out of love for the same area his friend
and fiery defender, Eugene Manlove Rhodes, wrote the
books which are the only ones we have that elevate
horse opera to the art of fiction. Fall's ranch, Tres Ritos,
was already famous when he acquired it. This he

owned, though inflationary fortunes are always inflationary debts and rich men of his species are always
short of solvency. Tres Ritos had about a hundred thousand acres; the family and corporate structure which he
later complexly merged it with owned (in some degree)
or controlled upward of a million acres.

Fall's type oppose governmental measures taken for
the public good; you see, they restrict opportunity. It is
significant that he opposed the establishment of the
U.S. Forest Service and, from its establishment on,
fought it. His kind all did; they still do. Naturally, he also
worked on it such personal frauds as he could. Once this
ran to grazing four thousand trespass sheep on Forest
Service ranges—four thousand more than he held permits and paid fees for. The Service called him. The second most powerful man in the Territory, he should have
been above reputation. "Replying [to the trespass no-
tice] on the letterhead of his Tres Ritos Ranch, Fall
wrote that the Forest Service would 'rue the day' and
promised 'punishment.'"[12] Now he had a second reason
to resent the creation of Gifford Pinchot and Theodore
Roosevelt.

As a Democrat, Fall had been a federal judge and Territorial Attorney General, though he disliked both jobs.
When he shifted to the gang with the heavier cannon,
he became just as powerful in the Republican machine.
As statehood approached, it was certain that he would
be one of the first two Senators. This is a period that
would reward expert study, for of the technical political
procedures in our system none requires greater skill
than to carry over into statehood the gang-control that
has been established in a Territory. Fall accomplished
the procedural tour de force and put the Senate of the
United States at the service of opportunity. That was
what he was there for.

As a side issue he made constant war on the Forest
Service. He had to: it was a public agency, it was the

basic conservation agency, it stood for the whole composite of values that opposed his gang and his kind. But this was only incidental to his career. Also, it turned out to be a mistake.

If we are to have a Warren Gamaliel Harding as President, we are certain to get a Daugherty, a Denby, and a Fall in the Cabinet. And if an Albert Bacon Fall goes into the Cabinet, he is certain to be Secretary of the Interior. (Harding, who greatly admired him, wanted to make him Secretary of State but let wiser men talk him out of the appointment; besides, Fall did not want the job, which was without wide opportunity.) He was prepared for the job: he took to his great office the skills he had learned and the values of his kind. The Teapot Dome and Elk Hill leases were in the cards.[13]

He got the aces into his hand fast. The Administration had been in office less than three months when he procured the transfer of the naval oil reserves to the Department of the Interior, President and Secretary of the Navy consenting, Attorney General certifying legality. I suppose one Cabinet officer has seldom treated another one with such arrogant disdain as Fall showed toward Denby, but the record was not to be public for some years. Once in the proper position, he held on—very likely, he was holding out. It was not till April and December of the next year, 1922, that he secretly, for a sum known to have been at least $360,000 transferred Elk Hills to Edward F. Doheny and Teapot Dome to Harry F. Sinclair. If he was running the price up, he was also showing iron self-discipline, for Tres Ritos, the land he loved, badly needed working capital.

But the first crisis in the Administration, which has never yet been forced wholly into the open, had occurred much earlier, in April or May of 1921. Fall had made a mistake. Also, Mr. Henry Slattery was looking into the activities of another Secretary of the Interior.

Fall was having the oil reserves transferred to the Interior Department by Executive Order. He drew up another Executive Order, transferring the Forest Service as well into his Department. The transfer would have destroyed the Forest Service and would have put an end, at once and forever, to the entire movement of the federal conservation of natural resources which had been gathering momentum since Powell, had been launched by T.R., and had started the United States on the long job of getting its forests, its soil, and its water into wise instead of destructive use. Transfer of Forest Service to Interior had been all along, as it still is, the shining goal of the piratical West that Fall symbolized. There would have been no public land to conserve by the time of the Dust Bowl, Hugh Bennett, and F.D.R.

Harding was entirely agreeable—why shouldn't he go along? Fall was his friend, the easy way was always his way, and he saw no reason why there should be unpleasantness; unpleasantness was what he most disliked in the public service. But Mr. Slattery had been at work. Rumors about the transfer of the oil reserves did not reach print for nearly a year and it took several years to bring out the full facts. But Henry Slattery had a sufficient idea of what was up within two weeks and he communicated it to the Secretary of Agriculture, the elder Henry Wallace. So when Harding prepared to act on his friend's desire and transfer the Forest Service to the Interior, there occurred the first revolt in the Administration and one of the oddest scenes, surely, that have ever taken place in the White House.

"Henry Wallace," Mr. Russell Lord writes, "coolly dropped a bomb into the President's lap as he sat there at the head of the Cabinet table with his official family gathered around. Secretary Wallace told him that if the Forest Service were transferred, he, Wallace, would resign from the Cabinet, call public mass meetings at places such as Omaha, Chicago, and Kansas City, and put the case against Fall and his colleagues—forests, oil, and everything—before the whole country."[14]

At no time in their careers as public servants had either the President or the Secretary of the Interior encountered this kind of official opposition. Harding disposed of the unpleasantness by making what is called a compromise. He would back Fall on transferring the naval oil reserves to the Interior but would not give him the Forest Service too. He learned nothing from the experience but Fall did—or from this experience and the amazing fact that he kept meeting others in Washington who did not accept the ethics of power. So many of them, and so many who insisted on letting the public know when things smelled bad, that after a couple of years he resigned his job. Not, however, till he had sold out Elk Hills and Teapot Dome to, presumably, the highest bidders, and had protected their purchasers against rival thieves. (He once called on the Navy or Marines to drive some hijackers out of Teapot Dome, which he had sold to Sinclair; he was an honest man and would stay bought.) When everything was squared away, he retired to Tres Ritos, paid his huge delinquent taxes, remodeled the ranch house, put up a lot of new fencing, bought some pedigreed bulls, and added a couple of adjoining ranches to his holdings. He was a cattle baron who loved the land, when the Teapot Dome scandal, which was eventually to send him to jail, broke out in public.

It is in the books as the worst corruption in an Administration which was spongy with corruption almost throughout. It *was* the worst, though the bribes paid Fall were minute as compared with the routine grafts of the Incredible Era, the common take of the little green house on K. Street for instance, and though the value of oil stolen was smaller than the take from a good many other thefts. What made it the worst was the spirit in which the opportunity was used and the position Fall held as trustee of the public resources. The transfer of the Forest Service would have meant a many times larger take in cash and ultimate catastrophe for the West, but it would have been precisely the same sort of thing, done in precisely the same spirit.

Nothing said here would have made any sense to Fall. He understood that he had been found guilty of a crime when a court said so, but he was quite incapable of perceiving that he had committed a breach of trust. He was a man who had got power, thus had achieved a position which enabled him to use power, and had then used it. Why not? It was no different from the land that you had, or someone had, taken from the Indians. You were given trusteeship over the public resources for the precise reason that trusteeship would enable you to cash in on them. That was what they were for; that was what your office was for; that was what power was for. I am confident that he felt virtuous according to what horse opera calls the code, in that the man who paid him the smaller bribe, Doheny, was an old *compañero* of his. They had been hardrock miners together and Fall greatly admired the coolness he had seen Doheny display once when shooting a man. You help out your friends, don't you?

Chapter Five
The Eighth City of Cibola

There are two visions of the West which can be neither fused nor fully differentiated. Both are creations of longing and desire.

I have mentioned the vision of illimitable fertility, the everlasting Eden, in Mr. Henry Nash Smith's phrase the Garden of the World. Out yonder is nature's treasure house and we'll do better in a new country where a man can stand on his own two feet. On the far side of the hill the soil is deeper than it is on these familiar acres, the crops more bountiful, the wind gentler, the winter shorter and less severe. Much of the Western character was shaped by the impact on this expectation of desert, drought, alkali, and dust.

The other vision is pre-American. Cibola, Quivira, El Dorado, innumerable palaces of porphyry and gold have always shimmered in the sunset light. If there had been no Western Islands, no America, it would not have mattered to the human mind, which would have gone on searching for them. What seems an ambiguity or contradiction in this mirage is not truly one. The substance is greed, cupidity, cruelty, treachery, and massacre. It is also courage, fortitude, gallantry, the unrest of aspiration, the hunger for knowledge, the will to achieve.

"We ever held it certain that going toward the sunset we would find what we desired." The man who wrote those words had experienced every conceivable failure, hardship, loss, desperation, and ignominy; he was preparing a hallucinated frenzy as fatal to the conquerors as to the conquered, which was to loose on the Southwest a cruelty whose scars have lasted for four centuries now. Also he embodied a human dignity that makes the man who reads him hold his head higher. Assuredly Cibola was a dream of loot and Quivira a mining stock promotion, as Quebec was a flyer in furs and Massachusetts Bay a real estate promotion. All four were also the honor of man.

No one need be bothered by contradictoriness and unreality in various of the areas where these two visions meet. "Wilderness," "the wild lands," "the western waters," "the virgin country," "the unspoiled West"—among the components of such phrases has always been a protean poetry. If the American West was to be an agrarian Utopia, it was also the earthly paradise. It made those who reached it larger than life size. Nature was pure and those who sought it virtuous. In one light they were Natural Man, uncorrupted and incorruptible, noble beyond our petty selves. But in another light, the virtue that was native to the wild lands was redemptive and regenerative. Wilderness would wash man's vileness clean.

Moreover, on the far side of the hill the country is mysterious and strange. Here at last longing could make a landfall in reality.

In the fall of 1873 there was a gold strike at Breckenridge, high in the Park Range of Colorado. (Breckenridge is almost a ghost town now. Also, it ranks high among the West's exhibits of the annihilation wrought by gold dredge; where a dredge has worked, the land and the streams can be brought back to the order of creation only in geological time.) Everywhere on the mining frontier, busted drifters scraped outfits together and headed toward the new bonanza. In November a party of twenty-one set out from Provo, Utah; it was a dangerous season and they had to traverse one of the most difficult areas in the Rockies. They were used up and close to starving when, deep in the mountains, they reached the junction of the Gunnison and Uncompahgre Rivers. Here they met the Ute band of Ouray, an intelligent chief whose weakness was a foolish friendliness toward white men. He fed them, told them it would be fatal to cross any more ranges, and invited them to stay with his people till the snows were gone. About half of them did wait for spring with the Utes but the others felt the tug too powerfully and, in two parties, they tackled the mountains. One party made it. Of the second, which numbered six, only one made it. His name was Alfred (sometimes he spelled it Alferd) Packer.

In mid-April 1874 Packer came down to an agency town on the western slope of the Cochetopas but the events for which he is remembered had occurred a long way to the west, at the foot of the Uncompahgre Peak. The six had come to feeding on wild rose hips and their boiled boots. Packer found the diet enfeebling, so he killed his five companions, fed on their corpses, and stowed their money and valuables in his possibles-bag. The scene was set in Hinsdale County and Lake City, a microscopic hamlet which was to be founded a couple of years later, calls the place "Cannibal Plateau." Besides Alfred Packer Lake City offers history only the period when it was the shipping point for ore from such rich mines as the Hidden Treasure and the Golden Fleece.

The crime was soon half proved, Packer made a kind of confession, and he was jailed. He escaped, as most prisoners in frontier jails did, and was not seen for nine years—by the end of which social organization was developing in the Rockies. In 1883 he was recognized while prospecting in the Fort Fetterman region of Wyoming. Malcom Campbell, a sheriff who was to be on the fringe of the Johnson County war a few years later, arrested him and sent him back to Hinsdale County. By now Lake City existed; he was tried there, found guilty, and sentenced to be hanged. Taken to Gunnison, where there was a stronger jail, he proved to be a tourist attraction and formal invitations to the hanging were printed. But a loophole in the law under which he was tried had lately been found. The Supreme Court of Colorado held that he could not be hanged but, since he had already been tried for only one murder, ordered a trial for manslaughter in consideration of the other murders. He was found guilty and sentenced to serve forty years. The sentimentality of the hardboiled West gushed like Old Faithful but for a long time did not succeed in getting him pardoned. Finally the Denver *Post,* then at the apogee of its Tammen-Bonfils phase, directed its famous sob-sister Polly Pry to procure mercy. She did the job, though she got both her employers seriously shot up in the course of it, and Packer was pardoned after serving fourteen years.[1]

So told, this is just a murder story garnished with cannibalism, which on all frontiers is less rare than we like to think. Observe now how it was transmuted on becoming a Western story.

The judge who sentenced Packer had been reared in the school of classic American oratory. His pronouncement of sentence is sown with flowers: ". . . You and your companions camped at the base of a grand old mountain . . . on the banks of a stream as pure and beautiful as ever traced the finger of God upon the bosom of the earth. . . . As the days come and go and the years of our pilgrimage roll by, the memory of you and your crime will fade from the minds of men. . . . Prepare to meet thy God; prepare to meet the spirits of thy murdered victims; prepare to meet thy aged mother and father, of whom you have spoken and who still love you as their dear boy. . . . "

The tradition is different. Western humor was the life-saving response of nerves stretched taut with the intolerable, and Western humor found Alfred Packer precious. There are as many versions of the judge's sentence as there are storytellers in saloons, but a fair representative would be: "Alfred Packer, you blackhearted cannibal, stand up. I sentence you to be hanged by the neck till you are dead, dead, dead, and may God have mercy on your soul. Why, you man-eating son of a bitch, there was only six Democrats in Hinsdale County, and, by God, you et five of them."

The Western story goes on from there. In 1930 Will Rogers alluded to the cannibal in his newspaper column. Unhappily he named the wrong town, transferring a business asset from Lake City to Del Norte. Instantly the Lake City *Silver World* rose up "in defense of veracity and community pride and spirit, to take up the challenge and give the whole story as it occurred. Unless this is done, Lake City is threatened with the loss of much of that on which its glory is founded."

Similarly, Denver laid fifteen tons of concrete over the coffin of Buffalo Bill, lest Cody, Wyoming, steal the bones for Rotary. The fear was not without justification or precedent.

In 1953 a price war broke out in the Dakotas. The Sioux thaumaturge Sitting Bull had no high regard for white men, once remarking for the record that he preferred the companionship of dogs, and presided over the killing of a good many of them, notably at the Little Big Horn. White men returned his feeling in kind; at Wounded Knee the 7th Cavalry avenged the defeat into which its stupid Colonel had led it by massacring a lot of unarmed Sioux of both sexes and all ages. But the heroic Seventh did not get Sitting Bull with his people. It had been anticipated by other representatives of our culture, who shot the aged prophet in his tent while he was in a trance of the ghost-dance religion, a pathetic evangelism which taught that the millennium was at hand and would be presided over by an Indian Jesus.

That was in 1890. They buried him at Fort Yates, just outside the North Dakota village of the same name. His bones were left there when the old military post was abandoned. Sixty-three years after he was murdered, some men of business vision at Mobridge, South Dakota, decided that Sitting Bull could be tourist bait. They prevailed on an agency Indian, undoubtedly with cash, to request that the visionary be dug up and reburied with his people, the Hunkapas, who are in South Dakota. Realizing that they had missed a chance, North Dakota chambers of commerce set up delaying actions. But their predecessors hadn't laid enough concrete over him, only a slab that a wrecker's derrick proved able to lift. So on an April dawn, a Mobridge committee dug up Sitting Bull, transported him over the state line, and buried him, with lots of concrete, on a hill above town. North Dakota claims that in their haste they got only a third of the bones and that hence the tourist should visit what after all constitutes a working majority. Two patriot-antiquarians got so emotional about their loss that one shot the other.

I cannot explain why the romantic principle chose only one Western type for its tabernacle in fantasy, relegating other types to supporting roles. The dime novel was deeply devoted to The Scout, who guided troops in the Indian country. In historical fact, the scouts were surviving mountain trappers technologically unemployed. Newspaper correspondents accompanying the troops added their praise to the yellowback novelist's, and the costumes and liturgies of the early Wild West shows were certainly impressive. But no substantial image of The Scout resulted and in the Old West he has only a walk-on part.

It is hard to understand why romance has not taken up certain lieutenants and captains of the Topographical Engineers who in the 1840s and 1850s conducted exploring expeditions in the mountains and deserts. They were a remarkable group—even the paranoid Fremont was a first-rate frontiersman—and they did a remarkable job. The combat army at the time of the wars with the Plains Indians, however, offered iconography nothing that could be used. Following the Civil War the Army sank to the lowest estate it had ever known, and the strategy and tactics it had learned in that war proved to be one more set of preconceptions unfitted to the Western realities. Moreover, the high command sent singularly few good officers west. Crook was the best of them, the only one with enough originality to work out military methods that could cope with the country and adversary. Such men as Gibbon, Miles, and Canby were rule-book ritualists and Howard's principal excellence was at shooting squaws. Most field officers proved themselves asses at the first opportunity and were apparently assigned to active service to keep them from fouling up the paperwork back East. They graded down to the absolute fool, Custer. Romantic image-making would have had to utilize not the troops but their quarry, such men as Joseph, Red Cloud, Crazy Horse, Two Moon, Dull Knife, Mangus Colorado, and Cochise. Presumably we will delay that step as long as the Indians retain any property worth taking from them, and the Southwestern reservations are rich with uranium deposits.

Most surprising, however, is the failure of romance to make use of the trapper, the mountain man. His experience ran to all the fundamental themes, most of all the enduring one of man against the hostile land. If mythology had grown out of history, the sun god of the Old West would wear buckskins. Instead he wears chaps. The election fell on the cowboy.

This is to say that the eighth city of Cibola is what Walter Webb called the Cattle Kingdom, and the mass dream which utilizes it as the Old West was manufactured after the fact and outside the area. The historical referent is a period of no more than twenty years. Its components are the open range, the cattle trails, and the inflation. The inflation began to collapse in 1885 and the winter of the Big Freeze, 1886–1887, merely finished the job. Thereafter methods of cattle ranching changed so radically, and so many new forces began to affect the West, that only vestiges of the Cattle Kingdom remained, even in Wyoming and New Mexico. As myth the Old West is set in the earlier era. When fiction or the screen seems to be bringing it down to a later time, nothing but the costumes are changed.

The myth comes into this book because, though it was made in the East, it went on to victimize the West. But it is a fascinating phenomenon in itself. Its interest is on the one hand its great commercial importance and on the other its tawdriness and absurdity.

Students have worked hard to find genuine folklore in the Cattle Kingdom but have turned up practically nothing except some songs. There are a lot of them and yet far from enough to supply the demands of the assembly line, which has to provide its own. The ballads that ooze from Western stations all day long and that the singing cowboys croon on the screen are by ASCAP.[2] Like folk songs everywhere the genuine ones tend to be either maudlin or humorous. It is notable that many of the humorous ones express the corrosive disenchantment which I have said was the essence of Western humor—a fact which makes difficulties for European critics, who accept them as straight—and that others

satirize and burlesque the cattle business. It is equally
notable that they contain not the slightest trace of the
Old West; if this music is an honest expression of the
cowboy of the Cattle Kingdom, he did not romanticize
his trade. Many are uproariously obscene and some are
very fine indeed. Such a song as "The Old Chisholm
Trail" is enduring folk art.

In the later production it is fair to distinguish from
the Tin Pan Alley species a few songs by talented people, all of which employ the mythological substance. By
a good deal the best of these is "Spanish Johnnie" and
the reader may be surprised to learn that its words were
written by Willa Cather. Miss Cather forbade its publication but since her death her wish has been disregarded.

The graphic arts, significantly, have seldom been
able to approach the Old West in a serious mood, and
contemporary Western painters show little interest in
the cattle business. Charlie Russell, who saw Montana
in the last years of the Cattle Kingdom and whose paint-
ing was instinctively reportorial, gave us about all we
have that issues from a genuine feeling for the life he
was a part of. Frederic Remington was only a little later
but his fervent romanticism kept him from seeing what
he looked at and his poster-like paintings are a powerful
buttress of the Old West myth. It is worth pointing out
that both Remington and Russell were better artists in
bronze than on canvas.

As this indicates, the myth of the Old West is a literary creation, but it is one which will not rise to literature. It has had practically no writers of consequence.
Charlie Russell's divided soul makes him an interesting
exhibit. As a humorist he is realistic, caustic, and disenchanted and well outside the myth, but at any moment
his eye may begin to swim with mirage, whereupon his
medium changes to nostalgia and tears. Only once has
the Old West risen to the art of fiction, at the hands of

Eugene Manlove Rhodes; only one other good novelist has tried to work with it, Conrad Richter, and he failed to lift it above horse opera.[3] A few first-rate writers of non-fiction, most of them émigré Easterners, have worked expertly and devoutly with the myth and are in fact its principal creators. It can be most agreeably examined in the books of the best of them, Struthers Burt, but the classical expositions are to be found in earlier and more voluminous writers, such as Emerson Hough. Yet writers whose names can be cited do not matter, neither names nor writers matter; the literature of the myth is impersonal and all but anonymous.

The movies, which more often than fiction offer criticism something worth dealing with, show why. And here, purely for convenience in reference, let me differentiate horse opera from the Western story, in both fiction and the movies. The Western story is the more inclusive form and sometimes deals with other Western images, cliches, and types. But its principal and commonest subspecies is the cowboy story and I limit the term "horse opera" to this form.

The movies have movement and immediacy at the disposal of their illusion, and since Technicolor they have had the inestimable assistance of the landscape, beautiful, terrible, and overwhelming. Moreover, *le western* has benefited from Hollywood's steady advance in narrative techniques, which contrasts so sharply with its failure to advance in content. So sometimes it produces admirable melodrama. Melodrama is not concerned with motives or credible experience, it ignores emotion, it asks only a momentary acceptance, it is for itself alone. Its essence is tension, objectified conflict, suspense, the intensifying rhythm of action that produces a moment of dramatic culmination. At its most expert, therefore, *le western* can be pure cinema.

But there are not many such films; it appears that there need not be any at all. The genre is puerile: devoid of character and even of personality, naive beyond anyone's power to express, formalized and formularized. It is fabrication by interchangeable parts. Often quite literally. The half-hour films of television are composed largely, often entirely, of stock shots. A producer will put together in Hollywood an entire series, thirteen or twenty-six items, from material shot in a couple of weeks on location. On location the creative process is methodical, by blueprint: one man chasing Autry, two men, three men, four men chasing Autry; Autry chasing one man, two men, three men, four men; two, three, four men shooting at each other; fist fight involving two, three, or four including Autry; the same excluding him; general brawl inside saloon, general brawl outside saloon, general brawl in travel shot both inside and outside; man in checked shirt, in dark shirt, in light shirt, in big hat, hatless, on pinto, on palomino, on bay; various falls from various horses; sheriff as conspirator, sheriff on our side; runaway with blonde, with brunette; Autry kissing blonde, blonde kissing Autry, but these not in close-up for we may want to change the blonde.

It does not matter; the mass dream needs merely some familiar symbolic stimuli and plenty of violent movement. And the full-length horse opera, whether quickie, B picture, or feature, differs from the television product only in that not many of its shots are from stock. As drama it is all stock. There will be a lot of galloping. There will be one fist fight or a number, and one general brawl or several. There will be one dry-gulching (murder from ambush, and always of course by a baddie), several six-gun duels and probably a mass gunfight, and shooting will culminate in a walkdown. The filling will depend on which subhead has been chosen, but whether this is the blood feud, rustling, the range war, the gunman in hope of reformation, or whatever, the standard components will be present. But there will be nobody acting from recognizable motives and evoking emotion in the audience.

Empty and absurd as it is, however, horse opera on the screen is a considerably more respectable art than it is in prose. The movies are anonymous because they are created by committee action, but horse opera in fiction is anonymous because of the essential fatuousness of its content, which has no gloss of cinematic illusion. Nobody writes a horse opera, for the writer has been slain by the absurdity of his material, and the art of fiction cannot abide anonymity.

About a hundred and fifty book-length Westerns are published every year; perhaps seventy-five percent of them are horse operas. Set aside from ten to twenty by writers of considerable skill, about which I will make a further point in a moment. The others have no more content than the B films, put together from stock situations in stock sequences, without the content of fiction. This is the standard packaged article; its best producers—Henry Herbert Knibbs, William MacLeod Raine, Clarence Mulford—are fourth-rate writers. Their narrative is clumsy, their characters are plot functions with names, their technical address and manner are amateurish. From this top level, the genre grades steeply downward to semi-illiterate bathos resembling the work of Mickey Spillane. When Mr. Raymond Chandler remarked that the lowest grade of fiction gets printed only in the detective story, he revealed that fortune had protected him from the contact with horse opera.

These books, mechanical assemblies of conventions and cliches without relevance to experience, are accepted by hundreds of thousands of people. Add those who read the sub-basement stuff in the pulp magazines, and the audience must be numbered by the million. The packaged goods verify what I have pointed out about the movies; the mass dream requires only some stimuli associated with the Old West.

The ten or twenty novels a year which I have set apart are written by expert craftsmen who have chosen to produce popular romantic fiction in terms of the Old West. They are pros, technically deft and ingenious and original within the rigid limitations of their form— which is to say fertile in the contrivance of switches and gimmicks. They write good narrative and some of them render their landscapes with feeling and subtlety. As historical novelists—for horse opera is historical fiction— they are scrupulously faithful in their period detail.

Yet their work lacks the persuasive plausibility, the superficial warmth, the appearance of dealing with genuine if unimportant portions of experience that popular light fiction by men of similar competence frequently has in other fields—light fiction about the suburbs, the country club, or the college campus for instance. Their form has developed too great a solemnity to experiment with comedy, and it never rises above the threshold of pathetics though it pretends to work with heroism, the testing of individual man, human aspirations and failure, and passions whose counterparts in experience are among the most powerful men can feel. The cowboy simply will not live for these writers, nor the situations in which they place him nor the accessory characters with which they surround him. Some of them are clearly trying to elevate entertainment fiction to a serious status but their books are without serious substance. They contain no experience a reader can share or identify himself with and no emotion that he can respond to with emotion of his own. They are not a picture of the world or of its people that can engage belief. They are simply the clichés of the fourth-raters more pretentiously and more skillfully rendered.

Once more, for the purposes of the dream this does not matter. But it matters for the purpose of this book, and we must look more closely at the basic absurdities of horse opera.

Parents of pubescent boys used to attribute to ten-cent yellowbacks about the Wild West the same evils they now attribute to comic books in which green three-legged creatures from outer space raise electronic welts on the back of naked intergalactic cuties. The dime novel made use of cowboys for about a generation, in two roles. One was a low-down no-good, an outlaw who ended as he richly deserved to. The other, an Epworth League character, helped the romantic lead to solve the mystery of his birth. On orthodox literary principles we would have expected the second one to figure in the development of horse opera, but so far as I can see he did not. And the dime novel appears to have lost interest in cowboys at about the time when more ambitious literature was beginning to take him up.

Nor, so far as I can see, does horse opera owe anything to the fashion of "local color" which during the 1870s and 1880s filled quality group magazines with quaint originals from various upcountry regions who spoke a lingo that was alleged to flow unchanged from a fountainhead in the Book of Common Prayer. Perhaps the Egglestons, Craddocks, and Freemans of that era avoided cowboys because of the Beadle taint. Nevertheless when the Western story does appear, in the 1890s, it is a highly evolved form, and a critic who had not looked into the earlier material would assume that it was a composite of Beadle and local color formulas.

Instead, the formulas must be ascribed to journalism. During the period of the cattle trails, the cowtowns, and the open range, the stock business was well reported. Texas, Kansas, and Kansas City newspaper files are the historian's best source today, and at first the roving journalist who wrote for magazines read these papers carefully and kept his eyes fixed on the same set of facts. But about 1880 this tony correspondent began to find in cows and cowpokes a glamour which up to then had escaped his attention. He filled

Harper's, Scribner's, and the *Century* with tidings that gallantry roamed the high plains and that the narrow code of the East would not hold in horizon land. There had arisen a person in a big hat whose grammar would seem deplorable in the drawing room but whose nature it was to see right through the drawing room's shams. This type loved horses, respected good women, respected the feminine principle in the soiled doves of the saloon, and when working at his trade performed heroisms that must evoke the deepest admiration in the Eastern breast. In fact nothing so completely showed up the falsity, timidity, prudery, and artificiality of the East as association with a man in leather pants. Such a man was muscular, he was brave, he told the truth, he stuck to his partner, he scorned to shoot an unarmed enemy, and if Miss Mary Eleanor Wilkins' New England nun would consent to come west he would make her fruitful, lawfully.

These reports enriched the literary topsoil for about five years, and Mr. Owen Wister could then go west. He did so in 1885. He was to give the Cattle Kingdom a place-name: Wyoming.

Wister appears to have suffered from the imperfectly described nervous disturbance that afflicted so many Ivy League patricians of his time who had aspirations toward the arts, and this "neurasthenia" appears to have been the reason for his going west. He gratefully discovered that Wyoming had one's own kind in quantity, Philadelphians, Bostonians, men of good clubs, younger sons and even titles from England and Scotland. He visited the ranches of these well-born stockmen and became a habitué of their Cheyenne Club. (One of his earliest hosts later became the Gentlemen's field commander in the Johnson County War.) He returned for other summers, shot big game, got about widely and by the mid-Nineties had seen most of the West. He met lots of the magazine correspondents' natural noblemen and watched them working at their glamorous trade. He met "desperadoes" too and all the other startling and quaint characters of the Cattle Kingdom. He listened to their talk—and to the ideas of the Gentlemen.

As was proper for one with a Main Line inheritance, Mr. Wister had a law degree. But he really aspired to the arts and Wyoming crystallized his ambition. If he could believe in the efficacy of prayer, he said, he would "petition to be the hand that once and for all chronicled and laid bare the virtues and the vices of this extraordinary phase of American social progress." He was not to achieve this ambition—instead he invented horse opera— but it was an ambition of great, and artistically admirable, seriousness. And one must attribute much significance to the episode that seems to have crystallized this decision out of the solution of desire and doubt in which it had been building up for some years.

He saw a cowman, moreover one who was a Gentleman, in a fit of insane rage beat a horse with revolting cruelty and gouge out one of its eyes. An intolerable cruelty had been inflicted on Owen Wister as well. This was Wyoming, it was the abode of heroism and gallantry, it was Cibola. Yet in Cibola this dreadful, symbolic thing could happen. The country demanded an interpretation in art, but it had had none. "No one has touched anywhere near it. A few have described external sights and incidents but the grand total thing—its rise, its hysterical and unreal prosperity, and its disenchanting downfall, all this and its influence on the various sorts of human character that have been subjected to it—has not been touched by a single writer that I, at least, have heard of. The fact is, it is quite worthy of Tolstoy or George Eliot or Dickens. Thackeray wouldn't do."

The last two sentences show that Wister understood what was required. The West was proper material for serious fiction, and in the humility of an artist he proposed to do what he could. But the preceding sentences reveal the inhibiting factor: the West was merely what he had seen and heard of the afterglow of the Cattle Kingdom.

No literary conflict was ever fixed in clearer amber for the critic to examine. "I begin to conclude from five seasons of observation, that life in this negligent, irresponsible wilderness tends to turn people shiftless, incompetent, and cruel. I noticed in 1885 and I notice today [1891] a sloth in doing anything and everything, that is born of the deceitful ease with which makeshifts answer here." In this amazing statement there is an exact equipoise between sight and blindness, perception and nonsense. The sightless eye was to win—perhaps to a man of Wister's lineage, a member of Dickey and Porcellian, at that moment of time and point in space, no other outcome was possible.[4] The outcome, however, is abundantly foreshadowed in the context I have been quoting from, his letters of 1891. In order to enjoy its fullness one must be able to recognize the names of his Wyoming associates and know their places in the hierarchy and in events. But no such familiarity is needed to read the signs. I quote two passages. Just before the skies opened for his illumination he had written, "On the way here [the geographical center of Cibola; he was at the Powder River] yesterday, passed emigrants on their way from Black Hills to Oregon. Three slow crawling wagons ('prairie schooners') with their long teams. A woman riding straddle, several other women, and any amount of children. The women do their work, and the children are begotten and raised along the journey. A miserable population. These people, it seems, have been moving in this way pretty much all over the continent west of the Missouri, settling nowhere." And the last sentence but one in the letter of 1894 with which his daughter chooses to end her selections from this correspondence reads, "There's nothing makes this world seem so little evil as to meet good men in their humbler walks of life."

Well, he tried. He tried harder than was logically to be expected, and the truth is he came nearer succeeding than, granted the data, a critic could have predicted. And the vision of his good eye got no help from his own kind or from the arbiters of literature. *Harper's* for August 1892 carried the first of his stories about "the virtues and vices of this extraordinary land"; the same magazine was to publish everything else that came from his illumination. In January 1894 it ran "Balaam and Pedro," in which Wister described the precipitating episode, the flogging and blinding of the horse. *Harper's* was then edited by Henry Mills Alden, who thought of Wister's stories as mere vehicles for the art of Frederic Remington, and who had the most delicate sensibilities in American criticism—which is quite a statement, considering that Richard Watson Gilder's prudery was in full vigor. Mr. Alden did not permit Pedro's eye to be gouged out and he inflicted on the story such further, if now unascertainable, softening that Wister was in despair. But the editor's treatment was a much lighter blow than one which called his whole intent into question, the disapproval of the friend whom he all but deified. Bowdlerized as the story was, it nevertheless shocked Theodore Roosevelt, who rebuked him for brutality and told him that the office of literature was to exalt and inspire, not to disgust.

Wister did not restore the gouged eye, or apparently any other detail that Alden had excised, when he worked the story into *The Virginian.* Yet the nature of the book would not have been changed if he had embodied in it all the incidental brutalities he had seen or heard about. His fiction reveals that he would not see out of his good eye, either. He was inclosed in the Old West; he was one of the artificers who made it up.

The Virginian is a novel published in 1902 but put together, not too smoothly, from short stories that had been published in *Harper's* during the 1890s. It was preceded in 1897 by a collection of short stories from the same period, but without the mythological figure, called *Lin McLean*. A literary critic might agree with me in thinking the earlier book somewhat the better fiction; it is more amusing and, dealing with unimportant aspects of the life at hand, reports them more truly. But that judgment is meaningless. *Lin McLean* is significant only so far as it shares the qualities of *The Virginian*, which in its earlier and its later form created Western fiction—created the cowboy story, the horse opera novel, the conventions, the clichés, the forms, the values, and the hero. The cowboy story has seldom produced anything as good and, apart from Rhodes, it has not even tried to do anything different.

Some preliminary remarks are called for. A fine comic sense informs much of the book and, curiously enough, this was the hint that the Western story first acted on. Through the late 1890s and the first years of the next decade, the story about cowboys was thought of as an exercise in humor. As such it sometimes rose to excellence. Henry Wallace Phillips' stories about Red Saunders are good reading still. The Wolfville stories of Alfred Henry Lewis, though they invented some of the most painful stylistic mannerisms of the form, can be highly amusing. This strain reached its apogee (apart from the humor that is so central in Gene Rhodes) in the work of Harry Leon Wilson. The humorous cowboy story was sometimes capable of burlesque and even travesty, sometimes expressive of the corrosive disenchantment I have referred to, and clearly was the best chance *le western* had to achieve realism. There is no trace of the Old West in it; though there is sometimes fantasy, there is never the myth. But this strain withered away, unquestionably because it was irreverent, and the cowboy story concentrated on the remainder of *The Virginian*.

Also, I point out a surprising fact: the Virginian is permitted a casual and assured success in the seduction of women which the form has never since ventured to imitate. (It would conflict with a provision of the code: the cowboy reverences womanhood.) On the other hand, it is made clear that he has the humility to pattern his clothes, when not in costume, on the tailoring to be seen at the Cheyenne Club, so that he can appear in the fine old houses of Bennington, Vermont, without causing mirth, and that though noble by virtue of his Western domicile he accepts tuition in English literature from his well-born schoolmarm.

Again, the Virginian has no name. One context reveals that back home his friends called him Jeff, a nickname, but not even the schoolmarm for whom he serves his seven years ever confides to the reader the name she will bear as a married woman or the Christian name she will whisper in love passages between paragraphs. Wister was unconsciously symbolizing the anonymity of the genre he was creating.

The fundamental fact, the fact that must be fully understood, is that the themes of the book are from the Johnson County War. Wister has scrambled his time-sequences and in the last few pages says flatly that the events of that superb social comedy are still to come. But they have already occurred, and especially they have occurred to the Virginian himself. The book is the Gentlemen's apologia. Its artistic problems originate in their ethics and purposes. An abiding irony of literary history is that mere accident fastened on horse opera and the myth of the Old West, a dilemma which never would have arisen if Wister had not come from the Main Line.

The Virginian is a hero. Popular Romance has to have a hero, indeed it does not have to have anything else, but in the genre Wister was inventing this particular one became The Hero. A cowboy righting wrongs, doing justice, avenging injury, triumphing over peril, eradicating evil, and shooting people. Shooting bad people.

Shooting Johnson County "rustlers"; that is, quite uncultivated persons who have small landholdings and
small herds.

By origin the Virginian is one of those "good men in
the humbler walks of life" who make "this world seem
so little evil." But "this negligent, irresponsible wilderness" is intensely democratic; the natural patricians of
the Old West can rise to equal status with the Gentlemen. As an employee of one of them he adopts the values of the well born and adds their manners to his own.
Miss Mary Stark Wood of Bennington, of one of those
gracious houses on Monument Avenue, though the family fortune has been lost and she has been courted by a
wealthy parvenu—Miss Wood encourages him to read
elevating literature and he improves his spelling by
himself. As I have remarked, he appreciates good tailoring, and it is to be said further that the Episcopal
Bishop of Wyoming heartily admires him. (I believe
that at the time Wyoming was *in partibus infidelium,* so
the Bishop's acceptance of murder as a folkway may be
understood as one of the compromises necessary to the
conversion of the heathen.) Having patterned himself
on the Gentlemen and executed their justice, the Virginian marries Miss Wood, becomes a ranch owner, pos-
sesses coal lands, and rises to wealth. In short, such is
the miracle of Cibola that he can move naturally among,
on the one hand the Frewens, Barbers, Gardiners, and
Penroses, and on the other the Careys, the Warrens, and
the Kendricks.

Till he went to work for Judge Henry the Virginian
was a ramblin' cowboy and so, necessarily in the Old
West, had shot an unspecified number of men. But he is
able to tell Miss Wood's mother that he has "never killed
for pleasure or profit" and is not "one of that kind, always preferring peace." Here is one of the bedrock reasons why *The Virginian,* and horse opera with it, was
prohibited from becoming serious fiction. Wister be-

lieved that this declaration was true, and it was as he understood it, but it originates in Cibola—for the Gentlemen both killed and hired killing for profit. The declaration sets forth another bedrock necessity: The Hero must be a goodie. He acquires an Adversary, and his genre acquires its type villain, in Trampas, to whom in the second chapter he speaks the line that has become immortal, "When you call me that, smile."[5] Trampas is a rustler, so eventually The Hero must kill him; another necessity is established. And the form acquires still another one when Miss Wood saves The Hero's life. (After he has been shot by Indians, a remarkable achievement in eastern Wyoming in the 1890s.)

Rustlers are preying on the Gentlemen's herds and must be killed. One of them is, or rather has been till lately, The Hero's best friend, his pardner. But The Hero has to help hang him in protection of the Gentlemen's commercial hegemony. The failure of horse opera to become serious fiction pivots on this necessity and on Judge Henry's explanation of it to Miss Wood. I repeat that Wister tried hard, and he tried hardest here, confronting what is in terms of art the problem of his novel. He honestly attempts to solve it as an artist but he cannot make the grade. It turns out that in one portion of Cibola small property owners have organized a county: they have stolen the courts from the Gentlemen. The Gentlemen have no recourse but to repossess the government by means of murder. Judge Henry tells Miss Wood that murder is all right, and in fact according to the strictest principles of American democracy and the evolution of law, when it is done—in this instance hired—by the Gentlemen. Miss Wood has little difficulty believing him, for she might have been the heroine of "The Great Divide," but The Hero feels an inner conflict and has a hell of a hard time. For obeying a major provision of the code requires him to violate a provision that had not been previously understood to be a lesser one. Steve, the hanged baddie, has been his pardner, and he feels some revulsion on discovering that property transcends not only law but friendship too. Still, there is alleviation: Steve dies game.

Horse opera might have been spared the basic dilemma which it has never solved if Wister had ever faced the question of what happened when the courts of Laramie County, as distinguished from Johnson County, tried either a sheepman or a small cattle rancher, that is a baddie, who had committed a tort against a Gentleman. He discussed this commonplace every time he visited a friend or dropped into the Cheyenne Club. But the essence of Wister is that he saw no artistic problem in the commonplace and none in murder as a business method.

It was the Old West that supplied the Virginian as Hero with his past, his mannerisms and stage properties, and his code. It was the art of fiction that set up as the central action of the book the pursuit and lynching of Steve, with the unavoidable accompaniments. But it was the vanishing hegemony of the Gentlemen that provided the evasion and capitulation, Judge Henry's lecture on the place of law in society. That did it: Wister could not be the West's Tolstoy nor even its unsuitable Thackeray, and the literary form called horse opera had been invented. But he was lavish and went on to give the form its supreme effect.

Having saved The Hero's life and accepted his employer's position on murder as an economic measure, Miss Mary Stark Wood of the patrician East plights him her troth. (The Old West will supply ennobling landscapes for the honeymoon; besides tailoring, the Harvard Club will supply an approved kind of ring.) The two set off for town, where the Bishop of Wyoming will marry them, but on the way they see Trampas. The Hero must kill the baddie or the baddie will kill him.

There is no option; the code will not permit him either to avoid the baddie or to have him jailed. A problem remains: what explanation shall he give his bride? Somewhere in these contrivances, motive as a component of human behavior, occasionally present up to now, makes its final exit from horse opera. It has never yet returned.

Meeting the Bishop of Wyoming, The Hero listens to the Christian's advice to run away for at least his wedding night, rejects it, and says good-bye, the Bishop murmuring as he leaves, "God bless him! God bless him!" Though Miss Wood has divined what is to come, he tells her and will not yield when she falls on her knees and begs him, "For my sake. For my sake." So, "'I have no right to kiss you any more,' he said. And then, before his desire could break him down from this he was gone and she was alone."

The Hero's friends make sure that no minor baddie will do the job for Trampas. "Then he walked out into the open, watching." His friends follow at the indicated distance, "because it was known that Shorty [an earlier victim of Trampas'] had been shot from behind." Presently, "A wind seemed to blow his sleeve off his arm and he replied to it, and saw Trampas pitch forward. He saw Trampas raise his arm from the ground and fall again, and lie there, this time still. A little smoke was rising from the pistol on the ground, and when he looked at his own gun he saw the smoke flowing upward out of it. 'I expect that's all,' he said aloud."

That is the first walkdown. But the scene is not ended:

> The Virginian walked to the hotel and stood on the threshold of his sweetheart's room. She had heard his step and was upon her feet. Her lips parted and her eyes fixed on him, nor did she move or speak.
>
> "Yu' have to know it," said he. "I have killed Trampas."
>
> "Oh, thank God!" she said; and he found her in his arms.

I ask the reader to visualize this scene and to accept its action and emotions, identifying with them as he does with a successful scene in a serious novel. To assist him I print the same scene from a contemporary horse opera, where it is the last one in the book, as it is not in *The Virginian*. I could have taken it from any of scores of books; I choose Luke Short's *Saddle by Starlight* because it is the one I have read most recently.

"Luke Short" is a pseudonym, employed by the author because it was the name of an actual Western gunman. (Perhaps this fact reveals something about the genre.) He is a voluminous producer of horse opera; some devotees account him the best practitioner since Ernest Haycox.[6]

In this passage The Hero is Sam, the Trampas figure is Heth, and Miss Wood's apparition is Julia. Some interesting variations have gone into the walkdown; among them, the reader must understand, is the fact that Heth is on horseback.

> . . . And in that feral moment of expectancy Sam felt an unaccountable pleasure. "You'll not live to say so, Sam," Heth said. [To say that he has identified the subsidiary baddies.]
>
> Then as if doggedly accepting one more burden, Heth savagely roweled his horse, pointing him straight at the rail. With an iron clamp on the reins, Heth drove his mount not over the tie rail, but into it, and the wooden crossbar split and parted at the impact. Unrelenting, Heth roweled him onto the plankwalk, driving him at Sam, and at the same time reaching bent-armed for his gun.
>
> Heth shot first, as if his urgency could not bring him to Sam quickly enough. Sam raised his gun and could see nothing along its barrel except the lunging chest of Heth's horse, and he shot. The horse's knees folded, and he fell with a violence that splintered the plankwalk. Heth was thrown forward over his mount's neck and landed heavily

on all fours, not thirty feet from Sam. The horse's hindquar-
ters swung up in a crazy cartwheel of momentum and then
crashed across Heth's boots, pinning him to the plankwalk.

No sound of pain escaped Heth. For one bitter second he
struggled to free himself, and then he raised his gun in a
wild thrust, as if trying to club Sam. When Sam looked
down his barrel and saw the grey patch that was Heth's
face line in front of him, he began to squeeze
the trigger. Heth's gunshot made a violent blossom of
orange in the darkness, and merged with his own shot.

Then, arms outspread, he took a half-step to put his
back against the wall of the bank, momentary blindness
leaving him defenseless. When it was gone what he saw
then was only the dark form of a big man lying on his
face, head cushioned on his arm, a pistol slack in his out-
thrust limp hand.

Only then did Sam hear the swift and light footsteps
coming toward him at a run. He turned and saw Julia
close to him, and with an instinctive gesture to bar her
from the sight of Heth he raised his arm. Julia was never
to know what was behind that mistaken gesture. She
read it as natural, and came into his arms. And Sam, sensible now, held her closely.

THE END

Not all horse operas include the walkdown but those
which omit it have its equivalent in man-to-man conflict.
For it has become in *le western* what critical terminology
calls the obligatory scene. Plotting, which nowadays is
both more complex and more skillful than in Wister's invention, works out so that The Hero can triumph only
by means of it or that the Trampas figure can prevent
him from triumphing only by the same means. Across
an open space they approach each other. All that the
code requires is a fair draw; The Hero will be the faster.
Yet it is a higher *noblesse* if The Hero permits Trampas
the first shot, as both the Virginian and Sam do in the
scenes I have quoted. In the second one, a gimmick lets

Sam give Trampas not one first shot but two. The second scene also shows the influence of the screen; it takes place at night, which permits the lighting effects. Another common Hollywood addition happens not to be used here: tension will be added to the walkdown if The Hero comes into it straight from a fist fight that has used him up badly, or if he has suffered damage to his gun arm.

The culmination that adds a clinch to both scenes is less universal but is very common nevertheless. It will be enhanced if The Hero is wounded, though not seriously, in the exchange of shots. It delivers into the arms of his love a character who in serious fiction would be feeling whatever whirlpool of emotions a man feels who has just killed another man while being himself shot at.

The walkdown has evolved as the supreme embodiment in fiction of the Old West. It and the kiss that comes as the fulfillment of murder show why horse opera cannot become fiction. They are empty of experience, of motive and emotion. The Old West exists outside the art of fiction; it is an absurdity.

Very few literary critics have so much as alluded to the cowboy story; in a dogged search through the usual media I recently found only two articles. One was by Mr. Delmore Schwartz, who neglected to tell us what he meant by what he was saying. The other, by Mr. Leslie Fiedler, was preposterous; as a student of the West and a reader of fiction I could find nothing true or sensible in his piece. A few amateur Freudians, notably Mr. Gershon Legman, profess to find in horse opera the same sadistically displaced sex they find in Mickey Spillane and innumerable other data which they say establish the castration of American men by their mothers and wives. They do not convince me. The thesis would require the killing to be either purgative or orgasmic to either The Hero or the reader, and would require some

kind of content in the subsequent three paces that take
The Hero into Miss Wood's arms. Assuredly, there has
never yet been enough reality to produce desire or even
horror. Both the murder and the clinch, wholly without
motive and emotion, are dissociated from actuality; they
are as formalized as a do-si-do in a barn dance.

I have found a number of discussions of horse opera
in the professional journals of psychoanalysis. The au-
thors have seen some movies and may have read some
cowboy fiction, though there is an odd failure to mention any by name, but they appear to be ignorant of the
historical West, of the Old West myth, and of the writing of fiction. They seem to be extending their basic theories outward to include another phenomenon *a priori*
rather than examining the phenomenon. They rightly
recognize horse opera's hero as The Hero. They go on to
say that he stands for half of a split, the other half being
Trampas. The two represent the good father and the
bad father. The murder of the latter represents the pri-
mal scene but also since he is a baddie it is permissive
murder of the reader's father. The conflict allays the
reader's anxiety about his own oedipal conflict. (Has
psychoanalytical criticism any other position about any
literature?) Because The Hero is omnipotent, they add,
his triumph inhibits such wishes to grow up as a reader
may have—though why this any more than its common
contrary in art, why it does not fulfill those wishes in
fantasy and therefore assist them, does not appear. At
any rate, the heart of the psychoanalytical position appears to be that reading horse opera is regressive. For
all I know, this may be true.

The point seems to be that, since serious novelists es-
chew the Old West and since it is only a formal technical exercise for the pros who write horse opera, such enlightenment as we may find must be sought in the
audience. I now enter the explanation offered me by a
native Westerner who is an authority on the history of

the West, especially the stock business. He is a biographer, a bibliographer, and a writer of fiction—including some horse opera.

Like the rest of us, he concentrates on the symbol. Horse opera's cowboy, he concedes, is a complete phony, but he insists that the symbol is one of personal decision, of a man's power to settle the problems of his life by his own will and action. "The whole progress of events [preceding the walkdown] has led up to a climactic resolution of The Hero's problems which he has personally elected to resolve in this fashion." The Old West is a place where a man can act to make his will good.

"How many men today have mastered the art of living in *this* trackless wilderness at the height of function? Man today spends his time in functions which are a part of some whole which he cannot control and but poorly understands. . . .

"I have long suspected that the Anglo has as deep a fascination with Death, with the Moment of Truth, as the Spaniard he affects to despise for that fascination. . . . In [horse opera's] glorification of the folk heroes, our confused, fanatical, fearful ant-crawling in a circumscribed orbit about this cooling cinder finds release. Those were the days! And those were the men who could take fell circumstance between their own two hands and wring it dry, shake it out, hang it up, and never regret the lack of a detergent. That this involved a choice between Life and Death, a choice which incidentally they could elect to accept or duck, simply adds to the vicarious orgasm. Here is the mainspring then: that a man *could* make a direct personal decision and *would* make it stick, whether he stood or fell thereby. You must accept the fact that the popular mythology of the persons or events involved has little or no relation to reality."

My correspondent's thesis makes better sense than any other I have heard. Also, it puts the acceptance of

the tawdry and preposterous content of the mass dream
on grounds rather more creditable to the human race.

But it leaves unexplained the West's victimization by
the myth of the Old West.

The cowboy rode a horse. So he was a *caballero,* a
knight. Men on foot were lesser folk. . . . When a newspaper referred to the cowboy as a hired man on horseback, which is an accurate designation, the offense so
wrought upon the other and romantic part of Gene
Rhodes's heart that he wrote a poem which has Hector
and David admitting to their company, and that of the
Cossacks and Saracens, "This new brown comrade for
the old brown clan, the great-hearted gentlemen who
guard the outer wall." This in turn appeals so eloquently
to the romantic fraction of Frank Dobie that he recently
spoke of it as "the strongest, noblest, and most moving
poem that the Southwest can claim."

I quote Struthers Burt, a man who was capable of
blistering realism about the contemporary West and yet
was one of the architects of the Old West: "Somehow or
other a man on a horse feels different from his fellows.
Somehow or other all he does is colored and accentuated
by his position. A little above the ground, his mind, his
voice, his hands controlling casually but instinctively
the silken thing between his legs. [Meaning his horse,
and see what can happen to a good writer.] Whatever
the horseman does is just a trifle more gallant, more
swaggering, than the gestures and actions of a footman;
his vices are more dashing, his virtues freer. There's fan-
fare to a horse."

Over the years fiction has created for this *caballero*
an amazing protocol, a set of ceremonial forms as rigid
as the rituals of a religious sect and as elaborate as the
Court of Love—all enforceable, understand, by gunfire
or a lynching rope. And all retrospective. By comparison
it reduces to nonentity the code of chivalric conduct

invented by long dead moonlight-and-honeysuckle novelists and now accepted as once real by historians of a
fading myth, the Old South. From "When you call me
that, smile" on, it has kept proliferating till by now its
bulk and intricacy are a considerable hazard to the
horse opera that invented it, which frequently has to interrupt the narrative to construe a statute, aware that
it may be talking over the reader's head.

As we have seen, the code postulates that the cowboy was brave, gay, gallant, dashing, swaggering, arrogant, and all the more so when the pressure was on;
that his pride was stupendous and his honor on a hair
trigger; that he was so loyal to his friends, his outfit,
and his job that there was never a question but that he
would gaily and gallantly give up his life for them when
the sacrifice was demanded; that he was kind, gentle,
gracious, smiling, considerate. And so on. Some articles
of the code say merely that cowboys were required to respond intelligently to the demands of their trade, but
most of them are formal rules covering ritualistic situations. They are thought of and written about in the present tense.

On greeting a stranger the cowboy raises his hat or
at least touches its brim with his gun hand. When drinking at a bar, he holds his glass in his gun hand. This is
to assure those whom it may concern that he is not, at
the moment, going to shoot anyone. Also, if he accepts
a drink from any enemy, that closes the contention; as
Mr. Ramon F. Adams puts it, "If still seeking revenge,
the recipient of the drink must pick a new quarrel. An
infraction of this provision of the code will make the vi-
olator an outlaw in the graces of his fellowmen."[7] In the
same courteous and cautionary spirit, when meeting a
stranger on the trail he and the stranger dismount, both
being scrupulous not to get on the far side of his horse.
Approaching a camp or a house, he will hail it far off,
halt till invited to approach, and stay in the saddle till

invited to alight. Before entering a house he will hang
his belt and gun from the saddle or dispose of it in some
other patently pacific way.

You see, the cowboy has a .45 on his hip; Col. Colt's
pacifier is the *caballero's* rapier. At any moment there
may be a formal trial at arms. The code's provisions in
regard to it are as formal as those of a mediaeval tour-
ney; I have already mentioned some of them above and
they are far too numerous and detailed for further spec-
ification here. Here the code becomes richly cosmic, especially in the eyes of a historian. At more than a few
yards the hand gun is an unsatisfactory weapon; historically the West did its serious shooting with a rifle or
a shotgun whenever possible. Whenever possible, too,
shooting took the form of drygulching, and if God was
with you the victim would be unarmed. See the newspapers and the court records. And why not? The two
principal reasons for shooting someone were business
and self-defense against other businessmen. Horse opera
tells us that *caballeros* were courtly about murder,
whereas other Western types were likely at any moment
to turn into baddies.

It goes on and on, and always there is some filament
leading back to the .45.[8] There is no reason to carry the
analysis further but I add that, apart from the trial at
arms, the strictest commandments deal with courtliness toward women. All my authorities agree here and
horse opera has always supported them. (But as Mr. W.
H. Hutchinson points out, since Ernest Haycox it has
made the second feminine lead a soiled dove.) I find Mr.
Adams most engaging. "No other class of men look upon
women with greater reverence," he says. And, "No matter who she is, not what her station in life, the cowman
holds respect for her." And, "A woman may live alone,
miles from anyone, but she has no fear of any true Westerner. She is as safe as a church and she knows it. If any
man, at any time, under any circumstances, mistreats a

woman, he is culled from society. Men refuse to speak to him, doors are shut against him, and he is probably killed sooner or later, even if someone has to get drunk to do it."

One remembers that there were two sexes in the cattle country and still are, and that the behavior of the sexes toward each other has on other frontiers and in all other portions of America covered the whole range of variation. But we deal here with Cibola. "There were no gods then," Gene Rhodes puts it, "and circles had no centers."

"That lusty pioneer blood is tamed now, broken and gelded like the wild horse and the frontier settlement. And I think that I shall never see it flowing through human veins again as it did in my Uncle Jim Brewton riding a lathered horse across his shaggy range or standing in his massive ranch house, bare of furniture as a garret, and holding together his empire of grass and cattle by the fire in his eyes." Jim Brewton had been an army officer and had fought Indians in New Mexico, where his empire now is. That empire is an expanse of the Public Domain, the public range land, "larger than Massachusetts with Connecticut thrown in." And his word is the law, "not dead sentences in a book, but a moving finger writing on a cottonwood tree where all who rode could very plainly read."

These are the opening sentences of a book not easily classified; it is by the most gifted writer who has so far written fiction about the Cattle Kingdom, but it is also horse opera. . . . There is an organization called The Westerners which has local branches in various cities, East and West. The locals are called Corrals. Members are Possemen and the chairman is the Sheriff. The secretary may be the Deputy in Charge of Ritin' and Readin', the Keeper of the Tally, or the Registrar of Brands. Meetings are Roundups. Such titles suggest the travesty of the Baker Street Irregulars but the groups are much more like the Daughters of the Confederacy. They are devotees and acolytes, high priests, tenders of a flame. They are from all walks of life but they meet as book collectors, antiquarians, bibliographers, and historians. Also as pedants, precisians, doctrinaires, hairsplitters, fanatics, and true believers. A Roundup usually features the reading of a paper into which has gone admirably careful scholarship; in the hierarchy of learning, they belong to the species of local historians who establish the groundwork of small certainties and probabilities without which history cannot operate. Also they are litigants, crusaders, canonists, partisans, and feudists. Whom Billy the Kid had been visiting on that fatal evening, what the exact derivation of "dogies" is, where Albert J. Fountain was buried and by whom, what took Calamity Jane to Natrona County in 1892—innumerable such questions are debated till sects form, war on one another, split, and realign. Novelists and screenwriters have a professional stake in the Old West, but The Westerners are exclusively for love and worship. They are the cult who do most to maintain it.

. . . Yet the forms of law exist to annoy Colonel Brewton and a couple of his cowpokes are on trial, pro forma, for having shot (not fatally) a nester who had had the foolish daring to file a location claim on the public range that is part of the Colonel's larger-than-Massachusetts ranch. Crowds of dirty and snarling nesters are in town, in Salt Fork, for the trial; one of them has been killed by a stranger, who has been lynched. You cannot doubt that the villagers of Salt Fork who compose the jury will, touching their forelocks, find the Colonel's cowpokes not guilty. It is made clear or at least alleged that the nester was run off the Colonel's landgrab not because he wanted the land but because he wanted to plow it. . . . There is a chestnut here, a cliché, but there is also a valid point. The Colonel's empire cannot quite be located on the map. Mostly it seems to be in western New Mexico, in the vicinity of Gallup, but sometimes it seems to spread out from the valley of the Rio Grande in the east-central portion of the state. But it is quite true that growing wheat on land so steep and high that it should have remained grazing range has been one of the principal destroyers of the West. But it is the lesser of the two. Wheat-growers have not ruined a tenth as much land as the Colonel Brewtons. If the Sea of Grass which the elegist of the lusty pioneer blood is remembering is in fact in east-central New Mexico, then the destroyers were not the nesters but the cattle kings and their lesser successors. This sea rises to the stirrups of all who have written their memoirs or, more recently, recorded them on tape for Mr. Lou Blachley's foundation—and throughout New Mexico the universal testimony is that the range went because too many cows were grazed on it.[9]. . . Colonel Brewton states the case for the unbroken soil—and states it to the district attorney who has just lost the assault case and who will be Evil and Cowardice in this drama. He also remarks that, though his kind took the land from the Indians, he feels "a little charity for the nester who waited until the country was safe and peaceable before he filed a homestead on someone else's range who had fought for it."

. . . Cheyenne, Pendleton, and Calgary are the big names but major circuits include various other cities and road shows tour the East. There are minor circuits, and in little towns back in the hills the boys come in from the ranches on Saturday afternoons and stage small rodeos that in some ways are more fun than the big ones. The rodeo is an authentic, autochthonous Western festival. Those Saturday afternoons in the whistle stops supply the only resemblance to the original festivals; the others are theatrical performances by professionals. This fact has to be realized but does not in the least diminish the effectiveness or the excitement of the show. Half the program or more is made up of acts that have no relation to the cattle business or the cowboy's vocation, steer-riding and rope-twirling for instance. The costuming represents a theatrical evolution; by now it has become overspecialization of the kind that renders organisms unfunctional. The hats, chaps, shirts, boots, spurs, saddles, and accessories are part of show business. Cowgirls too are a theatrical invention. But as the production has developed, so has skill—and half the skills exhibited at a rodeo were basic in the cattle business as it used to be. They are genuine and superb; the programmed performers are unquestionably much more expert than the waddies of the Cattle Kingdom whom they represent ever were.[10]

. . . On the day when Colonel Brewton expresses his baronial scorn of hinds and clods to the district attorney, his bride comes to Salt Fork. She is Miss Cather's Lost Lady. She bears the Colonel three children but one of them is the son of the district attorney, for she has fallen in love with that defender and inciter of untouchables. She prepares to go away with him but unspeakable dishonor occurs, for he will not stand by her side and let the Colonel shoot him with "an untamed violence, like a prairie fire rimmed with black smoke, flaring in his dark eyes." The Lost Lady disappears, no one knows where.

. . . The dude ranching business began as a seasonal accessory of working cattle ranches but developed into a specialty. Nowadays most dude ranches that run any cattle at all do so for the sake of entertaining and educating their clients. The dude ranch is another admirable Western contribution to the national culture. Most of them are located in spectacular mountain country—and the finest mountain scenery can be reached only on horseback. They provide a kind of vacation that serves all the needs for recreation and re-creation of a harried, metropolitan people. Cowpokes who work on them are paid considerably higher wages than they could get on a cattle ranch. Rightly, for they not only have to costume the part and not only have to be expert at all the skills they are called on to exhibit but have to have learned the difficult job of guarding greenhorns in the wilderness. They have to be actors too, as well as performers. And they too have begun to specialize. Many go south in the winter to practice their trade in Florida and along the Gulf coast. Others spend the off season in the now booming Western horse business—riding horses, gaited horses, schooled horses, race horses. (An amusing local specialty has developed. In the vicinity of Reno the normal stay at a dude ranch is six weeks. Women getting divorces tend to suffer sexual anxiety; ranch proprietors must provide interns who will alleviate it.)

... The nesters in the Salt Lake Fork country are from the humbler walks of life but no good men among them make the world seem little evil. They are unshaven, poorly dressed, personally soiled tenant farmers, backwoodsmen, steamboaters, and cotton choppers, too damned worthless to have got ahead back where they came from. The craven district attorney, who by political means (that is to say vilely, because not by the Colonel's will) has become a federal judge, is their leader. Colonel Brewton's eyes are "red coals like the implacable Indian pueblo fires that are never allowed to go out." The judge directs the nesters as they steadily whittle away the Colonel's Cross B range by getting legal title to it from the federal government and planting it to wheat. (Also, drinking next year's wheat away at bars which of right and justice should be patronized only by his loyal servitors.) "The people who had waited till the West was safe and the pioneering done were barking and snapping round [his] legs like a pack of dogs." The years pass, drought comes, no more wheat will be grown, and the Sea of Grass has been destroyed.

(The destruction of land is indeed the greatest Western tragedy. The destruction of range land is part of that tragedy, and its destruction by wheat growing is part of that part. But tragedy here is felt in terms of a class war; sansculottes are uprooting the natural rulers of society.)

... The dudes like the costumes of the cowpokes, so do transient tourists, and so do Western city-dwellers. In any town the biggest store on Main Street is called "Western Outfitters" or the equivalent. Higher sums than you might think can be paid for a saddle. Boots too are fantastically expensive, though Sears-Roebuck and other cheap lines undercut the market. They have grown more elaborate over the years, with flamboyant figures and sewing, two-tone leathers in novel dyes, and by now lastex inserts. The big hat is offered in a dozen pastel colors and a dozen basic models, with brims up to six inches wide. (Fashions in hats change often, with Hollywood and the rodeos calling the turn.) There are cheap hats, some made of plastics, to match the cheap boots but the true believers scorn them and pay up to fifty dollars for the best trade article; the truest believers have both hat and boots made to order at much higher prices. Shirts are the aurora, the dawn, the sunset, the rainbow, and the atomic burst, with pearl buttons, fancy stitching, and sometimes built-in dickeys. Belts are hand-tooled, with a lot of silver and sometimes turquoise. Bandanas are bedsheet size, of mixed colors, printed with pictures and legends. There are short string ties and somewhat longer ones with the heads of longhorns and other symbols embroidered on them. A corresponding, more diversified, and more expensive line of goods, climaxed by attractive riding pants with high crotch and tight seat, is offered transient cowgirls.[11]

. . . Drought is destiny and the judgment of God but God has other judgments too. Though the Colonel has willed that there be no stain on the Lost Lady's name, all New Mexico knows who was the father of the younger boy. He has bad blood in him; his father was a coward and defended nesters. So as he grows up he is the maverick. He becomes a gambler, and at one establishment he makes an arrangement with a woman who deals monte. The proprietor detects the cheating, he draws his gun, and the boy shoots him, fatally. Killing is hardly reprehensible but cheating at cards is a dishonor, and when the Colonel says as much, the boy lights out. He turns outlaw, joins Butch Cassidy's Wild Bunch, is chased by posses, is advertised as wanted for a dozen crimes. Finally he is cornered in an abandoned shack. The federal judge is going to be summoned to talk him into surrendering, though of course this obligation too he will cravenly evade, but the Colonel goes. "Then he raised his shaggy head in a semblance of that old untamed gesture of a mossy-horned lead steer smelling wolves or water. I had never seen him lift it so slowly but when the face came up, I saw with a feeling for which there are no words that somewhere in that old Indian-fighter frame still remained the breeding place of the whirlwind and the thunderbolt." He rides to the shack—this is the walkdown—but the wounded boy does not shoot. Presently he dies game. But the word of his last escapade has penetrated the far places and the Lost Lady comes back to the Cross B just as the boy's body gets there. Husband and wife are reunited, and the boy's tombstone says that he is their son.

. . . A writer in *Harper*'s recently protested the appearance in Eastern vacation areas of people wearing the rodeo costume, and the spread there of institutions calling themselves dude ranches. Both infestations are common—Hope County, Westchester, Dutchess County, Long Island, the Poconos, the Great Smokies, the

Adirondacks and Catskills, the Berkshires, the Franconias, the Maine and Florida beaches. There are cowboy crooners everywhere. Along all highways you can see signs inviting you to dine and dance at Joe's Nite Club to music by Salida Pete's Melody Cowboys, and if you accept you will find them, dressed like Gene Autry. But I cannot sympathize with the writer's grievance. However offensive they may be, cowpoke jazz and phony dude ranches are surely among the least regrettable consequences of the Old West, and after all it was an Eastern invention. The complainant would have done well to glance at the evidence out West.

In fantasy land high school and college drum majorettes are cowgirls. Courses are given in rope twirling. At the most expensive preparatory schools in the United States a cow pony is provided for every pupil and he is taught to read brands and for all I know to bulldog steers. At ordinary schools the last tune played at dances is "Good-bye, old paint, I'm a-leavin' Cheyenne" or one of its Times Square counterfeits. Those Times Square compositions drone from the local radio station, whose announcers, weather forecasters, and news reporters are called Cowboy Larry and speak the lingo. Where there is television they wear the costume too, often including chaps, and the local Betty Furness has both sides of her wide hat brim turned up or down, a bandana round her neck, a short skirt, and a wide belt studded with silver longhorns. The movie houses run double features in which first Alan Ladd and then John Wayne clean up the cowtown or win the range war with a walkdown. In all seasons all males are in big hats, from the two-quart "stockman's hat" that was John B. Stetson's first model on up to a large gallonage. High school boys wear the one with a flat crown and rolled brim that the cake-mixer has on, the one that is supposed to be Texan though New York State yokels were wearing it in the first quarter of the Nineteenth Century. There is a midsummer carnival called Old West Week or something similar, a shopping fair. Now all males must grow hair on their faces or apply it with gum arabic, and both sexes must be in costume. Druggists and bank clerks pitch down Main Street in unfamiliar boots, tripping over property spurs, and the phraseology of the advertising matter is from Alfred Henry Lewis.

It is unfelt, silly, and for the most part harmless. Except that it conditions political behavior no one could object to it. Yet behind the advertising it does represent a faint fantasy and a nostalgia for something idiotically misconceived.[12] If the druggist and the bank clerk were to wear peaked denim caps to Rotary luncheon and once a year were to put on striped bibbed overalls and go to the carnival carrying cotton waste and an oilcan with a long spout, bystanders would be moved to laughter rather than belief. Somehow nostalgia is accepted as dignified when the druggist takes to the Old Chisholm Trail firing six-guns with both hands at tenderfeet and baddies—prefiguring a hired man on horseback who did a hard and uninteresting job in circumstances of considerable discomfort, a hired man who was of humble intelligence or he would have been working at some other job, was on the average barely literate, and smelled of horse sweat and cow dung. Nostalgia for one of the West's businesses, conceived as spectacular and liberating, gallant and swaggering, with a six-gun on the hip. In the bunkhouses of "Out Our Way," Mr. J. R. Williams draws his buckaroos in the long undershirts and drawers which the brutal weather of the West required cowboys to wear and still does, but the fantasy covers these common work clothes with the stage costumes that no cowpoke ever wore till they started riding in rodeos for the entertainment of tourists.

Mr. Richter became an important novelist when he turned to other frontiers, and this fact highlights what happened when he wrote *The Sea of Grass*. Its sensitive prose is the more shocking in that it expresses the same falsities as *Saddle by Moonlight.* Accepted in its own terms, what is the novel? It is a declaration that the world has declined from its greatness and come upon evil days, that worth and virtue and freedom have vanished. The declaration is common enough in the novel, it is one of the standard themes, and clearly Mr. Richter makes it with a full and bitter heart. But he evokes no belief, he does not even evoke respect. His tragedy turns out to be a venture in pathetics, in nostalgia and tears. The heroic way of life he looks back to is a fictitious feudalism, maintained in a barbaric society, by violence on behalf of a small and ridiculous master caste. The attributes of the tragic hero are a capacity for rage and a constant readiness to kill someone—that is all. Only half of Gene Rhodes's declaration, that is, was true; circles indeed had no centers then but there were gods. Mr. Richter mourns their passing but his sorrow is without dignity. For he is following a mirage. What nostalgia uses to rebuke the degenerate present is a false image, an Old West that never existed.

Chapter Six
A Certain Mentality

The government of New Mexico never belonged exclusively to cattlemen. There were too important interests in sheep and minerals and too obedient a vassalage whom the *ricos* could maneuver, fight, and if necessary even vote as they might see fit. The best that the cattle kings could get was a share in an unstable coalition. So that our sole experiment in dictatorship by cowmen was made in Wyoming. It lasted about thirty years and the state has not yet recovered from it.

There was some quickly exhausted gold in the vicinity of South Pass but no other minerals worth talking about except oil, the development of which had to await the twentieth century. Wyoming Territory was organized in 1869, to trim the principality of Brigham Young and to provide a stronghold on the Mormon frontier.[1] Through the next generation the only important interest in Wyoming besides stockgrowing was the Union Pacific Railroad. That the two could be served with great benefit to both was shown by the career of Willis Van Devanter.

The first herds had come to Wyoming before the Territory was organized and the Cattle Kingdom may be said to have begun in 1870. By 1871 the establishment of a stock association was a necessity. There were changes of name and structure but in 1879 it took the name it has had ever since, the Wyoming Stock Growers Association. It was the government of Wyoming.

The political instrument was dual. The Association could act in its own person or as the Territory. The Territory delegated some functions of sovereignty to the Association; others remained official. Some Association activities were paid for with Territorial funds; some officers of the Association were Territorial officials. The Territorial legislature was in the Association's keeping; so was the appointive power. As a private body the Association could control its membership and provide its own regulations for the conduct of the dominant business in Wyoming. Then as the Territory it could enact the regulations into statutory law and, if necessary, back them up with the militia. Like any trade association it had its blacklist and its security service. It was an organization of big operators, individual ranchers or representatives of syndicates and corporations.

The inflation collapsed in 1886 and the Big Freeze came in the following winter, 1886–1887. The two phenomena may be taken as the end of the Cattle Kingdom. But by then too an adverse interest which had been building up gradually had become formidable—operators of small cattle ranches, sheep ranchers, and an increasing number of dirt-ranchers who were stealing the range of the bigshots by homesteading it and getting title to it from the federal government. Politically they had no recourse except to join the Democratic Party. Furthermore by now another railroad, the Cheyenne and Northern, had come to Wyoming, and a third, the Burlington, was on the way.

A serious and unforeseen embarrassment had begun in 1884 when a Democrat, Grover Cleveland, was elected President. National agitation for reform of the land laws and correction of the abuses committed under them had reached such intensity that it had to be acted on—and by a President who would act firmly. Mr. Cleveland inconvenienced cattlemen everywhere, even in Democratic Texas and the Southwest, by enforcing the land laws.[2] But in Wyoming his worst offense consisted of appointing Democrats to Territorial offices, thus taking the government away from the Association and giving it to unimportant people whom the Association was already calling, generically, "rustlers." Historical texts, which have been written in the spirit of *The Virginian,* speak of the Democratic governor as "unfortunate." At least his appointment was too bad, and even worse was the appointment of certain judges and U.S. deputy marshals. And up north Johnson County, where small ranchers and dirt-farmers had for some time been notably recalcitrant toward their betters, got entirely out of Association control.

Suddenly home rule had become desirable for Wyoming. The Association had no reason to doubt its ability to restore the old-time religion if it were freed from Presidential appointments and Congressional supervision. Wyoming must be a state.[3] That was easy as soon as Harrison became President and Congress was Republican. Wyoming was admitted as the forty-fourth state in 1890. The Association took control again. Francis Emroy Warren, whom Cleveland had removed and Harrison had restored as Territorial Governor, became Governor of the state. He was the owner of the 7XL and later, going into the sheep business as well, became one of several claimants of a popular Western title, "the greatest shepherd since Abraham." He was Governor for a few weeks only. According to plan, he resigned and was succeeded by the Secretary of State, who appointed him to the U.S. Senate. (He served there for thirty years.) The Secretary of State who thus became Acting Governor was a young Philadelphia physician named Amos W. Barber, rich, well-born and well-connected, and a choice spirit at the Cheyenne Club. (In *The Virginian* he becomes "Dr. Barker.") The senior Senator from the new state is even more interesting. Owner of the CY (which became the C Lazy Y) and other ranches, Joseph Maull Carey was the legal intelligence of the Association. He had been one of its organizers and was its president for four years, during which he also served as Territorial Delegate to Congress. He remained Delegate after retiring from the presidency, and introduced and steered the statehood bill. He had originally gone to Wyoming on appointment from President Grant as attorney-general of the Territory. He held that office when the Association was formed and thereafter served on the Territorial Supreme Court. Nothing could be clearer.[4]

With statehood everything should have been squared away. But most shockingly it proved that the Association could not restore the good old days, and the Wyoming cattle business got steadily worse. Some hard-minded members of the Association understood that a revolution of the Western cattle business was well under way and that a social revolution was going on at the same time throughout the West. The hard-minded were able to profit from both revolutions, making unobtrusive use of the failure of their brethren in the Association to understand what was happening. That failure was astonishing. So far as most of the cattle barons were concerned, all that was needed to restore the Cattle Kingdom was enough caste solidarity to deal with some interlopers. So Wyoming had a class war.

Only in the twentieth century have efficient methods of conducting the Western cattle business been developed. The most inefficient period of an inefficient business was the Cattle Kingdom, the period of large-scale operations based on the free use of the unfenced public domain. And this was at its least efficient in the climate and geography of Cibola or Shangri-La, in Wyoming.

Like all Western businesses, the cattle boom was financed by Eastern and foreign capital. Mr. Wister found Wyoming so reassuringly Ivy League because Laramie County and later the Powder River country were attractive to young millionaires from Boston, Newport, New York, and the Main Line, who could be manorial patrons, big game hunters, and practically-English sportsmen in magnificent natural surroundings while at the same time, so the theory was, the mating habits of neat cattle would rather more than double their investment every second year. Eastern Wyoming was full of such names as Sturgis, Brooks, Biddle, Lyman, Agassiz, Gardiner, Shaw, Higginson, Oelrichs, Teschemacher, Lodge, and the like. Because the imperially-minded British and Scots were eager to invest in bonanza ranching that had established a proper feudal order, it was also full of titles, younger sons, emergent middle-class millionaires, M.P.'s, and retired army officers. With a sprinkling of similar elegants from Europe, including an Austrian archduke.

They had a glorious time in a glorious country. At their home ranches—comparatively small and sometimes the only land they or their corporations actually had title to—they built what would have been hunting lodges in the old country. Usually of logs, they were spectacularly sited and luxuriously furnished, with fine libraries, the walls hung with sporting prints and mounted heads of big game. Elegant tallyhos and victorias mingled with the ranch buckboards and chuck wagons, for use in Cheyenne or to torture guests on the trails that led out from it. Many of them made a cere-

mony of dinner and formal dress, French wines, and
roasts of buffalo, venison, elk, bighorn, or what you will
fulfilled a sportsman's fantasy.

Most of the young elegants saw their outfits for only
a month or so in the spring, at the time of the calf
roundup, and a shorter time in the fall at the beef
roundup, after which they went hunting for a month—
in the Bighorns and perhaps on to the Wind Rivers or
even the Tetons. They would go east for the Season and
the Britishers would return to Parliament or their family estates. Summers were pleasant in the little railroad
town they had remodeled into Shangri-La's first cowtown. Cheyenne never has been handsome but it is cool
and it was easily adapted to fashionable diversions.
There was the exciting Western festival called the
rodeo—as Frontier Day, Cheyenne's was to be the first
famous one—and there were amateur saddle racing, amateur theatricals, tennis on the only courts between St.
Paul and San Francisco, gymkhanas, and even riding to
hounds.[5] And there was the Cheyenne Club. It did not
represent such massive wealth as analogous clubs in the
mining country did, at Butte, Helena, Denver, and later
Colorado Springs. But it was a lot more genteel. "It was
a cosmopolitan place," John Clay says. "Under its roof
reticent Britisher, cautious Scot, exuberant Irishman,
worldly New Yorker, chivalrous Southerner, and delightful Canadian all found a welcome home." Another nostalgic memorialist says that it exceeded all others in the
consumption of champagne. . . . There were some ruder
members too, the hard-minded who had pushed their
way into the hegemony but were without lineage, and
as the deflation went on there were more of them.

Pleasant as it was to be suzerains of the public's
range and make enormous sums of money—on paper if
you were American, ten percent a year or more in hard
cash, paid for by the sale of seed stock that diminished
capital, if you were British—there was an unfortunate

drawback. The elegants did not know the cattle business. Some of them tried to learn it and of these some
did learn it, after a costly educational process; most did
not. There were those who did know it. Some of them
were experienced stockmen, the firstcomers or Texans
who had come up the Long Trail and stayed. Others
were the elegants' foremen, who were top hands or else
agents of the British syndicates.

The foremen were the people who actually ran the
ranches that the elegants owned. Quite a few of them
stole their employers' calves, put their own brands on
them, presently were in the cattle business, and were
also in a position to clean up when the crash came. This
was a custom of the country. Cowpokes laid off for the
winter, discharged cowpokes, and ramblin' cowpokes
rounded up such unbranded stock—mavericks—as they
could find and always found a market for them. Foremen expected to buy such calves and sent the hands out
to look for them when the market was inactive. This was
"mavericking" and was not regarded as rustling. But
stealing one another's branded cows and brandblotting
them, that is rustling, was only conventionally disap-
proved. The big outfits stole one another's stock as opportunity offered. The prime reason for the establishment of the Stock Association had been to referee
among bigshots who were rustling, in the hope of eventually establishing that rustling did not pay. There were
very few small spreads in Wyoming when the Association had its legislature pass a maverick law.

When the deflation came it at once illuminated the
bad business practices of the Cattle Kingdom in
Wyoming. The famous "book count," by which business
deals, including bank loans and the sale of herds and
ranches, were conducted on the basis of a mathematical
formula, was prevalent throughout the cattle country,
but was no less disastrous in Wyoming because of that
fact. Three percent a month was standard interest on

loans. The foremen of the syndicate, as I have said, had been paying dividends out of capital. The Ivy League ranchers had kept going by floating loans and selling shares among their fashionable friends. And really tough operators—railroads, stockyards, and packing plants—had got a stranglehold on them which could not be broken.

And when drought and hard winters came, the Cattle Kingdom paid the inexorable penalty for its worst blindness and folly. In order to expand their operations, to keep abreast of their notes, and to hold their own against one another, the barons had disastrously overstocked the range. Overgrazing had steadily reduced the productivity of the range. The original grasses could not reseed themselves in quantity, sometimes not at all. They were replaced by less nutritious species, by weeds, sometimes by dust. In vast areas less than twenty years of high, wide, and handsome ranching—on some of the finest rangeland in North America—had reduced productivity by nine-tenths. (Even today, few ranges in eastern Wyoming can support half as many cows as they could have supported without deterioration when the big herds began to arrive from Texas and proceeded to overcrowd them.) This meant that a given area could feed fewer cows—the rancher lost capital. It also meant that the cows grazed on it put on less weight and succumbed more easily to drought and winter—so he lost more capital.

When payday came a lot of prominent people got squeezed out of the cattle business. Loans were refused, mortgages were foreclosed, corporations were reorganized, herds and holdings were reduced. The men were separated from the boys, or rather the pros from the amateurs. The hard-minded, efficient ranchers in the main survived, and it was notable how many resident managers had become ranch-owners. The new trend was toward smaller operations, home pasturing, winter feeding, and the growing of hay. But prosperity didn't seem in a hurry to come back and by now the small operators and farmers were making serious inroads. They filed homestead claims on lands that lay along watercourses, the remaining stands of good grass, and meadows and hillsides that were favorable for the production of hay. This barefaced steal of the Association's range forced members of the Association to file extensively (also fraudulently) on land they had been using free and to buy big chunks of Union Pacific land, which had a grant of alternate sections twenty miles wide on both sides of its tracks and all the way across Wyoming. No matter how cannily this was done—in patterns that facilitated domination of larger areas—it was expensive. And Wyoming now witnessed a curious reversal of practice, the big operators building fences to shut out the little ones. Fence wars resulted but nesters were as handy with pliers as employees of big operators.

Understand, the upstarts had no damned right to ranch or farm in Wyoming; it was the private fief of the Wyoming Stock Growers Association, which at the moment had about a hundred members. They owned two million cows, the state government, the courts, the handy instrument known as the Livestock Commission, and the avenues of approach to the Federal government. Anybody who defied, opposed, or even criticized the Association was a rustler and was liable to trouble.

Trouble was made for quite a number of such rustlers but terrorism did not stop small ranchers and farmers from progressively carving up the range. All dying oligarchies behave stupidly. The Association blacklisted upstarts, but upstarts went on ranching. The Association divided the State into roundup districts, named official roundup dates, prohibited any other roundups, and had its arrangements made the law of Wyoming. It went on to authorize its agents to forbid the sale or transportation from Wyoming of any cattle bearing the brands of suspected rustlers—to confiscate them and sell them for the profit of the Association. A suspected rustler was any cowman not a member of the Association whom any member cared to name. This too was made statutory law—in effect forbidding anyone who did not belong to the Association to engage in the cattle business in Wyoming.

Non-members were now outlaws but still the system did not work satisfactorily. In Johnson County it did not work at all. Up north there were too few bigshots and too many small ones, and the latter simply took control. The Association could not get its representatives elected to positions of power; it could not get grand juries to indict, petit juries to convict, courts to issue writs, or sheriffs to make arrests. So the citizens of Johnson County were rustlers. Certainly some of them were—rustling was an old Wyoming custom. Certainly too some of them were frontier riffraff, drifters preying on whomever they found at hand—a lot of the same kind were drawing pay from the Association. The point is not rustling, it is the class conflict. In the main Johnson County was composed of the ordinary folk of the changing agricultural frontier, farmers and small cattle ranchers, of the same mores and morals as anyone else of the time and place, of average decency and honesty. But the world had changed, the new era which was transforming the West was transforming Wyoming as part of it, and a ruling class was ceasing to rule. It didn't like what was happening.[6]

In the strictest tradition, the oligarchy decided to reverse the course of history. And shortly thereafter Johnson County formed the Northern Wyoming Farmers Stock Growers Association, announced that it would not abide by the Association's rules, and announced further that it would hold its own roundup, well in advance of the Association's. Note the date it set for its roundup: May 1, 1892.

In 1883 a man named Mosier who was accused—and guilty—of murder was in the Cheyenne jail. It was decided to save Laramie County the expense of a trial, and members of the Cheyenne Club were invited to share an interesting and exciting social experience. Mr. Charles A. Guernsey, for whom a Wyoming town was later named, declined with thanks. With some of his friends and the sheriff of Laramie County, however, he watched the lynching from the yard next door to the jail. He says the sheriff could have stopped it but didn't try. The mayor of Cheyenne, Joseph M. Carey, who was later Senator, did make a speech calling on the well-connected mob to break up, but it disregarded him and hanged Mosier from a light pole. "One of the boys from the [Cheyenne] Club who did participate," Guernsey's autobiography says, "told me afterward that he would never cease to regret the part he played, that the clang of the rail brought from the Union Pacific Yards with which they battered down the steel cage and cell doors to reach Mosier still rang in his ears."

Ugly as the roots, prologue, and aftermath of the Johnson County War were, its course was superb historical comedy and some day someone should write it as such. Here, however, it interests us only as it reveals a state of mind and illustrates the use of the political arm.

On the Sweetwater River, not far from the great historical landmark Independence Rock, a man named Averell filed a homestead claim on part of a Gentleman's public range. He was a graduate of either Yale or Cornell, a civil engineer, and he was promptly called a rustler. No doubt he was observing the local custom, and that was wrong for homesteaders. He also opened a saloon; it was patronized by increasing numbers of the nesters along the Sweetwater and by cowpokes who worked for the Gentlemen. He wrote letters for the Natrona County newspapers accurately describing the Association methods, applying accurately descriptive ad-

jectives to them, and naming names.[7] He forced three
members of the Association to prove up their claims in
the Sweetwater Valley, became something of a voice for
the small ranchers, and got his ranch made a U.S. post
office. Obviously an upstart and a trouble-maker.

Presently Averell was joined by one Ella Watson,
alias Kate Maxwell, who comes down in the literature as
Cattle Kate. She lived with Averell and filed a small
homestead claim. Some memoirs call her "handsome,"
an adjective of the period, though a photograph at the
University of Wyoming hardly justifies it. But she appears to have been a pleasant talker and she performed
an indispensable service in an area where women were
scarce. Some of her clients paid her fees with their employers' calves. She and Averell made frequent ship-
ments from their small corral. So presently a group led
by one of the parvenu Gentlemen and containing two of
those whom Averell had made legal difficulties for appeared at their spread and hanged both Averell and
Kate from a tree whose branch extended over a cut bank.

So far as my researches extend, horse opera has not
made use of this scene. Some disapproval was expressed
locally, and I find John Clay's comment interesting:
"The man wilted and begged for mercy, the woman died
game. This of course was a horrible piece of business
[the leader of the lynchers was foreman of a ranch in
which Clay had a stake], and in many ways indefensible
and yet what are you to do? Are you to sit still and see
your property ruined with no redress in sight?" The
code of the cowman is a literary invention. Cows, not
womanhood, were sacred.

Unhappily four witnesses had seen the lynching and
so there had to be some formalities. An indictment was
found—naming not one of the Gentlemen who had been
recognized but one of the thugs. (He had earlier performed similar services for coal-mine operators in Pennsylvania.) One witness was conveyed to the Eastern

seaboard, two disappeared, and one conveniently died. Indictment dismissed.

The Association had a private list, quite apart from the blacklist. The number of names on it is variously reported, usually as seventy, but it was being acted on methodically. A horse rancher was arrested on a false warrant and the deputy marshal who took him in custody hanged him in a gulch because "he looked guilty." There were no specific complaints against him, later research had turned up no evidence, and the deputy was not prosecuted.

Three officers and a footloose thug broke into a cabin to get one Nate Champion, whom the Association considered the most dangerous of the Johnson County "rustlers." Presumably his morals were not immaculate, though again there is no evidence.[8] It can be said certainly that he was a brave man and a good shot. This time he shot so effectively that he winged one of the gang and drove them all away so fast that they left identifiable possessions behind them. One of them was a somewhat discolored peace officer and semi-Gentleman who was calling himself Frank Canton. He had been, was, and was long to remain that favorite type of horse opera, the deputy sheriff doubling as the gun for hire, in Wyoming and elsewhere. Before the "rustlers" took the government of Johnson County away from the Association, he had been sheriff there while at the same time acting as an Association range detective. (He was wanted for murder in Texas and, the story is, eventually got a pardon from the Governor at the point of a gun.) Tears are shed for him and eloquent eulogies uttered in many memoirs, and it is pointed out that when he died he was one of the most reputable citizens of Oklahoma and adjutant-general of its militia. But in Wyoming he was a careless operator, or maybe only an arrogant one.[9]

This was November 1, 1891; the blueprints were well along. Near Buffalo, the seat of Johnson County, a young horse-breaker named Jones, against whom no accusation is made in the literature or even in rumor, was dry-gulched. Nobody doubted that Mr. Canton had acted for his principals. Two days later a Johnson County rancher was dry-gulched. Mr. Canton was seen departing in haste and he left his horse on the scene. It was remembered that the rancher had accused Canton of having murdered an elderly couple in Texas and that he had spoken forthrightly about the attempted murder of Nate Champion. A warrant was sworn out for Mr. Canton but he was of course released. With the leader of the gang who had lynched Averell and Kate (and whose subsequent activities are only partly shown in the records) he saw fit to leave Wyoming for a while. Young Dr. Barber refused to issue extradition papers. He came back to Cheyenne in March 1892 to join the Gentlemen's army, submitted to arrest, and on April 4 was bailed in the sum of $30,000. The bond was signed by some of the most patrician names in Wyoming, and the next day a military troop train arrived in Cheyenne from Denver.

The plans that had been worked out over more than a year were now being put into effect. The Association was going to invade Johnson County and shoot up the town of Buffalo, the center of the "rustlers." Or since the Association's executive committee was careful to hold no official meetings this year and to leave no records of friendly conversations, maybe we had better say that the Gentlemen were.[10]

Planning had been systematic. For a full year stories had been planted in Eastern newspapers and magazines saying that Johnson County was in revolt against the state of Wyoming. In the Eastern and the official imagination it was an area populated by multiples of Billy the Kid and the James brothers. It was foreseen that the Buffalo company of the National Guard might not sympathize with the Gentlemen's troopers, and indeed there was no certainty that companies in Natrona and Converse County would support the right side. So Dr. Barber had his adjutant-general issue a general order forbidding militia organizations to obey orders except from Cheyenne headquarters—in flat violation of a Wyoming statute which authorized local officials to call them out in emergency. A war chest of $100,000 was raised; it proved insufficient and had to be increased by assessment. Recruiting agents were sent to Idaho, Texas, and the Southwest to hire gunmen who would be sworn in as deputy sheriffs. Apparently it was thought that a hundred such could be hired and that they would be enough. Actually, apart from one Idahoan whose enlistment proved disastrous, only Texans were procured and only about thirty of them.[11]

Most of the Texans were qualified by experience for the job, having served as deputy marshals or sheriffs back home; some were even more unwholesome than the average of that type. They were hired for a given job; they knew what they were hired for; they were pros. Statements of the pay scale vary from a flat rate of a thousand dollars to base pay of fifty dollars a day plus fifty dollars apiece for every rustler killed. They assembled in Denver, where a couple of Association committeemen talked loudly to the press, and were taken to Cheyenne in a special Union Pacific train, with three carloads of saddle horses and extensive campaign equipment. At Cheyenne they were joined by a somewhat smaller number of Gentlemen who were going to be vigilantes. (Again, only about a third of those who had been expected to enlist actually showed up.) Also the equipment was completed; nothing is more revealing than the fact that the expeditionary force was free to draw tents, rifles, and ammunition from the U.S. Army post just outside of town, Fort D. A. Russell. The Association quartermasters provided dynamite, strychnine, and other useful material—including what every war party should have, a surgeon. Young Dr. Barber had a Philadelphia friend visiting him, a physician named Charles Bingham Penrose. His brother Boies Penrose was President of the State Senate of Pennsylvania and would soon begin his career in the U.S. Senate; his brother Spencer would soon be one of the richest mining operators in the West. Dr. Penrose was happy to join the Cheyenne Club hosts and their retainers—his enlistment was announced in that incredibly indiscreet newspaper interview in Denver—and Dr. Barber was happy to lend him a case of surgical instruments for which as Acting Governor of the sovereign State of Wyoming he had no present need.

The outfit was complete, a Cheyenne newspaperman and the correspondent of a Chicago newspaper climbed aboard, and the troop train—on the tracks of the Cheyenne & Northern now—took off for Casper, where the cavalry column would form. Telegraph operators were refusing messages that day, April 5, 1892. And just to make sure, the Gentlemen had had the wires cut in all directions.

It challenges belief: it defies belief. Here were fifty-odd pros and gentleman amateurs setting out to commit as large-scale a massacre as might prove feasible, in order to terrorize the inhabitants of Johnson County into flight or docile acceptance of Association rule. The oligarchy had backed up its instrument with its state government. Through its Senators it had squared the government of the United States and made requisitions on the U.S. Army. It had utilized its alliance with the railroads and the telegraph company. And yet!

The pros present no problem; they had been hired as technical experts to assist a commercial operation. They were working at their trade; most of them continued to work at it elsewhere after the campaign and quite a few died on the job. But what to make of the Gentlemen, near-Gentlemen, and eventual Gentlemen who were taking off for Casper in the most jocund mood to go hunting for unwashed and annoying persons as they had often hunted antelope? It is a tableau of inconceivable arrogance—and inconceivable idiocy too. Long ago a graybeard who had been a Sixth Cavalry trooper and had taken part in the final scene told me that the officers of the Sixth faced a considerable disciplinary problem; he said that he and his companions had to keep laughing out loud in ranks.

They were fools and their security measures had failed altogether. Association loudmouths had been interviewed in Denver and what they said there had gone out on the wires. Others in Cheyenne had issued idiotic proclamations calling for the "extermination" of Johnson County rustlers. The military special had been widely observed and checked up on. Though the telegraph company would accept no messages for Buffalo and presently had its wires down, someone thought to write a letter to the sheriff of Johnson County and it was promptly delivered. After the troop train departed, newspapermen and various casuals demanded to know what young Governor Barber was going to do about a large party of armed freebooters who had invaded Wyoming and were obviously disturbing the peace. The Governor, who was not a fool but only foolish, said that its presence had not been called to his official attention and that no action had been asked of him.

The military special paused to pick up the foreman of one of Senator Carey's ranches. It was decided, however, that you mustn't have a U.S. Senator's employee shoot people in the public view—a State Senator was in the army—and so he was dropped again and instructed to cut some more telegraph wires. The troops detrained at Casper and took to horse. Followed by the supply train, they rode fifty miles through uncomfortably cold weather to an Association ranch near the border of Johnson County. Here they spent the night and the next day—it was their happy belief that no one at all knew that anything whatever was going on. Here too young Dr. Penrose decided that the vigilante's life was not for him after all and stayed on at the ranch intending to go back to Cheyenne. The Cheyenne newspaperman and one of the Gentlemen also suffered second thoughts and departed. And now the code of the cowman got a notable vindication. It says that the cowman's hospitality is sacred. So up rode the foreman of a big Association outfit and reported that he had spent the preceding night at the KC ranch.[12] It had been leased by a "rustler" named Nick Rae who was on the Association's extermination list—again without evidence—and the foreman added that Nate Champion was there too. So the expeditionary force postponed its attack on Buffalo, made a night march to the KC, surrounded the ranch house, and prepared to commit its first murder.

It turned out that the job required all day. Two wandering wolf hunters had spent the night at the KC. Soon after daybreak they came out, separately, to the barn and were captured by the forces that had occupied it. (And became witnesses to murder.) Presently Nick Rae appeared in the dooryard and was shot. Champion carried him back inside the ranch house, where presently he died. Then Champion proceeded to hold off some fifty amateur and professional gunmen, who kept up a steady rifle fire on the squalid little shack. I repeat that this nester-rustler was a brave man. Following the earlier attempt to kill him, he had written a detailed description of it to the Buffalo newspaper. Now in intervals when he wasn't shooting at the concealed heroes, who felt no impulse to storm his one-man fort, he wrote in a pocket notebook a terse running account of the day. The journal of a man who knows that presently he will be dead, it is simple, hard, eloquent, and deeply moving. He caught a glimpse of one besieger long enough to recognize him as Frank Canton and wrote down his name.

By the end of the afternoon the heroes had figured out an expedient. They filled the wagon with hay, pushed it up against a blind wall of the ranch house and set fire to it. When the shack burned to the point where he couldn't stand it any longer, Champion came out shooting. Twenty-eight bullets hit him.

It had been amazing folly to spend a day shooting at Champion. Several casual passersby went on to Buffalo with word of what was happening; several more purposive neighbors, after riding over to take a look, did the same. (At Buffalo Association plans to have the sheriff murdered misfired.) Now the fools read Champion's brief diary and, merely cutting Frank Canton's name out of it, left it with his body, which they also vaingloriously placarded, "Cattle thieves beware." It would make a marvelous telling at the Cheyenne Club.

The murders of Rae (whose body was left to roast in the burning ranch house) and Champion were all the killing that the invaders were able to do. Two Texans contrived to shoot themselves accidentally, one of them presently dying of it, and Champion had winged another hero. With the sloppy job finished at last, the expedition now moved on to a member ranch for remounts. The next day they were continuing their march on the doomed town of Buffalo when a series of couriers riding hell-for-leather arrived and shocked them back to a sense of reality with news that Johnson County was not in flight but quite the contrary. The rustlers, their outlaw sheriff, a wicked parson, and in fact the whole dissolute and unwashed countryside—not one among them could have got past the membership committee of the Cheyenne Club—were mobilizing. Considerations that had not hitherto occurred to them now did, and with some force. They forted up at the T Open A on Crazy Woman Creek and set about frantically preparing to repel rudeness, connecting the various ranch buildings with a series of trenches and rifle pits.

The sheriff of Johnson County—duly elected and representing a legitimate and legal government, remember—was W. G. Angus. He called on the captain of the Buffalo company of the National Guard for help and was told the command would not be assembled without orders from the Governor. (The captain was reporting as often as possible to Dr. Barber.) He got the same answer from the colonel who commanded a squadron of the Sixth U.S. Cavalry at a small post named Fort McKinney just outside Buffalo, and this at least was regulation. So Johnson County organized its own assistance. Quite thoroughly: over three hundred uncultivated persons had surrounded the TA by the last reel, and more were riding in all the time. For two days the TA was under as hot a fire as the KC had been.

A cowpoke of unknown allegiance whom the defenders had captured en route volunteered to get word out, and succeeded in escaping the first night. Too bad that so much telegraph wire had been cut, but eventually he was able to get off a message to the Acting Governor. Dr. Barber had already heard a lot of alarming rumors that the secret invasion had backfired. He began to burn up the wires to Washington and to headquarters of the military department at Omaha. His telegram to President Harrison, asking that the Sixth Cavalry be ordered to the rescue, began, "An insurrection exists in Johnson County," which was a flat lie and highly interesting phraseology as well, and ended, "the lives of a large number of persons are in imminent danger," which was only too true. In Washington Senators Carey and Warren woke the President from sleep, not minimizing the emergency, and he directed the Secretary of War to issue the necessary orders.[13] He did so and the colonel of the Sixth, wiring back a corrective description of what had happened, saddled up Troops B, D, and H and trotted the fourteen miles to the TA. They arrived just after sunrise on their third day and raised the siege.

Just in time. The Johnson County folks were digging approach trenches and had almost finished the construction of a weapon that would have ended the war quite messily. They had captured the Gentlemen's supply train—weapons, dynamite, strychnine, and most of the reserve ammunition. They had chained two of the wagons together, piled them with logs to make them bulletproof, and were preparing to load them with dynamite and push them up against the principal stronghold and explode it. Forty-six *caballeros* of the cowman's code surrendered to the colonel, among them such proud Cheyenne Club names as Hesse, Tisdale, Debillier, Whitcomb, and Teschemacher. Two more of the boys had been winged.[14]

They had unquestionably committed murder and Sheriff Angus demanded that they be turned over to him for imprisonment pending trial. Both the colonel and Dr. Barber refused, quite rightly. As well turn a rustler over to the sheriff of Laramie County, with a light pole outside the jail. Thirty-nine indictments for murder were promptly found, however, and this too was right. Murder had been committed, and according to plan. . . . I know one son of a Gentleman-vigilante to whom the indictment seems an intolerable stigma.

Fort McKinney, whither they were taken, was uncomfortably close to Buffalo; so Dr. Barber directed the Sixth to remove them to Fort Fetterman, which was east of Casper. He and his Senators still had the President appalled by the open defiance of Johnson County to the law and its officers, and presently the defendants were moved on to Fort Russell, which was convenient to the Cheyenne Club. The Texans, being only hired hands, had to check in at night and so got pretty bored during the next two months, but members were not inconvenienced.

The two wolf hunters who had been captured at the KC and were eyewitnesses of the murders had, most foolishly, been released. They were now kidnapped at Casper and conveyed out to Wyoming to a running war of warrants and habeas corpus orders that was handsomely publicized by the Western press.[15] They ended up at, of all places, Westerly, Rhode Island—Oelrichs country?—where they spent eleven months of pleasant idleness at somebody's expense. Eventually they were released from custody and paid off with checks for $2500 apiece. The checks bounced.

The Association now got a genuine social scare. To the staggering surprise of the Cheyenne Club and its officials and associates, the state of Wyoming at large was shocked and angered by armed invasion, hired murder, and the subversion of government by the well-heeled. There was a lot of ugly talk; there were some ugly, if now inevitable, actions, the first of the sequelae that were to last for a long time. An Association foreman rode into Buffalo to pick up some of his employer's cows and got killed. The Association foreman who had tipped off the invaders to the presence of Champion at the KC met Champion's brother and killed him. The little weeklies were publishing the most outrageous items and epithets about the invasion and its managers; you could even hear some of them repeated approvingly in Cheyenne saloons. There was a series of mass meetings which adopted highly insulting resolutions and got them into the newspapers. It was a good thing that the Association owned the state government, but even so Dr. Barber and his Senators tried hard to get President Harrison to declare martial law in Wyoming, which would have made a safer and much neater game. They did not make the grade but they did get him to order six thousand more cavalry into the state before the preliminary hearing on the murder charge. (Unquestionably they were a restraining force, but rather on the possible willingness of witnesses than on violence. Plenty of sporadic violence followed and the troops made some of it.)

Nothing happened at the hearing of course or at the formal last act. The judge knew what his duty was and did it; the only thing worth noting here is the first appearance in a national news story of one of the defendants' counsel, a Mr. Willis Van Devanter. The Texans stayed in formal custody for a while, though they had reverted to the status of employees again and the amateurs kept them in their place. "The cattlemen shared many of their good things with them," Malcolm Campbell's book says, "but socially the deadline was drawn across the center of the room."[16] Most of them had gone home by the time the Association's judge dismissed the murder charges, when it was apparent that, the Association numbering the treasury of the state among its possessions, neither Laramie nor Johnson County could afford a trial.

"There was a jollification in a mild way at the Club," John Clay says of this outcome, "but it did not touch the bubbling enthusiasm of the old days." Mr. Clay was one of the agents of British syndicates whom the depression had advanced to great heights in the cattle business. He was by now the most influential cattleman in Wyoming and on his way to becoming the wealthiest one. He was President of the Association and an extremely shrewd man. His shrewdness included a decision to be far away when the plans he had helped to make were carried out; so he went to Scotland for the fishing. He devotes a chapter of his memoirs to the invasion, and its last paragraph is marvelously expressive.

> It cost the cattle-owners around $100,000. They responded freely, although it was the panic year of 1893. But money counts for little when placed beside nobility of character, of patient self-denial, of loyal friendship: the strong supporting the weak morally and financially. From the fiery furnace of trial and tribulation came pure gold, no tawdry counterfeit but the real stuff, repre-

sented by splendid examples of courage, honesty and ever-lasting belief in the justice of their cause. Against this were a few cattlemen, some of them oldtimers, who failed to support their friends, who before the raid were far from silent critics of Wyoming's tardiness in punishing the rustlers. They were absent at the hour of need, and among their fellowmen they were despised and a black mark put against their names. Politics was the cause of some retreating; cowardice and self-interest influenced others. But sufficient for the day is the evil thereof. Today Wyoming is a better state to live in, so far as property rights are concerned, than it was twenty-five years ago. The "invasion" cleared the air.

That is one way of putting it, a most elegant way; Mr. Wister's Judge Henry could not have improved on it.

Back at the ranch where he had stayed behind when the still exuberant raiders rode off to murder Rae and Champion, Dr. Penrose started out to drive to Cheyenne. It is a long way. For four or five days Wyoming boiled round him, with aroused and alarmed partisans of both sides galloping everywhere, laying up rifles and ammunition, and hearing and creating the wildest rumors. No one told the young tenderfoot about any of this; in great innocence of heart he drove his buckboard on through the cold April toward the Cheyenne Club. He reached Douglas, which was tense with conflict and certainly no Association town. He tied his team in front of the back and went in and asked if Dr. Penrose, of 1331 Spruce Street, Philadelphia, a friend of Acting Governor Amos W. Barber, could cash a check. The authorities—it is not clear just who they were or whether they were acting on Sheriff Angus's request to jail all suspicious characters— arrested him and told him that he would be sent to Buffalo to be tried for conspiracy and murder. To the frantic telegrams pouring into and out of Cheyenne, Washington, and Philadelphia were now added various piteous ones by Dr. Penrose. Dr. Barber, stimulated by Boies Penrose, found time among his urgencies to get off a marshal to Douglas, with a writ of habeas corpus. It was arranged not to receive Sheriff Angus's warrant for the young man till he could be got out of town on a locomotive. How could you let Johnson County try anyone or let anyone try a Penrose? There was another locomotive at Cheyenne and Dr. Barber, escorting him to it, told him he would be safe as soon as it crossed the line into Nebraska.

The Johnson County War brought many things to Wyoming besides what Mr. Clay calls pure gold. It made class conflict almost permanent, created alignments and feuds and political pressures and private passions which have not altogether lost their force even now, more than sixty years later, and produced a lot of dry-gulching, open murder, and miscellaneous gunfire— though these last must be seen as products of the feuds rather than directly of the war. Of this area of social turbulence I have no need to speak, for the relevant point is that the War was an extremely serious setback for the Association. Neither direct action nor direct control of the state would ever work again. Different methods must be used and the Association must keep itself dissociated from them, at least officially. It would never stop trying to make its oligarchical dictatorship of Wyoming absolute, it has not stopped even now, and it would always in large part succeed, as it does now, though also it would always fall short of what was desirable. John Clay manifested a clear understanding of much of this shortly after he got back from the fishing in Scotland. He brought up from the Southwest and put on the payroll of one of his ranches a former Army scout, Pinkerton operative, and range detective named Tom Horn, who though by no means the killingest of the psychopaths was on the whole the most repulsive one. The murder end of the cattle business must thereafter be conducted by individual ranchers or their employees.

The Association kept on losing the kind of power it had exercised, not least remarkably in that it had to become larger and less exclusive, admitting ranchers so widely that in the end all ranchers had to be considered eligible. Moreover, another kind of conflict that weakened it further was becoming acute and widespread. Sheep were coming to Wyoming in constantly increasing numbers, and of course they were grazing the cattlemen's public domain. Two of the cattlemen's grievances against them were entirely realistic and sound. Even when they were handled skillfully the great trail bands did fearful damage to the range adjacent to the trails, and when they were handled carelessly, as they often were, the area of damage was greatly increased. Furthermore, one kind of sheep operator appeared with the others, a type that was to become permanent down to the closing of the public domain twenty years ago and was to be feared and hated as well by sheep ranchers as by cattlemen—the nomad who had no range of his own and often no home ranch, who grazed his sheep only on public domain, moved about it as best suited him, and had no interest in taking care of any range. Yet I cannot say that either of these just grievances went any deeper than the primary one, the cattlemen's feeling of intolerable outrage that anyone except them should use the public range.

There followed in Wyoming more than two decades of range war between cattlemen and sheepmen. I have sufficiently described this kind of conflict in an earlier chapter and need say only that it *was* war, as the invasion of Johnson County was not. It was bloody and shameful. Clubbing, dynamiting, rimrocking, burning, throat-cutting, poisoning, every kind of sheepkilling— flogging, murder, dry-gulching, even massacre—raids by gunnysackers, by undisguised cowpokes, by merry-makers on the loose—blood feuds in the Bighorn Basin, guerrilla fighting in the Owl Creek Mountains, that enormous pile of bones at Scab Creek—deadlines decreed or negotiated, upheld, broken, circumvented. I have said that there were no convictions and few trials until very late along, which shows the power of the cattlemen was still great, though it was ebbing. And especially the power of the Association decreased—for this wild riding and killing had to be by individuals, not by Association decrees. The truth was that too many cattlemen were going into the sheep business, that the wealth represented by sheep was becoming too big, that the society of Wyoming was growing too complex, and even that opinion was divided and hot blood was turning cool.

It took a long time for cattlemen to accept coexistence with sheepmen, and longer to accept alliance with them. Reality was not readily accepted by a class of men who were caught in a fantasy of their own past, a fantasy which their own experience had proved false. But the possibility of widespread range war was ended when the federal government convinced even the fieriest that the grazing ranges in the national forests would indeed be open to sheep as well as cattle. The worst of it was clearly over and that date may be accepted as the end of an era, though the situation on the unreserved public domain (mainly desert ranges) was unchanged, though these ranges went on deteriorating, though the struggle for them was not ended and sometimes rose to violence, though some attitudes did not change and indeed have not yet changed, and though crisis was to follow crisis in a business which has never much possibility of stabilization and was repeatedly hard pressed.

Yet there is another date that will do as well for our purposes and is far more symbolic. In November 1903 Tom Horn was sentenced to be hanged, sentenced by the same judge who nine years earlier had dismissed the case against the invaders of Johnson County. And a year later, November 1903, he was hanged, in the Cheyenne jail. When he was hanged it was quite clear to all of those whom John Clay calls the oldtimers and to all of Wyoming besides that the oldtime hegemony of the big cattleman was over. For either the bigshots whose employee he had been since 1893, with time out for army service in the Spanish-American War, had been unable to spring him or had not dared to. Either way, it added up to plain proof that they no longer had enough power.

Horn himself, most of Wyoming with him, and it may be some of his later employers themselves expected that he would be bought free, pressured free, or freed by force—but he wasn't. There was no doubt that he had been working as a range detective, which is to say a murderer when need be, for the wealthiest cattlemen in southeastern Wyoming. (That we must specify a subdivision is another sign of drastic change.) How many actual cattle rustlers, no-goods, and mere rivals or enemies of his employers he had terrorized into docile behavior cannot be estimated or even guessed, nor how many he scared out of the state. Terror was his job, and his employers profited not only by the increased security of their herds but by the opportunity to lease or buy the ranges of the terrified, or to get them for nothing. How many he killed is not known either. It *is* known that he committed five murders in the interests of his employers, though two of them were in Colorado. It is known that for two of these he received a fee of three hundred dollars apiece, apart from whatever his salary may have been, and no one doubts that for the other three (plus five shots vainly fired in a fourth effort) he got $2100. No one doubted it when he was found guilty on the evidence, but the wealthy and powerful with whom he associated so openly and intimately and whose agent he was known to be were expected to take care of him. They didn't or they couldn't. What had been forced on them was often called cowardice locally, but it wasn't. It was the discretion of impotence, the inability to oppose the process of history, and they knew at last that the world had changed.

The Western cattleman was a victim of history—repeatedly. Time after time, wave after wave, development after development, history knocked him down and rolled over him. On its way west American society, building up its experience and enlarging its estate of habit and expectation and belief, developed institutions, customs, legal systems, political systems, fixed ideas, and fixed illusions. All these had been shaped by experience in regions of adequate water supply. To put it technically, in humid and subhumid regions. When American society reached the Hundredth Meridian, they were no longer adequate but they remained all-powerful. Some of them were merely inappropriate to the new conditions of life, more were disastrous. Most Western businesses, all the basic ones, even mining, suffered from the breakdown of our traditional institutions and the inertia of our inherited ways of thinking and feeling. But the cattle business suffered most.

Consider Wyoming east of the Continental Divide, the area in which all the actions glanced at in this chapter occurred, except the sheepkillings, which were statewide. In order to highlight the historical problems of the cattle business, let me generalize and simplify this area. And let me look at it *as if:* that is, with the perceptions of hindsight and in terms of an ideal society, as if men were wise and able to make their societies conform to their wisdom.

This portion of Wyoming, then, belongs to what I have been calling the high plains. It is part of the geographic region which the texts call the Great Plains and of the subdivision or province which they call the Northern Plains. (Associated with it are portions of Colorado, Montana, and the Dakotas, but disregard them.) It is a region of deficient rainfall. Also not much of it is fitted for large-scale dryland wheat-farming, and this fact is one of the few bits of good fortune vouchsafed its people. Disregarding very minute areas which are not numerous and cannot count here, only such parts of it should ever have been made cropland as could be irrigated at economic expense and were of sufficiently low altitude to permit intensive and diversified farming. Wyoming had had to learn (or rather partly learn) at the cost of much bankruptcy, human anguish, and social waste, that these parts amount to far less in sum than was believed from decade to decade and generation to generation. And in part is still believed. And I must point out right here that the intensity of the Western (and national) belief in irrigation has ignored, and still ignores, the fact that much irrigation has failed, that in many places which have been irrigated, irrigation has proved to be a bitter folly.

But most of this region, though again there are exceptions, is part of what must be considered the finest grazing range for beef cattle in the United States.[17] I remarked earlier in this book that the American cattle business has always been pushed back farther into worse lands. In terms of *as if*, this historical process should have ended when it reached the portion of the high plains to which eastern Wyoming belongs, the great cattle range. In the wise society this area would never have been plowed or irrigated except for the production of hay to feed cattle. (Again, with the exceptions already noted.) It is one of the basic and omnipresent paradoxes, and one of the tragedies, of the West that the great grazing range was not maintained solely as a grazing range. Not even in the beginning or for a moment may we forget that one reason for this basic paradox and tragedy was certain inherent attributes of the cattle business itself, and another reason was a certain state of mind—certain illusions and delusions—of Western cattlemen. But also the entire experience of the America people forbade. Historians are not supposed to be fatalists but in this respect I do not see that the historian of the West can be anything else. What has happened was foredestined to happen. And the reason was water.

Everything forbade, and first of all the landholding system which the Americans had developed, the system of land-ownership, and the system of subdividing the public domain and getting it into private ownership. These systems, which cannot be separated from one another, the American people had developed between 1620 and 1870. They had developed them as they moved inland from the Atlantic littoral, through the forest, across the prairie lands, and across the eastern or tall-grass portion of the Great Plains. Up to the point where the West begins, in the portions of the United States which get an average of twenty or more inches of rain per year. But they were no more applicable to the West than the woodscraft of our forest hunters was applicable to the deserts and mountains to which our fur-traders followed Lewis and Clark. But in two and a half centuries of experience, they developed an institutional rigidity and a network of social beliefs, sentiments, emotions, and illusions of such strength that experience in the climate and geography to which they were not applicable could not prevail against them.

In connection with the timber frauds, I pointed out that it was impossible to classify land according to its nature, as cropland, timberland, or rangeland. The classic American expectation of profit from speculation in land and from corrupt political manipulation of land titles enters here, and it would be impossible to overstate its importance. But we must add to this the force of the expanding nineteenth-century American economy with its extreme emphasis on individual action, and this reached one of its highest peaks in the first stage of the Western frontier. (The only stage in which the phrase "Western individualism" has meaning.) To classify land according to its potentialities and proper use would have been to restrict an American citizen's inalienable right to do what he pleased with his land and go broke in the process. Against the power of this sentiment it meant nothing at all that the Western geography and climate left the land in such a fragile equilibrium that if an individual misused his land the land of many others might be damaged, and not their lands only but their irrigation systems, their city water supplies, their mines, and their forests. The federal government might properly be called upon to relieve those who had gone broke from trying to use Western lands in ways which the natural conditions penalized with bankruptcy, and from 1870 on relief laws for Westerners who had been so penalized were a constant in Congress. But it was possible for the federal government to refuse to grant a citizen a homestead on the public domain on the ground that it was grazing land and that he would go broke if he tried to farm it.

And something else which I have already discussed came to bear right here with disastrous force: the mystical idea, born of our historical experience in regions of abundant rain, that the proper size of a family holding, the area that would support a family in comfort and independence, was 160 acres. There are many places in the West and perhaps some in the portion of Wyoming which I am discussing where 160 acres must be translated as permission to make a living from one and a half cows or seven and a half sheep.[18] We have seen that the 160-acre homestead became first the 320-acre homestead and then the 640-acre one, rising from the quarter-section to half-section to a section, as efforts to deal with the problems of the arid country were belatedly made. The efforts were unrealistic and the largest of the figures remained much too small. John Wesley Powell said that the *minimum* homestead in the arid regions should be four sections, 2560 acres, and we know now that there are few places in those regions where so small a ranch could, without irrigation, provide a living for a stockgrower. The result was to make the Western stockgrower a lawbreaker. One way or another, whether he was a small operator or a big one, he *had* to use more land than he was legally entitled to.

There was not only John Wesley Powell, the genius who understood the arid country and accurately foretold the turmoil and failure that in fact resulted from attempts to apply to it institutions which were not adapted to it—there was also the fully visible example of Texas. When Texas surrendered its status as a republic and was admitted to the Union, the treaty of annexation struck a bargain between the two parties. In return for the state's agreement to assume the national debt of the Republic of Texas, the United States relinquished to it all the unsettled, ungranted, and unclaimed land within its borders, which otherwise would have been added to the public domain. The state abandoned the theory of free grants of homestead and disposed of its lands only by sale. As early as 1880 it took the necessary step of classifying the lands of its arid region according to their nature, and thereafter it steadily increased the size of the grazing area which a purchaser could buy—from three sections to four, to eight, and eventually (after the turn of this century) twenty sections—making the family-size ranch in arid Texas up to 12,800 acres, whereas officially in the West it was at most 640. This was possible in Texas because of a complex of historical developments too involved to be examined here, though it may be summed up with the statement that the vital portion of the state's frontier experience occurred outside the American system. It was entirely impossible in the West. The mystical unit was 160 acres. Our experience in the humid regions, our conviction and belief, and our illusions all said it was. So did the imperative possibility of speculation, corruption of officials, inflationary financing, and graft.

The westering Americans were a land-hungry people, predominantly farmers in search of more or better cropland. And their inherent desires and instincts were stepped up by the land-grant railroads, which had lands to sell and hoped for freight to transport, by speculative corporations that had got hold of land or hoped to, and by the Western states themselves. It was altogether impossible to keep them from homesteading such portions of the public land as they thought could be farmed, or as they could be convinced by illusion or advertising could be farmed. So, like his predecessors to the eastward, the Western cattleman was always being pushed back to worse lands.

But that is only part of it, for other inexorable forces were exerted by the inapplicable institutions. Banking, for instance. The spread of interest rates on mortgages and loans, East and West, has always been one of the handicaps under which Western business at large has operated, but it was murderous to the cattlemen. The common figure I have quoted, three percent a month, represented in part a realistic judgment on the hazards of the cattle business, but it was also an established institution taking advantage of the natural situation. Together with the vise in which the railroads and the stockyards held the cattle barons, it made particularly poignant their illusion that they *were* barons—were a ruling class and the freest men on earth. (In the same illusion their national associations today cheerfully align themselves with the interests that exploit them.) What was needed was a credit system adapted to the nature of their holdings and the methods of their business. None was worked out during the Cattle Kingdom, and a fully satisfactory one has not yet been achieved. But one under which the cattle business could be conducted in reasonable accord with the conditions of the arid country was developed at the end of the first quarter of the twentieth century. By, of course, the federal government.

The pattern of settlement, the pattern of railroad lines, the subdivision of the Western states into smaller political units, the early legal codes and especially the law of water rights, even such institutions as public school systems—all these had characteristics developed in the humid country that affected the cattle business unfavorably as they affected other business in the rural West. But there is no reason to go into them here.

What was the answer? I am not sure that there was any, even in terms of *as-if*.

Certainly the Cattle Kingdom was not an answer, the free use of the unfenced range. It was possible for a single short period of history only, it was economically unsound, socially disastrous, and destructive of land. It was an absolute and complete subsidy of the Western cattle business by the people of the United States at large. Then, as we have seen, it inevitably led to overstocking the ranges, with the consequent deterioration of the ranges, which meant depreciation of the cattlemen's capital and had disastrous effects on the rest of the West. It must have led inevitably, too, to land monopoly by the wealthy, the exclusion of others from the cattle business, and the consequent social disaster that land monopoly has always meant. At the basis of our success as a democracy and a republic lies the fact that the United States has always made such monopoly impossible.

Yet the Western cattle business is most efficient when conducted in tolerably large units, though as I have said this fact also increased its vulnerability. Perhaps the wisdom of an *as-if* society would have contrived to institute at the beginning a system of leasing the public domain in efficient units, a system open on just terms to individuals, corporations, and cooperative associations of individuals. A system which would have given leases a sufficiently long term to assure stability, would have exacted a just price for the use of the range, and would have protected the range from deterioration. Again the West lost out because the process of history forbade and the nature of the West also forbade.

Nobody was going to make the early West cooperative and the federal government was not, by God, going to regulate the early West. In the end massive cooperations were being forced on the Western cattle business by a series of disasters and bankruptcies. In the end leasing and regulation were to be forced on it too so far as the public ranges were concerned, a kind of fee was to be exacted for the use of the range, and some of the ranges were to be repaired and protected. By, of course, the federal government.

Every step of the long process was violently opposed by the Western cattle business—down to the 1930s when, as we shall see, climactic catastrophes forced the cattlemen themselves to demand federal organization of the remaining unorganized ranges in the public domain, the desert and foothill ranges. That was far too late. And as soon as the immediate emergency was over, powerful elements of the Western cattle business at once began to demand the step-by-step repeal of everything that had been slowly and painfully achieved. They are still demanding it.

The present system—so far as the public ranges enter into it—is characterized by cooperative association, leased grazing ranges, fees, and federal regulation. Parts of it work very well; parts of it work badly; the parts that work best are most violently attacked by powerful elements of the Western cattle business. And it is certainly not the system of an *as-if* society, having been developed too late and too slowly and comprehending too little of the West. And, such as it is, it is a subsidy of part of the Western cattle business by the nation at large, including such parts of the Western cattle business as do not use the public ranges. (That is a subsidy of one-fifth of the business by the remaining four-fifths.) Cattlemen who graze their stock on the ranges in the national forests pay from a fifth to a third of what the grass would be worth on an open market. Those who use the other principal kind of public range, the lands administered by the Bureau of Land Management, pay from a fifteenth to an eighth. (Both get the further subsidy of range maintenance and protection.) Whereas those who lease ranges from Indian tribes usually have to pay almost full value and those who lease them from private individuals have to compete in the open market and pay par.

The raising of beef cattle (and of sheep) is the most primitive branch of agriculture. The technological revolution that has transformed farming has affected it very little. Not much of it can be mechanized, apart from the substitution of truck transport for trailing and the purely farming operations of home ranches. And this is most true of the range-stock business, which seems likely to decline in the West. Two developments are prophetic. Full home-ranching is on the increase—it is more intensive and more efficient, with irrigated pastures, home-grown feed, the shrewd purchase of commercial by-product feeds according to market opportunities, constant improvement of stock, and the use of machines so far as they can be used. And also the constant increase of cattle growing in the South seems likely to make some now unpredictable portion of the range-stock business incapable of competition.

The essential primitiveness of cattle raising may help to explain the persistence of sentiments that relate to the era of the free and open range but are oddly and dangerously anachronistic now. But it only helps, it does not explain in full. The great interest of those sentiments is their kinship with the basic paradoxes and illusions of the West.

From the beginning down to now there have always been influential numbers of cattlemen to oppose sheep-growing, farming, the creation and maintenance of public reservations, the use of such reservations for anything but grazing, the paying of fees for grazing them, the regulation of grazing on them, the application of scientific procedures to them, and anything else that such influential cattlemen may happen to disapprove. To oppose anything that interferes with the cattleman's will or impinges on his picture of himself. Wyoming was his in 1880 and sheepmen had no right to bring their bands into it and use his range. The West was his in 1888 and Harrison was acting unconstitutionally when he created forest reserves. The national forests were his in 1905 and Roosevelt was acting unconstitutionally when he permitted Gifford Pinchot to assess a fee for the use of their ranges and open them to sheep. The unorganized domain was his in 1934 and though it was permissible for the second Roosevelt to organize it in order to save the cattle business, he was acting unconstitutionally when he set out (but mostly failed) to improve it. The West is his now, and it is unconstitutional as well as against God for city water-chasers, farmers, dam-builders, industrialists, people who like to shoot deer, or even visitors to national parks to interfere with his use of his West. There he is, a cattle baron, a feudal overlord, bronzed and of hair-trigger honor and in a big hat, riding at the head of his proud but obedient cowpokes across a vast expanse in which from horizon to horizon nothing can be seen except cows wearing his brand, at a season and in a West that are forever 1880.

A minority of a minority, of a steadily diminishing minority. Only in Wyoming and Nevada is the cattle business the greatest value even in agricultural production. Elsewhere in the developing West, it is less important than other forms of agriculture and than the businesses and industries of the expanding economy. And in the cattle business itself, the 1880 sentiments are instruments only of the top crust, the big operators, and adverse to the other cattlemen, who are the bulk of the business. It is the national association, which these operators control, that succeeds (in great part) in inducing the Western cattle business to act as if 1880 still lingered on. As if *The Virginian* were this morning's newspaper and the thundering-herd epics of Hollywood were true. As if the Cheyenne Club must ride off to Johnson County and shoot some rustlers.

The trouble is that the bronzed barons of the top crust are able to excite much of the rest of the Western cattle business with the same fantasy. The much greater trouble is that repeatedly the West itself enters happily into the fantasy—the West of steel, aluminum, uranium, of the industrial complexes and the population rate that is shooting up like a rocket. That is the trouble—but it can be stated even more simply. The trouble is that 1880 is dangerous to the West for it damages land.

And to damage land is to destroy water.

Chapter Seven
Nemesis

August 1923. President Harding died at San Francisco on the 2d; in the earliest morning hours of the 3d Calvin Coolidge took the oath of office in his father's farmhouse at Plymouth, Vermont. On the 18th a seventeen-year-old girl named Helen Wills ended the long tennis championship of Molla Mallory. On the 21st the first transcontinental airmail flight reached San Francisco, flying time was twenty-six hours. Leafing through a file of the month's newspapers, one notices two serial stories: Ku Klux Klan riots were occurring widely, and on September 14 Jack Dempsey and Angel Firpo were going to fight for the heavyweight championship of the world.

I have twice had occasion to mention the zone of rich farmland at the western foot of the Wasatch Mountains in Utah. In one context I described the steep curve of the rainfall from the crest of the Wasatch, to Salt Lake City at their feet, and on to the Salt Desert forty miles farther west. In another I pointed out that this narrow zone, from two to ten miles wide, 160 miles long, and with an area of about 1200 square miles, held (in 1950) fifty-six percent of Utah's population and produced more than three-quarters of its agricultural wealth.

Of this zone, the most intensively cultivated part is Davis County. Its farms—mainly orchard and garden crops, though with considerable acreage in grains and sugar beets—have on the average the highest acre-for-acre value in the state. North to south it is about twenty-two miles wide. Beyond it to the south is Salt Lake County, with the largest city in Utah and the principal industrial concentration. Beyond it to the north is Weber County, with the second largest city, Ogden. North of Weber County is Box Elder County, which will need some notice here.

The west front of the Wasatch rises steeply above Davis County, very steeply. In twenty-two miles this front is gashed by eleven small canyons, which drop down from the ridge to the bench of ancient Lake Bonneville and the floor of Salt Lake Valley—to the rich farmland.[1] They are narrow canyons, their sides are even steeper than the west front, and some of them have still smaller, narrower, and more steeply-walled canyons entering them from the north or south. The west front is also furrowed by several small gulches, which in geological time will become canyons.

(I need also mention a village called Willard, ten miles north of Ogden, in Box Elder County, the county where the best Utah peaches are grown—I am not one to deny that they are the best in the world. Like the villages of Davis County, Willard is set in that narrow zone between the mountains and the salt flats that border Great Salt Lake. Like them too, it has a steep and narrow canyon coming down from the Wasatch ridge. In fact, Willard Canyon has walls which in some places are sheerer cliffs than any in the Davis County canyons.)

When you climb from the Davis County farmland to the Wasatch ridge, you are not able to see much of the green zone of orchards and fields, so steep is the slope, rising from an elevation of 4400 feet to one of 9200 feet in four and a half air-line miles. What you see instead is oppressive. Beyond that green park is a wide barrenness stretching westward to the bright and sterile waters of Great Salt Lake, from which rise barren, gray and rose-pink mountain islands. This dead expanse is made up of salt-flats and salt marshes intermingling in curves and striations of gray, white, sick green, and brown. At a little town named Farmington, the lake curves deeply eastward. Here at Farmington (and the resort called Lagoon which I had occasion to mention earlier) the cultivated zone of Davis County reaches its narrowest and is little more than two miles wide. Shoreline and salt water stretch northward to where, beyond Ogden and just short of Willard, a curving spur of the Wasatch closes off most of the vista. To the south, beyond Salt Lake City and almost hidden by smoke from the copper smelters at Garfield a small range called the Oquirrhs stretches westward from the Wasatch; the sulfur in that smoke has killed its vegetation and made it a desert range.

If you visit Davis County in July or August, you may witness one of the furious summer rainstorms characteristic of this region and of all the Great Basin, the Canyon Lands, and most of the Southwest. They originate in air masses which have come not from the west and the Pacific but from the southeast and the Gulf of Mexico. They are popularly called cloudbursts, and with reason. Usually they strike in late afternoon, and the rain they drop falls with a violence as great as that which accompanies a hurricane. Indeed with greater violence—for most of the fall is concentrated in the first stage of the storm. A cloudburst may last half an hour, several hours, or (merging with another storm in an ef-

fect that would require too much analysis here) two or
three days, but after the first stage it becomes a gentle
if steady rain. Whereas two inches of rain may fall in two
hours—a third of an inch in five minutes, half an inch in
ten minutes, three-quarters of an inch or even a full inch
in fifteen minutes. That is, for fifteen minutes it may fall
at the *rate* of four inches an hour. (Three times the rate
of the heaviest recorded fall in the Olympic rain forest.)
Occasions are recorded when for short periods the rate
was between seven and eight inches an hour. During
this stage of such a storm the rain is a solid wall of
water. The reader will remember that on the valley floor
the *total* rainfall of an average year is sixteen inches.

In a normal and healthy watershed in a terrain like
that of Davis County, such a storm will bring the little
mountain creeks from their summer trickle to the bank-
full high water they had at the crest of spring runoff. Beginning with the last quarter of the nineteenth century,
in many places throughout the length of the Wasatch
range the cloudburst floods frequently came over the
banks of creeks and did considerable damage. As the
years went on this phenomenon appeared in other Utah
ranges and in the high plateaus. An increasing number
of small-canyon creeks and the larger streams they join
flooded after cloudbursts, and the damage done by such
floods became more extensive.

One of the eleven small canyons of Davis County debouches just above Farmington and is named for it. In a
range heavily dissected by canyons most of which are
scenically pleasing, Farmington Canyon is commonplace,
and unattractive. A typical mountain creek flows down
it and at the point where its drop could best be utilized
it used to be dammed for a small installation of the Utah
Power & Light Company. Much farther up the canyon
there used to be a small mine too. Two generations ago
Farmington Canyon was denuded of such usable timber

as it had. But in 1923 there were willows and small cottonwoods along the creek, and some small poplars in places, and upstream from the power dam a sizable grove of aspens. On August 14, 1923 two small parties were camped on opposite sides of that grove, four boy scouts from Salt Lake City, and a young man and his wife from Ogden. The young woman was pregnant and her term must have been nearly fulfilled.

Late in the afternoon of August 14 there was a sprinkle of rain and then the western sky turned black, lightning began to flash, and the islands in Great Salt Lake were blotted out. Some time before 6 P.M. two men started from Farmington to drive a wagonload of supplies to the little mine—the road was steep and so uneven that a Model T probably could not have got beyond the dam. They creaked and strained past it and the grove of aspens, and shortly afterward the storm struck.[2] It struck with the usual barrage of thunder, savage gust of wind, and solid curtain of water as if a celestial dam had given way. The cloudburst lasted about forty minutes. Then in most of Davis County a gentle rain succeeded it, but in Farmington Canyon rain apparently stopped altogether for a time. (A characteristic freak of such storms.) The freight wagon must have halted on the primitive road, the horses must have been terrified, and the two freighters must have stood at their heads holding them by main force throughout the furious downpour. Presently they started out again, in twilight broken by occasional flashes of lightning, and now the canyon echoed with a sudden loud roaring. Because they knew what cloudburst had done to Farmington Creek over the last generation, the freighters leaped out, got the tugs and traces off the horses, and ran frantically up the side of the canyon to get above the flood. They got above it, and almost at once they saw it coming down the canyon, a wall of water between twenty and thirty feet high. But it wasn't water.

The front of that flood which they saw roll over their team and wagon "was alive with sparks, as if on fire." So one of them later told a reporter, and again he called it "a blaze of sparks." What was coming down Farmington Canyon was not a water flood. It was a river, or rather a glacier, of mud. Mud the consistency of newly mixed concrete. It was what Utah would soon learn to call a mud-flow or a mud-rock flow; the latter term is exactly descriptive. Upstream the violent rain had loosened portions of the mountainsides and they had collapsed into the rapidly flooding creek.

In a constricted canyon the mud glacier gathers force as other patches of soil thicken and build it up, and as it is pushed on by the runoff behind it, which it backs up in a rapidly enlarging reservoir just as an earth-fill dam does. It flattens whatever timber may be in the way (as this one did with the aspen grove), and crushes or rolls over whatever structures may be in the way as this one did with the little dam and generating plant. It moves more slowly than a flooded creek but frighteningly fast nevertheless. (Like the flow of rivers and glaciers, its movement is composite, slower at the edges than at the center.) Its force is so great that it gouges out the bed of the creek below the level that has been geologically stabilized, and it may forsake the bed of the creek and carve a channel of its own. The capacity of running water to carry silt increases in proportion to the square of the velocity of the flow increases, but in a mud-flow the viscosity of mud greatly increases this power. As it travels it picks up not only silt and gravel but rock fragments and boulders weighing hundreds of pounds, a ton, ten tons, on up to (at Farmington) three hundred tons. It was the grinding of such rocks and boulders against one another that made the front of the flow which came down Farmington Canyon that early evening blaze with sparks.

At the mouth of every canyon such as this there is an alluvial fan, which is magnificent farmland below the steep, boulder-littered slope at its beginning. The mud-flow keeps on gathering force as it travels down the canyon, but when it reaches the alluvial fan, it spreads, begins to lose its force, and progressively drops its load. When it has dropped all the load it ceases to be a mud-flow but, a fan-shaped avalanche, it may have traveled as much as two miles from the mouth of the canyon. It has covered whatever it crossed with a deposit of silt, gravel, rocks, and boulders which may be as much as thirty feet deep. And it is followed by the flood wa-ters which it has been damming up, whose debris-carrying power is only that of rapid water (the Colorado River, say) but which spreads more widely and travels farther.

The mud-flow at Farmington in August of 1923 reached more than a mile west of Farmington Canyon. It took out the telephone and electric service lines and the main high-voltage transmission line. It buried the main north-south highway and one railroad line under twenty feet of debris. It reached the tracks of an in-terurban electric railroad and about here it stopped, but the following flood covered this line and went on to wash out another railroad line beyond it. It leveled all houses, sheds, and farm buildings in its path. A girl run-ning home reached her house, which was on the edge of the flow, just as the flow did. As she opened the door, the house was sliced cleanly in two and the far half was carried away and crushed. On the other edge and far-ther west another house held firm and the family, tak-ing refuge on the second floor, saw the flow build up a wall of mud and gravel exactly even with the windows they were looking through. Spreading north and south the following flood waters reached the resort called La-goon, covered it with mud and miscellaneous flotsam, leveled a small tent settlement, and swept away sheds and amusement booths.

Here at Lagoon a man died of heart failure, trying to reach his children, who he mistakenly thought had been left in the tent-settlement. He was the only casualty of the water flood. The mud-flow killed six, or rather seven, the four boy scouts, the married couple, and their baby, which was delivered by a horrible operation. The woman's body was found in two parts, severed at the hips, and the baby's body separately from both. The bodies had been carried at least two miles from what had been the aspen grove.

South of Farmington Canyon another of the main ones I have mentioned, Parrish Canyon, poured out a similar mud-flow but the damage was less extensive. And thirty-two miles to the north the same storm struck the upper slopes of Willard Canyon and sent a mud-flow roaring down on the village of Willard. Because at the mouth of the canyon the arable strip is even narrower than at Farmington, the destruction here was spread over a smaller area but it was more intense. Some of the great Box Elder County peach orchards were buried in gravel.

The storm of August 14 had the heaviest concentration of rainfall that had ever been recorded at the Weather Bureau station in Salt Lake City. (Since then it has been exceeded several times.) It had a wide front and so damage was widespread. All the canyon creeks in the part of the west slope that it touched went to flood and most of them went over their banks. Larger streams in Salt Lake, Weber, and Cache Counties also flooded, washing out roads or making them impassable. Such larger streams cannot produce mud-flows; the cross section of the stream is too big and the canyons are too wide. No matter how much debris of soil and rocks is swept into them, they drop the burden too fast for the lava-like substance to be built up. Though as every newspaper reader knows the floods of such rivers can do enormous damage, they are of the familiar kind. And we must glance at a flood which reached one of these rivers following the storm of August 14, for the area it occurred in is part of the story I am telling.

The city of Ogden is some sixteen miles north of Farmington. To the east of it Ogden River has cut through the main range one of the most beautiful canyons in the Wasatch. It is about twelve miles long; a number of side canyons come into it. One of these, Wheeler Canyon, enters the story later. At the eastern end of Ogden Canyon is Ogden Valley, a lovely circular basin of the kind that the fur-traders called "holes." It appears as Ogden's Hole in the literature of the fur trade, named for the Hudson's Bay Company benefactor, Peter Skene Ogden. It is drained by three creeks from the mountains that ring it round, which join at its western edge to form Ogden River and are called North Fork, Middle Fork, and South Fork.

High up on North Fork, this August week, there was a boy scout encampment. There were occasional bursts of light rain on the afternoon of the 14th, and a steady fall began at about 7:30 P.M. By eight o'clock all the scouts were in their tents and in bed. I made it a little past eight when the big storm broke at Willard, which is thirteen or fourteen miles west but with the high and massive ridge in between. No matter how much rain fell on the ridge above Willard and neighboring mountain spurs, there was a lot left in the storm as it traveled east. Presently a river five hundred feet wide and at least five feet deep flowed straight across the scout camp. It took tents and equipment with it, including all lights and all the scouts' clothes except the pajamas they had on. No lives were lost; a heroic and ingenious scoutmaster succeeded in saving some of his charges and helped them save the rest.

Something is to be observed about this sudden flood. There was no canyon above the scout camp to canalize the runoff from the cloudburst. There was only the western foothill slope of Ogden Valley with the steeper slope of the east front of the Wasatch above it. The same slopes were above all of Ogden Valley and the same storm hit all parts with the same intensity, but only in this part was there a flash flood. Clearly special circumstances produced it.

No part of all this was without precedent in Utah, in Davis County, or even at Farmington.

A combination of steep slopes, thinly vegetated soils, and violent or prolonged rain is always likely to produce floods. There had been floods throughout the history of Utah; there always will be. But the floods of August 14, 1923 were distinctive, were various effects of a single cause. A process had been going on in Utah that few people fully understood, many misunderstood, and practically everyone disregarded. The sequel of the cloudburst of August 14 was a notification that this process had now reached a critical stage in Box Elder, Weber, and especially Davis Counties. The warning was disregarded.

Utah is a desert which, it seems certain, no one but the Mormons could have settled and made fruitful. Brigham Young was the greatest colonizer in American history. From an obedient and cooperative people he forged an instrument for the conquest of the arid land that succeeded repeatedly in areas identical with areas where non-Mormon attempts have failed. His shrewdest lieutenants spied out the land, locating the water sources, the favorable soils, and the good grazing ranges. To such areas the Church, which is to say Brother Brigham, sent out parties of colonists, made up not haphazardly but with strict regard to the problems they must solve. They were task forces—so many blacksmiths, so many mechanics, so many experienced farmers, so many stockgrowers, and as an estate of experience built up, men who had learned in earlier ventures how to deal with the desert. They were communities before they started, they were completely cooperative, and, bringing to the conquest of the desert the zeal of their religion, they built irrigation works, established farms, developed herds—and made Utah.

There are no better farmers than the Mormons, no better stockgrowers, and no desert-dwellers anywhere near so successful. And yet! Their conquest of the desert was not so complete as it appeared to be. The desert West which imposes its own terms on everyone imposed them on the Mormons. And one of the most admirable virtues of the Mormon people exposed their society to counterattack from the desert.

As the years ran on in Utah, it was said that floods and especially the floods that followed cloudbursts were more frequent and more destructive than they used to be. This is the kind of oldtimers' talk that rising generations shrug off as the brag or nostalgia of pioneers or, with a greater show of logic, as the effect on larger communities of what had been unimportant in small ones. The explanations were wrong. Floods in Utah *were* more frequent, more extensive, and more destructive than they had been in the generation of pioneers. It is possible even to work out a fairly dependable time-scale. About twenty-five or thirty years after the settlement of a new oasis in desert Utah, the streams that came down from the mountains began to flood out of their banks and (those that had them) out of their flood plains.

There are all degrees of flood in the mountains, from clear high water which picks up no topsoil and carries no debris except such vegetable litter as lies along the banks on up to such mud-rock flows as I have described. At a time of intense or prolonged rain a stream that has a healthy watershed will not begin to run high for a considerable period, will rise gradually, will stay within its banks without cutting them or scouring the stream bed, and will recede in a smooth curve. A stream that behaves otherwise is draining a watershed of which some part has been impaired.

Note always that these mountain floods are fundamentally different from those that make the national headlines with disasters at say, Kansas City. They are in small streams, not big ones; they are local, not general.

By 1923 Utah had had hundreds of these local floods. But the damage was local, it was gradual, and it had not produced general apprehension. Among them had been many mud-flows but most of these had not been in such densely settled areas as Davis County; they had been in small, thinly populated oases far out in the general desert. In 1896 Chalk Creek had brought a mud-flow to the desert town of Fillmore, below the Pahvant Mountains, and had produced others in later years, though after 1906 they began to be less common and less destructive. At the mountain-locked town of Manti in San Pete County, Manti Canyon had poured out floods and mud-flows in 1889, 1893, 1896, 1901, 1906, 1908, and 1909. Then—for a reason apparently understood but not brought to bear elsewhere—there had been no more, though cloudbursts which struck this watershed without affecting it created serious floods in neighboring ones. At an oasis named Paria, settlement had had to be abandoned—one of the few total failures of the Mormon effort. The little community of Escalante, at the foot of the Aquarius Plateau and looking off toward the majestic cliffs of the Kaiparowits Plateau, was in deep trouble, its economy wasting away because of recurrent floods. Various other small communities were in trouble. But these were not the three great oases of the state—Salt Lake Valley, Cache Valley, and the valley of the Duquesne. And the Saints knew that at best life was hard in the desert, that the Lord was wont to test His people with tribulation, and that there was no trial which could not be met with courage and hard work.

Yet even in the three great oases, with their abundant irrigation, there had been trouble. In July 1878, exactly thirty years after the settlement of Farmington Canyon and Steed Canyon, which is the next one south. Again in August 1912 a mud-flow had come out of Haight's Creek, which flows down one of the smaller gulches I have mentioned, a mile and a half north of Farmington Canyon. Though it was small and did not travel far it was a blatant warning which with the wisdom of hindsight we can see was unmistakable.[3]

The storm of August 14, 1923 proved that portions of vital watersheds in Davis, Weber, and Box Elder Counties had been seriously damaged. Only a few scientists, who were disregarded, understood that a process of land destruction which was almost universal in Utah was coming to crisis. Almost invisibly, except when violent symptoms manifested themselves, the garden which the Mormons had brought to be in the desert was being destroyed. Including its richest portion, Davis County.

No more mudflows came down to the Davis County farms till 1930, but floods were common everywhere in Utah. Warning signals were plainer.

I witnessed one of them. In the summer of 1925 my wife and I rented a cabin in Wheeler Canyon, which I mentioned above. A couple of miles west of Ogden Valley, it comes down to Ogden Canyon from a small, high amphitheater at the eastern foot of Mount Ogden that was called Wheeler Basin in my boyhood, though it is now Snow Basin. I knew the whole area intimately and I had known Wheeler Creek as a clear and lovely mountain stream. It was different now but I did not understand why or even wherein, though I went several times to look at the monstrous change that had been wrought at Willard two years before. Our cabin was on the steep eastern side of Wheeler Canyon, perhaps forty feet above the creek. In August a cloudburst brought a flash flood down the canyon, I think the first one it had ever had. I remember it as following the short and furious storm by about three-quarters of an hour and lasting no more than twenty minutes.[4] It could not have been more than eight feet high for it did not take away the hanging bridge to our canyon. But it did take away everything downstream from us that was lower than its crest. It dumped a lot of miscellaneous debris and filled a flume at the mouth of the canyon with sand, but though the greatest damage was visible it was understood only by the scientists: the bed of Wheeler Creek was gouged below the level of equilibrium that had been maintained since the ice age.

By next summer there was no mistaking the meaning of this flash flood. In Wheeler Basin, intolerably abused land had given up and let go. In 1926 and 1927 cloudburst produced floods in Wheeler Creek far more serious than the one I had seen. They made Wheeler Canyon unusable for any of the purposes to which the people of Ogden had put it.

Farm prices continued to sag, farmlands that had been so valuable in wartime were hardly worth their mortgages now, and worse came with the market collapse of October 1929. And 1929 turned out to be a drought year in the fertile zone at the western foot of the Wasatch.

So, it developed, was 1930. The water level in only half-filled storage reservoirs sank steadily lower. The inexorable rules of water rights cut down the amount of irrigating any farmer could do. Crop yields would be small at best; farms along the margins of irrigating systems might have no crops at all. Men stared at the shining Western sky as the Pueblo people had stared at the sky above Mesa Verde in the thirteenth century, fearfully, as if that brilliant blue had death in it. By the second week of July the fields of Davis County were prematurely gold

and turning brown. The scant water turned into them
sank swiftly out of sight.

Indeed on July 10 when a great storm passed over
Davis County, the hearts of many people lifted for a moment. The hot and dusty smell of drought was gone, the
air was alive, a woman's skin seemed smooth again. For
the most fortunate this exhilaration may have lasted
half an hour. . . . Next day farmers at the village of Roy,
which is just outside Davis County but further out from
the mountains, drove off to Weber Canyon to see the
damage they had heard about, and marveled. Roy had
got little rain to ease its drought, not enough, one of
them said, "to slick down a short haircut."

Because Weber Canyon is the one practicable pass
through the Wasatch Mountains everything bound east
or west in northern Utah uses it: the Union Pacific, US
30-S which is a main transcontinental highway, trunk
transmission lines, a trunk-line oil pipe, a trunk-line pipe
for natural gas. At its narrowest place, Devil's Gate, it
was once no wider than the bed of Weber River, less
than a hundred feet; railroad, highway, and pipe lines
had to blast their way through the sheer-walled spur
that here contracts it. It was the cliffs of Devil's Gate
that in 1846 made the Donner Party decide not to try to
force a way through Weber County and so started them
on the fifteen-day detour by way of East Canyon and
Emigration Canyon that led to their tragedy.

At Devil's Gate the storm of July 10, 1930 brought
down from the sides of Weber Canyon such quantities of
soil, gravel, and stone that they formed a dam from
forty to eighty feet deep and more than half a mile long.
Behind this barrier the waters of Weber River backed up
till they were powerful enough to burst it. First, however, they had to clear away four smaller dams farther
up the canyon, dams of identical stuff that had poured
out of side canyons. The highway was washed out in
many places, so were the Union Pacific tracks; trans-

mission lines were carried away; a power house and other structures in Weber Canyon were filled with silt; the high line canal that takes irrigation to one edge of Davis County and one of Weber County was filled in several places and cut in several others. About a hundred automobiles and trucks were marooned on the highway; many of them were destroyed.

The front of that storm was 150 miles wide. By a freak Ogden and its wastelands were missed, but solid sheets of runoff brought most Wasatch canyons into flood from Spanish Fork on the south to Cache Valley on the north. Above Brigham City in Box Elder County every bridge in Mantua Canyon was carried away. Parley's Canyon poured debris into the bench-land residences of Salt Lake City. Everywhere cattle and swine were drowned—hundreds of them and thousands of chickens.

It was worst in Davis County. In 1923 mud-flows had come out of two of the eleven principal canyons. Now the same two and three of the others poured out mud-flows which were worse than the earlier ones and were followed by the waters of worse floods. Cold lava from Farmington Canyon swept again over the farms and orchards, and the highway and the railroads. But now it was not the worst. The next town south of Farmington is Centerville. Three canyons projected mud-flows into it, the worst coming from Parrish Canyon, which had produced one in 1923. Below the mouth of this canyon was the most thickly built-up part of town; houses, stores, a school house were crushed, buried, or swept away.

Eleven canyons; five mud-flows, the worst of them from Parrish Canyon. The next one south of it is Centerville Canyon. The heads of Parrish and Centerville Canyons, high up the west front of the Wasatch, are separated by a sharp divide but are so close together that if that knife-edge should split a raindrop its halves would flow down separate watersheds. The canyons diverge as they move down the mountainside but they are only a mile and a half apart at the mouth. No mud-flow came out of Centerville Canyon and though the creek rose to high water it stayed within its banks and no flood came out of it, either. Still farther south, above the village of Bountiful, is Ward Canyon; it differs in no way from the others. No mud-flow and no flood came out of Ward Canyon.

A second cloudburst struck the west front on August 11, 1930 and a third one on August 13. Any portions of the Utah heartland that had been missed by the July storm now had that omission repaired. Across the flat where the boy scouts had made their encampment in 1923 another flash flood swept down to the North Fork of Ogden River. New floods gouged the floor of Wheeler Canyon deeper. Two west front canyons above Ogden sent floods into the city. In canyons above Salt Lake City mountainsides collapsed and buried roads; in the city, basements filled and cemeteries were dug up. Cedar City was inundated. The narrow gulch that holds the town of Bingham, just over the divide from the great copper mine, was flooded. So were Magna, Garfield, Tooele, Eureka, Provo; and in some of these, and elsewhere, the floods were mud-flows. Irrigation systems filled with silt. So did the storage reservoirs.

In each of these August storms and in a third one that came later mud-flows poured out of some or all of the five Davis County canyons that had erupted with them before, and out of four of the remaining six canyons that had not. Nine canyons spread mud and boulders over fields and orchards that had been among the richest in Utah, over homesites, transmission lines, highways, railroads.

But no mud-flow and no flood came out of Centerville Canyon or Ward Canyon.

This was 1930, a drought year, a depression year, perhaps the most anxious year the West at large had

ever known. And now no one could fail to see that Davis
County was sick and that the disease might prove fatal.
The price of farmland sank lower. Banks foreclosed
mortgages on Davis County farms. They refused to
make farm loans; then later, when they desperately
sought to make them, they could not get takers. For people were moving away. The fatal shadow that had
spread over the area was widening. In the next two
summers no mud-flows came out of the canyons but
floods did when the cloudbursts struck. Catch-basins
were built below the mouths of canyons, and masonry
walls and wing-dams to slow up and spread the floods,
divert them from certain areas, and make them drop
their mud. These measures were soon seen to be only
palliative at best, and there could be no doubt that
there would be more mud-flows. If Davis County were to
be saved, and by now many people doubted that it could
be, then measures must be taken that would be fundamental, radical, and indeed without precedent.

By 1933 the nature of the fatal disease was understood, and measures had been devised which, there was
hope, might arrest it. So in 1933 the towns, the county,
the state, and the federal government joined in a course
of radical treatment. The hope was that fifteen years of
it would save Davis County. In the event twelve years
proved to be enough.

What was the cause of the floods and especially the
mud-flows? High up in the Wasatch, mainly in small
basins just below the ridge, small but critical portions of
the watersheds that drained down those nine canyons
had been denuded of vegetation. Remember that this
high elevation was the humid island, the great reservoir
of the snow pack which provided the forty inches of
rainfall that irrigated the rich lands in the valley
below—and in the midst of it patches of desert had developed. They were bare and as hard as pavement;

when a cloudburst struck they were impermeable. The force of the rain was not broken by plants and water would not sink into the ground. So it carved gullies and ran down them, and the gullies multiplied and joined together in an efficient system, constantly impairing more of the steep slopes. There were such areas in every one of the Davis County watersheds that had produced mud-flows. In only one case, that of Parrish Canyon, did they add up to more than ten percent of the area of the watershed. These comparatively small patches of ruined land were the plague-spots that were steadily destroying Davis County.

When a cloudburst struck the high slopes, the furious water poured down the gullies in the denuded places and in those that were being denuded. It widened and worsened the latter not only by multiplying and widening the gullies but by what is called sheet erosion. Some of the material that composed the mud-flows was swept off these surfaces, but most of it came from the action of the gullies, some of which were fifteen feet deep or more. Rushing down these conduits, the water cut them wider and deeper, and sections of mountainside thus carved up collapsed into them. Accelerating as its mass increased and as the flood waters pushed it from behind, this torrent of mud reached the narrow canyons and was constricted and so built up greater power. From the bed of the creek and along the banks it picked up small boulders. At the mouth of the canyon it picked up big boulders from the glacial detritus.

The west slope of the Wasatch had never been heavily timbered; such usable timber as it had once had had been cut long ago. But this cutting had little of anything to do with the denudation, nor were the periodic brush and grass fires much to blame. Most of the slope had a thick cover of oak brush and above this there was a zone of shrubs and grass. There was plenty of vegetative cover on the west front of the Wasatch—plenty of leaf fall and dried litter and perennial and annual plants—to take the teeth out of a cloudburst. . . . If it had been allowed to stay in place.

It had not been allowed to stay in place, and that was the simple reason why Davis County as an agricultural society was being destroyed.

Too many cattle and sheep had been grazing these steep slopes and those high small areas of basin. The land had held out for a time against this overuse. It had always held out for a time—whose length varies with the conditions. Then it had begun to deteriorate. The vegetative cover, the grass and shrubs that held the soil in place, broke the force of rains, and let the water sink safely and productively into the ground—this cover had begun to grow thin. Thin and inferior. Less nutritious plants began to replace the original ones—which meant that stock would need more of them, which in turn meant that the new ones were less likely to reproduce themselves. The replacement plants were also less effective as cover—more widely spaced, less able to break the impact of rain, with root systems that led less of it into the ground. Still worse plants began to crowd out the replacements—more worthless as forage, less useful as cover. The more widely spaced inferior plants, more closely grazed, left less litter covering the soil. Bare spots appeared; the heavy rains (as well as the hooves of stock) hardened them. Rains ran off them instead of sinking into the ground. The runoff took with it plants and soil that would normally have stayed in place, so the bare spots widened. The bare spots widened, the areas thinly covered by replacement plants widened, and the action of both accelerated the processes that had produced both. Always more water ran off, and as it did so, it spread the impairment wider. Damage was cumulative—all across the west front of the Wasatch in Davis County, and, as has been shown, in some parts catastrophic.

These herds were the property of Davis County; they were not large and the sum of them was not great—though and the grass passed that area had grown smaller, and the supply of forage diminished. If they had been small enough, if they had been herded correctly, and if they had grazed thin slopes at only the proper times, it may well be that Davis County would have had no trouble. Some slopes are so steep, some soils so unstable, and some ecological balances so precarious that there are mountain areas which ought not to be grazed at all. But it is not clear that the west front in Davis County was wholly of this kind; at least its lower portions could have been grazed in safety if they had been grazed properly. The necessity is that the plant cover replace itself without loss. This means that only a certain percentage, which varies from place to place and species to species, of the cover be grazed off; the rest must come to seed and produce next year's growth. It also means that stock must not be allowed to graze any year's plant growth till that growth is well established. In any given place, both the number of stock that will graze the proper percentage and no more, and the spring or summer week before which they must be kept off that area, can be exactly determined. That is, both carrying capacity and grazing season are subject to wholly scientific determination and control. That being done, and provided always that the stock be properly herded, there is no reason why a range should not be maintained in full health and efficiency forever both as forage and as plant cover protecting the soil from erosion. All ranges can be permanent, safe, and productive. All should be.

Davis County had been overgrazed. The land had slowly deteriorated. A time came when deterioration became, in some areas, ruin. Ten percent of the Kay's Creek watershed, eleven percent of Farmington Creek watershed, and so on. Therefore the mud-flows and an agricultural society that was sick and all too obviously dying.

The town of Centerville got its domestic water from Centerville Canyon. Farther south, the town of Bountiful got its domestic water from Ward's Canyon. In order to protect their drinking water from *pollution*—not from flood damage—these towns had moved in time. With tax money they had bought portions of the watersheds that supplied them—and these portions they had fenced off, keeping stock away from them. And, by town ordinance, they had limited the number of stock that were allowed to graze the rest of those watersheds—arriving at the same number by empirical knowledge and perhaps some luck—and Centerville and Ward Canyons produced no floods or mud-flows.

The fatal disease of Davis County was a single and simple infection: overgrazing. Prevention of that disease had always been equally simple: suitable regulation of grazing. But, apart from Centerville and Ward Canyons, the disease had advanced so far that preventive and merely remedial measures were useless. Drastic treatment was required. Such treatment was provided and Davis County was saved.

I need not tell the great story of that victory in detail. A frightened population demanded—and permitted, as an unfrightened one usually will not—unified, cooperative, basic, and scientific action, and got it. The study that developed the program was made by scientists and engineers (geologists mainly) of the Utah State Agricultural College, the Soil Conservation Service, and the U.S. Forest Service—mainly the last, and only a small group all told.[5] The money that paid for the project was in part state but mostly federal. And it is a poignant fact that the waste and loss of the depression years were a favorable circumstance for Davis County. For the labor of the project was done by about half of a

company (the other half worked at other jobs) of the
Civilian Conservation Corps. About one hundred CCC
boys saved the west front—they and a handful of geologists, foresters, botanists, and soil experts.

The Davis County farmland and its society could be
saved if the vegetative cover of the west front could be
restored. But it could not be restored unless the sting
could be taken from the cloudbursts while it was growing back. So there were two problems.

Some of the west front was public land, a bedraggled
part of the remaining Public Domain. They were now
declared a part of the Wasatch National Forest, whose
principal area was east and south of Salt Lake City. Congressional appropriations were provided to buy from its
owners the rest of the west front (including the town
lands in Centerville and Ward Canyons) and this too
was added to the Wasatch Forest. Then all stock was ex-
cluded from the whole area.

The lower slopes of the west front, being less steep
than the upper ones, required little reconstruction.
With grazing ended, perhaps they might even have
slowly healed themselves, except for the continuing
damage from above. They were planted with various native grasses and with various alien ones which Forest
Service experiment stations had found adapted to the
soil and climate. Small checkdams of brush and earth
were built in such gullies as had formed, and various
quick-growing shrubs and trees were planted in them. It
was the areas of greatest damage on the upper slopes,
the areas which had produced the floods and mud-flows,
that required the drastic treatment. The treatment they
received was unique. Nothing like it on such a scale had
ever been done in the United States; for that purpose
nothing like it had ever been done in the world.

Briefly, at each of these denuded places on the upper
slopes, the mountainside was terraced from well below
the damaged part to well above it, sometimes all the

way to the ridge. They were built on the contour, they were banked and leveled, and at short intervals slightly lower dams were built across them. On the average, they were about twenty-five feet apart, a regular, uniform stairway ascending the slopes, and in total capacity capable of holding as much water as a cloudburst would produce—holding it till it could sink into the ground, as it would have done if the plant cover had been in place. Then a plant cover was provided: the trenches and the slopes between them were planted with the appropriate grasses and with young trees.

Even with the cheap labor of the CCC this was expensive repair work. Perhaps it would not have been economically justified in an area less valuable as farmland than Davis County—but it would not have been so expensive if the destruction of land had not proceeded so far. When misused land begins to deteriorate, the time to repair it is right then.

Restoration, the healing of the land, would begin at once; complete recovery would take many years. When work on the project started in 1933, the estimate was that the watersheds would be safely under control in fifteen years, that is by 1945. (Intervening storms might destroy portions of the system, which would have to be rebuilt, but would have a steadily diminishing, increasingly limited effect.) Actually the project was ended in its eighth year, for in 1940 CCC appropriations ceased, and thereafter only odd jobs could be done by the regular and always insufficient crews of the Forest Service itself. But that proved to be enough.

Five years after the project was abandoned, on August 19, 1945, the most violent rainstorm ever recorded in the region struck the Wasatch. In Salt Lake County to the south and Weber County to the north, disastrous floods followed, and a mud-rock flow just north of Ogden Canyon swept down to within two miles of the center of Odgen. But every creek in Davis County stayed within its banks.... Grass is deep now, in some places waist high, on the places that were bare and hard as concrete in 1930. The banks of creeks are thick with willows and brush, which in 1930 were as bare as the sides of excavations. The floors of the little basins are carpeted with grass and shaded with poplars and aspen. From the floor of the valley you can seldom make out the setbacks of the contour-trenches; grass has made them part of the land. Eventually they will not be visible at all.

The healing is not yet complete, even in the areas where the project was completed. That sorely beset stream, Farmington Creek, for instance, though it does not flood any more has not yet stabilized its bed, but because its watershed is secure, eventually it will. A minute gulch called Half-Way Canyon that comes into Farmington Canyon from the north does flood. Repair work on its small watershed was begun but could not be finished, and some sixty untreated acres produce the floods. Its future is uncertain, but natural processes may heal it. As I write (1955) they are slowly healing the watershed of Davis Creek, the northernmost of the Davis County canyons. It was scheduled for the full treatment but was left to the last and got none of it. Every big storm brings it to flood, and in 1947 it sent mud out as far as the highway. Removal of livestock from the watershed reversed the process and it has been slowly healing ever since, though because the creek bed was efficiently scoured out by the mud-flows of 1930, it may yet produce others—orchards and houses below its mouth are not yet safe.

And yet none of these things matter much. Half-Way Canyon is quarantined; if it never recovers, it is a small diseased patch completely surrounded by healthy land, and no one will suffer loss. Davis Canyon either is or is not quarantined; probably it is not a threat, and if it is the damage will be limited, small and constantly diminishing. So far as the most searching calculations can be trusted—I trust them entirely—Davis County has been saved from destructive flood. The farms now are richer and more valuable than they ever were. Fine houses and town buildings have been erected below the canyon mouths that gushed mud in 1930—on top of the debris that has been brought down. The crops come to harvest and the creeks stay in their banks. In the summer of 1954 I talked to various people in Centerville and Farmington who had suffered dreadful losses in 1930 but had only the haziest recollection of those floods. In the main, Davis County has forgotten them.

But I saw a more vivid demonstration in May of 1952. I was lecturing in California when the newspapers told of costly and very curious floods in Utah. I flew there to take a look at them—and they were curious indeed.

The Utah flood of May 1952 was no one's fault and could not possibly have been prevented. (Of course there were areas where the damage was greater than it would otherwise have been because those areas had been misused.) The preceding winter had left a record snow pack in the Wasatch. Spring was late and slow—the pack melted but little. Then at the middle of May there came an unprecedented heat wave, nearly ten days of summer temperature. The melting that would normally have been spread over two months was concentrated into little more than a week. Nothing could have held that run-off and there were floods the whole length of the Wasatch.

I saw it all. Many blocks of Salt Lake City were under water, and large and rapid creeks were flowing down several of its streets, confined between lines of sandbags. At the mouth of Weber Canyon the highway was washed out for hundred of yards and the Union Pacific had mobilized its manpower to channel the waters away from a mile of track. Provo, Spanish Fork, Ogden—all the big streams had inundated fearful areas. It was deeply gratifying to see Logan River, which was not in flood and which I will come back to later on. But if that was gratifying, then one felt a kind of awe in Davis County. Ward Creek, Centerville Creek, Parrish Creek, Farmington Creek, Stud Creek—all the creeks were bank full and stable, running high and running clear. Not one of them was even roily, not one came out of its bed. You looked, indeed you stared, seeing, but hardly believing what you saw. No one except the citizens of Davis County who were going about their lawful occasions—no one could help remembering the blaze of sparks that had played above that advancing wall of mud in 1923, and the dead baby, and the drowned land smothered. . . . .

It was possible, it had happened, the thing had been done.

[Bernard DeVoto's manuscript and typescript end here.]

Epilogue

For all the success of his encyclopedic understanding of an American West that had passed, my father, Bernard DeVoto, knew that the tides and tribulations of civilization would continue to dominate and eventually threaten the future of the lands that he loved and that belong to all Americans. In 1946 he began to publish the articles on conservation and the public lands that came to be the principal focus of his last years' work. It is not generally realized today that for a long time my father's was the only passionate voice raised in defense of America's natural resources, and the only national voice with a national audience. His exposé of the secret plan by the Western stockmen to hoodwink the 80th Congress into selling off the public lands was front-page news; it added the word "land-grab" to our vocabulary. The whims of national politics and corporate greed kept the same issues active during the next decade, and DeVoto's pen remained busy. As he wrote in 1955:

The reason why the landgrab did not succeed in 1947, and the reason why the continuing attack on the public lands system since then has not succeeded, is that journalism has kept the public informed about what was going on. *Harper's* and these articles have shared that public service—they have helped provide a reason why the attack is not going to succeed even now, with a President in the White House who is ignorant of the situation and piously indifferent to it, the landgrabbers in control of the Department of the Interior, and the chambers of commerce in control of the Department of Agriculture.

(The President was Eisenhower; his Secretary of the Interior was Douglas McKay, who, in 1956, would resign to run for Senator from Oregon against Wayne Morse, and lose; the Agriculture Secretary was Ezra Taft Benson.)

He might have finished *Western Paradox* had other matters not slowed its progress. One of the most egregious was the well-publicized plan to construct the Echo Park hydroelectric dam on the Colorado River that would have flooded Dinosaur National Monument in Utah. The attempt failed, but it had been a close call, and DeVoto did not live to learn how much his own efforts had helped defeat it.

During the year after my father's death, his library was acquired intact by Stanford University, which established an archive of his personal papers. Among these were the handwritten draft and typescript of *The Western Paradox*, both incomplete. My mother consulted several friends about what action to take with respect to the unfinished book. Among these were Wallace Stegner, who later wrote DeVoto's biography, and Arthur Schlesinger, Jr., who had been DeVoto's student at Harvard and had traveled west with him in 1940. Anne Barrett, an editor at Houghton Mifflin and a close friend of the DeVoto family, read the typescript closely and prepared an extensive outline, noting that DeVoto

himself had used some of the material for his penulti-
mate Easy Chair for December 1955.

In a letter to Stegner dated January 5, 1956, my
mother wrote:

> Benny left a book about two thirds finished—about the
> West today and you know how important that would have
> been. There was some talk about asking you to finish it,
> but Anne Barrett now inclines to believe that even you
> couldn't do it. Benny had six and a half chapters out of a
> possible nine in the first draft, and the first chapter and
> a bit more in the second draft. But she feels, and I agree
> with her, that what made his books uniquely DeVoto
> went in on third draft—the balance and bite pulling the
> structure together. Of course I hate having an unfinished
> book that would have meant so damn much to us all, par-
> ticularly the Democratic party—but if he had lived to be
> 90 there would still have been an unfinished book, and I
> simply will not have anything published that is not first-
> rate.

Forty-four years later, and ten years after my
mother's death, I still agree with this appraisal, in
which Stegner concurred. But at the same time, I have
decided to publish *Western Paradox,* for two reasons, of
which the first is my feeling that Bernard DeVoto's still-
vigorous reputation as a first-rate writer is not likely to
be impared by its publication, even granted the unfinished and sometimes unpolished state, which is more
than compensated for by the passion and vividness of
the writing itself.

The second and more important reason is that, de-
spite the passage of half a century, the issues brought
forth with burning eloquence in *Western Paradox* and
the accompanying essays are more timely and important than ever. The attempt put forward by the Republican 80th Congress to sell off the West's public lands
"has been held in check and it will not win this time. But

it will be repeated many times and the West intends it
to win." Fifty years later, the accuracy and foresight of
DeVoto's words have not changed. Today, under the combined pressure of vastly increased population, massive
corrupt interests, and elected representatives in Congress equally in thrall to big money and to the classic
myths of the West, the danger to the public lands has
probably never been greater. The defilement of major
areas of America's national forests through exploitive
and indiscriminate logging, dominated by the demands
of large timber corporations and wastefully financed at
public expense, is a familiar news item everywhere
today. The progressive destruction of watersheds from
overgrazing by cattle and sheep, again subsidized by
America's taxpayers, proceeds unabated and unre-
strained. The mining law of 1872, passed during the administration of President Grant and unamended in over
a century, permitted a public resource worth several bil-
lions of dollars to be sold for a pittance to a foreign corporation just two years ago.

　　Thus it may not surprise the reader to find that there
is little in *Western Paradox* that is seriously out of date,
nor is there much in the accompanying *Harper's* essays, ironclad documents of their time, that requires
correction or amplification today. Some annotation was
necessary, however, to explain the legal and political vi-
cissitudes of the half century since the main text was
written. Douglas Brinkley and Patricia Nelson Limerick,
renowned and expert historians, have no peers in their
knowledge of this complex field, and it has been my pro-
foundest joy to have their enthusiastic cooperation and
assistance. That they were able and willing to take time
from furiously busy schedules in order to annotate a
fifty-year-old torso has earned my everlasting thanks;
more than that, it is renewed testimony to the enduring
value of Bernard DeVoto's urgent message.

Had he lived, DeVoto might have added perhaps three more chapters. But his typescript of six chapters and an unfinished seventh were already fully drafted, with only a few details missing which he would certainly have provided at his next opportunity; we believe we have filled all of these gaps.

In two places in the typescript, DeVoto indicated a short passage to be cut out, because it would be handled later in a different chapter. We have left these in place, assuming that the reader will not seriously object when one or two paragraphs seem to recapitulate earlier material.

Though I believe that *The West Against Itself,* the title of DeVoto's pioneering essay, best illustrated the provocative essence of that very paradox which dominates the American West of our time, *Western Paradox* is a title that fully signals the content of the chapters it covers. For my father, were he around today, would still find a West struggling against an encroaching East and its own occasional short-sightedness, caught in the paradox of adolescent growth.

Mark DeVoto

Notes

Selected Essays

The West Against Itself

1. At the time of this essay's publication, DeVoto had been writing for *Harper's* for eleven years. [Ed.]

2. McCarran's three-year attack on the Grazing Service, a classic demonstration of how to assassinate a federal agency, had just succeeded when this article was written. The Grazing Service was abolished as such, being merged with the General Land Office, the historic (and often graft-ridden) custodian of the national domain, to form a new agency, the Bureau of Land Management, which took over its functions. BLM was so set up as to be entirely subservient to McCarran and the big stock interests he was stooging for, and from the beginning it was understaffed. The next year, 1947, he succeeded in getting its appropriations reduced to the point where it could not perform the functions originally assigned to the Grazing Service.

3. Subsequently a senator.

Sacred Cows and Public Lands

1. Under a later reorganization the parent committee has become the Committee on Interior and Insular Affairs.

Heading for the Last Roundup

1. This program has been halted by the Bureau of the Budget in the Eisenhower administration, a munificently spendthrift form of economy.

Conservation: Down and on the Way Out

1. It was defeated in the closing days of the session.

Western Paradox

Chapter One: To the Traveler's Eye

1. The young historian was Arthur Schlesinger, Jr. [Ed.]

2. Probably "Plundered Province." [Ed.]

3. When DeVoto wrote this there were 20 million people living in the West. By the end of 1999 there were 61 million. [Ed.]

4. For instance, women with deranged emotional lives try to find mother figures in their entourage in order to cover their own lack of motherliness by identifying themselves with these. Even then they do not have much feeling for the child, but they imitate the attitude of a loving mother so well that they themselves and the persons around them think that their motherliness is genuine. *Psychology of Women*, vol. 2, p. 273, and see p. 329. Dr. Deutsch also treats the subjective more technically and at greater length in *Psychoanalytic Quarterly*, vol. 9.

5. Exactness in these distances is not necessary for my purpose and in some of them could not be achieved anyway, but since there are always people to challenge figures printed in a book I make a statement that will apply to all distances in this one. I am making rough approximations and am here making them by map measurement. In small areas the large-scale Forest Service maps are the most accurate ones generally available; I use some later on but none in this passage. I use General Land Office maps of the states (the worst of all, and very bad), U.S. Army Map Service maps, regional and larger-scale aeronautical charts, and, whenever possible, the topographical quadrangles of the Geological Survey, usually those of 1:125000. Anyone who cares to think in inches, rods, or even furlongs, may cavil at these last as much as he cares to but they soothe my soul and I have spent a lifetime reading maps. I cheerfully grant the caviler that some of those from which the measurements in this passage were taken have not been revised since the 1890s when they were made and that some of them are merely triangulation. But I add that I don't know what the actual "sources" of some of these rivers are, and neither does anyone else for the concept is theoretical, and that no error herein is sufficient to land the reader on the wrong side of a ridge or descending the wrong stream.

6. Brown's Hole to the mountain men, some of whom for a while maintained Fort Davy Crockett there. It is the "Robber's Roost" of horse opera and earned its reputation. It was a hideout

for Butch Cassidy's "Wild Bunch" and many other Western outlaws, especially cattle rustlers. Tom Horn committed two of his known murders there. Even today the visitor avoids expressing interest in the cattle business.

7. This, the southernmost extension of the Parks, is known locally as the Mosquito Range.

8. Mount Whitney is the highest peak in the United States, 14,495 feet. This is 64 feet higher than Mt. Elbert in the Sawatch and 713 feet higher than Gannett Peak in the Wind Rivers. (According to the tables to which I adhere in this book for the sake of uniformity. Like map distances, the official heights of mountains depend on who is determining them. There is no such thing as an absolute height, or at least no such thing as a determinable one.) Being a single range and indeed a single massif, however, the Sierra is comparatively regular and so does not give such a continuous impression of precipitous ruggedness as many others do, for instance the Sawatch, the San Juans, the Uncompahgres, the Sawtooths, or the comparatively low Lewises.

Chapter Two: Damnedest Country Under the Sun

1. A number of bureaus and institutions compile rainfall statistics and the tables they publish sometimes differ. The differences are insignificant but make trouble for writers who use them. I confine myself almost altogether to the tables in the 1941 Yearbook of Agriculture, *Climate and Man,* and to the maps in that volume and those in the *Atlas of Agriculture* (1922).

2. When I made approximately this same statement in a magazine article I was deluged by telegrams from chambers of commerce in California and Arizona claiming the highest extremes and similar ones from North Dakota claiming the lowest ones. Peace, compadres, there is glory enough for all.

3. When asked by Eastern friends what guide book to take West, I invariably name this one and add Fenneman's *Physiography of the Western United States*. I am entirely serious; both are always with me when I am in the West, however briefly.

4. *Listen, Bright Angel,* p. 20.

5. The Weather Bureau, the Soil Conservation Service, and the Geological Survey all study droughts. But because they study them to different ends the differences in their results are a good deal more serious, for my purpose, than the differences in statistical tables that I have previously remarked on. I use them all as I best can and follow SCS oftener than the others. But there are some conflicts too great to be ignored, and I have referred these to my habitual consultants, who are in the Forest Service.

Chapter Three: Emptiness Can Affect the Unwary

1. These figures are from the Census of 1950 and so are all others I cite, except where I plainly note that I am using later estimates. A point of very great importance, which I hope the reader will bear in mind, is that halfway through the next decade they do not hold for New Mexico in the vicinity of Albuquerque, Arizona, California, Oregon, and Washington west of the Cascades, or the Eastern slope of Colorado. The population of these areas has continued to increase, following 1950, at rates which differ from one another but are all much higher than the rates anywhere else in the United States.

2. A few thousand less than Flint, Michigan; or than Wichita or Youngstown.

3. No one can foresee to what extent the Colorado River will be developed and so there is no way of guessing how much water Nevada will ultimately get from it. The present plans for development are the master illusion of the West. The Colorado River Compact allots 300,000 acre-feet a year of Colorado River water to Nevada. The Compact, in effect, directs fourteen ounces to fill a sixteen-ounce bottle, but this is the sole remaining water source of any importance in the state.

4. A minimum guess at the cost of this reclamation would be $1400 per acre; conceivably it might cost twice that, or four times. (One vision of the Central Arizona Project would have cost upward of $10,000 per acre.) Hay land in Utah is seldom worth $150 per acre. Accept that and add $90 per acre for the water right. The Project would spend $1400 to make an acre of forage-growing land worth $240.

5. There were also two "sanitariums" at thermal springs which had pools of hot, opaque, yellow, stinking water. A very great many such resorts were scattered about the mountain West. They were supposed to be medicinal and to be especially good for rheumatic and venereal complaints, but they were also patronized for sport. I suppose that a quarter of them still operate, even now. No one who has not swum in such water can imagine how revolting the experience is.

6. The other, which has been insufficiently publicized by Eastern architectural journals, is the admirably functional small house of the Southwest modeled on the evolution of Spanish-Indian adobe houses and sometimes still made of the same material. It has thick walls, small windows, usually an overhang, usually a galleria, and a patio. It is far more pleasant to live in and better to look at than any of the genres so far recognizable as such of the California show window and technocratic eclectic. Westchester ranch house is the prevailing style in "developments" outside of

California and the Southwest, and all too often in the Southwest. Subdivisions climbing the side of a hill above town are a depressing rash of it, ugly and incongruous.

7. Gold can be panned in many Western creeks, especially in Idaho, but only in such minute quantities that no one can make a living from it.

8. Far more so, and with security to boot, in the atomic towns, whether directly run by the government or leased to such corporations as General Electric. Here is as crazy a prohibition of all citizenship as ingenuity can work out. Since half the males are PhDs married to committeewomen of the League of Women Voters, there are spectacular guilts, neuroses, and manias as a direct result. Someone should give us a detailed account.

Chapter Four: Unregarded Inheritance from the Frontier

1. A statistical study would certainly show that Wyatt Earp is runner-up to Billy the Kid in the admiration of our contemporary romantics. He was, we are told, a noble gentleman, and the language used about him is on the border between worship and lust.

2. William A. Keleher, *The Fabulous Frontier,* p. 25.

3. Usually the summer and winter ranges are considerable distances apart, often several hundred miles. Formerly the bands of sheep—"flocks" is not a Western usage—were invariably trailed from one to the other and an impressive number still are, especially from Utah winter ranges to Colorado summer ranges. But in the main rail and truck transport have replaced trailing.

4. Arizona land frauds run to the picturesque. One character pirated Bright Angel Trail by means of false mining claims, and levied tribute on the Santa Fe Railroad, the Fred Harvey Company, and the people and government of the United States for quite a while. With unimpeachable technique, the gentleman got himself elected to the United States Senate, so that he could control appointments to the federal court in which effective action for his ejectment from a national park could be brought. Certain highly amusing aspects of this case have never been published.

5. It was also a tool that could be used against one's competitors and by small operators who were in a position to hold up a big one—false location as blackmail.

6. Mr. Henry Nash Smith calls this myth The Garden of the World and devotes a large part of his book, *Virgin Land,* to it. This is one of the basic Western books.

7. Both the Homestead Act and the Pre-emption Act forbade homesteading forest land, but no land was forest until it was classified as such.

8. Perhaps the reader may demur, since most of the great Mesabi iron deposits were fraudulently homesteaded at $1.25 an acre. But operating costs on the way to patent were far higher.

9. Pat McCarran made no impression on Eastern journalists till the very end of his life, when he belatedly got into the security racket and, in the immigration racket, came out from behind the disguises that had concealed his long and piratical activity. Even then they tended to regard him as a cheap, small-time, and rather inept operator. Nothing could have been farther from the truth: he was a brilliant man and his piracies were on a truly impressive scale. It is true that no crook was too small for him to form an alliance with, but it is also true that he was in lifetime alliance with the largest-scale crookedness of his region. In my time no other Senator has so constantly worked against the interests of the United States.

10. *The Autobiography of William Allen White,* p. 619.

11. A good many of Fall's opportunities have been described in books, more in newspapers. Still others are in court records and there are as many legends as anyone may care to listen to. For an undisputed case of the use of a fiscal agent, one who muffed his job, see William G. Shepherd, "How Carl Magee Broke Fall's New Mexico Ring," *World's Work,* May 1924.

12. Russell Lord, *The Wallaces of Iowa,* p. 227.

13. They had been thoroughly prepared at the Republican Convention, which smelled of oil even in the decorous newspaper reports. They were fully foreseen by those who had been defending the public interest. The autobiography of Josephus Daniels tells how he and his young Assistant Secretary, Franklin D. Roosevelt, did what was possible, during the last days of their administration, to prevent the anticipated theft. Perhaps I should point out that Daugherty had been an attorney of big oil companies and Denby, a friend and Congressional defender of Ballinger.

14. *The Wallaces of Iowa,* p. 228.

Chapter Five: The Eighth City of Cibola

1. I have followed Paul H. Gantt's excellent treatise, *The Case of Alfred Packer, the Man-Eater.*

2. Apparently Hollywood's preference for the phony would hold even if the supply of authentic ones was unlimited. When a film was based on the keelboat section of A. B. Guthrie's *Big Sky,* the most distinguished Western novel, a sequence called for Canadian boatmen to sing a Canadian boatmen's song. There were at hand hundreds of *voyageur* songs, which are as notable as Negro spirituals and often very beautiful. There was also a handful of Ameri-

can songs from the Western waters. Neither would serve. The director used an African veldt song, "Brandy Leave Me Alone."

3. When this chapter was still in first draft, Mr. Richter published a philosophical treatise called *The Mountain on the Desert*. I have read it diligently but must report that I do not understand it. It has overtones of the desert mysticism exemplified by Mary Austin a generation ago and kept thinly alive still in the salons of Santa Fe and Taos but I take it to be primarily a metaphysics of energy, teleological, anti-Freudian, and strongly influenced by the atomic theories that issue from Los Alamos, all establishing that the spirit of man has a better chance in New Mexico than elsewhere.

4. The complete comment on Wister's snobbishness was made by Alexander Woollcott in a review of *Roosevelt: The Story of a Friendship*. Under the title of "Wisteria" it is reprinted in *While Rome Burns*.

5. The spatial limitations of the theater frustrate horse opera. Otherwise this line would have had stern competition from one in "The Great Divide," by William Vaughn Moody, which was being taught as the best American play when I was an undergraduate. Its drama is the difference between the liberating individualism of the West and the sin-conscious timidity of the East. Just before the final curtain, compressing the Virginian and the Old West into a single speech, the heroine says to the Hero, "Teach me to live as you do."

6. But in my judgment Mr. Frank O'Rourke runs well ahead of the field.

7. "The Cowman's Code of Ethics," *The Brand Book*, Denver Corral of the Westerners, June 1949. Mr. Adams, a scholar and the author of a standard bibliography of Western outlaws, believed so intensely in the Old West that it is going on outside his study window as he writes—in Dallas, I think. This article is the best codification of cowpoke protocol but it is very far from being exhaustive. (Significantly, Mr. Adams originally wrote it as a lecture for a writers' conference.) Many additional specifications of the code are scattered through Philip Ashton Rollins' *The Cowboy* and similar books.

8. Horse opera's long affection for the rare and usually military caliber .44, which today's careful writers have abandoned, probably goes back to the fact that that was the gun which went root-a-toot when Frankie shot her ever-lovin' man.

9. I remind the reader of a fundamental fact discussed in an earlier chapter, that in the West proper the tall grass was mostly on the foothills, not the flats.

10. The trick riding and trick falls of Hollywood are by stunt men, not rodeo performers.

11. Of late years the collection and publication of early Western photographs has confirmed the historian's findings about the actual work clothes of the Cattle Kingdom, but their testimony relating to shirts and head gear has been ignored by horse opera and the Western Outfitters. In the West of my boyhood work shirts were mostly black, and Saturday (not Sunday) best shirts for town were blue or black and white checks. (Forty-nine cents and made for the working cowboy still by such famous firms as Big Yank.) Ranch hands, like newspapermen, liked to wear vests because the pockets were handy. It is an odd and perhaps lamentable fact that the work clothes of Levi Strauss were not widely known in the West till after the First World War, and I have not found the common noun "levis" in print earlier than 1926.

12. We must not understate the commercial stake. Manufacturers of everything that can be associated with horse opera cash in and their advertising is on a national scale. During one vogue everything a child could wear, use, or eat had a Hopalong Cassidy trademark. In the spring of 1955 a variant named Davy Crockett rose to national leadership. When the editor of *Harper's* ran a couple of paragraphs of acid comment on Crockett and the Alamo campaign, the magazine received, besides editorials of denunciation from every newspaper in Texas, hundreds of protesting letters that were obviously written by children. It turned out that advertising agencies had directed retail outlets to stir up the children to write them.

Chapter Six: A Certain Mentality

1. It was composed of portions of Utah, Idaho, and Dakota Territories. As the DAH notes, "Wyoming contains lands obtained from the Louisiana Purchase, Texas Annexation, the Oregon Treaty, and the Mexican Cession of 1848." It lies on both sides of the Continental Divide and of the 42nd Parallel.

2. Perhaps most outrageously of all, the laws forbidding the erection of private fences on the public domain.

3. Precisely this sentiment is behind the ten-year campaign of the two national stock associations to get the national forests transferred to the states, which I treat at length later. With the forests in state ownership, stockmen would be able to dispose of forest grazing ranges as they might see fit without interference by the damned long-haired, swivel-chair bureaucrats in Washington who take orders from Russia. The stock business has changed very little, and its sentiments have not changed at all, since Abel's time. During the height of the landgrab brawl in 1948 I heard an opposition orator in Casper, Wyoming, representing the interests

of water users, refer to Cain as the most maligned figure in history—"All he ever did was to shoot a stockman—is that bad?"

4. The essence of the political point of view I am describing is
that so honorable a man as Carey perceived nothing unethical in
the system he was so conspicuously advancing. He was a powerful
businessman associated with powerful businessmen and able to
subvert government to the service of their interest. No fraud is
alleged. It is true that in the universal illusion of the time—universal except for John Wesley Powell and his associates—he became the author of what is called the Carey Act, under which a lot
of cattle companies fraudulently acquired a lot of desert range.
(And the Western states were stuck with a lot of land that has
proved unsalable.) But he thought it a service to reclamation. And
in his later career he did notable services to reclamation. He envi-
sioned an agricultural Wyoming—so, though he was a stockman,
he was frequently attacked by his caste.

5. I have always heard about the pink coats but, checking up
for purposes of this paragraph, I have been unable to find any
printed mention of them.

6. My account so far could have been based, though it is not,
solely on Maurice Frink's *Cow Country Cavalcade,* a history of the
Wyoming Stock Growers Association, published in 1954 and subsidized by Association funds. The last section of the book is heavily charged with propaganda for the stockmen's side of the continuing struggle over the public lands. But its earlier portion is
sound history. I had not expected to live long enough to see so
frank a book on the subject come out of Wyoming.

7. Socially it was a good deal later than the Association
thought. In general the Wyoming newspapers—small weeklies—
opposed Association control of the state. Even a Cheyenne paper
was critical.

8. In itself this means little, of course. Evidence about rustling
in a documentary form and left on the record for historians to use
seldom exists.

9. Mr. Frink's *Cow Country Cavalcade,* turning discreet, says
that in the Johnson County War "he played a part the full story of
which does not show in the records." This superb understatement
refers to the Association records and to Canton's part before the
invasion.

10. Separate out from the invaders Frank Canton, two or three
others of his type, and the salaried thugs. Of the rest a historian
must say that they were a lot of damned fools—arrogant but inconceivably silly and footless fools. The historian knows that they
had been skillfully guided to their consummate folly by a group of
those whom I have called hard-minded, who were using the Association (and the Cheyenne Club) for their own purposes, who

stood to profit from the invasion, and who suffered no inconvenience in its aftermath.

11. Figures are almost as untrustworthy as those carried by the
scarehead press at the time. In the outcome forty-six invaders surrendered and thirty-nine were indicted. No other figures are certain. The most reliable printed source is A. S. Mercer, *The Banditti
of the Plains*. Printed in Cheyenne and confiscated—as obscene
literature—by Association officials, the first edition is one of the
rarest of Western Americana. In 1954 it was reprinted by the University of Oklahoma Press with an invaluable introduction by
William H. Kittrell. The only scholarly study of the Johnson County
War ever made is by Wayne Card, in *Frontier Justice*. Innumerable
ambiguities and lacunae still exist and always will.

12. Now the site of a hamlet called Kayce, Wyoming.

13. The Secretary was Stephen B. Elkins, who later became
Senator from West Virginia. He had a distinguished career in the
Territory of New Mexico, where as a member of the ruling oligarchy he had mastered the use of government as an instrument
of business.

14. The Idaho recruit succeeded in hiding out and soon made a
most embarrassing detailed confession, which A. S. Mercer was
happy to publish. According to Wyoming legends, several others
had succeeded in getting away by night; they are variously
thought of, depending on which side the narrator takes.

15. Obviously this farce could not have succeeded if the Attorney General of the United States had not adopted the official view
of insurrection in Johnson County.

16. *Malcolm Campbell, Sheriff,* by Robert B. David. Campbell
was a first-rate sheriff and, though a friend of and sympathizer
with the bigshots, an honest man, so honest that the Association
had contrived to get him out of the state during the invasion. This
fact makes all the more interesting the use of the first person and
the eyewitnesses' testimony in the book. Mr. David, its author, had
a lively imagination but he also obviously had a lot of information
from various invaders. One of them is identified by Mr. Kittrell as
the company foreman who had spent the night with Rae and
Champion and told the invaders where they were.

17. Simplifications and flat statements are at their most dangerous here and let me protect myself from at least the charge of
ignorance. Nature came close to creating a paradise for Western
cattle growers in the sand hills of Nebraska and another one for
those whose operations are limited to feeder stock in the flint hills
of Kansas. Both are too small and too special to count on the level
of generalization I must maintain here. Also, my generalizations
about the Western cattle business apply to them too, in part.

18. That is, from a range with a "carrying capacity" of one "animal unit" per hundred acres per year. I avoid the technical terms of land specialists as much as possible but will be forced to use these two occasionally. The carrying capacity of a given area of land is the number of stock that can be grazed on it with full benefit to the stock and no damage to the range. Because there are summer, spring and fall, and winter ranges, and because the growing season is a vital factor, it must be stated in months. An animal unit is one cow or horse, or five sheep or goats. Calves and lambs don't count and are not figured in. It has always been the assumption of stockgrowers who use public ranges or private ranges under lease that trespass stock—stock in excess of those their permits or leases call for—don't count, either.

Chapter Seven: Nemesis

1. Beginning at the north, they are the canyons of Kay's Creek, Bair's Creek, Sheppard Creek, Farmington Creek, Steed Creek, Davis Creek, Ford Creek, Barnard Creek, Parrish Creek, Centerville Creek, and Ward Creek.

2. The storm was reported copiously but sloppily by the newspapers of Ogden and Salt Lake City. The stories omit a number of vital facts one would expect to find; the times I give are those which I have worked out as probable. The appearance of the flood at Farmington is given at various times from 6:30 to 10 P.M. I judge that it came out of the canyon at about 7:30.

3. *Deseret News,* July 25, 1878; Salt Lake *Semi-Weekly Herald,* July 31, 1878; Kaysville *Weekly Reflex,* Aug. 8, 1912. To anticipate, these three mud-flows resulted *primarily* from small burned areas in the three watersheds. Fresh growth covered the burns so quickly that there were no followups.

4. I may be wrong in both memories but it is revealing that I cannot check them, for this flash flood gets only a single and non-statistical paragraph in the newspaper story of the general storm.

5. So novel and unprecedented was the problem that the geological evidence was open to various interpretations. Nothing in the whole story is more remarkable or exhilarating than the fact that the Forest Service geologists, on whose hypotheses the project was based, interpreted the evidence in a way that their colleagues in the Geological Survey sharply challenged. Not only the empirical results but the later studies of many geologists have proved them right.

Bibliography

"I am a professional writer, a journalist, and am proud of the craft. As a journalist I have ranged pretty widely. I am an educated man and am willing to write about anything I am informed about and interested in. A bibliography of my work would stretch a considerable distance—from *Liberty* to the *Psychoanalytic Quarterly,* from coterie magazines of the fragrant Twenties which were issued in editions of thirty-two on hand-made paper to their principal emetic *The Saturday Evening Post,* from the program of the Harvard-Yale game to the confidential reports of *Consumer's Research,* from the private annals of the Social Science Research Council to the throwaways of a good many agitations. I have even appeared in the *New Republic.*"
—Bernard DeVoto

"The Reasonableness of World-wide Conciliation," *Ogden Standard,* May 10, 1913.

"The Doctor," *The University Pen,* December 1914. Short story. Reprinted in a special anniversary issue (1947) of the University of Utah literary magazine *Pen.*

The Crooked Mile. New York: Minton, Balch, 1924.

"Children Best Part of Novel," *Evanston News-Index,* Dec. 16, 1924. Review of Mrs. Edward (Mary Borden) Spears, *Three Pilgrims and a Tinker.*

"Lesion," *Guardian,* December 1924. Short story.

"America by the Frontier Formula," *Chicago Evening Post Literary Review,* Dec. 26, 1924. Review of Frederick L. Paxson, *History of the American Frontier.*

"An American Tragedy," *Saturday Review of Literature,* Dec. 27, 1924. Review of Stewart Edward White, *The Glory Hole.*

"An Inconclusive Symposium," *Chicago Evening Post Literary Review,* Jan. 16, 1925. Review of Malcolm R. Thorpe, ed., *Organic Adaptations to Environment.*

"Sees Paradox in Dual with Vatican," *Evanston News-Index,* Jan. 20, 1925. Review of Alfred Loisy, *Duel with Vatican.*

"Lake Land's Spell Lives in This Book," *Evanston News-Index,* Jan. 27, 1925. Review of Charles B. Reed, *Four-Way Lodge.*

"Mencken Beheads Heedless Corpses," *Evanston News-Index,* Jan. 27, 1925. Review of H. L. Mencken, *Prejudices, Fourth Series.*

"This Is True Epic of American Land," *Evanston News-Index,* Feb. 3, 1925. Review of Mary Austin, *A Land of Journey's Endings.*

"Paint Future in Sad, Glad Colors," *Evanston News-Index,* Feb. 24, 1925. Reviews of Gerald Heard, *Narcissus;* and F. C. S. Schiller, *Tantalus.*

"God—Litterateur," *Guardian,* March 1925.

"Digging up Literary Remains of Conrad," *Evanston News-Index,* Mar. 3, 1925. Review of Joseph Conrad, *Tales of Heresy.*

"Puts 'Arrowsmith' with Great Novels," *Evanston News-Index,* Mar. 10, 1925. Review of Sinclair Lewis, *Arrowsmith.*

"Van Doren in Appraisal of J. B. Cabell," *Evanston News-Index,* Mar. 17, 1925. Review of Carl Van Doren, *James Branch Cabell.*

"A Naturalist in Paradise," *Chicago Evening Post Literary Review,* Mar. 20, 1925. Review of Robert Cushman Murphy, *Bird Islands of Peru.*

"This Science of History," *Chicago Evening Post Literary Review,* Mar. 20, 1925. Reviews of Jacques De Morgan, *Prehistoric Man;* and C. E. Fox, *The Threshold of the Pacific.*

"Sin Comes to Brattle Street," *Saturday Review of Literature,* Mar. 21, 1925. Review of B. H. Lehman, *Wild Marriages.*

"Blind Man's Buff Is Not Hémon's Best," *Evanston News-Index,* Mar. 24, 1925. Reviews of Louis Hémon, *Blind Man's Buff;* and Elmer Davis, *The Keys to the City.*

"Perfect Comedian Is Aldous Huxley," *Evanston News-Index,* Mar. 31, 1925. Review of Aldous Huxley, *Those Barren Leaves.*

"What Causes This Honing for Arcady?" *Evanston News-Index,* Apr. 7, 1925. Review of Robert Nathan, *Jonah.*

"The Stop of Blood," *Saturday Review of Literature,* Apr. 18, 1925. Review of Percy Marks, *Martha.*

"Writer Foresees Doom of Mankind," *Evanston News-Index*, Apr. 21, 1925. Review of Stanton H. Coblentz, *The Decline of Man*.

"Scientists Show Secrets to Public," *Evanston News-Index*, Apr. 28, 1925. Reviews of F. G. Crookshank, *The Mongol in Our Midst;* J. B. S. Haldane, *Gallinicus;* and J. C. Patten, *The Passing of the Phantoms*.

"Kreymborg Tells Tale of Moderns," *Evanston News-Index*, May 5, 1925. Review of Alfred Kreymborg, *Troubadour*.

"Ghosts as Social Assets," *Chicago Evening Post Literary Review*, May 8, 1925. Review of Charles G. Harper, *Haunted Houses*.

"On Making History an Exact Science," *Evanston News-Index*, May 19, 1925. Review of Frederic L. Paxson, *A History of the American Frontier*.

"Indoor Morality Outdoors," *Chicago Evening Post Literary Review*, May 22, 1925. Review of Earle Amos Brooks, *A Handbook of the Outdoors*.

"Ellen LaMotte Tells of Opium Trade in East," *Evanston News-Index*, May 26, 1925. Review of Ellen LaMotte's *Snuffs and Butters*.

"Adventures of a Scholar Tramp," *Evanston News-Index*, June 2, 1925. Review of Glen H. Mullins, *Adventures of a Scholar Tramp*.

"Frontier Days and Industrial Emergence," *Chicago Evening Post Literary Review,* June 5, 1925. Review of Theodore Calvin Pease, *The Story of Illinois*.

"Our First International Gentleman," *Chicago Evening Post Literary Review*, June 5, 1925. Review of George S. Hellman, *Washington Irving, Esquire*.

"Everything about Prehistoric Man," *Chicago Evening Post Literary Review*, June 12, 1925. Review of George MacCurdy, *Human Origins*.

"The Odyssey of Mormonism," *Saturday Review of Literature*, June 27, 1925. Review of M. R. Werner, *Brigham Young*.

"New and Old Poems by Mr. Nicholson," *Evanston News-Index*, Aug. 11, 1925. Reviews of J. U. Nicholson, *King of the Black Isles;* and *The Drum of Yle*.

"Is the New Woman Superior to Old?" *Evanston News-Index*, Sept. 7, 1925. Reviews of Anthony M. Ludovici, *Lysistrata, or Woman's Future and Future Woman;* and Dora Russell, *Hypatia, or Woman and Knowledge*.

"'Prometheus' Seeks to Annihilate Bunk," *Evanston News-Index,* Sept. 14, 1925. Reviews of H. S. Jennings, *Prometheus;* and Vernon Lee, *Proteus;* and H. F. Scott Stokes, *Perseus.*

"'Quo Vadimus' Tale of the Golden Age," *Evanston News-Index,* Sept. 16, 1925. Reviews of D'Albe, *Quo Vadimus;* and Wright, *The Conquest of Cancer.*

"Timothy Dexter Was American Nobleman," *Evanston News-Index,* Sept. 21, 1925. Review of J. P. Marquand, *Lord Timothy Dexter.*

"The Good Old Days—Best in Southwest," *Evanston News-Index,* Sept. 30, 1925. Review of Owen P. White, *Them Was the Days, from El Paso to Prohibition.*

"Bojer's 'Emigrants' Fine Work of Art," *Evanston News-Index,* Nov. 4, 1925. Review of Johan Bojer, *The Emigrants.*

"Here Is Genuine American Poetry," *Evanston News-Index,* Nov. 18, 1925. Review of John G. Neihardt, *The Song of the Indian Wars.*

"Alexander Writes of Indian Dramas," *Evanston News-Index,* Nov. 25, 1925. Review of Hartley Alexander, *Manito Masks.*

"Aaron Burr Is Vindicated," *Chicago Evening Post Literary Review,* Nov. 27, 1925. Review of Samuel H. Wandell and Meade Minnigerode, *Aaron Burr.*

"Morale of Enemy Objective of War," *Evanston News-Index,* Dec. 2, 1925. Review of B. H. Liddell Hart, *Paris or the Future of War.*

"Bercovici Writes of Melting Pot," *Evanston News-Index,* Dec. 9, 1925. Review of Conrad Bercovici, *On New Shores.*

"'Murder at Smutty Nose' Enthralling Book of Crime," *Evanston News-Index,* Dec. 10, 1925. Review of Edmund Pearson, *Murder at Smutty Nose.*

"'Prairie' Faithful to Midland Creed," *Evanston News-Index,* Dec. 16, 1925. Review of Walter J. Mullenburg, *Prairie.*

"A Working Philosophy of Liberty," *Chicago Evening Post Literary Review,* Dec. 18, 1925. Review of Hendrik Van Loon, *Tolerance.*

"Newton Produces a Literary Gem." *Evanston News-Index,* Dec. 23, 1925. Review of A. Edward Newton, *The Greatest Book in the World.*

"'First Forty-Niner' Story of the West," *Evanston News-Index,* Dec. 30, 1925. Review of James A. B. Scherer, *The First Forty-Niner.*

The Chariot of Fire. New York: Macmillan, 1926.

"Bertrand Russell on 'What I Believe,'" *Evanston News-Index,* Jan. 6, 1926. Review of Bertrand Russell, *What I Believe.*

"American Husband Finds a Champion," *Evanston News-Index,* Jan. 20, 1926. Review of Alexander Black, *American Husbands.*

"Hauptmann Novel Joyous Allegory," *Evanston News-Index,* Feb. 3, 1926. Review of Gerhart Hauptmann, *The Island of the Great Mother.*

"Interpretation of Indians Pleasing," *Evanston News-Index,* Feb. 10, 1926. Review of Eda Lou Walton, *Dawn Boy.*

"See Machine Age Bringing World Chaos," *Evanston News-Index,* Feb. 10, 1926. Review of Garet Garrett, *Ouroboros or the Mechanical Extension of Mankind.*

"1925 Short Stories Disappoint Critic," *Evanston News-Index,* Feb. 17, 1926. Review of Edward J. O'Brien, ed., *The Best Short Stories of 1925.*

"Reformer Writes Brilliant Document," *Evanston News-Index,* Feb. 24, 1926. Review of Frederick C. Howe, *The Confessions of a Reformer.*

"Southwest Glorified by C. F. Lummis," *Evanston News-Index,* Feb. 24, 1926. Review of C. F. Lummis, *Mesa, Cañon and Pueblo.*

"Utah," *American Mercury,* March 1926. [The DeVoto Papers— housed at Stanford University—include the annotated page proofs signed and dated Dec. 13, 1925.]

"Huxley Gives Dope about Traveling," *Evanston News-Index,* Mar. 3, 1926. Review of Aldous Huxley, *Along the Road.*

"Your Future Morality Is Safe," *Evanston News-Index,* Mar. 10, 1926. Review of C. F. M. Joad, *Thrasymachus.*

"'The Oldest God' Is Robust Irony," *Evanston News-Index,* Mar. 17, 1926. Review of Stephen McKenna, *The Oldest God.*

"Norris Shown Too Much Profundity," *Evanston News-Index,* Mar. 24, 1926. Review of Charles G. Norris, *Pig Iron.*

"The Paradox of D. H. Lawrence," *Evanston News-Index,* Mar. 24, 1926. Review of D. H. Lawrence, *The Plumed Serpent.*

"Memories of One Lucky American," *Evanston News-Index,* Mar. 31, 1926. Review of Walt McDougall, *This Is the Life.*

"Mrs. Wembridge's Further Moronia," *Evanston News-Index,* Mar. 31, 1926. Review of Eleanor R. Wembridge, *Other Peoples' Daughters.*

"Americana Vaunts Two Masterpieces," *Evanston News-Index,* Apr. 7, 1926. Reviews of Walter Noble Burns, *The Saga of Billy the Kid;* and George H. Devol, *Forty Years a Gambler on the Mississippi.*

"Ammunition for an Attack on Babbitt," *Evanston News-Index,* Apr. 21, 1926. Review of Duncan Aikman, *The Home Town Mind.*

"The Mauve Decade from Two Angles," *Evanston News-Index,* Apr. 28, 1926. Reviews of Thomas Beer, *The Mauve Decade;* and Floyd Dell, *Intellectual Vagabondage.*

"Jurgen Performs in Cabell Novel," *Evanston News-Item,* May 5, 1926. Review of James B. Cabell, *The Silver Stallion.*

"Stribling Scores in 'Teeftallow,'" *Evanston News-Item,* May 5, 1926. Review of T. S. Stribling, *Teeftallow.*

"South Lambastes Minnigerode Book," *Evanston News-Index,* May 19, 1926. Review of Meade Minnigerode, *Some American Ladies.*

"A Critical Analysis of the Sacco-Vanzetti Case," *Evanston News-Index,* June 1, 1926. Review of Felix Frankfurter, *The Case of Sacco and Vanzetti.*

"'Americana' Shelf Gets New Volume," *Evanston News-Index,* Oct. 6, 1926. Review of P. F. Byrne, *Soldiers of the Plains.*

"Saving the Sophomore" by Richard Dye. *American Mercury,* November 1926.

"Vestige of a Nordic Arcady," *American Mercury,* November 1926.

"Mr. Nathan Gets Hilarious over the American Drama," *Evanston News-Index,* Nov. 17, 1926. Review of George Jean Nathan, *The House of Satan.*

"Names 'Doctor's Memories' Year's Most Interesting," *Evanston News-Index,* Nov. 24, 1926. Review of Victor C. Vaughan, *A Doctor's Memories.*

"The Mountain Men," *American Mercury,* December 1926.

"Will James Gives West Its True Color and Loveliness," *Evanston News-Index,* Dec. 1, 1926. Review of Will James, *Smoky.*

"Dr. Collins Treats Tabooed Subjects with Ripe Wisdom," *Evanston News-Index,* Dec. 10, 1926. Review of Joseph Collins, *The Doctor Looks at Love and Life.*

"'Wild Bill Hickok' Hastily Done but It Reads Well," *Evanston News-Index,* Dec. 10, 1926. Review of Frank J. Wilstach, *Wild Bill Hickok.*

"College and the Exceptional Man," *Harper's,* January 1927.

"Harry Kemp Exhibits His Life in Greenwich Village," *Evanston News-Index,* Jan. 12, 1927. Review of Harry Kemp, *More Miles.*

"'The Hard-boiled Virgin' Is Caviar for the Particular," *Evanston News-Index,* Jan. 12, 1927. Review of Frances Newman, *The Hard-boiled Virgin.*

"Seitz's Book 'Dreadful' in Format," *Evanston News-Index,* Feb. 2, 1927. Review of Don C. Seitz, *The Dreadful Decade.*

"'The Delectable Mountains' Adds to Burt's Reputation," *Evanston News-Index,* Feb. 2, 1927. Review of Struthers Burt, *The Delectable Mountains.*

"George Washington the Man Shown without Sentiment," *Evanston News-Index,* Feb. 9, 1927. Review of W. F. Woodward, *George Washington, The Image and the Man.*

"'Chevrons' Is Truth about American Army in France," *Evanston News-Index,* Feb. 16, 1927. Review of Leonard Mason, *Chevrons.*

"Sinclair Lewis Continues Progress in 'Elmer Gantry,'" *Evanston News-Index,* Mar. 16, 1927. Review of Sinclair Lewis, *Elmer Gantry.*

"Asbury Writes Definitive History of Methodist Mind," *Evanston News-Index,* Apr. 6, 1927. Review of Herbert Asbury, *A Methodist Saint.*

"'Revolt in the Desert' Is Destined for Immortality," *Evanston News-Index,* Apr. 27, 1927. Review of T. E. Lawrence, *Revolt in the Desert.*

"Figures and Events of 1926–7 Run in Review," *Evanston News-Index,* May 11, 1927. Review of Grant Overton, ed., *Mirrors of the Year.*

"The Great Medicine Road," *American Mercury,* May 1927.

"The Argonaut Makes Its Debut," *Evanston News-Index,* June 5, 1927. Review of Arthur D. Howden Smith, ed., *The Narrative of Samuel Hancock.*

"In Search of Bergamot," *Harper's,* August 1927. Short story.

"The Co-Ed: The Hope of Liberal Education," *Harper's,* September 1927. Reprinted in *Forays and Rebuttals* under the title "The Co-Eds: God Bless Them." [Reprinted in *College Readings in Contemporary Thought,* ed. Kendall Taft and others, Boston: Houghton Mifflin, 1929.]

"Footnote on the West," *Harper's,* November 1927.

"Front Page Ellen," *Redbook,* November 1927. Short story.

"Sons of Martha," *Saturday Review of Literature,* Nov. 19, 1927. Review of T. Morris Longstreth, *The Silent Force.*

"Sleeping Dogs," *Saturday Evening Post,* Nov. 19, 1927. Short story.

"Casehardened Men," *Saturday Review of Literature,* Dec. 10, 1927. Review of Walter Noble Burns, *Tombstone.*

"A Social Experiment," *Saturday Review of Literature,* Dec. 24, 1927. Review of Judge Ben B. Lindsey and Wainwright Evans, *The Companionate Marriage.*

The House of Sun-Goes-Down. New York: Macmillan, 1928.

"Farewell to Pedagogy," *Harper's,* January 1928. Reprinted in *Forays and Rebuttals.*

"This Must Not Get Out," *Redbook,* January 1928. Short story.

"English A," *American Mercury,* February 1928.

"Father of Waters," *Saturday Review of Literature,* Feb. 4, 1928. Reviews of Harold Speakman, *Mostly Mississippi;* and Lyle Saxon, *Father Mississippi.*

"Mr. Ford's New York," *Saturday Review of Literature,* Feb. 18, 1928. Review of Ford Madox Ford, *New York Is Not America.*

"'A Chick among You,'" *Saturday Review of Literature,* Mar. 3, 1928. Review of Philip Guedalla, *Conquistador.*

"A Yearbook of Folly," *Saturday Review of Literature,* Mar. 10, 1928. Review of Charles Merz, *The Great American Band Wagon.*

"Image and Symbol," *Saturday Review of Literature,* Apr. 28, 1928. Review of Harvey W. Root, *The Unknown Barnum.*

"Jewry in America," *Saturday Review of Literature,* May 5, 1928. Review of Ludwig Lewisohn, *The Island Within.*

"Ranch Wondering," *Saturday Evening Post,* June 2, 1928. Short story.

"Afternoon of a Biologist," *Harper's,* September 1928. Short story.

"Tools for the Intellectual Life," *Harper's,* October 1928.

"Teamwork," *Redbook,* October 1928. Short story.

"The Popular Proverbs of Baron O-No," *Saturday Evening Post,* Oct. 27, 1928. Short story.

"An American Myth," *Saturday Review of Literature,* Nov. 10, 1928. Review of Richard J. Walsh and Milton S. Salsburg, *The Making of Buffalo Bill.*

"Gaily the Troubador," *Redbook,* November 1928. Short story.

"Editions of 'Typee,'" *Saturday Review of Literature,* Nov. 24, 1928. Letter to the ed.

"Victoria Woodhull," *Saturday Review of Literature,* Dec. 29, 1928. Review of Emanie Sachs, *The Terrible Siren: Victoria Woodhull.*

"The College Angel," *Redbook,* December 1928. Short story.

"Exit Robin Hood," *Saturday Evening Post,* Dec. 29, 1928. Short story.

"A Hymn to America," *Saturday Review of Literature,* Jan. 5, 1929. Review of Thomas Williamson, *Stride of Man.*

"The Maddest of All Follies," *Redbook,* January 1929. Short story.

"Northwestern," *College Humor,* January 1929. Reprinted as "The Coeds Were Real—The Boys Were Shadows" in *The College Years,* Hawthorn Books, 1958.

"A History of Revivalism," *Saturday Review of Literature,* Apr. 13, 1929. Review of Grover C. Loud, *Evangelized America.*

"Our Local Guelphs," *Saturday Evening Post,* Apr. 27, 1929. Short story.

"Brave Days in Washoe," *American Mercury,* June 1929. Reprinted in *Mark Twain's America.*

"Frontier America," *Saturday Review of Literature,* June 1, 1929. Review of John P. Fort, *Stone Daugherty.*

"The Penalties of Wisdom," *Redbook,* September 1929. Short story.

"The Centennial of Mormonism," *American Mercury,* Jan. 1930. Reprinted and expanded in *Forays and Rebuttals,* and contracted in *The Mormon Century Book.* (Manuscript and/or typescript copy in the DeVoto Papers)

"Byron Satterlee Hurlbut," *Harvard Graduates,* March 1930.

"Sea Goddess," *Redbook,* April 1930. Short story.

"The Long Chance," *Saturday Evening Post,* Apr. 19, 1930. Short story.

"The Precarious Attitudes of Robeson Ballou," *Saturday Evening Post,* July 26, 1930. Short story. [Manuscript and/or typescript copy in the DeVoto Papers]

"From a Graduate's Window," *Harvard Graduates,* September 1930.

"Literary Censorship in Cambridge," *Harvard Graduates,* September 1930.

"The Hand of Fear," *Redbook,* November 1930. Short story.

"Back Bay Nights," *Saturday Evening Post,* Nov. 15, 1930. Short story.

"From a Graduate's Window," *Harvard Graduates,* December 1930.

Review of S. F. Morison, *The Development of Harvard University, Harvard Graduates,* December 1930.

Review of Robert Hillyer, *The Gates of the Compass, Harvard Graduates,* December 1930.

"You Jack o' Diamonds," *Saturday Evening Post,* Jan. 10, 1931. Short story.

"From a Graduate's Window," *Harvard Graduates,* March 1931.

"The Frivial Wick," *Saturday Evening Post,* Mar. 28, 1931. Short story.

"We Brighter People," *Harvard Graduates,* March 1931. Reprinted as "The Well-informed, 1920–1930" in *Forays and Rebuttals.*

"Civilized People," *Redbook,* May 1931. Short story.

"Webersham: The Leland Affair," *Saturday Evening Post,* May 2, 1931. Short story.

"From a Graduate's Window," *Harvard Graduates,* June 1931.

"The Real Frontier: A Preface to Mark Twain," *Harper's,* June 1931. Reprinted with additions in *Mark Twain's America.*

"Summer's End," *Redbook,* September 1931. Short story.

"Prig's Progress," *Saturday Evening Post,* Sept. 12, 1931. Short story.

"From a Graduate's Window," *Harvard Graduates,* September 1931.

"The Matrix of Mark Twain's Humour," *The Bookman,* October 1931. Reprinted with additions in *Mark Twain's America.*

"From a Graduate's Window," *Harvard Graduates,* December 1931.

"The Dying Rose," *Saturday Evening Post,* Dec. 5, 1931. Short story.

"Mark Twain and the Genteel Tradition," *Harvard Graduates,* December 1931. Reprinted in *Mark Twain's America.*

Mark Twain's America. Boston: Little, Brown, 1932; New York: Chautauqua Institution, 1933; Boston: Houghton Mifflin, 1951.

Review of Clara Clemens, *My Father: Mark Twain, New England Quarterly,* January 1932.

"Accolade," *Saturday Evening Post,* Jan. 16, 1932. Short story.

"College Education for the Intelligent Few," *Current History,* March 1932. Original title: "A Dilemma of the Modern College."

"From a Graduate's Window," *Harvard Graduates,* March 1932.

Anonymous, "Grace before Teaching: A Letter to a Young Doctor of Literature," *Harvard Graduates,* March 1932. Reprinted in *Forays and Rebuttals.*

"New England: There She Stands," *Harper's,* March 1932. Reprinted in *Forays and Rebuttals.*

"In Re Mark Twain," *Saturday Review of Literature,* Apr. 2, 1932. Letter to the editor.

"In Barrasca," [sic] *Saturday Evening Post,* Apr. 23, 1932. Short story.

"From a Graduate's Window," *Harvard Graduates,* June 1932.

"Tom, Huck, and America," *Saturday Review of Literature,* Aug. 13, 1932. Reprinted in *Mark Twain's America.*

"The Second Act Curtain," *Saturday Evening Post,* Sept. 3, 1932. Short story.

"The Skeptical Biographer," *Harper's,* January 1933. Reprinted in *Forays and Rebuttals.*

"Sinclair Lewis," *Saturday Review of Literature,* Jan. 28, 1933. Reviews of Sinclair Lewis, *Ann Vickers;* and Carl Van Doren, *Sinclair Lewis.* Reprinted as "Ann Vickers by Sinclair Lewis" in *Forays and Rebuttals.*

"The Rocking Chair in History and Criticism," *Forum,* February 1933.

"American Life," *Saturday Review of Literature,* Mar. 4, 1933. Review of Arthur M. Schlesinger, *The Rise of the City.*

"The Home-Town Mind," *Saturday Evening Post,* Apr. 1, 1933. Short story.

"Bully Boy," *Saturday Review of Literature,* Apr. 8, 1933. Review of Walter Blair and Franklin J. Meine, *Mike Fink.*

"A Primer for Intellectuals," *Saturday Review of Literature,* Apr. 22, 1933.

"DeVoto and Pareto," *Saturday Review of Literature,* May 20, 1933. Letter to the editor.

"Mr. DeVoto Wins," *Saturday Review of Literature,* July 22, 1933. Letter to the editor.

"The Girl Who Saved Herself," *Collier's,* Aug. 26, 1933. Short story.

"Jonathan Dyer, Frontiersman: A Paragraph in the History of the West," *Harper's,* September 1933. Reprinted as "The Life of Jonathan Dyer, Frontiersman" in *Forays and Rebuttals.* [Reprinted in *Rocky Mountain Reader*, New York: Dutton, 1946, 60–76.]

"Pareto and Bassett Jones," *Saturday Review of Literature,* Sept. 2, 1933. Letter to the editor.

"Sentiment and the Social Order: Introduction to the Teachings of Pareto," *Harper's,* October 1933.

"Pareto and Fascism," *New Republic,* Oct. 11, 1933. Letter to the editor.

"The Faculty First," *Harvard Graduates,* December 1933.

"One Part Cheesecloth," *Saturday Evening Post,* Dec. 9, 1933. Short story.

We Accept With Pleasure. Boston: Little, Brown, 1934.

"Champion Preferred," *Collier's,* Jan. 6, 1934. Short story.

"How Not To Write History," *Harper's,* January 1934. Reprinted as "Thinking about America" in *Forays and Rebuttals.*

Review of James T. Adams, *Henry Adams, New England Quarterly,* March 1934.

"Choice of Weapons," *Collier's,* Apr. 14, 1934. Short story.

"Nature's Wise Plan," *Collier's,* May 5, 1934. Short story.

"Exiles from Reality," *Saturday Review of Literature,* June 2, 1934. Review of Malcolm Cowley, *Exile's Return.* Reprinted as "Exile's Return" in *Forays and Rebuttals.*

"Hail Hale," *Saturday Review of Literature,* June 30, 1934. Letter to the editor.

"The Bulfinch House," by John August, *Harper's,* July 1934. Short story. (Bernard DeVoto sometimes wrote under the *nom de plume* John August.) [Manuscript and/or typescript copy in the DeVoto Papers]

"Snapshots," by John August, *Harper's,* August 1934.

"The West: A Plundered Province," *Harper's,* August 1934. Reprinted as "The Plundered Province" in *Forays and Rebuttals.*

"The Obvious Thing," *Saturday Evening Post,* Sept. 29, 1934. Short story.

"There's Something about a Wedding," *Saturday Evening Post,* Oct. 27, 1934. Short story.

Review of Harry Hartwick, *The Foreground of American Fiction, New England Quarterly,* December 1934.

"Up from the Sextette," *Saturday Evening Post,* Dec. 1, 1934. Short story.

"Manhattan Jitters," *Redbook,* December 1934. Short story.

"The Second Proverb," *Liberty,* 1934. Short story.

"The Timid Profession," *Saturday Evening Post,* Feb. 9, 1935. Short story.

"She Had To Be Understood," *Collier's,* Mar. 9, 1935. Short story.

"Streamline Version of Harold Bell Wright," *Saturday Review of Literature,* Mar. 30, 1935. Review of Lloyd C. Douglas, *Green Light.* Reprinted as "Green Light" in *Forays and Rebuttals.*

"Fossil Remnants of the Frontier: Notes on a Utah Boyhood," *Harper's,* April 1935. Reprinted in *Forays and Rebuttals.*

"A Novel Hammered Out of Experience," *Saturday Review of Literature,* Apr. 27, 1935. Review of James Boyd, *Roll River.*

"Trust Company Child," *Collier's,* May 25, 1935. Short story.

"The Importance of Pareto," *Saturday Review of Literature,* May 25, 1935.

"Candlelight in Westover," *Saturday Evening Post,* July 6, 1935. Short story.

"It's My Town," *Collier's,* July 27, 1935. Short story.

Review of Fred L. Pattee, ed., *Mark Twain Selections, New England Quarterly,* September 1935.

"View from the Top," *Collier's,* Sept. 21, 1935. Short story.

"Classy Literature," *Saturday Review of Literature,* Oct. 5, 1935. Review of Joseph Freeman, ed., *Proletarian Literature in the United States.* Reprinted in *Forays and Rebuttals,* in chapter entitled "Proletarian Literature in the United States."

"Hemingway in the Valley," *Saturday Review of Literature,* Oct. 26, 1935. Review of Ernest Hemingway, *Green Hills of Africa.* Reprinted in *Forays and Rebuttals,* in chapter entitled "Green Hills of Africa."

"The Greatness of Mark Twain," *New York Times Book Review,* Oct. 27, 1935. Reviews of Albert B. Paine, ed., *Mark Twain's Notebook;* and Edward Wagenknecht, *Mark Twain: The Man and His Work.*

"Solidarity at Alexandria," The Easy Chair #1, *Harper's,* November 1935.

"A Violent, Fighting Pioneer," *Saturday Review of Literature,* Nov. 2, 1935. Review of Man Sandoz, *Old Jules.* Reprinted in *Forays and Rebuttals.*

"The Absolute in the Machine Shop," The Easy Chair #2, *Harper's,* December 1935. Reprinted in *Forays and Rebuttals.*

Forays and Rebuttals. Boston: Little, Brown, 1936.

"Memento for New Year's Day," The Easy Chair #3, *Harper's,* January 1936.

"Life Begins So Soon," *Collier's,* Feb. 1, 1936; Feb. 8, 1936; Feb. 15, 1936; Feb. 22, 1936; Feb. 29, 1936; Mar. 7, 1936; Mar. 14, 1936; Mar. 21, 1936; Mar. 28, 1936; Apr. 4, 1936. Serialized fiction. Unpublished in book form. [The DeVoto Stanford bound copy is entitled "Senior Spring."]

"The Folk Mind," The Easy Chair #4, *Harper's,* February 1936.

"Terwillinger in Plato's Dream," The Easy Chair #5, *Harper's,* March 1936.

"The Subject Races," *Cosmopolitan,* April 1936. Short story.

"Another Consociate Family," The Easy Chair #6, *Harper's,* April 1936. Reprinted in *Forays and Rebuttals.*

"Genius Is Not Enough," *Saturday Review of Literature,* Apr. 25, 1936. Review of Thomas Wolfe, *The Story of a Novel.* Reprinted in *Forays and Rebuttals.*

"The Consumer's Automobile," The Easy Chair #7, *Harper's,* May 1936.

"The Editor-elect," *Saturday Review of Literature,* May 30, 1936. Announcement of DeVoto's editorial policies.

"What the Next Hour Holds," The Easy Chair #8, *Harper's,* June 1936. Reprinted as "What the Next Hour May Bring Forth" in *Forays and Rebuttals.*

Review of Edward Wagenknecht, *Mark Twain: The Man and His Work, New England Quarterly,* June 1936.

"Mark Twain and the Limits of Criticism," *Forays and Rebuttals.* Paper read before the American Literature Section of the MLA, Jan. 1, 1936.

"On Beginning To Write a Novel," signed "Anonymous," *Harper's,* July 1936. [Identified as DeVoto's work in Mattingly, *Bernard DeVoto: A Preliminary Appraisal.*]

"Notes on the Red Parnassus," The Easy Chair #9, *Harper's,* July 1936.

"How To Live among the Vermonters," The Easy Chair #10, *Harper's,* August 1936.

"John Dos Passos: Anatomist of Our Time," *Saturday Review of Literature,* Aug. 8, 1936. Review of *The Big Money* and other works.

Review of Walter and Margaret Hard, *This Is Vermont, Saturday Review of Literature,* Aug. 22, 1936.

"A Puritan Tercentenary," The Easy Chair #11, *Harper's,* September 1936.

"A Generation beside the Limpopo," *Saturday Review of Literature,* Sept. 26, 1936. Reprinted in *Minority Report.*

"Prize Novels," *Saturday Review of Literature,* Sept. 26, 1936. Editorial.

"Reviewing Reviews," *Saturday Review of Literature,* Sept. 26, 1936.

"One Man's Guess," The Easy Chair #12, *Harper's,* October 1936.

"Civilization in the U.S.A.," *Saturday Review of Literature,* Oct. 3, 1936. Review of Gilbert Seldes, *Mainland.*

"The 42nd Parallel," *Saturday Review of Literature,* Oct. 3, 1936. Editorial.

"The Code Napoleon," *Saturday Review of Literature,* Oct. 10, 1936. Editorial.

"Crackerbox Commentator," *Saturday Review of Literature,* Oct. 10, 1936. Review of Westbrook Pegler, *'Taint Right.*

Review of Idwal Jones, *China Boy, Saturday Review of Literature,* Oct. 10, 1936.

"Reviewing Reviews," *Saturday Review of Literature,* Oct. 10, 1936.

"Horizon Land (1)," *Saturday Review of Literature,* Oct. 17, 1936. Editorial. Reprinted in *Minority Report,* in chapter entitled "Costume Piece."

"Beyond Studs Lonigan," *Saturday Review of Literature,* Oct. 24, 1936. Review of James T. Farrell, *A World I Never Made.*

"Eppur Si Muove," *Saturday Review of Literature,* Oct. 24, 1936. Editorial. Reprinted in *Minority Report,* in chapter entitled "Overlooking the Campus." (Printed as "Eppur Si Move.")

"Mirrors of Forty-fifth Street," *Saturday Review of Literature,* Oct. 24, 1936.

Review of T. J. Maloney, ed., *U.S. Camera, 1936, Saturday Review of Literature,* Oct. 31, 1936.

"Unemployed Writers," *Saturday Review of Literature,* Oct. 31, 1936. Editorial.

"Witchcraft in Mississippi," *Saturday Review of Literature,* Oct. 31, 1936. Review of William Faulkner, *Absalom, Absalom!* Reprinted in *Minority Report.*

"On Moving to New York," The Easy Chair #13, *Harper's,* November 1936. Reprinted in *Minority Report.*

"Stercoraceous Comment," *Saturday Review of Literature,* Nov. 7, 1936. Editorial. Reprinted in *Minority Report,* in chapter entitled, "Overlooking the Campus."

"Delphic Apollo in Illinois," *Saturday Review of Literature,* Nov. 14, 1936. Review of Edgar Lee Masters, *Across Spoon River.*

"Realism for Children," *Saturday Review of Literature,* Nov. 14, 1936. Editorial.

"Political Coda," *Saturday Review of Literature,* Nov. 14, 1936. Editorial.

"Minority Report," *Saturday Review of Literature,* Nov. 21, 1936. Reprinted as "Monte Cristo in Modern Dress" in *Minority Report.*

"The Reference Shelf," *Saturday Review of Literature,* Nov. 21, 1936. Editorial.

"Regionalism or the Coterie Manifesto," *Saturday Review of Literature,* Nov. 28, 1936. Editorial.

"Seed Corn and Mistletoe," The Easy Chair #14, *Harper's,* December 1936. Reprinted in *Minority Report.*

"Passage to India," *Saturday Review of Literature,* Dec. 5, 1936. Reprinted in *Minority Report.*

"Reviewing Reviews," *Saturday Review of Literature,* Dec. 5, 1936.

"Sir:" *Saturday Review of Literature,* Dec. 12, 1936. Editorial. Reprinted in *Minority Report,* in chapter entitled "On Notions."

"Vardis Fisher in Salt Lake City," *Saturday Review of Literature,* Dec. 12, 1936. Editorial.

"Reading for Pleasure," *Saturday Review of Literature,* Dec. 19, 1936. Editorial.

"The American Scholar," *Saturday Review of Literature,* Dec. 26, 1936. Editorial. Reprinted in *Minority Report,* in chapter entitled "Overlooking the Campus."

"Tyranny at Longfellow School," The Easy Chair #15, *Harper's,* January 1937.

"The Brahmin Way of Life," *Saturday Review of Literature,* Jan. 2, 1937. Review of John P. Marquand, *The Late George Apley.*

"A Hard Life," *Saturday Review of Literature,* Jan. 2, 1937. Editorial.

"Gargantua in Modern Dress," *Saturday Review of Literature,* Jan. 9, 1937. Review of Francois Rabelais translated by Jacques Le Clercq, *Gargantua and Pantagruel.*

"How To Be a Publisher (1)," *Saturday Review of Literature,* Jan. 9, 1937. Editorial.

"The Library Crisis," *Saturday Review of Literature,* Jan. 16, 1937. Editorial.

"Reviewing Reviews," *Saturday Review of Literature,* Jan. 16, 1937.

"Reviewing Reviews," *Saturday Review of Literature,* Jan. 30, 1937. Editorial.

"The Test of Time," *Saturday Review of Literature,* Jan. 30, 1937. Review of W. Somerset Maugham, *The Moon and Sixpence.*

"The Future of the Longfellow School," The Easy Chair #16, *Harper's,* February 1937.

"The Specialist," *Saturday Review of Literature,* Feb. 6, 1937. Editorial. Reprinted in *Minority Report,* in chapter entitled "On Notions."

"My Dear Edmund Wilson," *Saturday Review of Literature,* Feb. 13, 1937. Editorial. Expanded as "Autobiography: or, As Some Call It, Literary Criticism," in *Minority Report.*

"About-face of Mr. Stearns," *Saturday Review of Literature,* Feb. 20, 1937. Editorial. Reprinted in *Minority Report,* in chapter entitled "Back Eddies."

"Magistrate Curran's Opinion," *Saturday Review of Literature,* Feb. 20, 1937. Editorial.

"The First WPA Guide," *Saturday Review of Literature,* Feb. 27, 1937. Editorial.

"Distempers of the Press," The Easy Chair #17, *Harper's,* March 1937. Reprinted in *Minority Report.*

"The Bonnie Blue Flag," *Saturday Review of Literature,* Mar. 6, 1937. Editorial. Reprinted in *Minority Report,* in chapter entitled "Costume Piece."

"Don't Miss Old Faithful," *Saturday Review of Literature,* Mar. 6, 1937. Editorial.

"Master of Two Dimensions," *Saturday Review of Literature,* Mar. 6, 1937. Review of W. Somerset Maugham, *Theatre.*

"Reviewing Reviews," *Saturday Review of Literature,* Mar. 6, 1937.

"The Pulitzer Prize in History," *Saturday Review of Literature,* Mar. 13, 1937.

"'William Dean Howells," *Saturday Review of Literature,* Mar. 13, 1937. Editorial.

"Amateur History," *Saturday Review of Literature,* Mar. 20, 1937. Editorial.

"The Chosen People," *Saturday Review of Literature,* Mar. 20, 1937. Review of Pierrepont B. Noyes, *My Father's House.*

"Agitated Ladies," *Saturday Review of Literature,* Mar. 27, 1937. Editorial.

"Author and Publisher," *Saturday Review of Literature,* Mar. 27, 1937.

"Perils of Pauline," *Saturday Review of Literature,* Mar. 27, 1937. Editorial. Reprinted in *Minority Report,* in chapter entitled "On Notions."

"Soliloquy in Arizona," *Saturday Review of Literature,* Mar. 27, 1937. Review of J. B. Priestley, *Midwest on the Desert: Excursion into Autobiography.*

"Not a Personal Essay," The Easy Chair #18, *Harper's,* April 1937.

"At the Cannon's Mouth," *Saturday Review of Literature,* Apr. 3, 1937. Editorial. Reprinted in *Minority Report,* in chapter entitled "Back Eddies."

"In Pursuit of an Idea," *Saturday Review of Literature,* Apr. 3, 1937. Review of Josephine Johnson, *Jordanstown.*

"Reviewing Reviews," *Saturday Review of Literature,* Apr. 3, 1937.

"Enlightened Research," *Saturday Review of Literature,* Apr. 10, 1937. Editorial.

"Reviewing Reviews," *Saturday Review of Literature,* Apr. 17, 1937.

"The Modern Keyhole," *Saturday Review of Literature,* Apr. 17, 1937. Editorial. Reprinted in *Minority Report,* in chapter entitled "Back Eddies."

"Horizon Land (2)," *Saturday Review of Literature,* Apr. 24, 1937. Editorial. Reprinted as "Continental Divide" in *Minority Report.*

"'Liberal' Equals N^{nx}," The Easy Chair #19, *Harper's,* May 1937. Reprinted in *Minority Report.*

"Germany in the Vortex," *Saturday Review of Literature,* May 1, 1937. Review of Erich Maria Remarque, *Three Comrades.*

"Nymph," *Saturday Review of Literature,* May 8, 1937. Editorial. Reprinted in *Minority Report,* in chapter entitled "On Notions."

"The Pulitzer Prize Winners," *Saturday Review of Literature,* May 8, 1937.

"Proposal to Contributors, Proposal to Publishers, Proposal to a Pulitzer Committee," *Saturday Review of Literature,* May 15, 1937. Editorial.

Review of James T. Farrell, *Can All This Grandeur Perish?,* *Saturday Review of Literature,* May 22, 1937.

"The Writer's Congress," *Saturday Review of Literature,* May 22, 1937. Editorial. Reprinted in *Minority Report,* in chapter entitled "Crackle on the Left."

"Always Different, Always the Same," *Saturday Review of Literature,* May 29, 1937. Reviews of Burton Rascoe, *Before I Forget;* and Malcolm Cowley, ed., *After the Genteel Tradition.* Reprinted as "Plus Ce Change" in *Minority Report.*

"Reviewing Reviews," *Saturday Review of Literature,* May 29, 1937.

"The Frustrated Censor," The Easy Chair #20, *Harper's,* June 1937.

"Invitation to the Waltz," *Saturday Review of Literature,* June 5, 1937. Editorial. Reprinted in *Minority Report,* in chapter entitled "Crackle on the Left."

"Rhapsody in Green," *Saturday Review of Literature,* June 5, 1937. Reviews of Charles Edward Crane, *Let Me Show You Vermont;* Frederick F. Van de Water, *A Home in the Country;* and Vrest Orton Weston, *And So Goes Vermont.*

"A Date for Thursday," by John August, *Collier's,* June 12, 1937. Short story. Original title, "An Hour on Sunday."

"Opportunities," *Saturday Review of Literature,* June 19, 1937. Editorial.

"Reviewing Reviews," *Saturday Review of Literature,* June 19, 1937.

"English '37," *Saturday Review of Literature,* June 26, 1937; July 3, 1937; July 10, 1937; July 17, 1937; July 24, 1937; July 31, 1937; Aug. 7, 1937; Aug. 14, 1937; Aug. 21, 1937; Aug. 28, 1937; Sept. 4, 1937. Subtitled "The Novelist and the Reader." This material is used as the basis of chapters VII through XI in *The World of Fiction.* Each installment printed on editorial page.

"The Cestus of Hygiea," The Easy Chair #21, *Harper's,* July 1937.

Review of Kenneth Roberts, *Northwest Passage, Saturday Review of Literature,* July 3, 1937.

"Reviewing Reviews," *Saturday Review of Literature,* July 17, 1937.

"Gettysburg," The Easy Chair #22, *Harper's,* August 1937. Reprinted in *Minority Report.*

"Reviewing Reviews," *Saturday Review of Literature,* Aug. 14, 1937.

"Page from a Primer," The Easy Chair #23, *Harper's,* September 1937. Reprinted in *Minority Report.*

"Reviewing Reviews," *Saturday Review of Literature,* Sept. 18, 1937.

"The Lineage of Eustace Tilley," *Saturday Review of Literature,* Sept. 25, 1937. Review of Walter Blair, ed., *Native American Humor, 1800–1900.*

"What of the Night?" *Saturday Review of Literature,* Sept. 25, 1937. Editorial. Reprinted in *Minority Report,* in chapter entitled "On Notions."

"The WPA Guides," *Saturday Review of Literature,* Sept. 25, 1937. Editorial.

"Desertion from the New Deal," The Easy Chair #24, *Harper's,* October 1937.

"A Sagebrush Bookshelf," *Harper's,* October 1937.

"Death of the Sentence," *Saturday Review of Literature,* Oct. 2, 1937. Editorial. Reprinted in *Minority Report,* in chapter entitled "Rule or Ruin."

"Grammarian's Funeral," *Saturday Review of Literature,* Oct. 9, 1937. Editorial. Reprinted in *Minority Report,* in chapter entitled "Rule or Ruin."

"Reviewing Reviews," *Saturday Review of Literature,* Oct. 9, 1937.

"Writing for Money," *Saturday Review of Literature,* Oct. 9, 1937. Reprinted in *Minority Report.*

"Tiger, Tiger!" *Saturday Review of Literature,* Oct. 16, 1937. Editorial. Reprinted in *Minority Report,* in chapter entitled "Lycanthropy."

"Rats, Lice, and Poetry," *Saturday Review of Literature,* Oct. 23, 1937. Editorial. Reprinted in *Minority Report,* in chapter entitled "Lycanthropy."

"The Logic of Sentiment," *Saturday Review of Literature,* Oct. 30, 1937. Editorial. Reprinted in *Minority Report,* in chapter entitled "On Notions."

"The Liberation of Spring City," The Easy Chair #25, *Harper's,* November 1937. Reprinted in *Minority Report.*

"Writing American History," *Saturday Review of Literature,* Nov. 6, 1937. Editorial.

"Books and Cameras," *Saturday Review of Literature,* Nov. 6, 1937. Editorial.

"Pseudo," *Saturday Review of Literature,* Nov. 6, 1937. Editorial.

"Dictionaries for Children," *Saturday Review of Literature,* Nov. 13, 1937. Editorial.

"Mene, Mene," *Saturday Review of Literature,* Nov. 20, 1937. Editorial.

"Our Dried Voices," *Saturday Review of Literature,* Nov. 27, 1937. Editorial. Reprinted in *Minority Report,* in chapter entitled "Back Eddies."

"Five-Cent Christmas Card," The Easy Chair #26, *Harper's,* December 1937.

"Christmas Tonic," *Saturday Review of Literature,* Dec. 4, 1937. Editorial.

"Reviewing Reviews," *Saturday Review of Literature,* Dec. 4, 1937.

"The Faculty Style," *Saturday Review of Literature,* Dec. 18, 1937. Editorial. Reprinted in *Minority Report,* in chapter entitled "Overlooking the Campus."

"Fiction Fights the Civil War," *Saturday Review of Literature,* Dec. 18, 1937.

"Great Circle," *Saturday Review of Literature,* Dec. 25, 1937. Editorial. Reprinted in *Minority Report,* in chapter entitled "On Notions."

"Good and Wicked Words," The Easy Chair #27, *Harper's,* January 1938. Reprinted in *Minority Report.*

"Ace in the Hole," *Saturday Review of Literature,* Jan. 1, 1938. Editorial.

"The Critics and Robert Frost," *Saturday Review of Literature,* Jan. 1, 1938. Review of Richard Thornton, ed., *Recognition of Robert Frost.*

"Shallow Waters," *Saturday Review of Literature,* Jan. 8, 1938. Editorial.

"Report on Photography," *Saturday Review of Literature,* Jan. 15, 1938. Editorial.

"The Test of Time," *Saturday Review of Literature,* Jan. 22, 1938. Editorial. Reprinted in *Minority Report,* in chapter entitled "Back Eddies."

"C-Plus Fiction," *Saturday Review of Literature,* Jan. 29, 1938. Editorial.

"Friday Afternoon at Country Day," The Easy Chair #28, *Harper's,* February 1938. Reprinted in *Minority Report.*

"The Second Step," *Saturday Review of Literature,* Feb. 5, 1938. Editorial.

"Romans à Clef," *Saturday Review of Literature,* Feb. 12, 1938; Feb. 19, 1938; Mar. 5, 1938. Reprinted on editorial page.

"Faulkner's South," *Saturday Review of Literature,* Feb. 19, 1938. Review of William Faulkner, *The Unvanquished.*

"Fiction Drowned in Talk," *Saturday Review of Literature,* Feb. 26, 1938. Review of Aline Bernstein, *The Journey Down.*

"Those Who Can Write," *Saturday Review of Literature,* Feb. 26, 1938. Editorial.

"The Game and the Candle," The Easy Chair #29, *Harper's,* March 1938.

"Mark Twain: A Caricature," *Saturday Review of Literature,* Mar. 19, 1938. Review of Edgar Lee Masters, *Mark Twain: A Portrait.*

"U.S. One," *Saturday Review of Literature,* Mar. 19, 1938. Editorial.

"A Demurrer," *The Middlebury College News Letter,* March 1938. Speech in acceptance of Honorary Litt. D. in 1937.

"Notes on Centennial," The Easy Chair #30, *Harper's,* April 1938.

"Reminiscence," *Saturday Review of Literature,* Apr. 2, 1938. Editorial.

"The River," *Saturday Review of Literature,* Apr. 9, 1938. Editorial.

"Sweet English," *Saturday Review of Literature,* Apr. 9, 1938. Letter to the editor.

"Notes on the American Way," The Easy Chair #31, *Harper's,* May 1938.

"New England Via W.P.A.," *Saturday Review of Literature*, May 14, 1938.

"The Fallacy of Excess Interpretation," The Easy Chair #32, *Harper's*, June 1938. Reprinted in *Minority Report*.

"Fiction and the Everlasting If: Notes on the Contemporary Historical Novel," *Harper's*, June 1938.

"The Day We Celebrate," The Easy Chair #33, *Harper's*, July 1938.

"On Moving from New York," The Easy Chair #34, *Harper's*, August 1938. Reprinted in *Reader's Digest*, November 1938. Reprinted in *Minority Report*.

"Letters from America," The Easy Chair #35, *Harper's*, September 1938.

"Vacation," The Easy Chair #36, *Harper's*, October 1938.

"DeVoto to Edit Mark Twain Papers," *Saturday Review of Literature*, Oct. 15, 1938. Letter to the editor.

"Snow White and the Seven Dreads," The Easy Chair #38, *Harper's*, December 1938. Reprinted in *Minority Report*.

"The Mark Twain Papers," *Saturday Review of Literature*, Dec. 10, 1938.

"Mark Twain Papers," *Saturday Review of Literature*, Dec. 10, 1938. Letter to the editor.

Troubled Star, by John August. Boston: Little, Brown, 1939.

"From Dream to Fiction," The Easy Chair #39, *Harper's*, Jan. 1939. Reprinted in *Minority Report* and *The World of Fiction*.

"Hoop Skirts and Buena Vista," The Easy Chair #40, *Harper's*, February 1939.

"Wisdom Lingers," The Easy Chair #41, *Harper's*, March 1939. Reprinted in *Minority Report*.

Review of Cyril Clemens, *My Cousin Mark Twain*, in *Saturday Review of Literature*, Mar. 11, 1939.

"Home Thoughts from Vermont," *Pan*, March 1939. The *Pan* was published in protest to the censorship of the *Pen* by University of Utah authorities. It was published off-campus and issued from a café near the campus.

Review of James Boyd, *Bitter Creek*, *Saturday Review of Literature*, Mar. 18, 1939.

"The Paring Knife at the Crossroads," The Easy Chair #42, *Harper's*, April 1939.

"G. and S. Preferred," The Easy Chair #43, *Harper's*, May 1939.

"Mark Twain about the Jews," *Jewish Frontier,* May 1939. Reprinted in *Jewish Frontier Anthology, 1934-1944.* New York: Jewish Frontier Association, 1945.

"What's the Matter with History?" The Easy Chair #44, *Harper's,* June 1939.

Review of Thomas D. Clark, *The Rampaging Frontier, New York Times Book Review,* June 25, 1939.

"Aftermath of a Cocktail Party," *New Republic,* June 28, 1939. Letter to the editor.

"Unrest in the Kitchen," The Easy Chair #45, *Harper's,* July 1939.

"Thou and the Camel," *Cosmopolitan,* July 1939. Short story.

"The Terror," The Easy Chair #46, *Harper's,* August 1939. Reprinted in *Minority Report.*

"Millennial Millions," *Saturday Review of Literature,* Aug. 26, 1939. Review of Vardis Fisher, *Children of God.*

"Doom Beyond Jupiter," The Easy Chair #47, *Harper's,* September 1939.

"Meditation in Fading Sunlight," The Easy Chair #48, *Harper's,* October 1939. Reprinted in *Minority Report.*

"Freud's Influence on Literature," *Saturday Review of Literature,* Oct. 7, 1939.

"The Sound of Silk," by John August, *Collier's,* Oct. 21, 1939. Short Story.

"The Oncoming," The Easy Chair #49, *Harper's,* November 1939. Reprinted in *Minority Report.*

"Widower's House," *Saturday Review of Literature,* Nov. 4, 1939. Review of Havelock Ellis, *My Life.* Reprinted in *Minority Report.*

"Luke II, I," The Easy Chair #50, *Harper's,* December 1939.

Rain Before Seven, by John August. Boston: Little, Brown, 1940.

Minority Report. Boston: Little, Brown, 1940.

"American Novels: 1939," *Atlantic,* January 1940.

"The Threshold of Fiction," The Easy Chair #51, *Harper's,* January 1940. Used in *The World of Fiction.*

"Father Abraham," The Easy Chair #52, *Harper's,* February 1940.

"Anabasis in Buckskin," *Harper's,* March 1940.

"The Engulfed Cathedral," The Easy Chair #53, *Harper's,* March 1940.

"Freud in American Literature," *Psychoanalytic Quarterly*, April 1940.

"Maternity Floor," The Easy Chair #54, *Harper's*, April 1940. Reprinted in *Reader's Digest*, May 1940.

"Remember the Pink Lady?" The Easy Chair #55, *Harper's*, May 1940.

"Nineteenth Anniversary," Easy Chair #56, *Harper's*, June 1940.

"Position Maintained," Easy Chair #57, *Harper's*, July 1940. Reprinted as "Preface Continued," in *Minority Report*.

"Letter from Santa Fe," The Easy Chair #58, *Harper's*, August 1940.

"Notes from a Wayside Inn," The Easy Chair #59, *Harper's*, September 1940.

"Road Test," Easy Chair #60, *Harper's*, October 1940.

"All Quiet Along the Huron," The Easy Chair #61, *Harper's*, November 1940.

"Main Street Twenty Years After," *Harper's*, November 1940. Reprinted in *Reader's Digest*, December 1940.

"To Our New Prophets," The Easy Chair #62, *Harper's*, December 1940.

Review of Franklin Walker and G. Ezra Dane, eds., *Mark Twain Travels with Mr. Brown*, *The New York Herald Tribune Weekly Book Review*, Dec. 29, 1940.

"The Mugwump on November 6th," The Easy Chair #63, *Harper's*, January 1941.

"Holidays, 1940," The Easy Chair #64, *Harper's*, February 1941.

"Easy Steps for Little Feet," The Easy Chair #65, *Harper's*, March 1941.

"Manifest Destiny," The Easy Chair #66, *Harper's*, April 1941.

"Mark Twain vs. Winston Churchill," *Reader's Digest*, April 1941. Reprinted from *Mark Twain in Eruption*.

"What to Tell the Young," The Easy Chair #67, *Harper's*, May 1941.

Review of Clifford Dowdey, *Sing for a Penny*, *The New York Herald Tribune Weekly Book Review*, May 11, 1941.

"For the Boys of '41," *Woman's Day*, June 1941.

"Stephen Foster's Songs," The Easy Chair #68, *Harper's*, June 1941. Revised and included in *The Year of Decision*.

"The Image of Napoleon," The Easy Chair #69, *Harper's*, July 1941.

"Touring New England," *Harper's,* July 1941.

"Either—Or," The Easy Chair #70, *Harper's,* August 1941.

Review of Thomas Beer, *Hanna Crane* and *The Mauve Decade,* *The New York Herald Tribune Weekly Book Review,* Aug. 24, 1941.

"Under Which King, Bezonian?" The Easy Chair #71, *Harper's,* September 1941.

"Information Please," *Saturday Review of Literature,* Sept. 27, 1941. Letter to the editor.

"Portico with Images," The Easy Chair #72, *Harper's,* October 1941.

"Report on the Summer Quartet," The Easy Chair #73, *Harper's,* November 1941.

"Lee Foster Hartman," The Easy Chair #74, *Harper's,* December 1941. Reprinted in memorial volume: *Lee Foster Hartman, Editor of Harper's Magazine, 1931–1941, Harper's,* 1941.

Mark Twain At Work. Cambridge: Harvard University Press, 1942.

Advance Agent, by John August. Boston: Little, Brown, 1942.

"The Writer's Project," The Easy Chair #75, *Harper's,* January 1942.

"The Lord Helps Those ...," *Reader's Digest,* January 1942. Reprinted from *Mark Twain in Eruption.*

"Lecture to a Woman's Club," The Easy Chair #76, *Harper's,* February 1942.

"The Civilian Outpost," The Easy Chair #77, *Harper's,* March 1942.

"Toward Chancellorsville," The Easy Chair #78, *Harper's,* April 1942.

"Lincoln to the 164th Ohio," The Easy Chair #79, *Harper's,* May 1942.

"Sedition's General Staff," The Easy Chair #80, *Harper's,* June 1942.

"B. DeV. Also," *Saturday Review of Literature,* June 13, 1942. Letter to the editor.

"Commencement Address," The Easy Chair #81, *Harper's,* July 1942.

"The Year of Decision," *Atlantic,* July 1942; August 1942; September 1942; October 1942; November 1942.

"Give It to Us Straight," The Easy Chair #82, *Harper's,* August 1942.

"Triangular Bandages Go on Babies," The Easy Chair #83, *Harper's,* September 1942.

Review of Richard G. Lillard, *Desert Challenge, The New York Herald Tribune Weekly Book Review,* Sept. 20, 1942.

"Dead Center," The Easy Chair #84, *Harper's,* October 1942.

"The Confederate Military System," *Saturday Review of Literature,* Oct. 24, 1942. Review of Douglas Southall Freeman, *Lee's Lieutenants,* vol. 1.

"Wanted: More News!" The Easy Chair #85, *Harper's,* November 1942.

"Wait a Minute, Dorothy," The Easy Chair #86, *Harper's,* December 1942.

"War Is the Life I Live," *Woman's Day,* December 1942.

The Year of Decision. Boston: Little, Brown, 1943.

The Easy Chair #87, *Harper's,* January 1943. Entitled in DeVoto's hand in his bound copy "A Psychiatrist on War." (The next eighty "Easy Chairs" rarely have titles. When DeVoto has titled them in his own copy it has been noted. At times *Harper's* supplied titles on the cover or in the index and they have also been noted for reference.)

"Parkman's Early Diaries," *Saturday Review of Literature,* Jan. 16, 1943. Letter to the editor.

The Easy Chair #88, *Harper's,* February 1943. Entitled in DeVoto's hand in his bound copy "To Be Filed, Probably."

The Easy Chair #89, *Harper's,* March 1943. Entitled in DeVoto's hand in his copy "Writers and the War."

"The End in View," *Woman's Day,* March 1943.

"An Exciting Batch of Assorted Prejudices," *The New York Herald Tribune Weekly Book Review,* March 14, 1943. Review of Rose Wilder Lane, *The Discovery of Freedom.*

The Easy Chair #90, *Harper's,* April 1943. Entitled in DeVoto's hand in his copy, "The Worst Mistake."

The Easy Chair #91, *Harper's,* May 1943. Entitled in DeVoto's hand in his own copy, "Distress under the Elms."

"Mr. Freeman's Continuing Study," *Saturday Review of Literature,* May 29, 1943. Review of Douglas Southall Freeman, *Lee's Lieutenants,* vol. 2.

The Easy Chair #92, *Harper's,* June 1943. Identified on *Harper's* cover as "The Egypt of the West."

"Seed Time of the New World," *The New York Herald Tribune Weekly Book Review,* June 27, 1943. Review of Stephen Vincent Benét, *Western Star.*

The Easy Chair #93, *Harper's,* July 1943.

The Easy Chair #94, *Harper's,* August 1943.

The Easy Chair #95, *Harper's,* September 1943.

The Easy Chair #96, *Harper's,* October 1943.

"A Natural History of Politics," *New York Herald Tribune Weekly Book Review,* Oct. 17, 1943. Review of Wilfred E. Binkley, *American Political Parties.*

The Easy Chair #97, *Harper's,* November 1943.

"Go Ahead and Holler," *Reader's Digest,* November 1943.

The Easy Chair #98, *Harper's,* December 1943.

The Literary Fallacy. Boston: Little, Brown, 1944.

The Woman in the Picture, by John August. Boston: Little, Brown, 1944.

The Easy Chair #99, *Harper's,* January 1944. Identified in *Harper's* index as "Mr. and Mrs. Charles A. Lindbergh."

The Easy Chair #100, *Harper's,* February 1944.

The Easy Chair #101, *Harper's,* March 1944.

"Geopolitics with the Dew on It," *Harper's,* March 1944.

The Easy Chair #102, *Harper's,* April 1944.

"They Turned Their Backs on America," *Saturday Review of Literature,* Apr. 8, 1944. Reprinted in *The Literary Fallacy* as part of the concluding chapter, and in *The Saturday Review Treasury* under the title "The Great Feud," New York: Simon & Schuster, 1957.

"First of the Great Lakes To Be 'Discovered,'" *New York Herald Tribune Weekly Book Review,* Apr. 9, 1944. Review of Fred Landon, *Lake Huron.*

The Easy Chair #103, *Harper's,* May 1944.

"Older Than God," *Woman's Day,* June 1944. Reprinted in the *Chicago Daily News,* July 12, 1944.

The Easy Chair #104, *Harper's,* June 1944.

The Easy Chair #105, *Harper's,* July 1944.

The Easy Chair #106, *Harper's,* August 1944.

"The Maturity of American Literature," *Saturday Review of Literature*, Aug. 5, 1944.

The Easy Chair #107, *Harper's*, September 1944.

"On 'The Road Back' Following Three Wars," *New York Herald Tribune Weekly Book Review*, Sept. 17, 1944. Review of Dixon Wecter, *When Johnnie Comes Marching Home*.

"The Falsity of Geopolitics in an Air Age," *New York Herald Tribune Weekly Book Review*, Sept. 24, 1944. Review of Hans W. Weigert and Vilhjalmur Stefansson, eds., *Compass of the World*.

"Let's Not Play College Again," *Woman's Day*, October 1944.

The Easy Chair #108, *Harper's*, October 1944.

"Short Course in American History," *Good Housekeeping*, October 1944.

The Easy Chair #109, *Harper's*, November 1944.

The Easy Chair #110, *Harper's*, December 1944.

The Easy Chair #111, *Harper's*, January 1945.

"How Do *You* Feel about Compulsory Military Training?" *Woman's Day*, February 1945.

The Easy Chair #112, *Harper's*, February 1945.

The Easy Chair #113, *Harper's*, March 1945.

The Easy Chair #114, *Harper's*, April 1945.

The Easy Chair #115, *Harper's*, May 1945.

The Easy Chair #116, *Harper's*, June 1945.

"Mr. DeVoto Explains As to Use of the Name, Mark Twain," *The Twainian*, June 1945. Letter to the editor.

The Easy Chair #117, *Harper's*, July 1945. Reprinted as "On a Note of Triumph," in *The Easy Chair.*

"Well, How Neurotic Are You?" *Woman's Day*, July 1945.

The Easy Chair #118, *Harper's*, August 1945.

"The Great Story of Plymouth Plantation," *New York Herald Tribune Weekly Book Review*, Aug. 5, 1945. Review of George F. Willson, *Saints and Strangers*.

"Yarbs and Doctor Stuff," *New York Herald Tribune Weekly Book Review*, Aug. 12, 1945. Review of Madge E. Pickard and R. Carlyle Buley, *The Mid-west Pioneer*.

The Easy Chair #119, *Harper's*, September 1945.

"When Social History Becomes Literature," *New York Herald Tribune Weekly Book Review*, Sept. 16, 1945. Review of Arthur M. Schlesinger, Jr., *The Age of Jackson*.

The Easy Chair #120, *Harper's,* October 1945.

"America's West and Mid-West in Literature," *New York Herald Tribune Weekly Book Review,* Oct. 14, 1945. Reviews of three anthologies.

"The Rare and Exciting Exercise of Thinking," *New York Herald Tribune Weekly Book Review,* Oct. 21, 1945. Review of Charles P. Curtis, Jr., and Ferris Greenslet, eds., *The Practical Cogitator.*

Review of Walker D. Wyman, *The Wild Horse of the West, American Historical Review,* October 1945.

"Barker Up the Wrong Tree?" *Harper's,* November 1945. In the "Personal & Otherwise" column.

The Easy Chair #121, *Harper's,* November 1945.

"A Reactionary Decision," *Author's League Bulletin,* November 1945.

"A Revaluation," *Rocky Mountain Review,* Autumn 1945.

The Easy Chair #122, *Harper's,* December 1945.

"The Case of the Prophet, Joseph Smith," *New York Herald Tribune Weekly Book Review,* Dec. 16, 1945. Review of Fawn M. Brodie, *No Man Knows My History, The Life of Joseph Smith.*

"The Flapper's Revolution," *Woman's Day,* January 1946.

The Easy Chair #123, *Harper's,* January 1946.

"Yankee Seafarer, Companion of Capt. Cook," *New York Herald Tribune Weekly Book Review,* Jan. 13, 1946. Review of Helen Augur, *Passage to Glory.*

Review of Henry Miller, *The Air Conditioned Nightmare, New York Herald Tribune Weekly Book Review,* Jan. 27, 1946.

The Easy Chair #124, *Harper's,* February 1946. Reprinted as "The War of Rebellion," in *The Easy Chair.*

"Mark Twain's 'Letter from the Recording Angel,'" *Harper's,* February 1946. Introduction to the story.

"Mountain Time," *Collier's,* Feb. 2, 1946; Feb. 9, 1946; Feb. 16, 1946; Feb. 23, 1946; Mar. 2, 1946.

"The Other Side of Some Mark Twain Stories," *New York Herald Tribune Weekly Book Review,* Feb. 10, 1946. Review of Samuel Charles Webster, ed., *Mark Twain, Business Man.*

The Easy Chair #125, *Harper's,* March 1946. Reprinted as "The Confederate Anachronism," in *The Easy Chair.*

"A Revaluation," *Improvement Era,* March 1946. This is a reprint of "A Revaluation," printed in *Rocky Mountain Review,* Autumn 1945.

"Hot Seat," *Harper's,* April 1946. In the "Personal & Otherwise" column.

The Easy Chair #126, *Harper's,* April 1946.

The Easy Chair #127, *Harper's,* May 1946.

"An Englishman Accomplishes the Impossible," *New York Herald Tribune Weekly Book Review,* May 12, 1946. Review of Graham Hutton, *Midwest at Noon.*

The Easy Chair #128, *Harper's,* June 1946.

"The Decision in the *Strange Fruit* Case: The Obscenity Statute in Massachusetts," *New England Quarterly,* June 1946.

"When the Goths Took Harvard," *New York Herald Tribune Weekly Book Review,* June 30, 1946. Review of Helen Howe, *We Happy Few.*

The Easy Chair #129, *Harper's,* July 1946.

The Easy Chair #130, *Harper's,* August 1946.

"Fenimore Cooper's Further Literary Offenses," *New England Quarterly,* September 1946. DeVoto introduces the first publication of this Mark Twain manuscript.

The Easy Chair #131, *Harper's,* September 1946.

The Easy Chair #132, *Harper's,* October 1946.

"A Great Explorer of the West," *New York Herald Tribune Weekly Book Review,* Oct. 6, 1946. Review of Stanly Vestal, *Jim Bridger: Mountain Man.*

"Wake Up and Meet These Great Americans," *New York Herald Tribune Weekly Book Review,* Oct. 27, 1946. Review of Stewart H. Holbrook, *Lost Men of American History.*

The Easy Chair #133, *Harper's,* November 1946.

"Westward—The Passion of Three Centuries," *New York Herald Tribune Weekly Book Review,* Nov. 10, 1946. Review of Jeannette Mirsky, *The Westward Crossings.*

"The Nebraska Heart of Boston," *New York Herald Tribune Weekly Book Review,* Nov. 24, 1946. Review of Frances W. Dahl and Charles W. Morton, *Dahl's Boston.*

"The Anxious West," *Harper's,* December 1946.

The Easy Chair #134, *Harper's,* December 1946.

"The Trail That Blazed America's Way West," *New York Herald Tribune Weekly Book Review,* Dec. 15, 1946. Review of the editors of *Look, The Santa Fe Trail.*

"The Glamour of Montana in Its Past and Present," *New York Herald Tribune Weekly Book Review,* Dec. 22, 1946. Review of Joseph Kinsey Howard, ed., *Montana Margins.*

Across the Wide Missouri. Boston: Houghton Mifflin, 1947.

Mountain Time. Boston: Little, Brown, 1947.

The Easy Chair #135, *Harper's,* January 1947.

"The West Against Itself," *Harper's,* January 1947. Reprinted in *The Easy Chair.*

The Easy Chair #136, *Harper's,* February 1947.

"John Steinbeck's Bus Ride into the Hills," *New York Herald Tribune Weekly Book Review,* Feb. 16, 1947. Review of John Steinbeck, *The Wayward Bus.*

The Easy Chair #137, *Harper's,* March 1947.

The Easy Chair #138, *Harper's,* April 1947. Reprinted in *Reader's Digest,* July 1947.

"The Great American Desert of Salt Water," *New York Herald Tribune Weekly Book Review,* Apr. 20, 1947. Review of Dale L. Morgan, *The Great Salt Lake.*

The Easy Chair #139, *Harper's,* May 1947.

Review of Townsend Scudder, *Concord: An American Town, America in Books,* May 1947.

Review of Clifford Dowdy, *Experiment in Rebellion, America in Books* (History Book Club), May 1947.

"Writing for Money," *The Writer,* May 1947.

"Marco Polo's Ford," *Woman's Day,* May 1947.

"Queen City of the Plains and Peaks," *Pacific Spectator,* Spring 1947.

"Historian on Tour," *Woman's Day,* June 1947.

"The National Parks," *Fortune,* June 1947.

The Easy Chair #140, *Harper's,* June 1947.

"Club's First Dividend 'The Stuff of Enchantment,'" *America in Books,* June 1947.

The Easy Chair #141, *Harper's,* July 1947.

"Club's Dividend for August Called 'The Stuff of Enchantment,'" *America in Books,* July 1947.

"Roadside Meeting," *Woman's Day,* July 1947.

The Easy Chair #142, *Harper's,* August 1947.

"A Hank of Tall Yarns, Folklore and Fantasy," *New York Herald Tribune Weekly Book Review,* Aug. 24, 1947. Review of Ben C. Clough, ed., *The American Imagination at Work.*

"S.R.L. Founder," *Saturday Review of Books,* Aug. 30, 1947. Review of Henry Seidel Canby, *American Memoir.*

"Doctors along the Boardwalk," *Harper's,* September 1947. Reprinted in *The Easy Chair.*

The Easy Chair #143, *Harper's.* September 1947.

"Adventurer Too Soon," *Pacific Spectator,* Autumn 1947. Publication of chapter 10 of *Across the Wide Missouri.*

The Easy Chair #144, *Harper's,* October 1947.

"Our Unpremeditated War with Mexico," *New York Herald Tribune Weekly Book Review,* Oct. 26, 1947. Review of Alfred Hoyt Bill, *Rehearsal for Conflict.*

Review of Clarence D. Jackson, *Picture Maker of the Old West, America in Books,* October 1947.

Review of A. R. M. Lower, *Colony to Nation, America in Books,* October 1947.

The Easy Chair #145, *Harper's,* November 1947.

"Those Two Immortal Boys," *Woman's Day,* November 1947.

"Club Dividend for December Called 'Riotously Funny, Irresistible,'" *America in Books,* November 1947.

Review of Robert Kinkaid, *The Wilderness Road, America in Books,* November 1947.

The Easy Chair #146, *Harper's,* December 1947.

"Explorers Who Brought In the Northwest," *New York Herald Tribune Weekly Book Review,* December 21, 1947. Review of John Bakeless, *Lewis and Clark.*

"Editorially Speaking," *America in Books,* December 1947.

The Easy Chair #147, *Harper's,* January 1948.

"Editorially Speaking," *America in Books,* January 1948.

"I Had the Funniest Dream Last Night," *Woman's Day,* February 1948.

The Easy Chair #148, *Harper's,* February 1948.

"Editorially Speaking," *America in Books,* February 1948.

Review of Paul Wellman, *Death on Horseback, America in Books,* February 1948.

The Easy Chair, #149, *Harper's,* March 1948. Reprinted in *The Hour.*

"Talking Point," *Reader's Digest,* March 1948.

"Editorially Speaking," *America in Books,* March 1948.

"April Dividend an American Classic," *America in Books,* March 1948.

"More Americans Than Not," *New York Herald Tribune Weekly Book Review,* Mar. 28, 1948. Review of Geoffrey Gorer, *The American People.*

Review of Clarence P. Jackson, *Picture Maker of the Old West: William H. Jackson, American Historical Review,* April 1948.

"Injustice," *Harper's,* April 1948. Letter to the ed.

The Easy Chair #150, *Harper's,* April 1948.

The Easy Chair #151, *Harper's,* May 1948.

"Editorially Speaking," *America in Books,* May 1948.

Review of Richard Lillard, *The Great Forest, America in Books,* May 1948.

The Easy Chair #152, *Harper's,* June 1948.

"Peter Pan, U.S.A.," *Woman's Day,* June 1948.

The Easy Chair #153, *Harper's,* July 1948. Reprinted as "Statesmen on the Lam," in *The Easy Chair.*

"Sacred Cows and Public Lands," *Harper's,* July 1948. Reprinted in *The Easy Chair.*

"The Desert Threat," *University of Colorado Bulletin,* July 1948.

The Easy Chair #154, *Harper's,* August 1948.

"Crisis of Man in Relation to His Environment," *New York Herald Tribune Weekly Book Review,* Aug. 8, 1948. Review of William Vogt, *Road to Survival.*

"The Good Teacher," *Woman's Day,* September 1948.

The Easy Chair #155, *Harper's,* September 1948.

"Conservation and the Coming Crisis," *New York Herald Tribune,* Oct. 11, 1948.

The Easy Chair #146, *Harper's,* October 1948.

"What Land Policy for America?" Annual Forum, *New York Herald Tribune,* Oct. 18, 1948. Reprint of speech.

"What Counts Is the Job," *The Writer,* October 1948. Reprinted from *Harper's,* The Easy Chair, April 1948.

The Easy Chair #157, *Harper's,* November 1948.

The Easy Chair #158, *Harper's,* December 1948.

"Reply to a Reply," *Harper's,* December 1948. Letter to the ed.

"Enigmatic Friend of Indians," *New York Herald Tribune Weekly Book Review,* Dec. 19, 1948. Review of Lloyd Haberly, *Pursuit of the Horizon.*

"For Public Control of Lands," *The Land,* Winter 1949.

"Water Runs Downhill," *Woman's Day,* January 1949.

The Easy Chair #159, *Harper's,* January 1949.

The Easy Chair #160, *Harper's,* February 1949.

The Easy Chair #161, *Harper's,* March 1949.

"The Absentee-owned Economy of the West," *New York Herald Tribune Weekly Book Review,* Apr. 10, 1949. Review of Ray B. West, ed., *Rocky Mountain Cities.*

"The U.S.A.," *The International House Quarterly,* Spring 1949.

"David Copperfield and the Beanstalk," *Woman's Day,* May 1949.

The Easy Chair #163, *Harper's,* May 1949.

The Easy Chair #164, *Harper's,* June 1949.

Review of Howard H. Peckham, *The Journals and Indian Paintings of George Winter, 1837–1839, Mississippi Valley Historical Review,* June 1949.

The Easy Chair #165, *Harper's,* July 1949.

"The Life and Wife of a Writer," *Woman's Day,* August 1949. Reprinted in *Women and Children First* by Cady Hewes.

The Easy Chair #166, *Harper's,* August 1949.

"Time without a Theme," *Saturday Review of Literature,* Aug. 6, 1949.

The Easy Chair #167, *Harper's,* September 1949.

"The Colleges, the Government and Freedom," *American Association of University Professors Bulletin,* Autumn 1949. Reprinted from The Easy Chair #167.

"Due Notice to the F.B.I.," The Easy Chair #168, *Harper's,* October 1949. Reprinted in *The Easy Chair.*

"Restoration in the Wasatch," *The American Scholar,* October 1949.

"Water Runs Downhill," *Outdoor America,* October 1949.

"Derbies Are Male," by Cady Hewes, *Woman's Day,* November 1949. Reprinted in *Women and Children First* by Cady Hewes.

"The Spectral Evidence," The Easy Chair #169, *Harper's,* November 1949.

"To 1864, When Lincoln Made U.S. Grant General-in-Chief," *New York Herald Tribune Weekly Book Review*, Nov. 6, 1949. Review of Kenneth P. Williams, *Lincoln Finds a General*.

"Our Contemporary, Jonathan Edwards," *New York Herald Tribune Weekly Book Review*, Nov. 20, 1949. Review of Perry Miller, *Jonathan Edwards*.

"Due Notice —," *Harper's*, December 1949. Letter to the editor.

"For the Wayward and Beguiled," The Easy Chair #170, *Harper's*, December 1949. Reprinted in *The Hour*. Other reprints are entitled "An Appreciation of the Martini Cocktail," or "A Bit of Rhetoric on the Topic of Gin and Vermouth."

"The Novel Is Always a Story," *The Writer*, December 1949.

"Lesson of Davis County," *Reader's Digest*, December 1949. Reprinted from *American Scholar*, Autumn 1949.

The World of Fiction. Boston: Houghton Mifflin, 1950.

"Parable of the Lost Chance," The Easy Chair #171, *Harper's*, January 1950. Reprinted in *The Easy Chair*.

"The Invisible Novelist," *Pacific Spectator*, Winter 1950, chapter 9 of *The World of Fiction*.

"Professor or Professional?" *Woman's Day*, February 1950.

"Year-end Megrims," The Easy Chair #172, *Harper's*, February 1950.

"Almost Toujours Gai," The Easy Chair #173, *Harper's*, March 1950. Reprinted in *The Easy Chair*.

"The Christopher Papers," The Easy Chair #174, *Harper's*, April 1950.

"The World Wives Live In," by Cady Hewes, *Woman's Day*, April 1950. Reprinted in *Women and Children First* by Cady Hewes.

"A Major New Landmark in the Critical Study of the American West," *New York Herald Tribune Weekly Book Review*, Apr. 9, 1950. Review of Henry Nash Smith, *Virgin Land*.

"The Camel on the Moon," *Woman's Day*, May 1950.

"Wanted, an Umpire," The Easy Chair #175, *Harper's*, May 1950.

"State of the Nation (Spring)," The Easy Chair #176, *Harper's*, June 1950.

"From New England the Yankee Went His Curious Way," *New York Herald Tribune Weekly Book Review*, June 11, 1950. Review of Stewart H. Holbrook, *The Yankee Exodus*.

"Research By Air," The Easy Chair #177, *Harper's,* July 1950. Original titles included "South Pass By Air," and "Ox Team West By Air."

"We Grew Up with Danger," *Woman's Day,* July 1950. Original title: "This Nettle, Danger."

"Shall We Let Them Ruin Our National Parks?" *Saturday Evening Post,* July 22, 1950. Reprinted in *Reader's Digest,* November 1950.

"A Fine New Talent on Ol' Man River," *New York Herald Tribune Weekly Book Review,* July 23, 1950. Review of Richard Bissell, *A Stretch on the River.*

"Our Hundred Year Plan," The Easy Chair #178, *Harper's,* August 1950.

"Ninety-day Venus," The Easy Chair #179, *Harper's,* September 1950. Reprinted in *The Easy Chair.*

"Tame Indian, Lone Sailor," *New York Times Book Review,* Sept. 24, 1950. Review of Walter Van Tilburg Clark, *Watchful Gods and Other Stories.*

"The Century," *Harper's,* October 1950. Reprinted in *The Easy Chair.*

"The Constant Function," The Easy Chair #180, *Harper's,* October 1950.

"Gone Are the Days," *Woman's Day,* October 1950. Original title: "The Old Home We Never Wanted."

"But Sometimes They Vote Right Too," The Easy Chair #181, *Harper's,* November 1950. Reprinted in *The Easy Chair.*

"Here Is the Civil War—America As It Really Was—Magnificent and Vile," *New York Herald Tribune Weekly Book Review,* Nov. 19, 1950. Review of Henry Steele Commager, ed., *The Blue and the Gray.*

"The Lush Life of the Primitive Continent," *New York Herald Tribune Weekly Book Review,* Nov. 26, 1950. Review of John Bakeless, *The Eyes of Discovery.*

"Shop Talk," The Easy Chair #182, *Harper's,* December 1950. Reprinted in *The Easy Chair.*

"On the Writing of History," *Chicago History Quarterly,* Winter 1950. Letter to the editor.

The Hour. Boston: Houghton Mifflin, 1951.

"Homily for a Troubled Time," *Woman's Day,* January 1951.

"Letter to a Family Doctor," The Easy Chair #183, *Harper's,* January 1951.

"The Ex-Communists," *Atlantic,* February 1951. Reprinted in *The Easy Chair.*

"Men, Women and Eight Cylinders," by Cady Hewes, *Woman's Day,* February 1951. Reprinted in *Women and Children First* by Cady Hewes.

"Our First Testing," The Easy Chair #184, *Harper's,* February 1951.

"Two-Gun Desmond Is Back," The Easy Chair #185, *Harper's,* March 1951. Reprinted in *The Easy Chair.*

"Whiskey Is for Patriots," The Easy Chair #186, *Harper's,* April 1951. Reprinted with changes in *The Hour.*

"Why Professors Are Suspicious of Business," *Fortune,* April 1951.

"Documented Novel of the Old Northwest Fur Trade," *New York Herald Tribune Weekly Book Review,* Apr. 1, 1951. Review of Walter O'Meara, *The Grand Portage.*

"Spring Clearance," The Easy Chair #187, *Harper's,* May 1951.

"Dull Novels Make Dull Reading," The Easy Chair #188, *Harper's,* June 1951.

"The Watchers on the Wall," *Woman's Day,* June 1951.

"Your Land and Mine —," *Harper's,* June 1951. Letter to the editor.

"Pocket Guide to Horse Opera," by Cady Hewes, *Woman's Day,* July 1951.

"Foul Birds Come Abroad [sic]," The Easy Chair #189, *Harper's,* July 1951.

"The Only Man To Paint the Rocky Mountain Fur Trade," *New York Herald Weekly Book Review,* July 22, 1951. Review of Marvin G. Ross, *The West of Alfred Jacob Miller.*

"Listen Sister," by Fairley Blake, *Atlantic,* July 1951. Reprinted with changes in *The Hour.*

"An It in the Corner," The Easy Chair #190, *Harper's,* August 1951. Reprinted in *The Easy Chair.*

"Ordeal by Poetry," The Easy Chair #191, *Harper's,* September 1951.

"Anyone Can Talk to a Genius," by Cady Hewes, *Woman's Day,* October 1951. Reprinted in *Women and Children First* by Cady Hewes.

"Two Points of a Joke," The Easy Chair #192, *Harper's,* October 1951.

"A New Approach to Our History, Visual and Revealing," *New York Herald Tribune Weekly Book Review*, Oct. 21, 1951. Review of Marshall B. Davidson, *Life in America*.

"Crusade Resumed," The Easy Chair #193, *Harper's*, November 1951.

"The Smoke Jumpers," *Harper's*, November 1951. Reprinted in *The Easy Chair*.

"Wayfarer's Daybook," The Easy Chair #194, *Harper's*, December 1951.

The Course of Empire. Boston: Houghton Mifflin, 1952.

"The Monster in the Home," by Cady Hewes, *Woman's Day*, January 1952. Reprinted in *Women and Children First*.

"The Sixty-Cent Royalty," The Easy Chair #195, *Harper's*, January 1952.

"These Lands Are Yours," *Woman's Day*, February 1952.

"Why Read Dull Novels?" The Easy Chair #196, *Harper's*, February 1952.

"The Third Floor," The Easy Chair #197, *Harper's*, March 1952. Reprinted in *The Easy Chair*.

"Stevenson and the Independent Voter," The Easy Chair #198, *Harper's*, April 1952.

"The Seventh Pocketbook," *Mademoiselle*, March 1952.

"Personal and Otherwise," *Harper's*, April 1952. Letter to the editor.

"Hurried Crossing," *Woman's Day*, May 1952.

"Les Amis des Deux Fishboulettes," The Easy Chair #199, *Harper's*, May 1952.

"Next to Reading Matter," The Easy Chair #200, *Harper's*, June 1952.

"Women in the Military Services," *Woman's Day*, June 1952.

"Transcontinental Flight," The Easy Chair #201, *Harper's*, July 1952.

"Vermont Is the Vermonters," *Reader's Digest*, July 1952. Reprinted from *Harper's*.

"Flood in the Desert," The Easy Chair #202, *Harper's*, August 1952.

"Boyhood Years That Shaped Mark Twain's Great Art," *New York Herald Tribune Weekly Book Review*, Aug. 31, 1952. Review of Dixon Wecter, *Sam Clemens of Hannibal*.

"The End of the Stalwarts," The Easy Chair #203, *Harper's*, September 1952.

"Turning Point for Lewis and Clark," *Harper's*, September 1952. Excerpt from chapter 11 of *The Course of Empire*.

"An Old Steal Refurbished," The Easy Chair #204, *Harper's*, October 1952.

"What Wendell Willkie Meant to His Party, His Country and the World," *New York Herald Tribune Weekly Book Review*, Oct. 12, 1952. Review of Joseph Barnes, *Willke*.

"Remainder Shelf," The Easy Chair #205, *Harper's*, November 1952.

"Transcontinental Flight," *Reader's Digest*, November 1952.

"Masterly Report on Civil War Generalship," *New York Herald Tribune Weekly Book Review*, Nov. 2, 1952. Review of Kenneth P. Williams, *Lincoln Finds a General*.

"The High Country," *Woman's Day*, December 1952.

"Samuel Hall, Gent," The Easy Chair #206, *Harper's*, December 1952.

"Twenty-nine Who Pictured the Old West," *New York Herald Tribune Weekly Book Review*, Dec. 14, 1952. Review of Harold McCracken, *Portrait of the Old West*.

"Preliminary Forecast," The Easy Chair #207, *Harper's*, January 1953.

"Virus Infection," by Cady Hewes, *Woman's Day*, January 1953. Reprinted in *Women and Children First* by Cady Hewes.

"Billion Dollar Jackpot," The Easy Chair #208, *Harper's*, February 1953. Reprinted in *The Easy Chair*.

"Extracts from the Speeches of the National Book Award Winners," by Archibald MacLeish, Ralph Ellison, and Bernard DeVoto, *New York Herald Tribune Weekly Book Review*, Feb. 15, 1953.

"Twenty-Hour Vigil," The Easy Chair #209, *Harper's*, March 1953. Reprinted *The Easy Chair*.

"Celebrating 150 Years of the Louisiana Purchase," *Collier's*, Mar. 21, 1953. Reprinted as *The Louisiana Purchase*, Crowell-Collier. Original title: "Traveling the Louisiana Purchase."

"The Case of the Censorious Congressman," The Easy Chair #210, *Harper's*, April 1953. Reprinted in *The Easy Chair*.

"The Indian All Round Us," *Reader's Digest*, April 1953.

"The New England Hill Country," *Woman's Day*, April 1953.

"The Sturdy Corporate Homesteader," The Easy Chair #211, *Harper's,* May 1953. Reprinted in *The Easy Chair.*

"Topic One," by Cady Hewes, *Woman's Day,* May 1953. Reprinted in *Women and Children First* by Cady Hewes.

"Ore for the Rouge," *Lincoln and Mercury Times,* May–June 1953.

"The Visual Instrument," The Easy Chair #212, *Harper's,* June 1953.

"TV, a Minority Report," *Reader's Digest,* June 1953.

"Heading for the Last Roundup," The Easy Chair #213, *Harper's,* July 1953. Reprinted in *The Easy Chair.*

"Homicide in the Home," *Woman's Day,* July 1953. Reprinted in *Women and Children First* by Cady Hewes.

Review of A. P. Nasatir, ed., *Before Lewis and Clark: Documents Illustrating the History of the Missouri, 1785–1804, American Historical Review,* July 1953.

"Mr. Ford's Favorite Town—Dearborn, Michigan," *Ford Times,* July 1953.

"Summer Preface," The Easy Chair #214, *Harper's,* August 1953.

"Motel Town," The Easy Chair #215, *Harper's,* September 1953. Reprinted in *The Easy Chair.*

"Playtime Paradise," *Woman's Day,* September 1953.

"Let's Close the National Parks," The Easy Chair #216, *Harper's,* October 1953.

"Notes on Western Travel," The Easy Chair #217, *Harper's,* November 1953.

"Always Be Drastically Independent," The Easy Chair #218, *Harper's,* December 1953.

"Our Great West, Boom or Bust?" *Collier's,* December 25, 1953.

"Traveling the Louisiana Purchase," *Ford Times,* December 1953.

"My Career As a Lawbreaker," The Easy Chair #219, *Harper's,* January 1954.

"That Southern Inferiority Complex," *The Saturday Evening Post,* Jan. 16, 1954. Original title: "Who Has Slighted the South?"

"Disaster Long Ago," *Woman's Day,* February 1954.

"Parks and Pictures," The Easy Chair #220, *Harper's,* February 1954.

"What Makes a Real Martini?" *True Magazine,* February 1954. Original title: "The Martini Unadorned."

"The Impatient Patient," by Cady Hewes, *Woman's Day,* March 1954. Reprinted in *Women and Children First* by Cady Hewes.

"Intramural Giveaway," The Easy Chair #221, *Harper's,* March 1954.

"My Wife Is Many Cooks," by Cady Hewes, *Woman's Day,* April 1954. Reprinted in *Women and Children First* by Cady Hewes. Original title: "An Artist in the Kitchen."

"Norwalk and Points West," The Easy Chair #222, *Harper's,* April 1954. Reprinted in *The Easy Chair.*

"DeVoto's New England," *Harper's,* May 1954.

"Fantasy at Noonday," The Easy Chair #223, *Harper's,* May 1954.

"Follow Any Road," *Woman's Day,* May 1954.

"Victory at Sea," The Easy Chair #224, *Harper's,* June 1954. Reprinted in *The Easy Chair.*

"The Grand Coulee Is Grand," *New York Herald Tribune Weekly Book Review,* June 27, 1954. Review of George Sundborg, *Hail Columbia.*

"Alias Nero Wolfe," The Easy Chair #225, *Harper's,* July 1954.

"Cambridge Man," *Holiday,* July 1954. Autobiographical letter.

"The Link," by Frank Gilbert, *Esquire,* July 1954. Original title: "The Hidden." Short story.

"Wild West," *Holiday,* July 1954. Reprinted in *Reader's Digest,* September 1954. Original title: "Western Paradox."

"Conservation: Down and on the Way Out," *Harper's,* August 1954. Reprinted in *The Easy Chair.*

"Yankee Reserve," The Easy Chair #226, *Harper's,* August 1954.

"And Fractions Drive Me Mad," The Easy Chair #227, *Harper's,* September 1954.

"New England Revisited," *The Lamp,* September 1954.

"Culture at Two Bits," The Easy Chair #228, *Harper's,* October 1954.

"The White-Water Riverman," *Holiday,* October 1954.

"In the Horse Latitudes," The Easy Chair #229, *Harper's,* November 1954.

"Phaethon on Gunsmoke Trail," The Easy Chair #230, *Harper's,* December 1954.

The Easy Chair. Boston: Houghton Mifflin, 1955.

"Yankee Grand Tour," *Ford Times, New England Journeys* #2.

"One-Way Partnership Derailed," The Easy Chair #231, *Harper's,* January 1955.

"Service in Four-color Gravure," The Easy Chair #232, *Harper's,* February 1955.

"Airlines Need a Lesson in Traveler Relations," *Time,* Feb. 14, 1955. Reprinted from *Harper's.*

"Hazards of the Road," The Easy Chair #233, *Harper's,* March 1955.

"Guilt by Distinction," The Easy Chair #234, *Harper's,* April 1955. Reprinted in *The Easy Chair.*

"Current Comic Strips," The Easy Chair #235, *Harper's,* May 1955.

"The Zippered Egg Boiler," by Cady Hewes, *Woman's Day,* May 1955. Reprinted in *Women and Children First* by Cady Hewes.

"The Reference Shelf," *Writer,* June 1955.

"For the Record," The Easy Chair #236, *Harper's,* June 1955.

Review of Samuel Eliot Morison, ed., *The Parkman Reader, New England Quarterly,* June 1955.

"New England," *Holiday,* July 1955. Original title: "The Yankee Republic."

"Peter and Wendy in the Revolution," The Easy Chair #237, *Harper's,* July 1955.

"On the Record," *Harper's,* August 1955, Letter to the editor.

"Spread of an Infection," The Easy Chair #238, *Harper's,* August 1955.

"An Inference Regarding the Expedition of Lewis and Clark." Reprinted from the *Proceedings of the American Philosophical Society,* Aug. 30, 1955.

"And the DAR," *Harper's,* September 1955.

"Hell's Half Acre, Mass.," The Easy Chair #239, *Harper's,* September 1955.

"Outdoor Metropolis," The Easy Chair #240, *Harper's,* October 1955.

"Number 241," The Easy Chair #241, *Harper's,* November 1955. Reprinted in *The Easy Chair.*

"Birth of an Art," The Easy Chair #242, *Harper's,* December 1955.

"Essence of New England—Lincoln Gap, Vermont," *New England Journeys.*

"Tour Boston on Foot," *Ford Times, New England Journeys* #3.

Women and Children First, by Cady Hewes. Boston: Houghton Mifflin, 1956.

"Beating the Bali Hai Racket," The Easy Chair #243, *Harper's,* January 1956.

"Heavy, Heavy, What Hangs Over?" *Holiday,* March 1956. Original title: "Boredom de Luxe."

"Good Place to Grow In," *Lincoln-Mercury Times,* March–April, 1956. Original title: "Ogden."

"Two Days in Washington," *Woman's Day,* March 1956.

"Bread Loaf, Vermont," *Ford Times,* May 1956. Reprinted in *New England Journeys.*

"Uncle Sam's Campgrounds," *Ford Times,* June 1956.

"Let me tell you about the Wasatch," *Lincoln-Mercury Times,* July–August 1956. Original title: "The Wasatch."

"Your National Forests," *Holiday,* August 1956.

"Roads of the Past," *The Lamp,* Fall 1956. Original title: "Early Highways of the East."

"Coolidge's Grave in Plymouth," *New England Journeys* #4. Original title: "Plymouth Cemetery."

"DeVoto's Letters from Harvard," by Carolyn Hoggan, the *Pen,* Spring 1957.

"Astor and Astoria," *American Heritage,* August 1958. Excerpt from *Course of Empire.*

"The Champlain Corridor," *Ford Times,* February 1959.

Acknowledgments

On January 11, 1997, the centennial of Bernard DeVoto's birth, the University of New Orleans' Eisenhower Center for American Studies and the Historic New Orleans Collection teamed up to cosponsor a public retrospective on the Pulitzer Prize-winning author's life and work. New Orleans as a setting bore a special significance. After all, this was the capital of Louisiana both when it was in French as well as when it was in Spanish hands. The day before the convocation, participants were given a private tour of the Cabildo, the elegant Spanish government building on Jackson Square in the French Quarter that faces the Mississippi River. In an upstairs room where the polished hardwood floors echo with the footsteps of history, our panelists stood precisely where the transfer documents for the Louisiana Purchase were signed in 1803.

If the assemblage of first-rate scholars and DeVoto devotees who constituted the day-long panel were not already in a Western state of mind, they were immediately transported by the magnitude of what had occurred nearly two hundred years earlier in this room in the Cabildo, which is now part of the Louisiana State Museum. Although New Orleans, in both space and spirit, lies many hundreds of miles from the grassy expanse of the high prairies and the lofty spires of the Rocky Mountains, it was here that the young United States gained possession of the enormous Louisiana Territory, a land of geographic and topographic extremes that has inspired conflict and euphoria, boom and bust economic cycles, and expressions of creativity that span the artistic spectrum. It was in this historic room, on the banks of the Mississippi River, that the United States officially came into possession of what DeVoto lovingly referred to as the "American West."

The January 1997 centennial symposium—titled "Devoted to the American West"—produced an extraordinary gathering of minds. Speakers included best-selling historian Stephen E. Ambrose; son of the honoree, Mark DeVoto; then Director of the Historic New Orleans Collection, Jon Kukla, who was inspired by the event to write a bicentennial history of the Louisiana Purchase; *Harper's* editor Lewis Lapham; *Reader's Digest* contributor and author of *The Ugly American,* William J. Lederer; University of Colorado professor of history Patricia Limerick; longtime DeVoto friend, Dr. Herbert Scheinberg; author and historian Arthur M. Schlesinger, Jr.; and former editor of *Wilderness, American West,* and *American Heritage,* T. H. Watkins. Sadly, Watkins, to whom this book is dedicated, died February 23, 2000, at his home in Bozeman, Montana. He was a lifelong outdoors enthusiast. As a young man, working for Wallace Stegner, Watkins embarked on a career as a writer, editor, and thinker who embraced the natural splendor of the West. In 1997, Watkins took up his first teaching position, the Wallace Stegner Chair in the American Studies Department at Montana State University in Bozeman. Throughout his life, whether with pen or as a teacher, T. H. Watkins devoted his energies to thoughtful analysis and understanding of environmental issues, particularly as they impacted the American West. He is greatly missed.

The forum—which the C-SPAN network documented for television audiences—was held at Le Petit Théâtre du Vieux Carré, an historic French Quarter auditorium rich in ambiance and charm. The atmosphere created was one of academic stimulation and free exchange of ideas. Audience response was enthusiastic. Later that evening, the participants convened for dinner in the Rex Room at Antoine's, a famous New Orleans restaurant operated by the same family since 1840 and imbued with classic French Quarter flair. Over superb cuisine, such as crawfish étouffé, and delectable California wines that perfectly complemented the flavorful Louisiana fare, the conversation turned once more to DeVoto and his legacy. Those present felt that something should be done, a step should be taken to ensure that DeVoto's writings would remain accessible to future generations.

Out of this gathering grew the idea to compile a Bernard DeVoto reader, an anthology that would bring together published and unpublished conservation writings by this fearless scribe who knew and loved the West so well. Thanks must be given to each and every one of the symposium's panelists, all of whom enthusiastically embraced the idea of such a book, later to become *The Western Paradox: A Conservation Reader*. As the process of putting the reader together got underway, Mark DeVoto, Professor Emeritus of Music at Tufts University, offered full access to his father's unpublished historical writings. A true Renaissance man with a fine sensibility for the nuances of language, he maintained a high level of commitment and involvement throughout the project.

Patricia Limerick is best known as an historian at the University of Colorado–Boulder, where she is co-chair of the board at the Center of the American West. Professor Limerick's publications include *Desert Passages: Encounters with the American Deserts* (1985), *The Legacy of Conquest: The Unbroken Past of the American West* (1987), and most recently, *Something in the Soil: Legacies and Reckonings in the New West* (2000). With her background, she brought invaluable expertise to the task of co-editing *The Western Paradox*. Her scholarly understanding of the history of environmentalism and the pitfalls of triumphalism were the keys to maintaining the focus of the book. Professor Limerick, in a true labor of love, gave tremendously of her time, energy, and knowledge to see this book through to fruition. Special thanks also go to Professor Limerick's friend and associate, Grant H. Nelson, of Brigham City, Utah, who is one of Bernard DeVoto's longest running fans.

I would also like to acknowledge the staff at the University of New Orleans' Eisenhower Center for American Studies. Research Associate Andrew Devereux was especially active with manuscript editing. He worked diligently in the final stages, as production loomed, to pull all the loose ends together. My wife, Tammy Brinkley, was instrumental from the outset with her work on manuscript preparation and fact-checking. Matthew Ellefson, Erica Whittington, and Kevin Willey, all of the Eisenhower Center, contributed their painstaking efforts by compiling the manuscript, helping with the editing and proofing, and serving as contacts among all parties involved. All of these people were crucial in keeping the progress of the book on track.

Professor John Mack Faragher of Yale University and author of *Daniel Boone: The Life and Legend of an American Pioneer* and *Women and Men on the Overland Trail* wrote the reader's report urging Yale University Press to publish *The Western Paradox*. Without his backing, the project might never have progressed beyond a pipe dream. We are indebted to him for both his scholarship and his enthusiastic support.

Finally, the folks at Yale University Press deserve special recognition. Senior Editor Larisa Heimert was the consummate example of what an editor should be. Her intelligence, creativity, and professionalism were indispensable in keeping everybody on the same page and making certain that the book was completed according to schedule. Reprints Editor Ali Peterson displayed patience and humor from start to finish. It was a delight to work with both of them to bring *The Western Paradox: A Conservation Reader* to fruition.

Scholars have written at length about the "opening" of the American West and, later, the "closing" of the Frontier. Today parts of the West are experiencing some of the most tremendous economic and population growth anywhere in the country. In the West, the stage is set for conflicts of great magnitude, many of which eventually affect the rest of the nation. Differing conceptions of land ownership and land stewardship result in intense, sometimes bloody strife over resources and environmental issues. One example of this is the severe power crisis in which California repeatedly finds itself ensnared. What is clear is that the West remains a distinct region. Bernard DeVoto is one of the most eloquent and honest writers to have confronted this. Through this reader, future generations will now be able to pore over the words of this brilliant advocate and lover of the West who, nonetheless, was unflinching in addressing the problems that have plagued, and continue to haunt, this majestic region of natural beauty and geographical extremes.

Index

d